www.wadsworth.com

www.wadsworth.com is the World Wide Web site for Thomson Wadsworth and is your direct source to dozens of online resources.

At *www.wadsworth.com* you can find out about supplements, demonstration software, and student resources. You can also send e-mail to many of our authors and preview new publications and exciting new technologies.

www.wadsworth.com
Changing the way the world learns®

FROM THE WADSWORTH SERIES IN THEATRE

Anderson/Anderson, *Costume Design,* Second Edition
Barranger, *Theatre: A Way of Seeing,* Sixth Edition
Barton, *Acting: Onstage and Off,* Fourth Edition
Brockett/Ball, *The Essential Theatre,* Eighth Edition
Brockett/Ball, *Plays for the Theatre,* Eighth Edition
Dean/Carra, *Fundamentals of Play Directing,* Fifth Edition
Downs/Wright/Ramsey, *Experiencing the Art of Theatre: A Concise Introduction*
Downs/Wright/Ramsey, *The Art of Theatre: Then and Now*
Essig, *Lighting and the Design Idea,* Second Edition
Huberman/Pope/Ludwig, *The Theatrical Imagination,* Second Edition
Hudson, *Writing About Theatre and Drama,* Second Edition
Jonas/Proehl/Lupo, *Dramaturgy in American Theatre: A Source Book*
Madden, *A Pocketful of Plays: Vintage Drama, Vols. I and II*
McGaw/Clark/Stilson, *Acting is Believing,* Ninth Edition
Olivieri, *Shakespeare without Fear: A User-Friendly Guide to Acting Shakespeare*
O'Neill, *The Actor's Checklist,* Third Edition
Parker/Wolf/Block, *Scene Design and Stage Lighting,* Eighth Edition
Schneider, *The Art and Craft of Stage Management*
Shapiro, *An Actor Performs,* Second Edition
Shapiro, *The Director's Companion*
Worthen, *The Wadsworth Anthology of Drama,* Brief Edition
Worthen, *The Wadsworth Anthology of Drama,* Fifth Edition

Experiencing the Art of Theatre

A Concise Introduction

William Missouri Downs
University of Wyoming

Lou Anne Wright
University of Wyoming

Erik Ramsey
Ohio University

Australia • Brazil • Canada • Mexico • Singapore
Spain • United Kingdom • United States

Experiencing the Art of Theatre: A Concise Introduction

William Missouri Downs, Lou Anne Wright, and Erik Ramsey

Publisher: Holly J. Allen
Senior Development Editor: Greer Lleuad
Assistant Editor: Lucinda Bingham
Editorial Assistant: Meghan Bass
Senior Technology Project Manager: Jeanette Wiseman
Senior Marketing Manager: Mark D. Orr
Marketing Assistant: Alexandra Tran
Senior Marketing Communications Manager: Shemika Britt
Project Manager, Editorial Production: Jennifer Klos
Creative Director: Rob Hugel
Executive Art Director: Maria Epes
Print Buyer: Judy Inouye
Permissions Editor: Joohee Lee
Production Service: Katie O'Keeffe-Swank, Lachina Publishing Services
Text Designer: Marsha Cohen
Art Editor: Heidi Grosch
Photo Researcher: Stephen Forsling
Copy Editor: Barbara Armentrout
Illustrator: Marsha Cohen
Cover Designer: Marsha Cohen
Cover Image: Photo by Joan Marcus © Disney; Tsidii Le Loka as "Rafiki," original Broadway company production of *The Lion King*

Tsidii Le Loka is a Tony Award nominee and winner of several top industry awards, including Outer Critics Circle Award, Drama Desk Award, EW Award, Drama League Award for Outstanding Performance in a Musical (for originating the role of "Rafiki") in *The Lion King* on Broadway, and The Ivor Novello Award for International Achievement in Musical Theatre from The British Academy of Composers and Songwriters. Tsidii is the only starring artist to also contribute as a composer to the production. Her composition, "Rafiki Mourns," is included in the Grammy Award-winning album of *The Lion King* on Broadway.

Compositor: Lachina Publishing Services
Printer: CTPS

© 2007 Thomson Wadsworth, a part of The Thomson Corporation. Thomson, the Star logo, and Wadsworth are trademarks used herein under license.

ALL RIGHTS RESERVED. No part of this work covered by the copyright hereon may be reproduced or used in any form or by any means—graphic, electronic, or mechanical, including photocopying, recording, taping, web distribution, information storage and retrieval systems, or in any other manner—without the written permission of the publisher.

Printed in China
2 3 4 5 6 7 09 08 07 06

ExamView® and ExamView Pro® are registered trademarks of FSCreations, Inc. Windows is a registered trademark of the Microsoft Corporation used herein under license. Macintosh and Power Macintosh are registered trademarks of Apple Computer, Inc. used herein under license.

© 2007 Thomson Learning, Inc. All Rights Reserved. Thomson Learning WebTutor™ is a trademark of Thomson Learning, Inc.

Library of Congress Control Number: 2005936609

Student Edition ISBN-13: 978-0-495-00180-5
ISBN-10: 0-495-00180-5

Thomson Higher Education
10 Davis Drive
Belmont, CA 94002-3098
USA

For more information about our products, contact us at:
Thomson Learning Academic Resource Center
1-800-423-0563
For permission to use material from this text or product, submit a request online at **http://www.thomsonrights.com**.
Any additional questions about permissions can be submitted by e-mail to **thomsonrights@thomson.com**.

This book is dedicated to

David Hall,

Holly Allen,

Greer Lleuad,

and

Barbara Rosenberg,

each a very vital link in the
long chain that brought this book to publication.

BRIEF TABLE OF CONTENTS

TABLE OF CONTENTS

PREFACE

Tonight in the United States, over 80 million people will watch television, and another 10 million will take in a movie, but only about 200,000 will attend the theatre. Most students who take the introductory theatre course know little or nothing about theatre, but they're well versed in theatre's direct descendents: movies and television. To meet students where they are, *Experiencing the Art of Theatre: A Concise Introduction* uses popular screen entertainments as a touchstone to begin exploring the unique art of theatre. *Experiencing the Art of Theatre* challenges students to interpret, criticize, and appreciate the roles theatre plays in society through positive comparisons to television and film. From theatre's ritual origins to modern musicals, from controversies surrounding the NEA to the applicability of acting lessons to everyday life, this book provides a first step toward a deeper awareness of theatre's enduring significance.

Experiencing the Art of Theatre has three sections, each covering a distinct aspect of the introductory theatre course. Because most theatre departments stage their first play about four weeks into a semester, **Part 1, "Theatre Literacy,"** contains four chapters of background information to prepare students to attend their first theatre production as knowledgeable theatregoers. In these chapters, we

- Explore the differences between art and entertainment and their relationship in our culture today
- Discuss theatre's relevance to today's audiences
- Define the most common types of theatre: commercial, historical, political, experimental, and cultural
- Explain how screen entertainment differs from theatre in purpose, mediums, and financing
- Describe theatre's relationship to culture and how cultural diversity manifests itself in U.S. theatre today
- Discuss how theatre can give a voice to groups who are ignored by historical and commercial theatre
- Outline audience etiquette and how to go about finding plays
- Describe the role of criticism in the theatrical process and how professional criticism differs from the critical analysis students are asked to do in class
- Discuss how free speech and audience participation differ in regard to screen entertainment and theatre

By introducing students to these fundamental topics early on, we provide a bridge between what students already know about movies, television, and culture and what they need to know about theatre.

Part 2, "The Arts within the Art," gives students a firm background in the primary arts and techniques needed to create a theatre performance. We concentrate first on creativity and the ensemble, and then move to playwriting, acting, directing, and design. Whenever possible, we provide a look at the nuts and bolts, the how-tos, of the art rather than concentrating solely on appreciation of the art. We show the readers how they can use acting techniques, character analysis, story structure, ensemble work, and creativity in their own lives. By the time they are finished with this part of the book, students should be ready to see their second production with a fuller understanding of the spectrum of skills and talents needed to stage a play.

Part 3, "A Concise History," ties the major episodes of theatre history to the historical, social, and philosophical events that theatre has caused and reflected. These four chapters provide students with a broader understanding of theatre's role in society. They make theatre history interesting by drawing connections, making analogies, and tying together what might seem random events into a logical, unified whole. We've explored theatre through the ages with an eye toward providing a compelling story that students will find meaningful and memorable. This section is not meant to be a scholarly treatise but rather an exploration of one of the most exciting topics in theatre: theatre history. It starts with theatre's origins, describing the theatre of the ancient Greeks and Romans; the theatrical traditions of India, China, and Japan; and shadow theatre in the Islamic world. The next chapter explores theatre's revival in Europe, focusing on the major theatrical movements of the Renaissance, Elizabethan England, the Restoration, and the Enlightenment. We then move into a discussion of the "isms" of the nineteenth and twentieth centuries, including Realism and Naturalism, avant-garde forms, and post-war theatre in the United States. Part 3 ends with a chapter on the evolution of the musical, a fun and popular theatrical form with which students are often the most familiar.

With strong coverage of theatre history and current events in theatre, a highly accessible writing style, and intriguing and meaningful features, *Experiencing the Art of Theatre* reveals theatre's place in society and its relevance to students today.

Features of This Book

- **Thorough coverage of diversity in theatre.** Diversity is woven throughout the text narrative and in the examples, quotations, and photos. Additionally, Chapter 3, "Theatre and Cultural Diversity," discusses diversity in modern U.S. theatre, including the theatre of identity, the theatre of protest, and cross-cultural theatre. Chapter 10, "Theatre's Beginnings," includes not only ancient Greek and Roman but also Indian, Chinese, Japanese, and Islamic theatre traditions.
- **Entire chapter on creativity and the collaborative process.** Chapter 5, "Creativity and the Ensemble," compares technique and talent, describes the attributes of creative people, provides tips students can use to enhance their creativity, and outlines the steps of creative problem-solving. This thorough discussion of creativity leads into a description of the theatre ensemble and the collaborative process necessary to stage a play. Chapters 6–9 follow with in-depth coverage of the members of the creative team.
- **"From Stage to Screen" side-by-side comparisons of stage plays and their film versions.** This feature shows students how the same story can be told in the two mediums. The book features comparisons of seven plays and their cinematic counterparts: *Macbeth, Angels in America, The Crucible, Rope, Cosi, Hamlet,* and *Chicago.*
- **Spotlight boxes.** This feature provides behind-the-scenes looks at the people, places, trends, and events that have shaped theatre. Examples of Spotlight boxes are "The Life of an Actor: Don Cheadle" (in Chapter 7, "The Art of Acting") and "Puritans, Pilgrims, and the Beginning of Theatre in America" (in Chapter 11, "Theatre's Revival in Europe").
- **Spotlight on Diversity boxes.** To further highlight varied traditions and give students an understanding and appreciation of the many voices in theatre, some of these boxes focus on non-Western theatre and others on diversity in U.S. theatre. These boxes describe not only ethnic and cultural diversity in the theatre but also diversity of thought. Examples of Spotlight on Diversity boxes are "Color-Blind Casting" (in Chapter 8, "The Art of Directing") and "Let's Do the Time Warp Again" (in Chapter 4, "The Audience, Criticism, and Free Speech") about audiences who are expected to "misbehave."
- **Interesting and relevant timelines.** Throughout the history chapters, timelines relate theatrical events to cultural and social events to illustrate theatre's place in world history.
- **Pronunciation guide.** The glossary includes pronunciation tips for theatre terms that may be unfamiliar to students, as well as a pronunciation guide for the hard-to-pronounce names of the theatre artists discussed in the book.
- **Integrated InfoTrac® College Edition readings.** These readings from periodicals encourage students to experience theatre online and explore the concepts presented in the text. (See "Resources for Students" and "Resources for Instructors," which follow, for more about InfoTrac College Edition.)

Resources for Students

- **Book Companion Website.** This outstanding site features useful web links, access to InfoTrac College Edition, suggested reading, chapter outlines, glossary flashcards, chapter-by-chapter online tutorial quizzes, a final exam, and more.
- **InfoTrac® College Edition with InfoMarks™.** Four months of free anywhere, anytime access to InfoTrac College Edition, the online library, can be bundled for free with this text. InfoTrac College Edition puts cutting-edge research and the latest headlines at your students' fingertips, giving them access to an entire online library for the cost of one book. This fully searchable database offers more than twenty years' worth of full-text articles (more than 10 million) from almost 4,000 diverse sources such as academic journals, newsletters, and up-to-the-minute periodicals, including *Time, Newsweek, American Theatre,* and *Criticism.* Your students also have access to InfoMarks—stable URLs that can be linked to articles, journals, and searches to save valuable time when doing research—and to the InfoWrite online resource center, where students can access grammar help, critical-thinking guidelines, guides to writing research papers, and much more.
- ***Theatre-Goer's Guide.*** This brief introduction to attending and critiquing drama enhances the student's experience and appreciation of theatre as a living art. This essential guide can be packaged for free with this text.

Resources for Instructors

- **Instructor's Resource Manual.** Save time, streamline your course preparation, and get the most from the text. This indispensable manual offers ideas for class discussions and papers, lecture notes that go beyond the text, exam questions, and easy-to-use quizzes for busy professors.
- **InfoTrac®** ***College Edition Student Activities Workbook for Theatre, 2.0.*** This unique workbook can be bundled with this text. Each workbook features extensive individual and group activities, focusing on specific course topics that make use of InfoTrac College Edition. Also included are guidelines for instructors and students that describe how to maximize the use of this resource.
- **ExamView® Computerized and Online Testing.** Create, deliver, and customize tests and study guides (both print and online) in minutes with this easy-to-use assessment and tutorial system. ExamView offers both a "Quick Test Wizard" and an "Online Test Wizard" that guide you step-by-step through the process of creating tests—you can even see the test you are creating on the screen exactly as it will print or display online. You can build tests of up to 250 questions using up to twelve question types. Using ExamView's complete word processing capabilities, you can enter an unlimited number of new questions or edit existing questions.
- **WebTutor™** ***Advantage on WebCT and Blackboard.*** With the text-specific, preformatted content and total flexibility of WebTutor Advantage, you can easily create and manage your own custom course website! The program's course management tool gives you the ability to provide virtual office hours, post syllabi, set up threaded discussions, track student progress with the quizzing material, and more. For students, WebTutor Advantage offers real-time access to a full array of study tools.
- **Multimedia Manager/Instructor's Resource CD-ROM.** This CD-ROM contains an electronic version of the Instructor's Resource Manual, ExamView® Computerized Testing, and predesigned Microsoft® PowerPoint® presentations. The PowerPoint presentation contains text and images that can be used as is or customized to suit your course needs.
- **The Arden Shakespeare Critical Editions.** Recognized and respected as the preeminent Shakespeare series, the Arden Shakespeare Critical Editions, second edition, are known for their readability and reliability, including full annotations and richly informative introductions. The plays included in this series are *The Tempest, A Midsummer Night's Dream, Twelfth Night, Othello, Hamlet,* and *King Lear.* These critical editions are only available—

at a substantial discount—when packaged with a Thomson Wadsworth theatre title. Consult your Thomson sales representative for packaging options.

- ***A Pocketful of Plays: Vintage Drama.*** This collection of some of the most commonly taught plays satisfies the need for a concise, quality anthology that students will find inexpensive and that instructors will enjoy teaching. The plays are accompanied by source materials to encourage discussion and analysis, as well as comments, biographical and critical commentaries, and reviews of actual productions. The featured plays are Susan Glaspell's *Trifles,* Sophocles' *Oedipus the King,* William Shakespeare's *Hamlet,* Henrik Ibsen's *A Doll's House,* Tennessee Williams's *The Glass Menagerie,* and Lorraine Hansberry's *A Raisin in the Sun.* This collection can be packaged with *Experiencing the Art of Theatre* at a reduced price.

Acknowledgments

A very special thank-you goes to Mike Earl, Lee Hodgson, Larry Hazlett, and Karl Brake for their help with the chapters on design, and to Sean Keogh for his help with the chapter on musical theatre. Thanks also to Robert St. Lawrence for his historical insight into lighting design. All donated their time, their designs, and their thoughts, and we are very grateful.

We also send our gratitude to other colleagues who gave us valuable assistance, including the University of Wyoming's Rebecca Hilliker, Jack Chapman, Don Turner, Peter Parolin, Harry Woods, Ron Steger, Wolf Sherill, Billie K. Gross, Leigh Selting, Ted Brummond, and Kathy Kirkaldie; and Ohio University's Charles Smith and Maureen Wagner. Special thanks to Oliver Walter and Tom Buchanan at the University of Wyoming, and to Rich Burk, Andy Bryson, Tamara Linse, Aiose Stratford, Keith Hull, Lew Hunter, Dr. James Livingston, Linda deVries, Peter Grego, Robin Russin, William Streib, Billie Wright, Barbara Brunett Ramsey, and our amazing students, past and present, at the University of Wyoming and Ohio University. Thanks also to the many reviewers of this book, who are listed on the inside front cover.

And thank you very much to the Thomson Wadsworth publishing team: Holly Allen, publisher; Greer Lleuad, senior developmental editor; Meghan Bass, editorial assistant; Lucinda Bingham, assistant editor; Jeanette Wiseman, senior technology project manager; Mark Orr, senior marketing manager; Alexandra Tran, marketing assistant; Jennifer Klos, production project manager; Mary Noel, production project manager; Barbara Armentrout, copyeditor; Stephen Forsling, photo researcher; and Katie O'Keeffe-Swank, project manager, Lachina Publishing Services.

About the Authors

William Missouri Downs has won numerous awards for teaching the introduction-to-theatre course at the University of Wyoming, including five Top Ten Teacher awards from graduating classes, two Top Prof awards from Mortar Board, and four Extraordinary Merit awards from his colleagues. With an average of 450 students per semester, his introduction-to-theatre course is the one of the largest classes at the university.

Downs holds an MFA in acting from the University of Illinois and an MFA in screenwriting from UCLA. He studied playwriting under Lanford Wilson and Milan Stitt at the Circle Repertory in New York and was a member of the Denver Center for the Performing Arts Playwrights Unit. He has authored a dozen plays, including *Jewish Sports Heroes and Texas Intellectuals,* which took first place at the Mill Mountain Theatre's Festival of New Plays; *Innocent Thoughts,* winner of the National Playwrights Award from the Unicorn Theatre in Kansas; and *Seagulls in a Cherry Tree,* winner of the Larry Corse Prize for Playwriting. His plays have been produced from New York to Singapore, from the Kennedy Center to the Berkeley Rep. As director and dramaturg, he has staged three original productions (*Rainy Day People* in 2002, *Missionary Position* in 2003, and the rock musical *Good Morning Athens* in 2004), which were selected as Region VII finalists in the American College Theatre Festival. *Good Morning Athens* was also produced at the Kennedy Center during the national American College Theatre Festival.

In addition to writing plays and directing, Downs is the author of the books *Naked Playwriting* and *Screenplay: Writing the Picture* both published by Silman-James Press. Before coming to the University of Wyoming, he lived in Hollywood, where he wrote for such NBC sitcoms as *My Two Dads* (which starred Paul Reiser), *Amen* (Sherman Hemsley), and *Fresh Prince of Bel Air* (Will Smith). After many years in New York and Los Angeles, he now enjoys living in the wide-open spaces of Wyoming.

Lou Anne Wright holds an MFA in voice, speech, and dialects from the National Theatre Conservatory. She is a certified teacher of Fitzmaurice Voicework and has vocal-coached productions from Los Angeles to the United Kingdom. As an actor, she has appeared in regional repertory and University of Wyoming productions of *The Last Night of Ballyhoo, The Seagull, Who's Afraid of Virginia Woolf?* and many others. She also played the role of Judy Shepard in the HBO film *The Laramie Project.* As a writer, Lou Anne has co-authored the play *Kabuki Medea,* winner of both the Bay Area Critics Award for best production in San Francisco and the Jefferson Award for best production in Chicago. It was also produced at the Kennedy Center for the Performing Arts. She is co-author of the book *Playwriting: From Formula to Form,* published by Harcourt Brace. Her screenwriting credits include the film adaptation of Eudora Welty's *The Hitch-Hikers,* which featured Patty Duke and Richard Hatch, and for which she was nominated for the Directors Guild of America's Lillian Gish Award. She has won an outstanding teaching award for teaching theatre history, voice and dialects, and acting at the University of Wyoming.

Erik Ramsey holds an MFA in playwriting from the University of Nevada, Las Vegas. He currently teaches at Ohio University as head of the BFA Playwriting Program and shares duties with playwright Charles Smith running the MFA Playwriting Program (ohioplaywriting.org). His plays have been workshopped and produced around the country, and several of his short works have been published by Samuel French and Dramatic Publishing. He is a past winner of the John Cauble Award, which included production at the Kennedy Center, and in 2002 the *Orange County Weekly* praised his play *Exploded View* as a "dazzlingly smart, powerful, and off-center diagram of life . . . far and away the best small theater production of the year" in the Los Angeles area. As a professional dramaturg, he has consulted on the development of a number of award-winning plays, including Julie Jensen's *Dust Eaters,* nominated by the American Theatre Critics Association for best new play produced outside New York in 2004. His latest play, *Lions Lost in Translation,* has been developed, read, and workshopped at numerous regional theaters, including Cleveland Public Theatre, American Stage, Washington Shakespeare Company, WordBridge Play Lab, and Pittsburgh Irish and Classical Theatre.

1 Theatre, Art, and Entertainment

hy is a can of Campbell's tomato soup on a supermarket shelf called lunch, while the same can sitting on a pedestal in an art gallery is called a work of art? Similarly, why is Shakespeare's play Romeo and Juliet *hailed as art, yet many dismiss the 1996 movie version starring Leonardo DiCaprio and Claire Danes as lightweight teen entertainment? What makes something* art *has been a subject of debate for centuries. Some boldly proclaim that art is everywhere and everything. Others assert that only objects that express beauty can be considered art. Who is right? This chapter provides a discussion about art that will help you understand the nature and purpose of theatre, describes why theatre is a unique form of art, and defines the major categories of theatre. Additionally, this chapter explores the distinction between art and entertainment and the role both play in our lives.*

© Kevin Berne/Courtesy Berkeley Repertory Theatre

◀ ***On preceding page:*** The Secret in the Wings, *written and directed by Mary Zimmerman, Berkeley Repertory Theatre, 2005, featuring (l to r) David Kersnar and Christopher Donahue. (The inset features Mark Alhadeff.) This play features retellings of five strange and rarely told European fairy tales.*

I Art, or Not Art: That Is the Question

Often the word *art* conjures up Mona Lisa's odd smile or ancient Greek statues lacking arms. We tend to think of *art* as an object, as something stationary that hangs in a museum or provides a perch for pigeons in the park. But art is not always an object. **Theatre** is a *performing art* and therefore dynamic. Theatre is also ephemeral, always changing and unique because no two performances can ever be identical. No two Hamlets ever ask the question "To be, or not to be. . ." in precisely the same way.

However, before comparing categories of art, we should take a closer look at the word itself. Think about how often the word *art* appears in everyday conversation. It is used in a wide array of contexts but generally conveys three main ideas: art as "skill," art as "beauty," and art as "meaning." We've all heard the word *art* used to describe the skill of golfer Tiger Woods as he drives a ball 386 yards with a finesse that drops it just inches from the hole. In this sense, the word *art* means "skill," and it derives from the Latin word *ars,* synonymous with the ancient Greek word *technē,* which means "skill" or "technique." And the word *artist* describes a person who has a great deal of skill or talent or whose work shows considerable technical proficiency or creativity. In this sense, *art* can be Tiger's exceptional golf swing as well as your favorite mechanic's cleverness at keeping your 1964 Mustang in top running condition.

FOR MORE ON
AESTHETICS
"In consideration of aesthetics," Marilyn Brakhage, *Chicago Review,* Winter 2001

We use *art* in the second sense when we make such comments as "The sunset at the beach was a work of art." When we use the word *art* to describe something of great beauty, whether it's a real and magnificent sunset or an exact watercolor replica of that same sunset, we are talking about aesthetics. **Aesthetics** is the branch of philosophy that deals with the nature and expression of beauty. When this definition of *art* is taken to the extreme, it gives art no other purpose than to delight the eye, to please the ear, and to stimulate a pleasant experience. In this sense, an artist is simply someone whose creations are deemed aesthetically pleasing by an individual or by society.

In the third sense, *art* can be defined as "meaning." When Martin Luther King, Jr., gave his "I Have a Dream" speech on the steps of the Lincoln Memorial in 1963, he did not set out to create art but rather to address America about civil rights: "I have a dream that one day this nation will rise up and live out the true meaning of its creed: 'We hold these truths to be self-evident that all men are created equal.'" This speech is now often considered to be the single most important oration of the twentieth century because of its poetic and artful ideas. King's speech, his vision for America, is often referred to as a work of art because of its meaning and its message.

© Hulton-Deutsch-Collection/Corbis

Most people think of Martin Luther King, Jr., as a minister and a civil rights leader, not as an artist. Yet many of his speeches, including his "I Have a Dream" speech, could be considered art because they convey such deep meaning and were delivered with such oratorical skill.

Similarly, artists such as playwrights frequently use the word *art* in terms of meaning. Artists commonly view their art as their own interpretation or judgment of existence, rather than simply as an act of skill or a work of beauty. When the word *art* is used in this way, the implicit meaning is "this is life as I, the artist, see it. This is my personal take on things." Certainly, when artists set out to create meanings, they may choose to do so in a socially acceptable manner. They may even choose to support their meanings with great skill and beauty. However, an artist may also choose to ignore, intend to challenge, or utterly defy traditional social values and disregard common standards of technique and beauty.

Theatre, or any kind of art, that confronts or violates the popular understanding of skill, aesthetics, and meaning can be dangerous to create. What if the audience disagrees with the artist's interpretation, finds it offensive, or simply refuses to pay attention? Moreover, what if an artist's personal interpretation is deliberately repulsive, created with little talent, and evokes the opposite of pleasure? The idea that art can reflect no skill, contain little beauty, and be unpleasant is sometimes hard to comprehend.

Clearly, there is much disagreement about what art is. This is nothing new. For millennia people have been debating whether art is simply a means to create objects of beauty and pleasure or is a tool to educate, inform, influence,

Art is a selective re-creation of reality according to an artist's metaphysical value judgments. Man's profound need of art lies in the fact that his cognitive faculty is conceptual, i.e., that he acquires knowledge by means of abstractions, and needs the power to bring his widest metaphysical abstractions into his immediate perceptual awareness.

Ayn Rand,
American author and philosopher

FOR MORE ON
ART AND BEAUTY
"An argument about beauty," Susan Sontag, *Daedalus*, Fall 2002

Kobal Collection/Picture Desk

Because the notion of art is so closely tied to the notion of beauty, art that is unconventional, unfamiliar, or unpleasant can provoke a hostile response. This has been true throughout history. For example, the paintings of French impressionist Claude Monet, which are now adored by the general public, were considered shocking and controversial when they were first exhibited in 1874. More recently, work that is considered art by some—such as Oliver Stone's movie Natural Born Killers *(shown here), Chris Ofili's painting* Holy Virgin Mary, *and Karen Finley's performance piece* We Keep Our Victims Ready*—has been condemned by others.*

> I don't think art has a consensus. I don't think ten people in a room talking about art could agree about whether something is good or bad art.
>
> ***Richard Prince,***
> *American artist*

FOR MORE ON
PLATO, ARISTOTLE, AND ART
"Plato: The morality and immorality of art," James Sloan Allen, *Arts Education Policy Review,* November–December 2002

and incite—or is all of these things. For example, in ancient Greece comic playwright Aristophanes (ca. 450–ca. 388 BCE) said of the theatre arts, "The dramatist should not only offer pleasure but should also be a teacher of morality and a political adviser." Yet his near contemporary, Greek astronomer and mathematician Eratosthenes (276–194 BCE), said the function of the theatre arts was to "charm the spirits of the listeners, but never to instruct them." Similarly, Greek philosophers Plato (427–347 BCE) and his student Aristotle (384–322 BCE) disagreed about the nature of theatre. Aristotle believed theatre is a creation meant to interpret the world and awake the soul, but Plato maintained that art should be a tool of the state and promote the well-being of the body politic. (For more about Plato and Aristotle, see the Spotlight box "Plato, Aristotle, and the Theatre Arts.")

The ancient Greeks' discussion about art has continued for two thousand years. Later in this chapter we will further explore why we create art and what role it should play in society, but first let's define some basic qualities of art.

The Qualities of Art

A few years ago, a janitor in a modern art gallery accidentally left his grimy mop and bucket on the gallery floor overnight. The next morning the gallery manager was shocked to find patrons gathered around the mess, admiring it as a work of art. This story illustrates how difficult it is to provide an exact definition of a word like *art.* In fact, defining any word that expresses an idea can be a challenge, as you've probably noticed when you've looked up certain words in the dictionary and found that they mean a number of different things. For example, it's nearly impossible to find a definition for the word *game* that applies to all games. We can say that poker and baseball are both games, yet they have little in common. We can say that games are about enjoyment, yet how much enjoyment is there in losing? We can say that games involve winning and competition, yet some games, such as the dress-up games kids play, are not meant to be won.

In his book *Philosophical Investigations,* British philosopher Ludwig Wittgenstein (1889–1951) points out that trying to find all-encompassing definitions is not only difficult, but also introduces boundaries that limit our imagination. Instead, he suggests we define words by pointing out their "family resemblances," or the ways in which the many different meanings of a word resemble one another. So rather than nailing down the exact definition of the word *art,* let's list the five basic qualities that all works of art share to an extent: human creation, structure, subject and medium, and reaction.

Art Is Created by Human Beings The most defining quality of art is that only human beings create it. As the *American Heritage Dictionary* puts it, art is "a human effort to imitate, supplement, alter, or counteract the work of nature." From this definition it is easy to see how the word *art* springs from the same root as the word *artificial.* As Spanish artist Pablo Picasso (1881–1973) said, "Art is a lie that enables us to realize the truth." However, art is not a "lie" or "artificial" in the sense that it intends to deceive. Art is artificial only in the sense that it is not the actual object or idea it represents, but rather a human

Plato, Aristotle, and the Theatre Arts

Plato (427–347 BCE) was a teacher, a philosopher, and an amateur playwright with political ambitions. However, early in his career he was persuaded by his teacher, Socrates (ca. 469–399 BCE), that playwriting was a waste of time, so he burned all his plays. Later in his career he wrote a series of some thirty dialogues between Socrates and others. These dialogues, conversation-like plays meant to be read rather than performed, deal with art, drama, censorship, metaphysics, immortality, religion, humanity, and the mind. Plato's most famous student was Aristotle (384–322 BCE). Aristotle's early writing strongly supported Plato's views, but later he began to develop his own distinct philosophies. He wrote on such diverse topics as logic, psychology, and the natural sciences. His treatise called *Poetics* is the first known text on how to write a play. It outlines the elements and structure of a good tragedy—unfortunately, his treatise on how to write comic plays has been lost.

Plato and Aristotle had very different ideas about theatre and its role in society. Plato accused theatre people of promoting vice and wickedness and of being largely responsible for the corruption of his day. He reasoned that because playwrights and actors are unable to commit heroic acts such as leading armies and ruling cities, they must compensate for their own worthlessness by mimicking the actions of people who do. His vision of a perfect republic, ruled by philosopher-kings and soldiers, had no room for the theatre. But, if there *had* to be theatre, he felt it must be subservient to the state and to society. He also advocated banning plays that did not promote the well-being of the body politic. He justified this call for censorship by asserting that people are imitative animals and tend to become what they imitate. He cautioned therefore that if we allow theatre, we should ensure that it features only characters that are suitable role models.

Aristotle disagreed with his mentor. He felt that art and theatre do not stir undesirable passions but rather they awaken the soul. He would argue that seeing a play in which a son marries his mother, as in the ancient Greek tragedy *Oedipus Rex,* doesn't cause the young men in the audience to run out and propose marriage to their mothers. (As independent film director John Waters once said, "No story is that good.") Instead, he believed that good theatre fortifies us because it allows us to release repressed emotions in a controlled, therapeutic way. Plato's concerns about the dangers of theatre stemmed from his belief that all we have here on earth are imitations of perfection. Thus, in theatre an audience imitates the actions of actors, who imitate the actions of human beings, who are themselves imitations of the *idea* of a perfect human being. However, as Brazilian theatre director Augusto Boal explains it, Aristotle argued that art does not slavishly copy nature but instead clarifies, abstracts, interprets, and idealizes it. Therefore, art depicts the universal character of things and includes the lessons the artist has learned by living and observing nature.

By Raphael, the Vatican, Rome. Photo © Ted Spiegel/Corbis

***Plato and Aristotle** (l to r), detail from Raphael's* The School of Athens *(1510–1511)*

interpretation of it. Therefore, snow-capped mountains, no matter how beautiful and inspiring, are not art because human hands did not create them, and those same mountains cannot become art until human hands interpret them through a medium such as oil paint on canvas.

© Richard Feldman

A cherry tree in full bloom is certainly beautiful, but because it was not created by human hands, it is not art. Yet when an orchard of cherry trees is interpreted as a metaphor for home, family, reversal of fortune, and, living in the past—as it is in the play The Cherry Orchard *by Russian playwright Anton Chekhov—it is transformed into art. This 2004 production was directed by Michael Greif at The Williamstown Theatre Festival in Williamstown, Massachusetts, and featured (l to r) Chris Messina, Linda Emond, Michelle Williams, Lee Wilkof, Reed Birney, and Frank Raiter.*

Art Provides the Perception of Order Art attempts to give structure, a meaningful form or order, to the visible and invisible aspects of life and nature. Artists select and arrange their perceptions of the world into unified wholes. If they cannot perceive a structure, then they impose structure. "It is the function of all art to give us some perception of an order in life, by imposing order upon it," said the poet T. S. Eliot. But why do we impose structure? We do so because we need art to help us make sense of our existence—art allows us, with our limited senses, to perceive what life and nature are trying to communicate. Structure develops when we begin to distinguish or impose patterns in our physical, emotional, psychological, social, and spiritual realities. Without these patterns there can be no art.

Aristotle spoke of structure when he said that art gives matter form. Matter is the raw material of nature—the matter of a statue is marble, the matter of music is sound, the matter of theatre is human interaction. Matter is pure potential. Form, on the other hand, is the *enactment* of potential. Form is what the marble, the sound, or the human interaction becomes in the hands of an artist. With form comes meaning and purpose. And so when an artist structures the sounds of nature (matter), we have the sound of a trumpet (form), and when an artist structures a block of marble (matter), we have a statue of Caesar (form). In this way, the structure of form reflects human intelligence and our ability to create order. In theatre, *structure* can refer to how a drama fits together as a recognizable progression of events through the arrangement and interconnection of story and character. The structure of art can be a precise blueprint or a loose method, but either way it is a design that helps an audience connect.

> Art is the layer that lies between the skin of truth and falsity—that which is false but not false, true but not true—that is what gives us joy.
>
> **Chikamatsu Monzaemon,** *Japanese playwright*

Art Consists of a Subject and a Medium Every work of art has a subject and a medium. The **subject** of the work is what that work is about, what it reflects and attempts to comprehend. The **medium** is the method, substance, and technique used to create the work. For example, the subject of an opera might be love and betrayal, and the medium is song. The subject of a dance might be the beginning of spring, and its medium is choreographed physical movement. Every type of art has a different medium that defines it and makes it unique. The **spatial arts**, such as sculpture and architecture, are created by manipulating material in space. The **pictorial arts**, such as drawing and painting, are created by applying line and color to two-dimensional surfaces. The **literary arts** are created with written language. Theatre is classified as a **performing art**, as are music, opera, and dance. The medium of the performing arts is an act performed by a living human being. In this way the performing arts are unique—they exist only in the time it takes an actor, musician, or dancer to complete a performance, and they necessarily have a beginning, middle, and end. Once a performance ends, the work of art no longer exists, leaving behind no tangible object such as a painting or a statue.

© Michal Daniel

One of the reasons why the plays of William Shakespeare continue to be staged and filmed today is that they tell timeless stories and evoke universal feelings. Although these plays were written hundreds of years ago, their plots and characters still amuse us, sadden us, call us to arms, inspire us, and make us think. Their ability to affect us in meaningful ways is what makes them art. This production of Othello *featured Keith David as Othello and Kate Forbes as Desdemona; it was directed by Doug Hughes at The Public Theater, New York, 2001.*

Art Makes You Feel Something Finally, in order for something to be a work of art, it must have an audience. (Interestingly, the word *theatre* is related to the Greek verb *theasthai,* meaning "to view as spectators.") Additionally, the audience must be affected—they must have a reaction to the art. If a work has no audience, or if the audience remains unmoved, then there is no art. As Russian author and philosopher Leo Tolstoy (1828–1910) said, "Art is a human activity which is passed on to others, causing them to feel and experience what the artist has felt and experienced. . . . It is a means of communication between people, uniting them in the same feelings. . . . As soon as the spectators are affected by the same feelings which the artist felt—that is art." Art provokes in us a reaction that causes us to consider, judge, emote, or perceive meaning in some way. Yet, each audience member views a work of art through the lenses of his or her own experiences, education, and interests. And because each of us understands and perceives differently, what is art to one audience member may not be *art* to another. This is the root of the difficulty in finding a definition of art on which all can agree.

An equally thorny problem is clearly determining the *purpose* of art. As you read in the Spotlight box "Plato, Aristotle, and the Theatre Arts," this question has been debated for centuries. And as we will see shortly, the purpose of art is closely related to the politics of art, or the worldview guiding the artist's choices.

FOR MORE ON
WHAT IS ART?
"Is computer-generated art really art?" Frank Rose, *Lotus,* May 1990

The Purpose of Art

When the *Mona Lisa,* one of the most famous paintings in the Western world, was stolen from the Louvre Museum in 1911, hundreds of people went to the museum and stared at the empty place where the picture had hung. For nearly two years, until the painting was recovered, the empty space was almost as popular as the painting itself. This story illustrates something about the depths of our feelings about art. But why did people stand there staring at a blank wall? What were they trying to remember? What did they miss?

Italian artist and inventor Leonardo da Vinci (1452–1519), the painter of the *Mona Lisa,* once said, "Although nature commences with reason and ends

It would be difficult to judge decisively whether art or nature is the greater teacher. Nature has more to tell us, but art is better skilled for utterance. Nature has so much to say that she has no patience for articulation. She thrills us with a vague awareness of multitudinous indecipherable messages; but she speaks to us in whispers and in thunders—elusive, indeterminate, discomforting. Art, with less to say, has more patience for the formulation of her messages; she speaks to us in a voice that has been deliberately trained, and her utterance is lucid and precise.

Clayton Hamilton,
American professor and writer

in experience, it is necessary for us to do the opposite—that is, to commence with experience and from this to proceed to investigate the reason." We humans have always had a need to understand and improve upon nature, to bring order to what seems to be a chaotic universe. Religion and philosophy help many people explain *why* natural events occur. For example, when a child dies of an illness, the parents are devastated. For some parents, their religious beliefs help them feel there is a higher plan for them and the child, which gives meaning to the death and helps them bear their grief. Assigning religious or philosophical meaning to death improves upon nature by refuting the view that natural events happen randomly and for no reason. Similarly, science helps explain *how* natural events occur. Science can tell the parents exactly what caused the illness and death of the child and perhaps how to prevent the death of other children. This knowledge helps the parents understand their child's illness and perhaps improve upon nature by advocating advances in diagnosis and treatment for other children.

Yet how does art help us understand and improve upon nature? Artists attempt to bring order to nature by creating work that expresses their own unique points of view about various aspects of nature. They voice their opinions, express their emotions, and interpret natural events to show us how the world is for them or how they think it should be. In creating art, artists explain or improve upon nature by adding to our understanding of it and ourselves. For example, let's say a mother creates a painting of herself sitting alone in a hospital room with her sick child. In reality, her spouse was always with her at their child's bedside, but by omitting her spouse from the painting, she conveys how alone she felt in her grief. The painting helps us understand

© Michal Daniel

Spanish playwright Federico García Lorca's Blood Wedding *(1932) is a good example of art that singles out aspects of life in order to explore their meaning. The play is based on a newspaper article about a bride who runs away with her childhood sweetheart and is subsequently murdered by the man she left at the altar. García Lorca used this story to explore not the actual event but aspects of it that interested him: desire, repression, ritual, and the constraints of community. This production was performed at the Guthrie Lab, Minneapolis, 2002, and featured Morena Baccarin and Rene Millan.*

what she was feeling and improves upon nature by showing us her state of mind, which would otherwise be invisible to us.

Artists isolate the aspects of nature they regard as essential and integrate them into a concrete, focused, and organized view of life. They select and arrange the stuff of life in order to emphasize certain elements. With this organization comes meaning and significance. As American theatre set designer Robert Edmond Jones (1887–1954) once said, "The world of the theatre is a world of sharper, clearer, swifter impressions than the world we live in." This selective aspect of art troubles some who believe the artist's duty is, as Shakespeare's Hamlet says, "to hold, as 'twere, the mirror up to nature; to show virtue her own feature, scorn her own image." In other words, some believe art should imitate life. Yet, if all artists were simply to create art that imitated nature, they would not be able to create meaning. Art would serve only to reflect what we already see and experience of nature, not help us understand it and improve upon it. Because it is not a mirror to nature but rather is based in opinion and interpretation, art is also inherently political.

The Politics of Art

Every time artists make a choice about what aspect of nature to select and arrange, they express a value judgment and reveal their dominant philosophy of life. In this way art is like politics in the broad sense that it reflects people's conflicting beliefs about how we should live, how society should be organized, and how the world is. "Politics" in this sense does not necessarily refer to elections, law making, and the schemes of the Republican or Democratic parties, but rather to the philosophical agenda the artist is pursuing by creating a work of art.

American philosopher and novelist Ayn Rand (1905–1982) interpreted the notion that art is political quite elegantly with the following example. Imagine that a beautiful woman in a lovely evening gown enters a ballroom. She is perfect in every way except for the fact that she has a rather large, ugly cold sore on her lip. What do we make of it? What does it mean? Not much—many people are afflicted with cold sores, and they are perhaps unfortunate but have little meaning. However, if a painter paints a picture of a beautiful woman in a lovely evening gown and portrays her with the same ugly cold sore, the blemish suddenly takes on great importance. This minor imperfection, says Rand,

> acquires a monstrous metaphysical significance by virtue of being included in a painting. It declares that a woman's beauty and her efforts to achieve glamour (the beautiful evening gown) are a futile illusion undercut by a seed of corruption which can mar and destroy them at any moment—that this is reality's mockery of man—that all man's values and efforts are impotent against the power, not even of some great cataclysm, but of a miserable little physical infection.

Artists select those aspects of existence they believe are significant, isolate them, and stress them to create meaning. The result is that artists' fundamental views of life are embodied within their art. Thus, at the core of every artist is a political individual who states an opinion that may challenge an audience's values and shatter their preconceptions.

> A work of art is the unique result of a unique temperament. Its beauty comes from the fact that the author is what he is. It has nothing to do with the fact that other people want what they want. Indeed, the moment that an artist takes notice of what other people want, and tries to supply the demand, he ceases to be an artist.
>
> **_Oscar Wilde,_**
> *Irish poet and dramatist*

However, art and what we commonly think of as "politics" often do run hand in hand. Many artists espouse political causes, actively support political candidates, state their political opinions publicly, or create art about specific political ideas. Bands such as the Clash and Rage Against the Machine are well known for the political nature of their songs and for their resistance to the corporate policies of the record companies that distribute their music. Film actors such as Leonardo DiCaprio and Nicole Kidman actively support political organizations—DiCaprio is a major contributor to the International Fund for Animal Welfare, and Kidman donates both her time and money as a Goodwill ambassador for the United Nations Children's Fund (UNICEF). South African playwright Athol Fugard has spent his life writing plays that attack apartheid, or state-sponsored racial segregation.

Artists, Entertainers, and Politics

Some artists and entertainers are not content to simply lend their names to political campaigns or to create works of art that confront the politics of their day. Rather, they jump directly into the business of politics. Vigdis Finnbogadottir, director of the Reykjavik Theatre, was elected president of Iceland, and movie stars Rama Rao of India and Joseph Estrada of the Philippines both became successful politicians in their countries. In the United States many actors and performers have gone on to successful careers in politics, including the child star Shirley Temple, song-and-dance man George Murphy, singer Sonny Bono, and actors Fred Grandy (*Love Boat*) and Ben Jones (*Dukes of Hazzard*). And, of course, we cannot overlook the former actor, movie star, and president of the Screen Actors Guild who became the fortieth president of the United States, Ronald Reagan, or the recently elected governor of California, Arnold Schwarzenegger, previously best known as the "Terminator."

Yet the road for artists into politics has often been perilous. Outside the United States, fame can be dangerous, especially if that fame is based on political ideas or art. For example, before Czechoslovakian playwright Václav Havel became president of the new Czech Republic in 1993, he was arrested so often by the former Communist regime that he carried his toothbrush with him—ready to go to jail on a moment's notice. Nigerian writer Wole Soyinka, the first black writer to win the Nobel Prize for Literature (1986), spent two years in solitary confinement secretly writing on toilet paper and discarded cigarette wrappers after he was arrested for his political views during Nigeria's civil war. Also in Nigeria, playwright Ken Saro-Wiwa was executed in 1996 by the government for his outspoken views against environmental pollution and the unfair business practices of the Royal Dutch/Shell Oil Company.

As Polish actor Zygmunt Hubner (1930–1989), former director of the Powszechny Theatre in Warsaw, said, "Beware of underestimating the theatre! The theatre is both a Shakespearean mirror of the world and also a lens that focuses the rays of many suns. And a lens can start a fire." That lens is the artist's interpretation of how the world is and should be. Often it is the artists who get burned, but on occasion art can also stoke an inferno that reduces tyranny to ashes.

© Robert Galbraith/Reuters/Landov

Arnold Schwarzenegger

© Petr Josek/Reuters/Landov

Artists often see their work as political, and some deal directly with political themes. For example, in the 1970s Czechoslovakian playwright Václav Havel wrote a series of one-act plays, Audience, Private View, *and* Protest, *in which the protagonist is a dissident playwright in trouble with the authorities. These plays reflected his own life as a dissident, frequently arrested for his "subversive" activities. Like many other artists, Havel went from creating political art to becoming a politician—in 1993 he became president of the new Czech Republic. He is pictured here with the Dalai Lama.*

FOR MORE ON
VÁCLAV HAVEL
"Saluting the playwright who became president," Peter C. Newman, *Maclean's*, August 17, 1998

As you can see from the Spotlight on Diversity "Artists, Entertainers, and Politics," the theatre arts often tend toward the political, both in ideas and in actions. This is due to the distinctive qualities that define the art of theatre.

This Wide and Universal Theatre: Theatre and Drama Defined

What makes theatre different from other forms of art? Theatre is unique in that it is the only art for which the medium and subject are exactly the same: the human experience. However, the human experience can be expressed on stage in a variety of ways. Many times when we say we're "going to the theatre," we are actually referring to attending a play: a story portrayed by actors on a stage and containing motivated plot elements that can be dramatic, comedic, musical, or some combination of the three. But "theatre" can be more than these traditional and recognizable story elements and forms.

What Is Theatre? What Is Drama?

The word *theatre* comes from the ancient Greek word *theatron,* which means "seeing place." The word *drama* comes from the ancient Greek verb *dran,* which means "to take action, to do, to make, or to accomplish." These meanings still apply today—theatre is about an audience witnessing a production or a theatrical event, whereas drama is a form of theatre that tells a story in which characters set out to do, to accomplish, or to take some sort of action.

In his book *The Empty Space,* English director Peter Brook states that all that is needed for theatre to occur is an empty space and someone to walk across that space while someone else watches. In later chapters we'll discuss the various types of spaces, or stages, used throughout history and today. At this point, simply note that, at its most basic, theatre requires only a space, a performer, and an audience. Story, characters, spectacle, costumes, lights, script, and sets are all unnecessary. They may improve the theatrical experience, but they are optional. As such, many events can qualify as a kind of theatre: weddings, award banquets, football games, political rallies, church services, or even a supermodel walking down a runway. Any time people get together with the common purpose of throwing the focus on a particular person, we have a theatrical event.

Drama is a form of theatre that tells a story about people, their actions, and the conflicts that result. **Conflict** is the key to the movement of a story and is what qualifies a theatrical work as a "play." Whether explicit or implicit, conflict is at the core of drama. As Professor David Ball, author of *Backwards & Forwards: A Technical Manual for Reading Plays,* puts it, "People who talk about, write about, or do theatre agree on little. But there is one thing: 'Drama is *conflict*!' we all cry in rare unanimity. Then we go back to squabbling over whether *Measure for Measure is* a comedy." Comedy is a subgenre of drama in which the conflicts work out to achieve a happy ending. The conflicts in comedy may be humorous or even ridiculous, but they are conflicts nonetheless, driving the story along. If there is no conflict, there is no power struggle, and if there is no power struggle, there is no story—whether lightly comedic or darkly dramatic. Without story, there may be theatre but not drama.

Both theatre and drama have three qualities that make them unique art forms. First, theatre is always live. This means that theatre cannot be replayed, like a film. If you hit the Rewind button, you can watch a movie again and again and it is always the same. This is not so in the theatre because no two performances are ever exactly the same. The differences from performance to performance may be subtle, but no matter how hard the performers try to act in the same way at each performance, there are always differences. So, if you go to the theatre on Monday night and tell a friend that you loved the performance, and your friend goes to the same show on Tuesday night and says that he hated it, you both may be right because the two of you did not see the same exact performance or see it with the same audience.

© Louie Psihoyos/Corbis

The Blue Man Group is a theatre group that performs synchronized productions mixing percussion-driven music and flashy special effects into a visual extravaganza. It's "must-see theatre," full of comedic bits and acrobatic routines, but because these performances don't tell a story, they don't qualify as drama.

The second quality that makes drama and theatre unique is that they are always about human beings. A painting might be about a flower, a poem might be about the stars, but theatre and drama can only be about human beings and human emotions. In other words, the medium and subject are exactly the same, even when expressed via other creatures, such as felines in the musical *Cats* or woodland fairies in Shakespeare's *A Midsummer Night's Dream.* These plays aren't really about fairies and cats but human emotions. In fact, theatrical performances that do not include any people are still about human beings. For example, in a puppet show, the puppets are controlled by human beings and express human emotions. If you watch performing bears at the circus, they don't act as bears. Instead, they wear human clothing, ride bicycles, and perform other acts that imitate human behavior. In contrast, if you watch bears at the zoo, it is not theatre because they are behaving as bears, not imitating human beings. At their most basic, theatre and drama always express something fundamental about the human condition with the intention to touch, arouse, inform, entertain, or even enrage the audience by portraying aspects of themselves.

The third quality that makes theatre and drama unique is that they are often collaborative forms of art, requiring more than one type of art and artist to produce. This is not true of most other forms of art, which are the product of a single individual. For example, art museums are often very quiet. They do not feature music, because it would interfere with the visual art. Similarly, we do not need music, dance, or a director to help us read a book. In contrast, plays often use lights, sound, movement, words, and actions. When you attend the theatre, more often than not you experience art made by an ensemble of artists. Often the final product is a result of how well all these artists coordinated their artistic visions. In later chapters we will explore in greater detail the various artists involved in crafting theatre.

Now that you've learned a bit about what makes theatre unique among the arts, let's explore the five most common categories of theatre: commercial, historical, political, experimental, and cultural.

The Common Categories of Theatre

There are many types of theatre, most of which are covered in greater detail in later chapters of this text. However, let's take some time here to survey the most common categories in order to understand the various roles theatre plays in society.

Perhaps the most familiar category of theatre is **commercial theatre,** which includes big musicals as well as comedies and dramas that are intended to be entertaining and profitable. Commercial plays offer safe themes, plenty of

© Joan Marcus

Commercial theatre offers safe themes, laughs, and spectacle, all of which are designed to appeal to a majority of the public and make a lot of money. Examples of successful commercial plays include the blockbuster musicals The Phantom of the Opera, The Producers, *and* Wicked, *all among the top ten highest-grossing shows on Broadway. Shown here is the 2003 Broadway production of* Wicked *featuring Kristin Chenoweth as Glinda and Idina Menzel as Elphaba, the future Wicked Witch of the West; it was directed by Joe Mantello.*

laughs, and spectacle designed to appeal to a majority of people, thereby filling lots of seats and ideally making lots of money. Big Broadway productions of Walt Disney's *Beauty and the Beast* and *The Lion King* are perfect examples of commercial theatre, but it can also include familiar plays appealing to the widest possible demographic staged by small local theatres. The commercial theatre has been around for thousands of years. As we will see next, most other types of theatre are not designed to be purely entertaining or to turn a profit.

Historical theatre presents dramas that use the styles, themes, and staging of plays of a particular historical period. And there is plenty of history to be staged, for theatre has been around for thousands of years and has reflected hundreds of styles and themes. From the classical forms of theatre that existed more than two thousand years ago, such as Sophocles' *Oedipus Rex,* to Shakespeare's *Hamlet,* to the dawn of modern drama with Ibsen's *A Doll's House,* historical theatre attempts to show how far humanity has come by presenting costumes, acting styles, language, and subject matter that express universal human concerns rather than ideas that are specific to the current generation. When you attend this type of theatre, you'll probably enjoy it more if you have some knowledge of history and do some research beforehand into the background of the particular playwright and theatrical style. When you attend historical theatre, you are not just being entertained, you are also getting a lesson in history. And one of those lessons may be that though a play is hundreds of years old, the themes are still very relevant.

© Michal Daniel

Historical theatre uses costumes, acting styles, and language of earlier eras, but the subject matter expresses universal human experiences. Examples of historical theatre are Euripides' Medea *(the power of jealousy and vengeance), Molière's* Tartuffe *(religious hypocrisy), and Eugene O'Neill's* The Hairy Ape *(the effect of industrialization on the worker and the frustration of class discrimination). Shown here is* Medea*, played by Barbra Berlovitz, with her children; the production was directed by Steven Epp at the Theatre de la Jeune Lune, Minneapolis, 2002.*

Political theatre allows playwrights, directors, and actors to express their personal opinions about current issues, trends, and politics. This type of theatre is a bully pulpit, an open mike, and a bullhorn that allows the artist to express ideas that are seldom heard in the mainstream media or in commercial theatre. Political theatre allows artists to ask an audience to join them in a protest or in calling for social change. It can also be theatre that is designed by "the powers that be" in order to control the hearts and minds of the people. For example, during World War II, Nazi Germany's rulers produced propaganda plays and highly theatrical political rallies designed to win the people over to their way of thinking.

Plays can also be experimental in nature. Just as automakers display concept cars that try out new designs, theatre artists also experiment with styles and ideas in **experimental plays** that push the limits of theatre. These plays might break down barriers by eliminating the distance between actor and audience, try out new staging techniques, or even question the nature of theatre itself. For example, The Living Theatre of the 1960s dedicated itself to staging such works as *Paradise Now* (1968) in which actors asked the audience to join them in a protest calling for a social revolution. Experimental plays are an attempt to reinvent theatre, for all art forms must avoid stagnation by constantly searching for what the future of the art form might be.

Finally, there is **cultural theatre**, which is designed to support the heritage, customs, and point of view of a particular people, religion, class, country, or community. This theatre celebrates human diversity by providing the audience a window into a world that is different from their own or by preserving the unique traditions of a particular society. As later chapters of this book will discuss, when you attend Japanese Kabuki plays, African ritual plays, or Navajo

© Yuriko Nakao/Reuters/Corbis

Cultural theatre supports the heritage, customs, and worldviews of a particular social group or country. This type of theatre celebrates the diversity of humanity by providing the audience with a window into a world different from their own. Examples of cultural theatre include traditional Chinese opera and Japanese Noh performances, ritual Maori dance ceremonies, and modern plays by playwrights such as Athol Fugard and Wole Soyinka, both from Africa. Here, Noh actors dance during a Takigi Noh performance at the Sensoji temple in Tokyo, 2004.

dance ceremonies, you reinforce your own culture or learn about other peoples' cultures by witnessing aspects of their religion, history, customs, folklore, or worldviews.

When attending the theatre, remember that any given performance doesn't necessarily fit neatly into just one of these categories. For example, a play can be both cultural and commercial, and another might be political and experimental. But knowing about these basic categories can increase your enjoyment of the theatre. For example, if you go to the theatre expecting a purely commercial production and find yourself watching an experimental play, you might not find it entertaining. In fact, you might be offended. Instead, try to keep an open mind, determine what type of theatre you're witnessing, and enjoy or study it for what it is rather than what you thought it would be. And remember that theatre is not always designed simply to entertain us. Sometimes it teaches us, sometimes it insults us, and sometimes it makes us think.

Fair Is Foul: Setting for Horror and Tragedy in *Macbeth*

One of the ways in which we understand films and plays is by classifying them into genres with familiar conventions. When we watch a comedy, a tragedy, or a thriller, we know what to expect of the story, setting, and tone. We know comedies will make us laugh and end happily, whereas we expect tragedies to involve dire conflict and end with sorrow or disaster. Some films and plays combine genres, so we have comedic dramas and melodramatic thrillers. One particularly interesting combination is director Roman Polanski's film *The Tragedy of Macbeth* (1971), a film that stays faithful to its theatrical source but also draws heavily on horror, a predominantly cinematic genre.

In William Shakespeare's play *Macbeth,* the title character, a courageous Scottish general, is visited by three witches who predict he will be crowned king of Scotland. He doesn't believe them initially, but ensuing events cause him to wonder if what they said could be true. He tells his wife, Lady Macbeth, about the prophecy. Ruthless and ambitious, she convinces him to fulfill it by killing the current king, Duncan. Although filled with doubt, he does as she says and takes the throne. And so begins a downward spiral of paranoia, murder, and madness as Macbeth slaughters rivals to maintain his position and guilt slowly drives Lady Macbeth insane.

Polanski takes this tragic story into the realm of

© Richard Termine

On stage, Lady Macbeth vainly tries to wash blood from her hands, blood only she can see. In this 2004 production, Kelly McGillis played Lady Macbeth; it was directed by Michael Kahn at the Shakespeare Theatre in Washington, DC.

From Stage to Screen

Kobal Collection/Picture Desk

On screen, warrior Macbeth (played by Jon Finch) defeats his enemies on a vast battlefield.

horror by using visual elements common to slasher films, such as bloody daggers, disturbing dream sequences, and gruesome murders. And with its references to thunderstorms, blasted heaths, and embattled castles, *Macbeth* lends itself to the sort of epic visuals that live theatre cannot easily offer. Polanski's *Macbeth* is filled with dark, miserable skies, exploiting the gloomy atmosphere that in horror movies signals impending doom. Terrible storms accompany the witches, and booming thunder heralds evil deeds as Duncan steps into the trap laid for him.

Polanski's powerful opening sequence demonstrates how film can use setting to underscore meaning. His first shot is of an empty beach at dawn—empty, that is, until we see the witches, disturbingly real as they chant incantations and bury gory charms in the sand. As fog begins to roll over the beach, they retreat, vanishing as they are obscured by the mist. The fog then lifts, revealing that the beach has become a bloody battlefield. The implication is clear: These witches operate in the natural world but manipulate it with unnatural powers.

Polanski also uses interior settings to reinforce Shakespeare's themes in a lavishly cinematic way. Our first view of Macbeth's castle is through close-ups of clean straw in an open courtyard full of bustling servants preparing a feast. This scene contrasts strongly with the menacing claustrophobia of the witches' hovel, where the feast is putrid and the "servants" are naked, distorted apparitions. Here we see an underworld that is both physically real and a metaphor for internal corruption. Later Polanski shows us the deliberately homey setting of a rival's castle, strewn with murdered children. These contrasts are truly sad and horrifying, symbolizing Macbeth's conflicting feelings of ambition and guilt. This conflict is the emotional crux of the tragedy, beautifully and brutally portrayed through cinema's lens of horror.

Aoise Stratford
Playwright

Art versus Entertainment

As you've read in this chapter, some categories of theatrical forms are considered more artistic or entertaining than others. But what exactly is the difference between art and entertainment? As we asked at the beginning of this chapter, why is Shakespeare's *Romeo and Juliet* considered art and director Baz Luhrmann's 1996 movie *William Shakespeare's Romeo & Juliet* considered entertainment?

The fundamental difference between art and entertainment is that artists create primarily to express themselves and communicate a particular perspective, whereas entertainers create to please an audience. The primary purpose of entertainment is to confirm an audience's values and beliefs. In other words, entertainment is meant to amuse us and make us feel good, not necessarily to challenge us. Entertainment generally shows us an agreeable mirror of ourselves and our ideas about how the world is or should be. Art may also confirm our values and beliefs, but artists do not necessarily *seek* to confirm them. True, artists often desperately want their audience to understand and appreciate their work, which is why they may pay attention to criticism and audience reaction. But artists do not always take an audience's opinion into consideration when creating work, whereas entertainers regularly do. Many, if not most, major movie and television producers show works-in-progress to test audiences before formally releasing the "product." These test audiences, usually recruited from a targeted age or social group, fill out questionnaires after the showing about what they liked and didn't like, what they thought about the story and the characters, and how the work could be improved. In essence, a test audience is a tool for producers to match the values of the product to the consumer, thereby making the product more entertaining and marketable.

What are values? **Values** are the principles, standards, or qualities considered worthwhile or desirable within a given society. Entertainers want to confirm our values because they want to make us feel good about who we are and what we believe so that we buy their product. Otherwise, we may turn the channel, buy a different CD, or spend our money on a different movie. For example, the reality-based TV show *Cops,* which depicts real police officers on the job, is pure entertainment because the bad guy is always caught. The show doesn't air the footage in which the bad guy gets away or the officers act unprofessionally. That footage wouldn't confirm the audience's values that criminals deserve to be punished and that police officers should protect the well-being of all citizens, even criminals. In this sense, *Cops* doesn't seek to assert that change is needed, that perhaps many police departments are under-funded, or that some police officers do not always treat criminals fairly.

Art, on the other hand, doesn't seek to confirm society's values, so it often solicits change. Unlike *Cops,* the play *Gangsters* by South African playwright Maishe Maponya likens state police officers to brutal gangsters who use their power as a tool of oppression. The play depicts the interrogation, torture, and death of a poet, absurdly accused of inciting dissent with her poetry, at the hands of two police officers. The play ends with the officers conspiring to cover up the cause of her death and then skulking off the stage, knowing that they probably will not be punished for their crimes. The fact that the police get away with murder does not confirm our traditional values that cops are the "good guys." Instead, it asks us to reflect on the possible abuses of power, which in turn prompts us to consider that change may be necessary. In this way, theatre can challenge us and make us think. Art and theatre often raise issues in a way that prompts us to imagine and possibly understand more than we did. As playwright David Hare says, "When people are confronted with a real work of art—then they discover that they don't believe what they thought they believed all along. In a way, the great art, the great subversive art, is art that makes you realize that you don't think what you thought you did."

FOR MORE ON

ART BY CENSUS

"Art by census: Should people get exactly what they ask for?" Carmi Weingrod, *American Artist,* October 1995

In short, screen entertainments generally present safe themes like "be yourself," themes that no one questions. Controversial themes that might challenge mainstream values are not often shown without the wrong being righted, the guilty being punished, and the evil being vanquished. Entertainment fulfills our expectations. Art, on the other hand, often inspires us to consider life's complexities and ambiguities. So, Shakespeare's play *Romeo and Juliet* is considered art because it is a timeless tale of star-crossed young lovers who die as a result of a senseless family feud—its simplicity and beauty prompt us to consider a tragic misunderstanding that could so easily have been avoided. And Baz Luhrmann's *William Shakespeare's Romeo & Juliet* is considered entertainment because, although it is an adaptation of the original play, its heavily edited retelling turns the tragedy into a clichéd action movie—one that its makers hoped teens would spend money to see again and again and again.

All this is not to say there is anything wrong with entertainment—we all need and enjoy entertainment, and there is nothing inherently wrong with paying money for it. From sitcoms to amusement parks to the Ice Capades, entertainment is a wonderful way to relax. It adds to the enjoyment of life and is often worth the price of admission. To most people, a life devoid of entertainment seems hardly worth living. Even in the harshest environments, people long to be entertained. For example, the USO (United Service Organizations) has been bringing entertainment to American soldiers on the front lines for more than sixty years, evidence of entertainment's ability to be therapeutic and increase morale.

A work can also be *both* art and entertainment. For example, the popular 1970s sitcom *All in the Family* and the HBO drama *Deadwood* are often considered both art and entertainment because they made people think and feel at the same time. Similarly, many independently produced movies, such as *Before Night Falls,* about the life of Cuban author Reinaldo Arenas, or *Dancer in the Dark,* about a man who lets an innocent, nearly blind woman hang for the crime he committed, are beautiful to look at but present disquieting themes that prompt an audience to consider the unfairness of life. And, of course, plays about serious topics, such as *Angels in America,* a heartrending story about living with and dying of AIDS in a conservative political landscape, often include entertaining moments that make an audience laugh and enjoy themselves.

But what happens when we indulge in a diet dominated by entertainment? In the United States, the entertainment industry influences many aspects of our daily lives, including the news we watch. Steven Brill, media watchdog,

University of Wyoming photo archives

Art and entertainment are not mutually exclusive. Entertaining works can be considered art, and art can be entertaining. Many plays that are highly respected for their artistic strength and integrity also feature entertaining moments or themes. This is true of plays throughout history, from Aristophanes' Lysistrata *(411 BCE), in which the women of Athens go on a sex strike to force their husbands to end the Peloponnesian War, to new plays such as* Festen *(2004), a dark drama about a disturbing family secret revealed through witty and, at times, very funny dinnertime banter. This 2004 update of* Lysistrata *by Sean Keogh, called* Good Morning Athens, *featured Stephanie Lovell, Heather Kaloust, Cheyenne Christian, Erica Edd, Devin Sanchez, Carly Schaub, Amanda Ryan Jones, and Lindsay Cozzens. It was directed by William Missouri Downs at the Kennedy Center for the Performing Arts.*

distinguishes between real news and vicarious news. Real news, he says, "is news that actually is important to you because it could affect your life, but you wouldn't necessarily know about it before it is brought to you," such as stories on the economy, elections, or corruption in the local police department. On the other hand, vicarious news "looks like news, but it's not really news that will affect your life as much as it is news that provides an entertaining respite from what else is occupying you." For example, in 2000 the story of six-year-old Cuban shipwreck survivor Elián González was not one that could directly affect the lives of many of us. However, according to the Center for Media and Public Affairs, it received more coverage on the major networks than the Columbine tragedy or the Oklahoma City bombing, events whose ramifications continue to affect us.

With a flick of a remote, we can usually find a TV program that makes us feel good about who we are and what we believe. Most popular movies and music do the same. What happens when we watch and listen to only what confirms our values? We may become apathetic and convinced of our own point of view, but more importantly, we can become intolerant of new ideas and alternative opinions of how the world is or should be. A steady diet of entertainment that reflects only our way of thinking limits our view of the world. Art and theatre help balance our diet—they challenge us, teach us, and sometimes even insult us by calling our values into question. In short, art and theatre guide us to a better understanding of our world and ourselves.

Curtain Call

All people, all countries, all societies on earth create and enjoy art and theatre. Societies in which different cultures and ideas collide usually have an abundance of diverse and creative theatre, whereas isolated cultures generally produce simple theatrical forms that do not change for centuries. Even in countries where the government controls and limits creative expression, theatre can thrive, albeit under restriction. Why are art and theatre such an integral part of all societies? As you've learned in this chapter, they help us understand and interpret ourselves and the world around us. Until we have all the answers about who we are and the environments in which we exist, art and the theatre will continue to be an important influence in our lives. As Robert Edmond Jones once said,

> Here is the secret of the flame that burns in the work of the great artists of the theatre. They seem so much more aware than we are, and so much more awake, and so much more alive that they make us feel that what we call living is not living at all, but a kind of sleep. Their knowledge, their wealth of emotions, their wonder, their elation, their swift clear seeing surrounds every occasion with a crowd of values that enriches it beyond anything which we, in our happy satisfaction, had ever imagined. In their hands it becomes not only a thing of beauty but a thing of power. And we see it all—beauty and power alike—as a part of the life of the theatre.

Summary

Philosophers, artists, and critics have been debating the meaning of the word *art* for thousands of years. Few have been in agreement, and even today the debate continues. Often when we use the word *art,* we are referring to a skill or a talent, the aesthetics of a piece of art, or the meaning inherent in a piece of art. Generally, artists see art as a means of finding or conveying meaning. They create art to educate, inform, influence, and sometimes even offend and enrage an audience.

Rather than attempt an all-encompassing definition of art, we may find it more useful to describe art in terms of the qualities that all works of art have in common. These qualities include human creation, structure, subject and medium, and reaction. By describing art in this way, we can embrace all the different forms art takes.

Art is important in our lives because it can bring order to what seems to be a chaotic universe. Religion and philosophy help us explain *why* events occur, science can explain *how* events occur, and art can fine-tune our understanding by expressing events in human terms. Artists isolate the aspects of nature they regard as essential and integrate them into a concrete, focused, and organized view of life. With this organization comes meaning and significance. In addition, every artist is a political individual who states an opinion that may challenge an audience's values, shatter their preconceptions, or help them see the world in a new way.

Theatre is a dynamic form of performing art that focuses on the human experience. All that is needed for theatre to occur is an empty space and someone to walk across that space while someone else watches. We often refer to theatre as drama, but in fact there is a difference. Drama is a form of theatre that tells us stories about people, their actions, and the conflicts that result. Conflict is the key to the movement of a story and is what qualifies a theatrical work as a "play." Conflict is at the core of drama.

Theatre is also a unique form of art because it is always live, it is always about the human experience, and it is a particularly collaborative form of art, requiring more than one type of art and artist to produce. There are many different categories of theatre, the most common being commercial theatre, historical theatre, political theatre, experimental theatre, and cultural theatre.

Theatre can be considered artistic, entertaining, or both. The fundamental difference between art and entertainment is that artists create primarily to express themselves and communicate their particular perspective, whereas entertainers create to please an audience. Entertainment is meant to amuse us and make us feel good, not necessarily to challenge our values and beliefs. Art may also confirm our values and beliefs, but artists do not necessarily seek to confirm them. This means that art is far more likely to have controversial themes that make us think.

The Art of Theatre Online

Use the *Art of Theatre* website at **http://communication.wadsworth.com/downs1** for quick access to the electronic study resources that accompany this chapter, including a digital glossary, a link to InfoTrac College Edition that you can use to find the For More On... InfoTrac College Edition readings listed below, a list of further reading, and a chapter quiz. When you get to the *Art of Theatre* homepage, click on the cover of the book you are using and you will be redirected to the website for your book. Then click on "Student Book Companion Site" in the Resource box, pick a chapter from the pull-down menu at the top of the page, and select an option from the Chapter Resources menu. The *Art of Theatre* website also includes links to interesting and informative theatre websites. Just click on the Theatre on the Web link in the Book Resources menu. The links to these websites are maintained and updated as needed.

Key Terms

aesthetics / 4
commercial theatre / 15
conflict / 14
cultural theatre / 16
drama / 14
experimental plays / 16
historical theatre / 16
literary arts / 9
medium / 9
performing arts / 9
pictorial arts / 9
political theatre / 16
spatial arts / 9
subject / 9
theatre / 4
values / 20

For More On . . .

Infotrac College Edition Readings

http://www.infotrac-college.com

2 Comparing the Living Stage, Silver Screen, and Home Theatre

An old theatre joke goes, "Theatre is art; film is a business; television is furniture." As with most humor there's a kernel of truth here. Theatre people usually do see what they do as an art, Hollywood film producers are often more concerned with profits, and television sets are as common as sofas. Of the three mediums, theatre in America today is the smallest—it's dwarfed by the "movie business" and "TV furniture." For example, when the hit mega-musical Cats *closed on Broadway after a record-setting 7,485 performances, it had been seen by almost 19 million people. Although that is certainly an impressive number, by comparison, on any given night more than 35 million Americans may watch a single episode of a hit sitcom. The average American spends about three hours per day watching television; children and teenagers watch even more. By the age of seventeen, the average American has*

© Ken Friedman/Courtesy Berkeley Repertory Theatre

◀ ***On preceding page:*** The Laramie Project *by Moisés Kaufman and the Tectonic Theatre Project, directed by Moisés Kaufman, Berkeley Repertory Theatre, 2001, featuring Greg Pierotti and cast members of the ensemble. This play explores the 1998 killing of gay college student Matthew Shepard in Laramie, Wyoming, via interviews with the townspeople there.*

spent 15,000–18,000 hours watching television, compared to 12,000 hours spent in school and only a few hours watching plays. Well over 1.3 billion movie tickets are sold in America yearly, which works out to five movie tickets per person. In contrast, only 0.23 theatre tickets per American are sold each year.

Although theatre, film, and TV all have some obvious elements in common, key differences make theatre unique in this age of DVD players, streaming video, and five hundred channels of "nothing to watch." Many of these differences grew out of the early part of the last century, described in the Spotlight "A Brief History of Screen Entertainments." These differences are in terms of audience, acting, directing, funding, control, and ownership. In this chapter, we'll look at each of these elements as they relate to the theatre and see why theatre remains vital and valuable today in the face of an avalanche of screen entertainments.

Audience: No Cell Phones, Please!

Movies and television require only passive participation. You can leave the theatre if you don't like a movie or hit Pause or Rewind on the VCR, and it will not affect the actors. However, in the theatre the performers can hear you and often see you. If the audience doesn't laugh at a line that the cast believes is funny, that affects them. If there is a lot of coughing, actors often interpret it to mean that the audience is bored, so they might try to speed up the pace. If an audience finds a performance amusing, the actors will "hold for laughs" to make sure the next funny line will be heard. And if a cell phone goes off or there is a disturbance in the audience, an actor might even be distracted enough to forget lines. Even when the audience is perfectly silent, cast members often say they can feel an "energy" coming from them. Backstage during the show and intermission they sometimes talk about whether the audience is "with them" and what they need to do to "win the audience over." One thing is certain: Give stage actors your full attention and they will do a better job. *New York Times* theatre critic Margo Jefferson says there is something almost "primal" about the relationship between a theatre audience and the actors because of their physical proximity and the power the audience has to affect the actors' performances. Theatre is sometimes called "the living stage" or a "living art"—movies and television separate the actor and audience with lenses and screens, whereas the theatre is immediate. Theatre always takes place in your presence.

> We're so accustomed to the unchanging nature of film (and recording and computer effects) that we're less tolerant of theatre's human fallibility. Nothing in our responses can change a movie; it's invulnerable, as no actor or play, however great, can be.
>
> ***Margo Jefferson,***
> New York Times *theatre critic*

Communication flows in only one direction during screen entertainments: from the TV screen to your easy chair, or from the big screen to your sticky megaplex seat. You can throw tomatoes at either screen and it won't change a thing about the show. The audience has only one choice: to watch or not to watch. This makes for a very different level of audience participation than at the theatre. For example, when was the last time you were at a movie where the audience applauded at the end? When you're watching TV, do you stand and applaud in your own living room? No matter how brilliant the acting, no matter how much the film or television show affected you, you don't usually applaud. Why? Because the performers can't hear you. There is no communication between you and them. In Yoruba, the western part of Nigeria, television is called *ero asoro maghese,* which means "the machine that speaks but accepts

A Brief History of Screen Entertainments

In 1893, Thomas Edison displayed the first commercial motion picture machine at the World's Columbian Exposition. Edison called his new contraption the *Kinetoscope.* Just two years later, Kinetoscopes were being installed in department stores, hotel lobbies, and drug stores all over the United States and Europe. Kinetoscopes were a box-like device with a view hole that allowed an individual to watch a silent sixty-second movie for about a penny per viewing. The first public exhibition of projected motion pictures happened on April 23, 1896, at the New York City Music Hall. Called *nickelodeons,* these movie projection devices soon became common. By 1910, there were over 10,000 nickelodeons in the United States.

Movies had a devastating effect on the theatre. In 1910, the cheapest theatres in the United States cost 25¢–50¢, but a movie cost only 5¢–10¢. By 1915, the number of touring theatre companies in the United States had been cut from 300 to 100 and soon fell to fewer than 10. By 1911, 1,400 legitimate stages had been converted to movie theatres. Even more theatres closed with the invention of talking pictures in 1927. Today, there are over 37,000 movie theatres in the United States, and movie screens outnumber legitimate stages by over twenty to one.

Television was developed in the 1920s but did not become common until the mid-1950s. With the first commercially successful home VCRs in the mid-1970s and DVDs in the 1990s, television has become a complete home entertainment package. Today, about 98 percent of homes in the United States have at least one television, 70 percent have cable, 91 percent have a VCR, and there are almost 300 national cable channels. These channels are owned by a small group of huge multinational media moguls such as News Corporation, whose television networks, from Fox in the United States to Star TV in China, reach 75 percent of the world's population. As Douglas Rushkoff says in his book *Media Virus!* television is more than a mirror of our culture, "it *is* our culture."

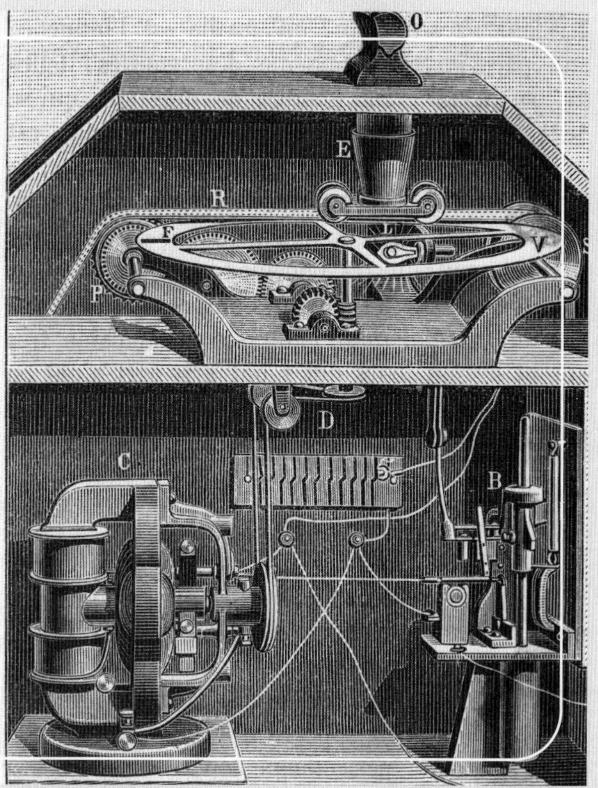

© Bettmann/Corbis

© Jay Yamada/Courtesy California Shakespeare Theater.

© Peter Cade/Stone/Getty Images

Theatre is live and immediate. The actors can hear and see you, and your reaction to them changes the production from performance to performance. With screen entertainments, communication flows in only one direction, but in the theatre communication is a two-way street. This is why theatre is often called a living art.

> We're tightrope walkers. When you walk the wire in a movie, the wire is painted on the floor, but when you walk it on the stage, it's a hundred feet high without a net.
>
> ***Al Pacino,*** *American actor*

> Think of this moment. All that has ever been is in this moment; all that will be is in this moment. Both are meeting in one living flame, in this unique instant of time. This is drama; this is theatre—to be aware of the Now.
>
> ***Robert Edmond Jones,*** *American theatre designer*

no reply." Theatre, on the other hand, accepts replies. Actor John Lithgow, who acts in films, television, and on the stage, says that performing in the theatre is "the purest form of acting" for it belongs to both the actors and the audience.

Theatre is a risky business. The unrepeatable nature of live theatre makes watching it like watching a high-wire act—something can always go wrong and you never know what you're going to get. Not only are no two performances exactly the same, but unless you read a review of a play before you see it, you probably know only the basics of the plot, not the specifics of the play's content. In contrast, movie studios and television networks advertise their products heavily before they're seen. Before you go see a movie or watch a television show, you usually have a pretty good idea of what to expect. Movies and television in the United States also have a rating system that warns you when one includes sexual content, violence, or adult language, and movie theatres even limit who can attend particular movies. All this information makes for a safety net not generally available in the theatre—most of the time you can avoid seeing material you think will insult you or challenge your values. In short, when you go to the theatre, you're often taking a chance. But this element of chance is also what makes live theatre exciting and rewarding to watch.

Acting: I'm Ready for My Close-Up

Many people think that what stage actors and movie actors do is essentially the same. In many ways it is, but it is also different in some key ways. Actors who work primarily on stage are often called "legitimate" actors. The term *legitimate* is not a form of snobbery but rather comes from eighteenth-century England where censorship laws required theatre companies to be licensed. A company of actors that had such a license was called "legitimate." Today, the term has come to mean a theatre that does only live plays, or an actor who acts only on stage in front of a live audience. Being a star of the legitimate stage requires years of training. Many movie actors also have considerable theatre training, although it's possible to become a movie star with a little charisma, a bit of talent, and a lot of luck. For example, supermodels such as Cameron Diaz have become successful movie stars, as have athletes such as Shaquille O'Neal, but you seldom see people with little or no theatre training acting on the legitimate stage.

Not that acting for the camera is easy. Movies are often shot out of sequence, so in the morning a film actor might start shooting a tender love scene, die that afternoon on the battlefield, and in the evening go back to finishing the love scene. And the movie-making process does not always allow for rehearsal time before shooting begins. There may be a dance number that must be rehearsed, or fight choreography to be learned, but generally the amount of rehearsal time for movies is far less than for a play.

Even after some rehearsal, if the film actor can't perform what the script or director calls for, doubles can fill in and perform the dance, jump off the high building, or sing the song. For example, in the movie *West Side Story,* Natalie Wood did not sing her own songs while playing the character of Maria. Rather than spending time and money training her to be a better singer, the film studio simply had her lip sync. A stage actress named Marni Nixon was the real singer in that movie—she also dubbed songs for Audrey Hepburn in the movie version of *My Fair Lady* and for Deborah Kerr in *The King and I.* But if you see *West Side Story, My Fair Lady,* or *The King and I* on stage, there can be no substitution. The actress playing the part must be able to act, dance, and sing.

Actors in films and TV are sometimes called "talking heads" because there are so many close-up shots in which an actor expresses an emotion with the face

Photofest

Photofest

When you see movie stars singing in films, you're often hearing someone else's voice. This process, called "dubbing," is common in movies. In the movie West Side Story, *the singing voice of Natalie Wood (at left) was dubbed by professional singer Marni Nixon (at right), who also dubbed Audrey Hepburn's voice in* My Fair Lady. *But you can't dub in theatre, so actors in musical theatre must sing their own songs.*

or even part of the face. Stage actress Dame Judith Anderson learned about close-ups in her first movie acting experience. The director called her aside and said, "Watch your eyebrows." He explained that when she moved her eyebrows on stage, it was a matter of only a fraction of an inch, but when she raised them in a close-up shot, it was the same as moving them three feet on screen. In the theatre, there is no such thing as a close-up. Everything is a wide shot, so actors must learn to express themselves with their entire body. Film actors also don't have to project their voices because the boom mike is always right over their head, just out of the frame. (In fact, if you watch closely enough, you can occasionally see the boom mike accidentally drop into the shot.) Screen actors don't have to use their bodies and voices to project emotions to reach the back row of a 500-seat auditorium.

© Photofest

Because many parts in plays require hoofers, from the competent to the accomplished, theatre actors are often trained in dance. Film stars are usually not as well trained. They may have to train hard for a few months before shooting difficult dance scenes. Or the director may have the film edited so that the best one- to five-second clips of an actor's dance moves are shown in quick succession, creating the illusion that the actor is a good dancer. The film rendition of Chicago *included all these possibilities. Catherine Zeta-Jones was a musical theatre pro in Europe before making it big in Hollywood; Renée Zellweger and Richard Gere required a lot of training prior to shooting; and skilled editing contributed to an entertaining musical full of splashy dance numbers.*

Additionally, screen actors often don't have to remember as many lines as stage actors. Many movies and most television shows generally have fewer lines of dialogue than plays, and screen actors seldom have to remember more than just a few minutes' worth of dialogue at a time. Screen actors often learn their lines on the day of shooting; sometimes they don't have to remember lines at all because cue cards and teleprompters can be placed just off camera allowing them to simply read their lines. This is especially true for television actors in many soap operas and live shows such as *Saturday Night Live.* Stage actors don't have it so easy. They must memorize thousands of lines of dialogue and long speeches before they dare to perform in front of a live audience—and if they forget their lines there is no one there to help.

But the most important difference is that in movies and TV, screen actors are allowed to fail. If they don't get it right on the first take, they can always try again. If they fail a hundred times in a row, they can still win an Oscar if they get it right on the hundred-and-first take. In contrast, stage actors must get it right the first time, night after night after night. For example, in the recent movie version of the stage musical *Chicago,* Richard Gere tap-dances, Catherine Zeta-Jones struts her stuff, and Renée Zellweger sings. They all look pretty good, yet the director had the luxury of cutting every few seconds to a new shot or to a different take, thereby covering up all their missteps and wrong notes. Generally, actors who train for the stage need more training, more hours of rehearsal, and perhaps even more talent, for there is no safety net in the theatre, no editor to make errors disappear, no cue cards or teleprompters, and no retakes or second chances. This is the very nature of the live theatre: Anything can happen!

| Directing: Direct and Indirect

Film is often called a director's medium because the director has a great deal of creative control. The director is all-powerful and tells everyone what to do, except for the producers, who bankroll the production. Directors can change the script, rewrite a scene, and control exactly what the audience will see moment by moment and shot by shot. If they don't like one take, they can shoot a scene repeatedly until they get what they want. Interestingly, the opposite is true in most television sitcoms and dramas. In television the directors often go unnoticed and are sometimes even subservient to the writers. Television is so fast-paced, delivering new ideas, scripts, and episodes each week, that it makes sense for the person in charge to be the one who produces those scripts: the writer or the producer.

As we will discuss in later chapters, theatre directors can also be very powerful, but they never have absolute control over every moment of the production. Each performance is different, and during each performance, actors make the moment-to-moment decisions about what the audience will see. In most instances the director chooses, or "casts," the actors, and during rehearsal the director will suggest, urge, and even demand certain things from them. Yet, once the curtain goes up, no director can bring it down to make adjustments. Nor does the theatre director have absolute control over the script—the playwright owns the copyright, except when the script is in public domain, which is the case for plays written long ago, such as Shakespeare's plays. The special collaborative aspect of play production usually makes theatre a little more democratic than film or television. You hear the words *ensemble* and *team* used often in the theatre but not always in film and television, even though these mediums also require a collaborative effort. As a result, in a good theatre production—one where egos are not battling for control, and collaboration is based on mutual respect—more voices are heard and more creative individuals are working together, rather than a solitary authority telling everyone what to do. In the theatre, there is no "director's cut."

Funding: Follow the Money

Another major difference between most theatre and screen entertainments is funding and profit. With only a few notable exceptions, such as the big Broadway production companies, theatres are generally nonprofit companies. "Nonprofit" companies do not have stockholders and pay no dividends or federal taxes. The Internal Revenue Service created nonprofit status for companies and organizations that are not designed for private financial gain and that provide the general public with charitable, educational, and recreational services, such as the United Way, the Red Cross, and the American Cancer Society. Most theatres apply for and receive nonprofit status because the sad fact is that most plays—and the theatre companies that produce them—lose money. If it weren't for tax exemptions, donors, and patrons of the arts, most theatres would cease to exist. Even without tax exemptions, theatres bring in little or no profit to pay taxes on. The exact opposite is true of most screen entertainments, where there are billions to be made and taxes to be paid.

Funding the Screen

Movies make money from ticket sales, video and DVD rentals, and the sale of movie rights overseas and to television. Over time, the profits on one movie can amount to hundreds of millions. Only a portion of that money comes from the movie theatre, even though news broadcasts now regularly report how much money the top movies make at the box office each weekend. In 2002,

> The initial release of the motion picture in movie theaters is becoming, to a large extent, little more than a preview trailer for the subsequent purchase of the DVD.
>
> ***Martin W. Greenwald,***
> *President of Image Entertainment*

FOR MORE ON
THE BUSINESS OF FILM
"Building knowledge about the consumer: The emergence of market research in the motion picture industry," Gerben Bakker, *Business History,* January 2003

Americans spent $12 billion to buy DVDs and videotapes of movies for home use. In fact, many movies now make more money from sales of DVDs than from the box office.

Television in the United States makes its money by selling commercial time. Time is critical to television. The more commercials a network can pack into an hour, the more money it can make. For example, on average MTV spends 18 minutes and 11 seconds per hour airing commercials; UPN, 17 minutes and 40 seconds; FOX, 16 minutes and 36 seconds. And the amount of commercial time continues to increase—Disney's ABC has augmented the amount of time given to commercials by 34 percent since 1989. Some programs garner so many viewers that advertisers pay outrageous sums to air their advertisements. The audience share of the 2003 Super Bowl was so high that ABC was able to charge over $70,000 per second for commercials. Income from basic cable network advertising was projected to exceed $23.5 billion and network advertising to go over $21.5 billion in 2005.

Funding Theatre and the Arts

When you divide the cost of a Hollywood blockbuster movie, which can cost upwards of $150 million to produce, by the tens of millions of people who will see it on the screen or on video, the production cost per audience member is tiny. The same is true of television. The sitcom *Frasier* cost between $4 million and $5 million per episode to produce, and *Friends* cost nearly $6 million per episode. On the other hand, a play costs far less to produce—anywhere from a few thousand dollars for a community theatre production to several million for a big Broadway production. However, when these costs are divided by the limited number of seats available, the cost per audience member can be high. In fact, it can easily be twenty, fifty, or even one hundred times more expensive per person. In that sense, theatre is expensive. For details about the costs of one production, see the Spotlight "Theatre Can Be Expensive."

The problem in funding theatre stems from the nature of theatre: It is a live medium. Theatre is labor intensive and comparatively low-tech, with few technological innovations to make it cheaper. Screen entertainments constantly benefit from technological advances that replace the expensive labor force once required to produce a movie or TV show. But in theatre, the cost of producing a play is continually on the rise precisely because it depends on human labor, much of which cannot be replaced by machinery. For example, the lighting changes for a play can be programmed into a computer, but no computer can predict what will happen during each live performance. It takes a human being to adjust the lighting based on the performers' needs. On the screen, an actor can adjust for technology. In the theatre, technology must adjust to the performer. Put simply, inspired human minds are always required backstage to support the inspired human minds and bodies onstage, as they attempt to inspire a live audience.

Another obstacle in funding theatre is that ticket sales at most nonprofit theatres cover only 50 percent of the cost of producing a performance. If most theatres had to depend solely on ticket sales, they would have to raise their prices to the point where only the very rich could afford a seat. In that case, theatre would become so scarce that most people would never see a play. So, to satisfy demand and make theatre available to more people, nonprofit theatres

Theatre Can Be Expensive

A play costs more per audience member to produce than any Hollywood movie. Whether you are attending a local community playhouse or the professional theatre, be prepared to pay more for your tickets. The most extreme prices are found on Broadway where ticket prices now hover around $100 per seat. This is because a typical Broadway production costs millions of dollars before the curtain even goes up, and between $300,000 and $500,000 per week after opening night. Costs include not only designing, building, and maintaining the costumes, sets, and lights, but also advertising, utilities, insurance, rental fees, maintenance fees, payroll taxes, union benefits, royalties, and salaries for actors, directors, stage crews, technicians, musicians, ushers, box-office personnel, accountants, and security.

Recently, producer Emanuel Azenberg opened his account books to a *New York Times* reporter to show how expensive it was to produce a play on Broadway. The play was Eugene O'Neill's *The Iceman Cometh* starring Kevin Spacey at the Brooks Atkinson Theatre. Before the curtain even went up on the opening night, $350,000 was spent to buy and rent the stage equipment and pay workers to set up the set, costumes, lights, and sound. Azenberg saved money by using the same set that was used when he produced the play in England, but it cost another $90,000 to adapt it to the Broadway house. The lighting and sound equipment budget was $75,000, which included $20,000 for the special light bulbs that cost as much as $700 each. Other pre-opening night costs included a dialect coach, a fight director, an assistant director, production staff, as well as salaries for actors and other members of the creative team during rehearsals—totaling over $300,000.

After opening night, weekly salaries, including payroll taxes and pensions, for everyone from actors to technical supervisors, came to $79,489.56 a week or $1,033,364.20 for the run of the play. This was kept low because star Kevin Spacey, who earns millions to be in a movie, agreed to do the play for only about $1,000 a week. The theatre itself cost $10,000 a week to rent plus a percentage of the show's gross income, plus thousands more to pay the theatre staff and box-office crews. To advertise the play before it opened cost $250,000, plus another $40,000 per week during the run. Miscellaneous expenses for everything from throat lozenges to coffee came to $2,500 a week. In the end, the play took an initial capital investment of $1.5 million and cost $250,000 a week to run for a total cost of $4.75 million. Even with a movie star name attached, and performing one of the most famous American plays of all time, Azenberg, the producer, only managed to break even. (For more information, see the *New York Times*, April 8, 1999.)

© Joan Marcus

Kevin Spacey in The Iceman Cometh, *directed by Howard Davies at the Brooks Atkinson Theatre, 1999.*

cut ticket prices and try to make up the difference through alternative forms of funding. A recent poll by the Theatre Communications Group questioned 262 theatres on the sources of their funding. It found that 59 percent of their income came from tickets and concession sales, and 41 percent had to come from outside sources, including grants and contributions. Individual contributors, corporations, foundations, and federal, state, and local entities keep theatre alive.

© Jerry Arcieri/Corbis

Compared with the cost of a movie ticket or a DVD rental, theatre tickets are expensive because the cost of a production must be divided among a few hundred or a few thousand audience members rather than millions.

Individual contributors to the arts, or **patrons**, come in all sizes. They range from billionaire philanthropists who give away millions to your average Americans who donate a few extra, hard-earned bucks. Most nonprofit theatres print a list of their donors in the program you're handed by the ushers. The people who contribute the least are listed as "donor" or "patron," while those who give greater amounts might be labeled "benefactor" or "producer" or given a creative name like "angel" or "protector." Most theatres are nonprofit, so donors' gifts are tax-deductible, meaning they don't have to pay federal income taxes on the money they've donated. Theatres also offer donors other benefits, such as special opening- or closing-night parties, first choice of seats, thank-you gifts, membership in patron clubs, and the opportunity to serve on the theatre's board of directors.

> Arts groups are notoriously undercapitalized, living year to year (or even week to week). As a result, even mild economic downturns can be devastating. In this era of free market fetishization, it may be difficult for many people to grasp, but the arts don't come close to paying their own way. They need welfare—public or private.
>
> ***Christopher Shea,***
> *American writer, in* The American Prospect magazine

Corporate funding for the arts, whether from the smallest "mom-and-pop" companies or mammoth corporations, is good for business. Small businesses, such as restaurants, will donate to a local theatre because a successful theatre in the neighborhood can increase dinner receipts. For every dollar a theatre spends, it brings in five dollars in goods and services for related or neighboring enterprises. Private parking lots, restaurants, taverns, coffeehouses, and retail stores reap the benefits of increased traffic, which boosts the local economy. Large corporations often make donations to gain political clout, tax write-offs, or publicity. Some corporations go even further to ensure their names are in the public eye by purchasing a theatre or the rights to its name. For example, in 2000 the Selwyn Theater on 42nd Street in New York City, originally named for theatre producer Arch Selwyn, was renamed the American Airlines Theater until at least 2010. Other corporations make donations to theatres to prove they are "giving something back" to the community. For example, for many years Texaco sponsored the live radio broadcasts of over 1,200 performances by the Metropolitan Opera. By creating an association with one of the greatest opera companies on earth, this sponsorship was intended to foster a perception that Texaco was interested in the public welfare. Sponsoring the arts also creates a venue for advertising disguised as philanthropy. As self-serving as this practice may sound, without Texaco many thousands of people would not have had the opportunity to ever hear live opera.

FOR MORE ON

CORPORATE FUNDING OF THE ARTS

"The corporate art of helping the arts," Stephanie French, *Public Relations Quarterly,* Fall 1991

Government funding, the money spent each year on the arts by federal, state, and local entities, is by far the most controversial method of maintaining a healthy arts community in the United States—even though it spends far fewer tax dollars on the arts than any other major industrialized nation. Here is a list of the dollar amount average taxpayers in ten countries pay per year to fund the arts:

Finland	$91.00	Netherlands	$46.00
Germany	$85.00	United Kingdom	$36.00
France	$57.00	Australia	$25.00
Sweden	$57.00	Ireland	$ 9.00
Canada	$46.00	USA	$ 0.33

The federal agency that disburses our arts tax dollars is the **National Endowment for the Arts (NEA)**. One of the smallest of all government programs, the NEA receives less than 1/100 of 1 percent (0.001%) of the federal budget. The average American pays over $500 per year in federal taxes for national defense and, as you can see in the list above, only about 33 cents per year to support the NEA. Few would begrudge the $500 we each spend on defense in today's uncertain world. However, the U.S. budget for the Marine Corps marching band is nearly *double* the budget for the NEA! Although we also pay state taxes and sometimes local city taxes to support the arts, all the combined taxes earmarked for the arts still average less than $5 per American per year.

President Kennedy finally earned the bipartisan support needed to create the National Endowment for the Arts (NEA), but he was assassinated in 1963 before his dream could be realized. In September 1965, President Lyndon B. Johnson signed into law the bill that created the National Endowment for the Arts as well as the National Endowment for the Humanities. The bill states in part, "While no government can call a great artist or scholar into existence, it is necessary and appropriate for the Federal Government to help create and sustain not only a climate encouraging freedom of thought, imagination, and inquiry, but also the material condition facilitating the release of this creative talent." The first NEA grant went to the American Ballet Theatre and saved

We have agencies of the Government which are concerned with the welfare and advancement of science and technology, of education, recreation and health. We should now begin to give similar attention to the arts.

John F. Kennedy,
President of the United States, 1961–1963

Courtesy National Archives

Before the NEA there was the Federal Theatre Project (FTP), established in the 1930s as part of Franklin Delano Roosevelt's New Deal social reforms. During its four-year existence, the Federal Theatre Project employed more than ten thousand theatre professionals and mounted over one thousand productions. Many plays staged during this time highlighted the social ills of the nation, such as Triple-A Plowed Under, *which dramatized the plight of farmers, and* One-Third of a Nation, *which studied the problems of the homeless in America. These sorts of plays got the Federal Theatre Project into deep trouble. By 1939, charges began flying that the FTP was dominated by Communists, and politicians accused it of portraying "un-American propaganda." Soon thereafter, funding was cut.*

the nearly bankrupt ballet company from extinction. Over the next thirty-five years, the NEA would become the largest single supporter of nonprofit art in America as it attempted to fulfill its mission "to foster the excellence, diversity, and vitality of the arts in the United States, and to broaden public access to the arts." Figure 2.1 shows the growth of state art agencies and performing arts groups between 1965 and 1999.

The NEA acts as an independent commission, and NEA panels do not have to get their decisions rubber-stamped by the Senate or the president. The law that created the NEA states: "No department, agency, officer, or employee of the United States shall exercise any supervision or control over the administration or operations of the NEA." It is to be an independent government institution, thereby facilitating artistic speech while limiting government interference and censorship. However, this very independence often inflames critics of public arts funding. When NEA funds have been used to support controversial projects, such as startling artworks about HIV/AIDS or "alternative" lifestyles, Senator Jesse Helms and other conservative critics have spearheaded numerous attempts to eradicate the NEA. Yet, as President Lyndon Johnson said when he signed the bill creating the NEA, "Freedom is an essential condition

© Joan Marcus

In 2003, the NEA awarded about $6 million to 260 theatre projects, including the celebrated Humana Festival of New Plays, sponsored by The Actors' Theatre of Louisville, the state theater of Kentucky. The Humana Festival has become a major force in introducing audiences to an eclectic mix of original plays by emerging playwrights. One of the festival's featured plays in 2003 was Omnium Gatherum *by Theresa Rebeck and Alexandra Gersten-Vassilaros, a unique look at the events of September 11. This play was later performed Off-Broadway and was named a 2004 Pulitzer Prize finalist.*

for the artist, and in proportion as freedom is diminished so is the prospect of artistic achievement."

To date, the NEA has given out over 140,000 grants and provided funding for a wide variety of artistic and cultural programs across the United States. It has supported concerts, theatres, film festivals, dance performances, orchestras, operas, poetry readings, and downtown renewal projects. It has helped museums with travel costs so that they can take exhibitions to inner cities and rural areas. It has invested millions in K–12 arts programs nationwide. It gives money to preserve historical paintings and public monuments. It helps showcase Native American art, helps fund the PBS *Great Performances* series, and even helped with the PBS documentary on the history of that American music creation known as rock and roll. The NEA has funded projects ranging from the design of the Vietnam Veterans Memorial in Washington, DC to the acclaimed documentary *Hoop Dreams* about two inner-city Chicago youths and their quest to become professional basketball players. When a symphony orchestra played at the memorial service for the victims of the Oklahoma City bombing, it was aided by a grant from the NEA.

The relatively minuscule funding our government invests in the NEA helps the national arts community pump nearly $37 billion into the economy and generates over $5 billion in revenue for federal, state, and local governments. Few, if any, other governmental programs can boast such a high return on such a small investment.

Control: Who Pulls the Strings?

The picture we have painted so far portrays those who control screen entertainments as being far more interested in the audience's values than in the artist's voice. Theatre, on the other hand, has been shown as more interested in the artist's voice than in the audience's values. However, there is no exact dividing line between them. Indeed, some commercial theatre productions, such as Disney's stage version of its films *The Lion King* and *Beauty and the Beast,* sometimes called **bourgeois theatre**, pursue maximum profits by reaffirming the audience's values just as rigorously as any big-budget Hollywood film, and many art and independent films stress the artist's vision as much as any noncommercial theatre. But generally speaking, Hollywood more often

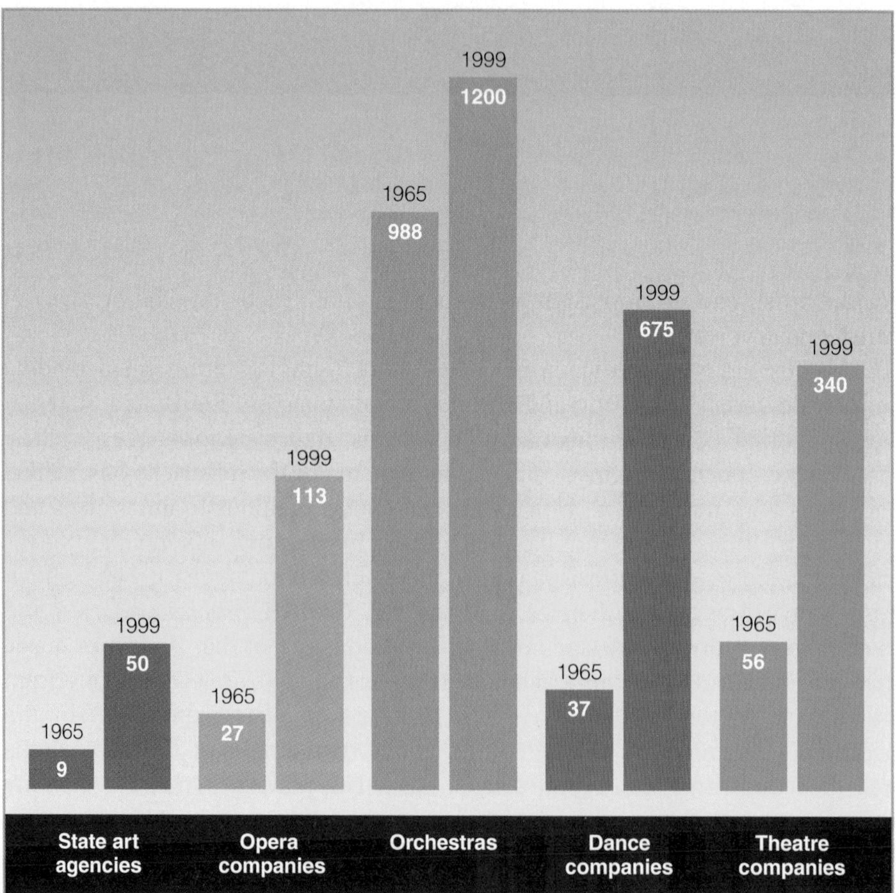

Figure 2.1 Growth of arts groups under NEA. *Since the establishment of the NEA, the number of state art agencies, professional orchestras, opera companies, dance companies, and professional theatre companies in the United States has increased dramatically. The numbers in this figure do not account for various non-professional or amateur art groups.*

SOURCE: National Endowment for the Arts

defines entertainment, and theatre more often defines art. This becomes even clearer when you look at the organizations that produce and fund—and therefore control—entertainments and art.

The Big Picture

Most Hollywood screen entertainments are produced by some of the largest, most profitable mega-corporations in the world. In contrast, smaller companies, independent producers, and even some "mom-and-pop" theatre companies produce most theatre. Even the largest of the theatre-producing organizations, such as the Shuberts, are minuscule when compared to the international media monoliths that control our screen entertainments. Essentially, only a handful of corporations now control almost the majority of entertainments and points of view available in movie theatres, on TV and radio, in magazines and newspapers, and even on bookstore and library shelves. These media moguls are part of huge multinational corporations with holdings in agribusinesses, airlines, transportation companies, banks, insurance companies, coal and oil producers, defense contractors, rocket and jet engineering firms, hotel chains, medical technology companies, and companies that build nuclear power plants and nuclear weapons. They are so large and so powerful that the United States isn't even a large enough market for their entertainment products. Most of their screen entertainments are manufactured in the United States, but a great percentage of the consumers live outside our borders (see the Spotlight on Diversity "Exporting Entertainment and Culture"). As discussed in Chapter 1, entertainment enterprises begin to make money by reaffirming the audience's values. Yet there is another reason for the decisions about the content of our entertainment: As the media moguls have gained more control, they have become increasingly interested in reaffirming their own values over those of their audiences.

Here is a small example of what can happen when only a few huge corporations gain control of our screen entertainments. In the mid-1970s, when numerous companies were competing for our entertainment dollars, approximately one out of every ten major movies shown in the United States was a foreign film. American movie theatres periodically showed the films of acclaimed and influential artists such as Akira Kurosawa, Satyajit Ray, Federico Fellini, and Ingmar Bergman. The availability of foreign films adds to a society's diversity because it helps us understand different cultural, social, and moral points of view. Twenty-five years later, only about one in every one hundred major films in the United States is foreign. It would seem that America's appetite for foreign films has waned, right? But the truth is that huge media corporations bought the majority of the movie screens and built huge megaplexes that drove the small, independent movie theatres out of business. These media moguls found that there was less profit in showing foreign films, so they loaded their mammoth 12- and 24-screen theatres with their own movies. Even if their own movies were in less demand, their costs were lower, so their income was higher. The result was fewer and fewer foreign movies available to us. The next group to eliminate foreign films was movie rental stores who saw demand for foreign films decrease because the new generations attending movies were not seeing or developing a taste for them. Instead, huge corporations dictated what entertainment was available and the public simply followed.

Exporting Entertainment and Culture

Americans certainly enjoy their entertainment—the amount of time and money American consumers spend on entertainment has risen at roughly twice the rate of overall consumer spending. In fact, Americans spend more money on entertainment than they pay for traditionally high-cost items such as health care. In the year 2000, the government listed motion pictures, television, radio, general amusements, and recreation as accounting for a greater part of the gross national product (GNP) than automobile sales, farming, or petroleum.

The United States not only produces more entertainment than any other country on earth but it also exports more entertainment. Hollywood makes so much money from film exportation that less than half of its current movie revenues come from the United States. Only India surpasses the United States in films made per year. India makes some seven hundred feature films per year, as opposed to Hollywood's average of about five hundred. But India makes movies primarily for its own market of over a billion people and seldom exports them. Hollywood, on the other hand, exports movies, television, and American culture all over the world. In 2001, Hollywood movies took 60 percent of the global box office. As an example, in Britain, U.S. movies account for 95 percent of the box-office revenues with an average of nine of the top ten films at any cineplex coming from America. The numbers are similar in Germany, Spain, and Italy. France is one of the few European countries in which a major provincial movie industry has survived, and that's only because French law states that 40 percent of the movies shown in France must come from France.

This cultural invasion through entertainment can have strange effects. For example, French police report that some French citizens are now demanding to be read their Miranda rights when they are arrested, even though they do not exist under French law. In Fiji, researchers assert that since the arrival of Heather Locklear's television presence on that South Pacific island, the old saying "you've gained weight," which is a traditional compliment, is no longer considered by many to be flattery.

Although the United States is tops in the world of screen entertainments, in the world of theatre it is a minor player. Per person, our attendance and funding of the theatre puts us below the top twenty-five of the world's major industrialized nations.

© Hoang Dinh Nam/AFP/Getty Images

A movie poster for Shrek 2 *in Vietnam*

© Patrick Baz/AFP/Getty Images

A movie poster for Terminator 3: Rise of the Machines *in Iran*

Kobal Collection/Picture Desk

Despite the success of certain foreign film genres, such as action martial arts movies like Zhang Yimou's House of Flying Daggers, *you'll have trouble finding a foreign film playing in your local theatres unless you live in a big city or in a college town. Big corporate movie companies have decided the average moviegoer doesn't have the patience to sit through a film with subtitles, so they continue to avoid foreign films. The distribution of these films is then left to independent companies, which are increasingly finding success with movies that tell stories from all around the world. These movies include* The Motorcycle Diaries *(pictured here),* Maria Full of Grace, *and* Good Bye, Lenin!

This is but one small example of what happens when screen entertainments are controlled by so few, and it is minor in comparison to what is happening to other forms of "content" and information. If this same handful of media conglomerates, owning both entertainment and news services, can control what world perspectives we see by filtering out movies from other countries, it can also control what *news* we see from other countries—and even what news we see about ourselves! An executive for News Corporation, Rupert Murdoch's media conglomerate that owns everything from the FOX television networks to major newspapers, said in 1998, "We paid three billion for these TV stations. We will decide what the news is. The news is what we tell you it is."

As a consumer you do have some small, but authoritative, power against the media giants: There is a button on your TV remote control labeled "off," and there is almost always a legitimate stage not far away where theatre professionals are plumbing the depths of the human condition for you to laugh at, rave at, rage at, weep, boo, and applaud where it makes a difference.

The Theatre Next Door

Although screen entertainments tend to be commercialized and globalized and have concentrated ownership, most theatre is less commercialized, more provincial, and locally controlled. But this does not necessarily mean that artists at a given theatre have the financial or civic freedom to produce any play they wish. For thousands of years the powerful and elite have subsidized theatre, from monarchs and czars, to wealthy citizens and the church. Those who control the funding have a tendency to control content. In short, the theatre has

© T. Charles Erickson/Courtesy Berkeley Repertory Theatre

Because legitimate theatres are locally controlled and funded, they can often present a wider diversity of views than movie theatres do. In contrast, major movie studios focus on producing blockbuster films that they think will appeal not only to the widest U.S. audience possible but will also translate well in an international market—that means big action movies, trite romantic comedies, and gross-out teen comedies. For a look outside the mainstream, many people turn to independent films or the theatre. An example is the dozens of black theatre companies throughout the United States that specialize in plays written by black playwrights, featuring black directors and actors, and whose content reflects the black experience, such as Zora Neale Hurston and Dorothy Waring's Polk County, *directed by Kyle Donnelly at the Berkeley Repertory Theatre, 2004–2005, and featuring Kevin Jackson and Kecia Lewis.*

always been a pawn to whoever controls the purse strings, and those who do not control the money often charge those who do with censorship. Joan E. Bertin, executive director of the National Coalition Against Censorship, points out that the impulse to suppress ideas comes from both sides of the political spectrum: "The left complains about art that is critical of feminists, civil rights advocates, and gay activists. The right usually objects to artworks that include nudity, have sexual or anti-religious themes, or denigrate patriotism or the American flag." The battle to control the funding of the theatre goes much deeper than government leaders and citizens worried about how tax dollars are spent. The core of the issue is *who* will control content and *who* will be able to promote their point of view and censor those who disagree.

But unlike screen entertainments that are dominated by a small handful of executives in massive companies with similar political agendas, theatre is liberated by a multitude of diverse, smaller, independent production companies. Hundreds of differing political points of view are promoted by thousands of theatres across the United States. As we stated in Chapter 1, art is political. Art has messages about how an artist thinks the world is or should be. A play contains an artist's opinions, values, and political views. Add this to the thousands of actors, playwrights, and directors in America, each working in theatres owned by different producing organizations with different funding sources, and you have a greater possibility that a wealth of diverse points of view will be expressed. Therefore, when you go to the theatre, you can see patriotic musicals and radical anti-government plays; stories that promote traditional "family" values and stories that champion diverse values; themes that endorse communism and themes that uphold capitalism; plays that glorify Christianity and plays that sing the joys of atheism. Some theatre companies promote African American, Latino, and Asian points of view, and others stage plays with gay, lesbian, and feminist themes. As long as theatre remains locally funded and controlled, a wealth of opinions can be expressed.

In short, a particular theatre may be controlled by corporate or local funding that restricts content, and groups may succeed in censoring, delaying, or even canceling a given production. Yet, with so many different theatres located in diverse areas and with diverse funding, more information, more points of views, and more diverse content can be disseminated. Theatre, therefore, has a much greater chance of being a forum for debate and controversy and providing a voice to those parts of our society about which the massive screen entertainments are silent.

Ownership: Copyrights and Cash

There are striking dissimilarities between a typical Hollywood screen entertainment and the theatre when it comes to who owns the words, ideas, or "content." A **copyright** is a legal guarantee granted by the government to authors, composers, choreographers, inventors, publishers, and/or corporations that allows them to maintain control and profit from their creative works. A copyright is similar to a patent. When you patent an invention, the

U.S. government grants you "the right to exclude others from making, using, offering for sale, or selling" your particular invention without your permission. A copyright, unlike a patent, protects the form of expression rather than the subject matter. When you copyright something, you affirm your exclusive right and ownership of your words, music, or other form of expression.

Playwrights copyright their plays, published or not. This means that in order to stage a play by a playwright who is living or has died within the last seventy years, you first must get written permission from the playwright or the playwright's agent, publisher, or estate. When a play is produced, a **royalty payment** must be made to the playwright or the playwright's estate. This payment is like rent, except that, instead of renting property such as a house or a car, you are renting the playwright's intellectual property. Also, because a play is copyrighted, directors, producers, actors, or anyone involved with the production cannot change, rewrite, or rearrange a script without permission from the playwright or the playwright's agent, publisher, or estate. Therefore, playwrights have the right to say who will perform their plays, the right to make money from the production or publication of their plays, and the right to decide what changes, if any, will be made. This gives playwrights one power: Their words, and therefore their thoughts, themes, and messages, cannot be altered without permission. So when a high school or community theatre cuts all the "dirty" words from a play in order not to offend their audiences, they are guilty of breaking the copyright laws of the United States.

FOR MORE ON

FUNDING THE ARTS AT THE LOCAL LEVEL

"State arts funding: The sad truth," Martha Ullman West, *Dance Magazine,* June 2003

© Richard Feldman

Playwrights copyright their work, so when producers, directors, or theatre companies want to stage a living playwright's work, they must get the playwright's permission first. Sometimes playwrights grant permission initially, but then object to script changes, unusual casting, or a particular interpretation of the play. For example, in 1984 playwright Samuel Beckett objected strongly to director JoAnne Akalaitis's decision to set his Endgame *in a decrepit subway station rather than in the "bare interior" he'd specified in his stage directions. This production featured Ben Halley, Jr.*

FOR MORE ON

PLAYWRIGHTS CONTROLLING THE COPYRIGHT

"*Best Little Whorehouse* playwright King won't let script be altered," Mike Maza, Knight Ridder/Tribune News Service, April 19, 2002

If the playwright has been dead for more than seventy years, the play passes into the public domain and the copyright no longer applies. Plays that are in the **public domain** are owned by the general public, and everyone has the right to produce, or change, them without permission from or payment to the playwright. For example, the plays of William Shakespeare (1564–1616) are now in the public domain and can be produced free of charge.

Things could not be more different for Hollywood screen and television writers. They, unlike playwrights, do not retain the copyright but instead sell their words outright. They are known as **writers for hire**. This means that instead of an individual writer owning her intellectual property, the Hollywood production company owns it and can hire other writers to change, rewrite, or rearrange the script however they see fit without the original writer's permission. Unlike the art of playwriting, which is dominated by solo writers who develop and own their words, Hollywood movies and television shows are often written by groups of writers who are hired to do the corporation's bidding and fired if they fail to measure up. Writers for hire are able to make considerably more money than playwrights. However, they usually make money by catering to the needs of the media conglomerates, not by sharing their own artistic visions of the world.

Rewriting is the intrusion of another mind, another personality, another ego, another ethos. Sometimes it is done with good intentions, good will, and sometimes it will seem to improve the script. But it is a violation of what lies at the heart of authorship and that's why . . . I was never happy writing for screen or for TV. I met some nice people, had some fun, and made some money, but was never satisfied.

David Karp,
Hollywood screenwriter

Unlike writers for hire, playwrights seldom make a living by writing plays. When a play is produced by a college or amateur theatre, the playwright might get as little as $50 per performance. Professional productions often pay a percentage of the gross box-office take (5–10 percent is common), which can lead to payments of several hundred to several thousand dollars per week, but these payments only last for a matter of weeks—until the play closes. If the play is produced by a big Broadway theatre, payments can rival or exceed a Hollywood screenwriter's paycheck, but this is extremely rare. Often, less successful playwrights agree to have their plays produced for no pay whatsoever in the hope of being discovered.

The playwright stands alone, has sole creative control of the script, and decides what can be changed. From the original idea to first draft to finished product, playwrights own their intellectual property. When you see a play, you are hearing the voice of the playwright, not of a committee. Emanuel Azenberg, the Broadway producer, said, "The wonderful thing about the theatre is the writer. Who writes a movie? The theatre is the writer's place." Unlike screenwriters, playwrights see their work produced as written. Unlike screenwriters, playwrights can be part of the total creative process, and unlike screenwriters, playwrights can know the joy that lies at the heart of authorship. When you see a play on stage, you are more likely to be experiencing a story that is true to the author's voice rather than one that has been rewritten to please the audience, the producers, or a multinational corporation.

FOR MORE ON

HOLLYWOOD AND WRITERS

"Living for the moment: As the preceding pages show, being a working actor or screenwriter can be tough. But it's nothing compared to being an aspiring actor or screenwriter," Tim Carvell, *Entertainment Weekly*, August 1, 2003

Curtain Call

Far more separates theatre from screen entertainments than most people take into account. True, one is live and the other only "shadows on a screen," but those shadows have far more financial power and it's concentrated in only a few hands. The media moguls of massive corporations have a huge effect on our lives. Not only do they reflect our values, which is problematic in itself, but they color their evening news programs, their newspapers, their movies, and their television shows with their corporate values or the values of other corporations that have the millions needed to buy air time.

This influence happens on several levels. Not only do corporations add their political points of view to the scripts, they also push their politics through their product advertisements. For example, the James Bond movie *Tomorrow Never Dies* had promotional deals with Heineken, Avis, BMW, and Smirnoff's vodka. These brands were, of course, all featured prominently. Several Hollywood stars have even signed contracts with cigarette manufacturers promising to smoke at least one cigarette per movie, while health care companies have hired agencies such as William Morris to help improve their image in television dramas and movies. These few media moguls have so much power they can influence laws in Washington and in foreign countries. They have driven legislation through Congress that increases their profits and makes them less accountable to the general public. And what do these huge corporations want from you, the audience? They want you to be good consumers. Theatres, by and large, seek to challenge you, not to make you "brand loyal."

The theatre is little, much smaller than it once was, but is it dying? Has it been defeated by the forms of screen entertainments that grew out of it during the early part of the last century? No. It is still very much alive, but its voice is a whisper compared to the roar of endless TV channels and megaplex cinemas. Yet as long as it is funded and uncensored, sometimes a whisper can change the world.

William Missouri Downs

Although theatre is no longer a dominant art form in the United States and Europe, it's still going strong. Popular plays and musicals still attract crowds, most big cities continue to enjoy thriving theatre scenes, playwrights keep on writing, and actors are still drawn to the stage. Here, theatregoers brave a rainy night to see Holly Hunter in By the Bog of Cats *by Marina Carr at the Wyndham's Theatre in London's West End.*

Summary

There are many differences between screen entertainments and the theatre. In terms of societal impact, one of the most important is that theatre attracts a relatively small audience. A play can run on Broadway for thousands of performances and still not be seen by as many people as watch a popular television show on a single night. Another key difference between theatre and screen entertainments is that theatre is a live, relatively interactive medium. When you watch a movie or a TV show, communication flows only one way: from the screen to you. In contrast, when you watch a play, you and the actors share communication—you each have a direct influence on the other. This is why theatre is called a living art.

Because it is live, theatre is a risky business. Many unfortunate surprises can occur in a live setting, but the show still must go on. As such, stage actors usually need plenty of rehearsal time in order to avoid making mistakes during a performance. Often, they also must be skilled in singing and dancing as well as acting. In contrast, screen actors are provided a safety net in the form of multiple takes, dubbing if they can't sing, and editing if they're not talented dancers.

In film, directors often have a lot of power and can directly influence what the audience will see. They control many aspects of the movie-making process because they can rewrite a script, influence the actors' performances, and dictate the editing of a movie. Stage directors usually do not have as much power or control. Because playwrights copyright their work, directors must obtain the playwright's permission to change a script, unless it is in the public domain. In addition, directors can do nothing to control the actors' performances once the curtain goes up on a performance. Similarly, directors of television programs have limited power over a production and are sometimes even subservient to the writers.

Theatre and screen entertainments also differ in how they are funded and in how profitable they are. Screen entertainments are often controlled by mega-corporations that expect their products—movies and TV programs—to make a profit. To help ensure that these products are profitable, corporations test audiences to make sure movies and TV shows are appealing and entertaining. These mega-corporations export American entertainment all around the world, open movies in dozens of theatres at once to maximize ticket sales, sell movies to home audiences in the form of videos and DVDs, and sell movie rights to lucrative overseas markets. Although some blockbuster plays and musicals turn a profit, many theatres cannot rely on ticket sales to cover the many costs of putting on a production. Consequently, most theatres seek additional funding from individual patrons, corporations, and government agencies such as the National Endowment for the Arts in order to make ends meet. Yet, because theatre is often locally controlled and funded, it can often present a wider diversity of subject matter and ideas than screen entertainments do.

THE ART OF THEATRE ONLINE

Use the *Art of Theatre* website at **http://communication.wadsworth.com/downs1** for quick access to the electronic study resources that accompany this chapter, including a digital glossary, a link to InfoTrac College Edition that you can use to find the For More On... InfoTrac College Edition readings listed below, a list of further reading, and a chapter quiz. When you get to the *Art of Theatre* homepage, click on the cover of the book you are using and you will be redirected to the website for your book. Then click on "Student Book Companion Site" in the Resource box, pick a chapter from the pull-down menu at the top of the page, and select an option from the Chapter Resources menu. The *Art of Theatre* website also includes links to interesting and informative theatre websites. Just click on the Theatre on the Web link in the Book Resources menu. The links to these websites are maintained and updated as needed.

Key Terms

bourgeois theatre / 40
copyright / 44
corporate funding / 36
government funding / 37
National Endowment for the Arts (NEA) / 37
patrons / 36
public domain / 46
royalty payment / 45
writers for hire / 46

For More On . . .

InfoTrac College Edition Readings

http://www.infotrac-college.com

The business of film / 34
"Building knowledge about the consumer: The emergence of market research in the motion picture industry"

Corporate funding of the arts / 37
"The corporate art of helping the arts"

Funding the arts at the local level / 45
"State arts funding: The sad truth"

Playwrights controlling the copyright / 46
"*Best Little Whorehouse* playwright King won't let script be altered"

Hollywood and writers / 46
"Living for the moment: As the preceding pages show, being a working actor or screenwriter can be tough. But it's nothing compared to being an aspiring actor or screenwriter"

7 Theatre and Cultural Diversity

We've all heard the age-old philosophical question "If a tree falls in the forest and no one is around to hear it, does it make a sound?" Philosophers have argued this question for centuries, but substitute the theatre for the tree and the argument becomes moot: If a play is performed and no one attends it, then the play has no effect on society, provides no entertainment, and makes no statement. In order for theatre—or, for that matter, communication—to take place, there must be someone to express an idea and someone to respond. In short, even if you have the ability and the freedom to speak, you don't have a voice in the political, social, or cultural arena unless someone can hear you.

Though we often think of theatre in terms of stars and spotlights, this chapter will focus on the ***theatre of the people,*** *where there are few stars or spotlights. This type of*

© Michal Daniel

◀ ***On preceding page:***
Top Girls, written by Caryl Churchill, directed by Casey Stangl, Guthrie Lab, 2003, featuring (l to r) Bianca Amato, Eunice Wong, and Sally Wingert. (The inset features Eunice Wong.) This play depicts the challenges working women face in the contemporary business world and society at large.

theatre provides a forum for everyday people to express themselves; it gives a voice to those who are seldom heard in the mainstream media. This goal is possible because of the very characteristics that distinguish theatre from television and film entertainments: Theatre is relatively low-tech so it can be done anywhere, anytime, and at low cost. Expensive lights, costumes, sets, and professional actors are *optional.* Additionally, local organizations often control theatre at the regional level, which means that theatre can represent the concerns of the *people,* not the government, the powers that be, or multinational media corporations.

The theatre of the people is what media researcher Jacob Srampickal calls the "popular theatre" in his book *Voice to the Voiceless, The Power of People's Theatre.* This is the theatre of the ordinary people, people who are determined to "free themselves from the political and socio-cultural constraints of the power structures." This is theatre for people and cultures that are intentionally or unintentionally neglected or stereotyped by the mass media. This type of theatre is what Brazilian director Augusto Boal called "theatre of the oppressed." (See the Spotlight "Augusto Boal and *The Theatre of the Oppressed.*") In this chapter we will explore theatre that gives a voice to the voiceless.

FOR MORE ON
AUGUSTO BOAL
"The theatre of the oppressed," Augusto Boal, *UNESCO Courier,* November 1997

I Critical Mirror: Art and Entertainment Reflect Culture

We all come from a culture, yet we are not always aware of it, particularly if we come from the dominant culture. Only when our culture is celebrated, denied, or contrasted with another culture do we become conscious of how much it affects our daily lives. **Culture** is the values, standards, and patterns of behavior of a particular group of people. Culture is expressed in a people's customs, language, rituals, history, religion, social and political institutions, and in its art and entertainment. However, culture is not the same as **pop culture**, short for "popular culture," which is the fads and fashions that dominate mainstream media, music, and art for a period of time.

We are not born with cultural knowledge. We learn about our culture by watching and imitating the behaviors of others and listening to their stories. The process by which we learn about our culture is called **enculturation**. Throughout history and in many societies, art and entertainment have often been sources of enculturation; they are tools for demonstrating culture.

As our culture changes, so do our art and entertainment. For example, back in 1962 the popular sitcom *The Dick Van Dyke Show* aired an episode featuring a black couple. It was one of the first times that black characters on a major sitcom weren't maids or gardeners or some other stereotype. Six years later, the sci-fi drama *Star Trek* portrayed the first interracial kiss on television. Captain James T. Kirk (William Shatner) locked lips with Lieutenant Uhura (Nichelle Nichols). This episode aired November 22, 1968, but was not shown in some parts of the United States where local channels thought it would challenge their audiences' values—in other words, question their culture. Only seven years later, the sitcom *The Jeffersons* featured an interracial couple, and it hardly created a ripple. Today, interracial relationships and nonstereotypical black characters are familiar on television. However, our entertainment did not lead the way; it followed the changing culture of the country.

Sometimes art and entertainment can suggest change rather than simply reflect existing culture. For example, in 1965 African American playwright

Augusto Boal and *The Theatre of the Oppressed*

Augusto Boal (b. 1931) made his reputation at the Arena Theatre in São Paulo, Brazil, where he experimented with new types of staging and acting that reached out to the common people. He wanted theatre to speak to the average people on the street—the poor and the disenfranchised—in their own language and with stories that addressed their situations. He felt that theatre should be controlled by the people and not by massive corporations or the government. He resisted the ideas spread by the dominant culture and instead made theatre a tool of self-expression. He wanted to help the common people develop a sense of their own identity and culture.

Boal also attacked the idea that theatre is a vicarious experience in which the audience sits in the dark. Instead, he wanted the audience to become part of the performance. In his theatre, the audience could stop the actors and suggest actions and solutions that the actors would then incorporate into the story. Once, when an actor could not understand a woman's suggestion, she went up on stage and acted out what she meant. For Boal, this represented the purpose of theatre: to make the audience not "spectators" but "spect-actors." Boal's theatre, which he called "a rehearsal for revolution," led to grassroots activism.

Shortly after the publication of Boal's book *The Theatre of the Oppressed,* a military junta took control of Brazil and Boal was arrested, tortured, and exiled. In exile, Boal organized the first International Festival of the Theatre of the Oppressed, gave theatre workshops all over the world, and established dozens of theatre companies whose community-based performances enabled common people to take political action. When the military junta in Brazil was overthrown, Boal returned to Rio de Janeiro. Today, he makes theatre for the people of Brazil, but he also continues to travel the world giving workshops on how to make theatre meaningful to people who have little political clout and whose voices are seldom heard in the mainstream theatre or media.

© Centro do Teatro do Oprimido do Rio de Janeiro

Director and author Augusto Boal initiated a revolutionary type of audience-participation theatre in his native Brazil. By giving audience members permission to stop a performance to suggest and demonstrate changes, Boal believes that they are transformed into "spect-actors" instead of mere "spectators" and can become empowered to initiate social change.

Douglas Turner Ward (b. 1920) wrote the play *Day of Absence,* about a small town from which all the black people suddenly disappear. The play satirizes the dominant culture of the day by depicting the white characters as suddenly adrift because they have no one to wash their clothes, take out the trash, and clean their yards. This biting satire did not support enculturation. Instead, it questioned the dominant culture of 1965 and helped change how Americans thought about race. More recently, the movie *A Day without a Mexican* (2004) considers what might happen if one day all the Latinos disappear from California. As time goes by, the state begins to deteriorate and it becomes apparent that the "California dream" is fueled in large part by Latino domestics, gardeners, farm and construction workers, athletes, and professionals. This movie makes the point that *all* cultures, not just the dominant culture, contribute to the well-being of a society.

Throughout the centuries, the theatrical talents of women were either largely ignored or squelched. Not until the mid-twentieth century did plays written by women become part of mainstream theatre. One of the first American women to write plays that presented women from a woman's point of view was Ruth Gordon, most famous today for her roles in the movies Rosemary's Baby *(1969)—for which she received an Oscar—and* Harold and Maude *(1972).*

© AP/Wide World Photos

I wrote my first play, *Uncommon Women and Others,* in the hopes of seeing an all-female curtain call in the basement of the Yale School of Drama. A man in the audience stood up during a post-show discussion and announced, "I can't get into this. It's about girls." I thought to myself, "Well, I've been getting into *Hamlet* and *Lawrence of Arabia* my whole life, so you better start trying."

Wendy Wasserstein,
American playwright

More often, though, art and entertainment reflect the voice of the dominant culture. For example, in its long history, theatre has not always given a voice to all people or reflected the many cultures in any society. Instead it has generally been controlled by the dominant culture: those in power, members of the upper class, government, religious institutions, and, in particular, men. For thousands of years, the dominant culture has controlled playwriting, directing, design, and acting through racism, sexism, discrimination, economic power, and social and religious customs. Throughout the centuries, women and minority racial, religious, and ethnic groups have usually been forced to stand on the sidelines. During most of Western and Eastern theatre history, not only was it considered improper for religious, social, or cultural reasons for women to write plays, but women were also not allowed to set foot on stage. Instead, men and boys played women's roles in drag. In England a few centuries ago, women were arrested for participating in theatre productions. In 1611, for instance, Mary Frith was arrested for acting on a public stage in London and charged with, among other things, "swearing & cursing & . . . usually associat[ing] her selfe [*sic*] with Ruffinly swaggering & lewd company."

Only in the last couple of decades has gender parity begun to seem possible in art and entertainment, reflecting a growing acceptance of the contributions of women to mainstream culture. For example, not until 1984 did a woman win a Tony Award for set design. Additionally, in the sixty-four years before 1980, only five women had won the Pulitzer Prize for Drama. Then in 1981 Beth Henley won it for *Crimes of the Heart;* in 1983 Marsha Norman won it for *'night, Mother;* and in 1989 Wendy Wasserstein won it for *The Heidi Chronicles.* According to figures compiled by the nonprofit theatre company Women's Project and Production, between 1985 and 1995 women wrote only 7 percent of new Broadway plays and 17 percent of Off-Broadway plays.

FOR MORE ON

WOMEN AND THEATRE

"Women & theatre: The companies they keep," Andrea Wolper, *Back Stage,* April 26, 1996 (includes list of women's theatre companies)

Then again, the old prohibition against women acting still seems to be in effect in Hollywood, mainly for older women. Holly Hunter, Kathleen Turner, Angelica Huston, Melanie Griffith, and other big stars have complained that roles dry up for women the minute they hit forty. Some of them have turned to the stage for work, where casting older women in lead parts is more common. For instance, Melanie Griffith took the role of Roxie Hart in the stage musical *Chicago* in 2003, and in 2005 Kathleen Turner received many positive reviews for her turn as Martha in the Broadway revival of Edward Albee's *Who's Afraid of Virginia Woolf?* Other top actors such as Jessica Lange have turned to cable and independent films. One of the reasons for this continuing gender bias may be that men write the majority of Hollywood movies. For example, from 1991 to 1997, male writers outnumbered female writers in Hollywood by about 5 to 1 in feature film and by 4 to 1 in television. Little has altered since then—only five current major network television shows (*CSI: Crime Scene Investigation, CSI: Miami, Cold Case, Judging Amy,* and *Joan of Arcadia*) have female head writers. Leah Krinsky, a writer for *Dennis Miller Live,* says, "It's a boys' club. There's a huge blind spot, and I don't know if it's biological, societal, or what. I know so many women who are so talented and funny, but they really have trouble finding work." A similar problem exists for minorities in Hollywood. Of the hundreds of Hollywood films made each year, minorities write, on average, only 5 percent. In the 1999–2000 season, 80 percent of the television shows had only one or no minority writers.

Photofest

As they get older, most women in Hollywood struggle to find substantial and interesting movie roles, whereas men are offered leading roles even into their sixties and seventies. Women also struggle to find directing jobs—in 2004, women directed only four of the top one hundred Hollywood films. Many older women turn to the stage or independent movies, such as Titus, *directed by Julie Taymor and starring Jessica Lange in the lead role of Tamora. Older women are also having greater success as movie executives. In 2005, women held top creative decision-making roles in four of the six top studios, including Universal, Paramount, Sony, and Buena Vista.*

Now that we've explored some ways in which theatre and screen entertainments have *not* given a voice to people outside the dominant culture, let's take a closer look at the theatre of the people. As you read at the beginning of this chapter, the theatre of the people provides a forum for people traditionally left out of the mainstream.

Theatre Can Promote Cultural Awareness

The purpose of the theatre of the people is to promote cultural awareness by giving a voice to all members of society. Allowing everyone a voice benefits society by increasing multiculturalism and helping to end stereotypes. **Multiculturalism** is the endeavor to overcome all forms of discrimination, including racism, sexism, and homophobia, so that people can coexist peacefully and attempt to achieve a pluralistic society. One of the fundamental conflicts of human existence is the difference between how we perceive ourselves and

> If we're going to have something that is called an American theater, then we have to allow room for the esthetic values of Hispanics, for Asians, African Americans, for all the racial and cultural groups that make up this society, as well as for the age-old tried-and-true values of the European American.
>
> ***August Wilson,***
> *American playwright*

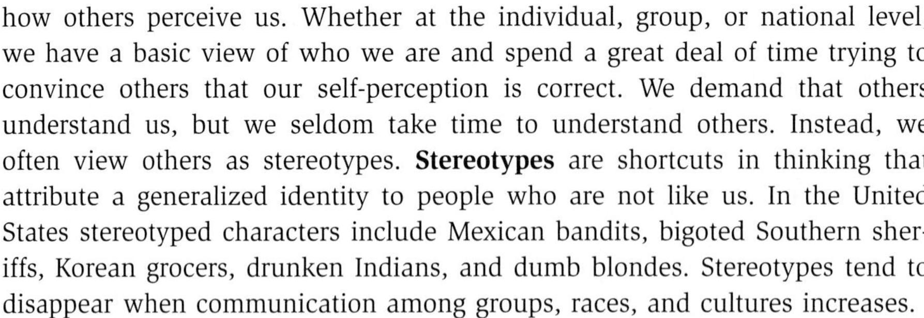

how others perceive us. Whether at the individual, group, or national level, we have a basic view of who we are and spend a great deal of time trying to convince others that our self-perception is correct. We demand that others understand us, but we seldom take time to understand others. Instead, we often view others as stereotypes. **Stereotypes** are shortcuts in thinking that attribute a generalized identity to people who are not like us. In the United States stereotyped characters include Mexican bandits, bigoted Southern sheriffs, Korean grocers, drunken Indians, and dumb blondes. Stereotypes tend to disappear when communication among groups, races, and cultures increases.

The theatre of the people attempts to increase communication by celebrating our differences, by highlighting our similarities, and by allowing everyone a voice. There are three basic types of theatre of the people:

FOR MORE ON
MULTICULTURALISM AND THEATRE
"The dilemma of multiculturalism in the theatre," Ethel Pitts Walker, *TDR,* Fall 1994

- *Theatre of identity* promotes a particular people's cultural identity and invites members of that culture and other cultures to experience that culture's joys, problems, history, traditions, and point of view.
- *Theatre of protest* objects to the dominant culture's control and demands that a minority culture's voice and political agenda be heard.
- *Cross-cultural theatre* mixes different cultures in an attempt to find understanding or commonality among them.

Of course, these types of theatre are not always separate. One play can include the characteristics of more than one type of theatre of the people.

Theatre of Identity

Theatre of identity promotes a particular people's awareness of themselves and their experiences, traditions, and culture. The plays of theatre of identity are written by members of a particular culture and staged by actors from that culture. This type of theatre gives a voice to a people and encourages audience members to reflect on, analyze, or reinvent their own self-perceptions. It gives a voice to groups that the dominant culture ignores or silences. This type of theatre is not closed to outsiders. On the contrary, theatre of identity often welcomes people of other cultures even though they might not completely understand the sensibility in these productions. Theatre of identity can present sugar-coated images of a culture, but it can also feature that culture's defeats and regrets. Images of imperfections are meant to strengthen the bonds of the community as it gives audience members of that culture a self-definition not available from the dominant culture. Cultural identity plays are performed in streets and small theatres in China, India, Latin America, Poland, and Nigeria—anywhere there are people who do not have a voice but have enough freedom to gather and form an audience. You'll read more about world theatre in Part III. In this chapter, we'll focus on American theatre.

In the United States, the theatre of identity grew out of the wide variety of traditions that make up our diverse population. People fleeing the French Revolution in 1789 started the French American theatre. One of the first African American theatres was founded in New York City in 1821, and some Spanish-language theatre was acquired with the conquest of the Southwest. In the 1800s

Photofest

Uncommon Women and Others is one of many plays by Wendy Wasserstein that reflect the joys and disappointments of women coming of age in the 1970s and 1980s. Wasserstein typically uses comedy to diffuse and explain such intimate topics as sexism, sexuality, and parent-child relationships. This 1994 revival of the play was directed by Carole Rothman at the Lucille Lortel Theatre, New York, and featured (l to r) Haviland Morris, Mary McCann, and Danielle Ferland.

German, Polish, Chinese, Norwegian, and Swedish theatres were founded across the country. These theatres reached their peak in the opening decades of the twentieth century because they provided art and entertainment for millions of new immigrants whose cultural and language differences, as well as outright discrimination, kept them out of mainstream American life. By the 1900s Finns in Oregon had the Astoria Socialist Theatre; Italians in San Francisco had their own theatre; and in New York City, Second Avenue was known as the **"Yiddish Broadway"** because so many Jewish theatres were located there. The first half of the twentieth century was also a time when the absence of plays written by women playwrights began to be corrected. Zona Gale (1874–1938), Georgia Douglas Johnson (1880–1966), Susan Glaspell (1882–1948), Edna Ferber (1885–1968), Ruth Gordon (1895–1985), Lillian Hellman (1905–1984), and many others were writing plays that presented women as successful scientists, businesspeople, legislators, and screenwriters who dealt with or fought against the male-dominated culture. Even though

The Second Avenue Theatre is one of the theatres in New York City that featured Yiddish plays in the early part of the twentieth century. There were so many of these theatres on Second Avenue that the area became known as the "Yiddish Broadway." Initially, many of these theatres premiered European Yiddish works that appealed to New York's many Jewish immigrants. Later, they featured new works based on the Jewish experience in America.

© Hulton Archive/Getty Images

their plays won critical acclaim, they were seldom included in popular anthologies, but these women let nothing stop them as they challenged stereotypes and stood up against a society that treated women as second-class citizens.

One of the strongest forms of theatre of identity in the United States is that of black Americans. Theatre performed by African Americans has been around for hundreds of years, but legitimate plays written by blacks, about blacks, and for blacks were rare until the twentieth century. Before that, black characters were mainly stereotypes written by whites and even performed by whites. (See the Spotlight on Diversity "Blackface, Redface, Yellowface.")

Willis Richardson (1889–1977) was the first black playwright to have a play on Broadway that was not a musical; his play *The Chip Woman's Fortune* appeared in 1923. Richardson went on to write about black historical heroes including Crispus Attucks, who was killed in the Boston Massacre; Alexander Dumas *père,* the biracial French playwright; and biblical characters such as Simon the Cyrenian, who carried the cross for Jesus. Richardson felt that too many plays by black writers were only about how black people were treated by whites. He said, "Still there is another kind of play: the kind that shows the soul of a people; and the soul of this people is truly worth showing." A few years later, in 1926, poet Langston Hughes said, "We younger Negro artists

Blackface, Redface, Yellowface

For most of U.S. theatre and film history, blacks, Native Americans, and Asians were discriminated against and even banned from appearing on stage or in films. As a result, whites played "ethnic" characters by wearing heavy makeup, which led to one of the most bizarre forms of theatre: the **minstrel show**. Minstrel shows originated in the nineteenth century and lasted well into the twentieth. These performances contained comic scenes, dance interludes, and sentimental ballads, all based on white people's perceptions of black life in the South. Black music was popular, but it was considered improper for whites to go to a theatre to hear black musicians, so whites would put on black makeup, called **blackface**, and perform as black people. Minstrel shows often contained skits with illiterate and foolish exchanges that made fun of blacks. Blacks did not attend minstrel shows; they were entertainment for white people only.

For many years in Hollywood films, it was considered acceptable for whites to play blacks as well as Native Americans and Asians. The first talking picture, *The Jazz Singer,* was about a Jewish boy (Al Jolson) who becomes a jazz singer. In the movie's final scene he performs in blackface in a minstrel show. In the 1950s, whites playing blacks finally fell out of favor, but the tradition of whites playing Asians and Native Americans continued into the 1990s. Katharine Hepburn, Fred Astaire, John Wayne, and Marlon Brando are some of the stars who played Asian roles in Hollywood films.

White domination of ethnic roles was challenged when the British producer Cameron Mackintosh (*Cats, Phantom of the Opera*) announced that the white British actor Jonathan Pryce was going to play the Asian male lead on Broadway in the hit musical *Miss Saigon.* Asian actors protested that they weren't even given a chance to audition. Actor B. D. Wong said, "If Asian American actors aren't good enough to play Asian roles, what are we good for?" At first, the actors' union protested. Asian actors announced that they would not allow "taped eyelids and yellowface" on a white actor. But when Mackintosh threatened to cancel the production, throwing many actors out of work, the union backed down. In the end, Pryce played the role, but he did not wear the eye prosthetics he had worn when he played the role in London. After he left the show, an Asian actor took over the part.

Is it right for whites to play blacks, or for Filipinos to play Chinese, or for Jews to play Italians? (The practice of casting actors regardless of their race is called color-blind casting. For more on this topic, see Chapter 8.) The actors' union said, "Jews have always been able to play Italians, Italians have always been able to play Jews, and both have been able to play Asians. Asian actors, however, almost never have the opportunity to play either Jews or Italians and continue to struggle even to play themselves." As recently as 1995, a book on stage makeup listed "ethnic appearances" including "Caucasian to Oriental" and "Caucasian to Indian," complete with before-and-after photos of a young white model made up to look like Fu Manchu. White to black makeup was not included. Today, the question remains: Should the theatre be color-blind or color-conscious?

© Joan Marcus/Photofest

British actor Jonathan Pryce originated the Asian lead role in the London run of the musical Miss Saigon. *His casting caused controversy when the play transferred to the United States, where the Actor's Equity union initially refused to allow Pryce to continue in the part because "it would be an affront to the Asian community." After pressure from the play's producer, Pryce joined the Broadway production. However, he agreed to perform without the eye makeup he had used in London to seem Asian.*

now intend to express our dark-skinned selves without fear or shame. If white people are pleased, we are glad. If they are not, it doesn't matter. We know we are beautiful. And ugly too." This comment summarized the black struggle for artistic independence that took place during the 1920s and 1930s, in the period known as the **Harlem Renaissance**. This was a time when black artists, actors, poets, musicians, and writers converged in Harlem and endeavored to tell the stories of their lives, their history, and their people contrary to white stereotypes of blacks.

During the civil rights movement of the late 1950s and 1960s, theatre of identity continued to grow. In 1959, Lorraine Hansberry (1930–1965) became the first black woman playwright to be produced on Broadway. It would take another twenty-five years for another African American playwright to succeed on Broadway. However, black playwrights, although they were still locked out of the mainstream commercial theatre, were finding a voice. Some of these playwrights are Amiri Baraka (b. 1934), whose *The Slave* (1965) deals with an interracial couple; Adrienne Kennedy (b. 1931), whose *Funnyhouse of a Negro* (1964) focuses on the human unconscious and the search for meaning and truth; and Douglas Turner Ward, whose *Day of Absence* mocks minstrel shows by having a black cast dress up in whiteface and play white characters.

By 1968 there were forty black theatre companies in the United States, and twenty years later there were over two hundred. However, many of these theatres suffer from unreliable funding and go in and out of business every few years. For example, the Tony Award–winning Crossroads Theatre Company in New Brunswick, New Jersey, recently had to close its doors but not before it became known as a trailblazing theatre that made a significant impact on American culture and black theatre literature. Some of the plays created by these influential theatres have even become mainstream Hollywood movies: *The River Niger* (1976), which starred James Earl Jones; *Ceremonies in Dark Old Men* (1975) with Glynn Turman; and Charles Fuller's Pulitzer Prize–winning *A Soldier's Play* (1981), which became the movie *A Soldier's Story* (1984) with Adolph Caesar and Denzel Washington.

Today, theatres that stress African American cultural identity still struggle for funding because their major purpose, unlike the mainstream commercial theatre, is not to make money but rather to promote cultural awareness and tolerance. Playwright August Wilson recently pointed out that few of the sixty-six major regional theatres in the United States are dedicated to preserving and promoting black culture. Wilson asserts that this inequality is "not only skewed toward whites and the so-called classical values of European theatre, but one that impedes the development of a truly American theatre and ignores the contributions being made by others of various ethnic and racial backgrounds."

Today, perhaps no two playwrights represent the growing diversity of the American theatre scene more than August Wilson (1945 - 2005) and Suzan-Lori Parks (b. 1964). Wilson grew up in the Hill district of Pittsburgh, Pennsylvania. He left school after daily barrages of racial epithets. Rather than tell his mother that he had dropped out, Wilson spent his youth at the public library, where he gave himself an education. In 1984 he had his first big success with *Ma Rainey's Black Bottom,* a play about black musicians struggling with their white bosses in the 1920s. The play was first produced by the Yale Repertory Theatre and later on Broadway. His second play, *Fences,* opened on Broadway

> We have never said that white reviewers cannot understand black theatre—if you can understand Duke Ellington and Ray Charles, you can understand black theatre.
>
> ***August Wilson,***
> *American playwright*

in 1987. It was set in the 1950s and tells the story of Troy Maxon, a garbage collector who has become embittered by the white-controlled system that has denied him the baseball stardom he feels he deserves. For this play, Wilson won the Pulitzer Prize. The following year he returned to Broadway with *Joe Turner's Come and Gone,* the story of a black man who was unjustly imprisoned in 1910. Then came *The Piano Lesson.* Set in the 1930s, it is the story of a man who wants to buy the land in Mississippi where his ancestors once worked as slaves. But in order to raise the money, he must sell the family heirloom, a piano. This play earned Wilson his second Pulitzer Prize for Drama. In Wilson's plays the white world is a major character but remains almost entirely offstage. Wilson said, "Blacks know the spiritual truth of white America. We are living examples of America's hypocrisy. We know white America better than white America knows us."

Suzan-Lori Parks represents a new group of young playwrights who are not waiting for the mainstream commercial theatre or the dominant culture to recognize their plays. Born in Fort Knox, Kentucky, she lived the transient childhood of an "Army brat." This allowed her to experience many different worlds, but friendships were hard to maintain so she entertained herself by staging puppet shows. After graduating from college in English and German literature, she moved to New York and started staging her own plays wherever she could find an empty space. Once, when she couldn't find a stage, she

August Wilson's Two Trains Running *uses sharp-edged humor and cutting social analysis to reveal the conflicts that African Americans face. Set in Pittsburgh in 1969 after the assassinations of Martin Luther King, Jr., and Malcolm X, the characters find themselves at a crossroads as they try to come to terms with their pasts and find self-respect in an inequitable world. This 2005 production featuring (l to r) Adolphus Ward, E. Milton Wheeler, James A. Williams, and Erika LaVonn was directed by Lou Bellamy at the Kansas City Repertory Theatre.*

© Don Ipock Photography/Courtesy Kansas City Repertory Theatre

© Michal Daniel

Topdog/Underdog by Suzan-Lori Parks is the dark comic tale of two brothers who vie with each other to come out on top. The brothers, named Lincoln and Booth by their father as a joke, experience an intense sibling rivalry and come to understand their shared history only through their obsession with the con game three-card monte. This 2001 Off-Broadway production featured Don Cheadle as Booth and Jeffrey Wright as Lincoln and was directed by George C. Wolfe at the Public Theatre in New York.

even used a garage at a gas station. To those who run into barriers she says, "To get a play done, you go to a place and do it, or you work your day job and then you do a play; you produce it yourself." Within a few years, she had graduated from garages to such notable theatres as the Public Theatre in New York and the Arena Stage in Washington, DC, and in 2001 her play *Topdog/Underdog* was produced on Broadway. A dark comedy about sibling rivalry between two brothers, Lincoln and Booth, *Topdog/Underdog* deals with oppressive systems within society. With this play, Parks became the first African American woman to win the Pulitzer. Parks succinctly summed up the ideas behind theatre of identity when she said, "I know where I am and who I am and what I do."

FOR MORE ON
SUZAN-LORI PARKS

"Whisper to a scream: Digging for Suzan-Lori Parks," Karen Wada, *Los Angeles Magazine*, June 2003

Theatre of Protest

The second type of theatre of the people could be called theatre of social agenda or theatre of militancy because its purpose is protest and change. **Theatre of protest** vents hostility toward the ruling class, race, or culture. Protest plays date back to the ancient Greeks. For example, Aristophanes' comedy *Lysistrata* (411 BCE) is often called the first anti-war play. Twenty-four hundred years later similar anti-war plays were produced during the 1960s and early 1970s as American students demonstrated against inequality and the Vietnam War. The French director Antonin Artaud (1896–1948) summed up the purpose of protest plays when he said, "The action of theatre, like that of plague, is beneficial, for, impelling men to see themselves as they are, it causes the mask to fall, reveals the lie, the slackness, baseness, and hypocrisy of our world." In other words, this type of theatre isn't presented to entertain but rather to demand justice.

One such theatre is El Teatro Campesino (The Farmworkers Theatre) founded in 1965 by Luis Valdez (b. 1940). Spanish-speaking theatre has existed in America since the late sixteenth century, but El Teatro Campesino became a new type of theatre that did more than celebrate Latino culture—it protested social injustice. Valdez and his theatre improvised plays to support Filipino and Chicano migrant farmworkers who, led by Cesar Chavez, were on strike against California grape growers. Performed on the backs of flatbed trucks, these plays were often cast with striking workers, which narrowed the line between performer and audience and made audience participation critical. The dialogue in *The Conscience of a Scab* and other plays was drawn from real conflicts the strikers experienced. The stories focused on the strikers' meager pay and poor working conditions, highlighting the oppressions perpetrated by the white growers. Valdez went on to write plays that addressed not only immediate local issues but also cultural identity and national issues. He has written about members of the Chicano community who deny their heritage as they attempt to blend into the American "melting pot" and has attacked Mexican

El Teatro Campesino began as the theatrical arm of the United Farm Workers, a labor union formed in the early 1960s that protested for fair wages and ethical treatment of Filipino and Mexican seasonal workers. Here, El Teatro Campesino members perform a scene from Las tres uvas, *a short play ridiculing the growers' strike tactics, describing them from the vantage points of a ripe grape, a rotten grape, and a raisin. Often performed from the back of a flatbed truck, plays such as this one were used to teach and boost the morale of the striking workers.*

© 1976 George Ballis/Take Stock

© Martha Swope

Luis Valdez's play Zoot Suit *dramatizes the powerful racial tensions of 1940s Los Angeles. Shown here is Edward James Olmos playing the part of El Pachuco in a 1979 production of the play, directed by Valdez at the Winter Garden Theatre in New York. The first Mexican American playwright to be produced on Broadway, Valdez observed that "until we [Mexican Americans] had the artists who could express what the people were feeling and saying, we wouldn't really register politically. Art gives us the tools of that expression."*

> We are a lot more varied, as a country, than we like to pretend to be. I mean, we give sort of a nodding recognition that the country is multiracial, for instance, but do not do a lot to really integrate, in a cultural-artistic sense, the real currents that flow in this country. That sort of thing has to happen of itself through the daily life of the people, through the daily cultural life.
>
> ***Luis Valdez,***
> *American playwright*

stereotypes found in mainstream theatre, television, and film. He has written that El Teatro Campesino's purposes are to "replace the lingering negative stereotype of the Mexican in the United States with a new positive image created through Chicano art, and to continue to dramatize the social despair of Chicanos living in an Anglo-dominated society."

Valdez's most famous play is *Zoot Suit* (1978), which is based on the Sleepy Lagoon murder trial and the famous Zoot Suit Riots, now often called the Sailor Riots. These riots occurred when American military personnel claimed that Mexicans wearing zoot suits had attacked them while they were on leave in Los Angeles during World War II. (A "zoot" is a flamboyant suit with wide lapels and oversized pleated pants popular among Mexican American youth in the 1940s.) In response to the allegation, over two hundred uniformed white sailors stormed into the heart of the Mexican American community in East Los Angeles and attacked anyone wearing a zoot suit. The police did nothing to stop the sailors' riot. After several days of rioting, when the Navy feared it had a mutiny on its hands, military authorities finally took steps to end the melee. None of the sailors was ever prosecuted, but many of the Zoot Suiters were.

Zoot Suit takes place in front of a giant newspaper that serves as a drop curtain. The headline reads "Zoot-Suiter Hordes Invade Los Angeles. US Navy and Marines Are Called In." The newspaper's fallacious headline becomes a symbol of Anglo racism. The play tells the story of Chicano consciousness and cultural survival in a country in which racism and violence are advocated by the press and the state. *Zoot Suit* ran for over eleven months in Los Angeles. It was also the first Chicano play to be produced on Broadway, and Valdez was the first Mexican American to direct on Broadway. Since *Zoot Suit,* Valdez has gone on to write many more plays and direct popular movies including *La Bamba* (1987).

Another example of theatre of protest is the modern performance art of Karen Finley (b. 1956), who tours the country performing one-woman plays about sexual abuse, violence against women, prejudice, censorship, AIDS, suicide, and the male domination of politics. Her most notorious piece, *We Keep Our Victims Ready* (1989), satirizes national events, questions the definition of obscenity, and confronts the dehumanization of women that reduces them to sexual objects. She also attacks the idea of a sole deity whose image is masculine, monolithic, and absolute, which she says results in a masculine-dominated society. Her performance includes a scene where she covers her naked body in chocolate and yams, almost like a tar-and-feathering, in order to symbolize the bruising abuse women suffer in our society. Taken out of context, these symbolic acts earned her the name "the chocolate-smeared woman." But Finley says, "My critics are people like Jesse Helms. The attacks don't come from people who have actually seen my work." Those who have seen her work, such as critics from the *New York Times,* praise her "highly visceral, startling monologues" in which she confronts pressing social issues. Theatre of protest is often censored or marginalized by the dominant culture, which doesn't want its views or traditions questioned. Such was the case when Finley was denied a grant from the National Endowment for the Arts because of what the head of the NEA called "certain political realities." Finley took her fight all the way to the Supreme Court (see the Spotlight "Diverse Beliefs and Values: Karen Finley and the NEA").

Diverse Beliefs and Values: Karen Finley and the NEA

SPOTLIGHT

In the last few years several complaints have been lodged against the National Endowment for the Arts (NEA) concerning the social and moral concepts behind the works of art it funds. (For more on the NEA, see Chapter 2.) With all the controversy, one might think that thousands of so-called questionable or obscene works of art must have been funded with federal tax dollars. But the truth is that fewer than 50 out of 140,000 works of art funded over thirty years have received complaints. Why would so few works of art—including Karen Finley's *We Keep Our Victims Ready*—cause such a stir? In his book *Culture Wars,* artist and writer Richard Bolton points out that many believe that artists are trying to introduce a progressive agenda into society, "an agenda based upon multiculturalism, gay and lesbian rights, feminism, and sexual liberation" that is intended to destroy traditional American values. Somehow this "objectionable" handful of artistic projects funded by the NEA—less than 0.001 percent of all the projects it has ever funded—is seen as a serious threat to the power structure of the United States.

In the 1990s Senator Jesse Helms tried to stop this "progressive agenda" with a law stating that every art grant given by the NEA has to take into consideration the general standards of "decency and respect for the diverse beliefs and values of the American public." Some said that the new law, when properly interpreted, had no practical effect. Others felt it was a far-reaching attack on the First Amendment's guarantee of freedom of speech. Finley, who was denied an NEA grant under the new law, immediately challenged the law in court. She felt that it discriminated against nontraditional artworks and that the "diverse beliefs and values" clause unconstitutionally suppressed ideas that challenged the general public's sensibilities.

David Cole, a professor at Georgetown University Law Center and a lawyer for the Center for Constitutional Rights, represented Finley before the Supreme Court. He argued that "one would be hard-pressed to find two people in the United States who could agree on what the 'diverse beliefs and values of the American public' are, much less on whether a particular work of art 'respects' them. . . . Decency is likely to mean something very different to a septuagenarian in Tuscaloosa and a teenager in Las Vegas." In the end the Supreme Court ruled 8 to 1 to uphold the new law. Everyone from Speaker of the House Newt Gingrich to President Bill Clinton claimed it to be a victory, while many people in the arts felt it was censorship and an attack on cultural freedom. Actor and former head of the NEA Jane Alexander said, "It is in decisions such as the Supreme Court's that liberties in our society are whittled away slowly and incrementally. Doors to diversity and variety silently close." The arguments before the Supreme Court raised many provocative issues: Does the government have the right to favor certain points of view? Does the NEA have the right to exclude grant applicants because they are not in tune with the dominant culture? Is it even possible to make a work of art that respects all the "diverse beliefs and values of the American public"?

© Terry Ashe/Time Life Pictures/Getty Images

Former head of the NEA, actor Jane Alexander answers charges in front of a congressional committee. Of the over 140,000 works of art funded by the NEA in its nearly forty-year existence, there have been only fifty complaints. But this was enough for some members of Congress to slash the NEA's budget and call for its demise. Although they succeeded in reducing its budget, the majority of their colleagues voted for its continued existence.

Today one of the best-known plays of the theatre of protest is Eve Ensler's The Vagina Monologues *(1996). Its monologues about female sexuality deal frankly with childbirth, sex, and rape.* The Vagina Monologues *continues to be performed around the world, often in connection with the V-Day initiative, a movement to end violence against women and girls throughout the world. On a local level, benefit performances of* The Vagina Monologues *are organized and performed by volunteers to raise awareness and funds for anti-violence groups.*

© Joan Marcus

FOR MORE ON

KAREN FINLEY

"Censorship crossroad: High court to hear Finley v. NEA March 31," Roger Armbrust, *Back Stage*, March 27, 1998

> The National Endowment for the Arts was funding work by those who were once rendered invisible by economic, ethnic, or gender differences. What previously had been a private, almost sequestered world, existing only within academia or in galleries, became public. People who had never had the same access that white, middle- or upper-class men have traditionally had were suddenly given means to create.
>
> **Karen Finley,**
> *American performance artist*

Cross-Cultural Theatre

Cross-cultural theatre borrows contrasting ideas from diverse cultures and joins them into a single work. At its most basic, cross-cultural plays borrow staging techniques from another culture to create a unique piece of theatre. At its highest level, cross-cultural theatre is an attempt to fuse various cultural rituals, myths, and styles in order to find parallels between cultures, including those of the writers and performers and those of each audience, and merge them in a performance that celebrates our diversities and similarities and promotes cultural pluralism. As Nigerian writer Ben Okri (b. 1959) said, "Literature doesn't have a country. Shakespeare is an African writer. . . . The characters of Turgenev are ghetto dwellers. Dickens's characters are Nigerians. . . . Literature may come from a specific place, but it always lives in its own unique kingdom."

Cross-cultural plays have been a part of the Western theatre experience for hundreds of years. Irish poet and dramatist William Butler Yeats (1865–1939) was influenced by the masks, mime, and dance techniques of Japanese Noh drama for his poetic dramas *Four Plays for Dancers* (1921) and *At the Hawk's Well* (1916). American playwright Thornton Wilder (1897–1975), who spent part of his childhood in China, adopted Chinese staging methods in his masterpiece *Our Town* (1938), a drama about life and death in a small New England town. In the play, Wilder used the character of a stage-manager/narrator to invoke the imagination of the audience, just as the Beijing Opera uses the character of the property man. Yet historically, many other Western cross-cultural plays have done little to promote understanding between cultures. For example, Gilbert and Sullivan's musical *The Mikado* (1885) and Puccini's *Madama Butterfly* (1904) were both influenced by Asian theatre but did little to portray nonstereotypical Asian characters or to promote cultural understanding.

Cross-cultural plays remain a part of the contemporary theatre. Japanese director and theorist Tadashi Suzuki (b. 1939) set the Greek tragedy *Trojan Women,* about the destruction of the ancient city of Troy, in post–World War II Japan and used both classical Japanese theatrical styles and modern Western staging. The play includes traditional Japanese music and Western punk rock, kimonos and sweatshirts, and a script spoken in both English and Japanese. One critic described the performance as "a controlled crash that celebrates both East and West and finds a common language." Similarly, Japanese director Shozo Sato stages Western classics such as *Medea, Faust,* and *Macbeth* in Japanese Kabuki style. Sato uses a multiracial cast of men and women, although Kabuki traditionally uses only men, and he adds a dash of "Kabuki soy sauce" in order to create what one critic called a "dramatic tension between the stylized beauty of the Kabuki tradition and the visceral action of Western stories."

The purpose of cross-cultural theatre is often to join people of diverse cultural backgrounds. This can mean that the performers come from one culture and the audience largely from another. For example, the play *Black Elk Speaks* (1994), which was adapted from an oral biography of a Sioux holy man, tells the story of white America's westward expansion from the Native American perspective. It is a story of broken promises, war, and the white man's quest for land and gold. When the play was originally produced at the Denver Center for the Performing Arts, it employed a cast of Native American actors, dancers, and singers from twenty North American tribes, but it drew an audience that was largely non-Indian. The play's purpose was to bring people together. As the director, who is white, said, "If Black Elk is saying anything, it is that the categorization is not red, white, yellow, and black . . . and all four have to live in this world together."

FOR MORE ON
NATIVE AMERICAN THEATRE

"Jane Lind: Alaskan-born theater artist puts Native American legends on stage," Holly Hill, *American Theatre,* October 1992

© Dan McNeil/Courtesy Denver Center for the Performing Arts

Black Elk Speaks *is an example of theatre as a vehicle for cultural interaction. Dramatizing the life of Black Elk, a Sioux holy man, and the struggles of Native Americans against the policy of Manifest Destiny, the play brings together the Native Americans who perform the play and the largely non–Native American audiences. This 1994 production featured Ned Romero as Black Elk and was directed by Donovan Marley at the Denver Center for the Performing Arts.*

Other cross-cultural plays expose the complexities among cultures by putting them on stage side by side. Such is the case with *M. Butterfly* (1988) by David Henry Hwang (b. 1957). This play explores the Western psyche and its stereotypical views of Asian culture, race, and gender. Hwang's play combines plot elements of *Madama Butterfly,* an Italian opera, with a story about a French diplomat who, after ten years, discovers that his Chinese mistress is not only a spy but also a man. This play uses a modified Japanese Kabuki stage and choreography from the Beijing Opera as it attacks the cultural blindness that pervades so much of the world—a blindness that reveals itself in many ways.

Cross-cultural theatre does have its critics. Some feel that cross-cultural plays mix cultures without grasping their ideological dimensions. These critics charge that intercultural borrowing merely reduces culture to an interesting stage technique. For example, the great-grandson of Black Elk was bluntly critical of the inclusion in *Black Elk Speaks* of non-Lakota songs, incorrect choreography, and sacred images that should not be put on stage. Other critics have charged that Shozo Sato's Kabuki versions of Western classics trivialize Japanese theatre because the Western actors lack traditional training and so cannot comprehend Japanese content or culture. But from another viewpoint, Ping Chong, a Chinese American creator of avant-garde dance-theatre who often employs Chinese and Japanese aesthetics, says, "I'm not going to allow myself to be ghettoized as an Asian American artist. I'm an *American* artist. The irony is that we are now ghettoizing ourselves by choice. I understand that this act is an affirmation of one's identity. That's important. But we cannot lose sight of the fact that we all live in a society where we have to coexist. It doesn't mean that I have to like your culture. But we have to be *sensitive* to each other's cultures."

I think one of the big problems, ultimately, in the efforts towards cultural diversity in the theater is whether the white establishment is willing to give up control. There have been a lot of well-meaning people, a lot of people trying to do things, but if you look at the administrative staffs of theaters, the decision makers there, nothing much has changed with them. As a result, tokenism remains far too prevalent.

David Henry Hwang,
American playwright

Photofest

Like many of his other plays, David Henry Hwang's M. Butterfly *blends Eastern and Western styles, incorporating elements from Kabuki theatre, Chinese opera, Western opera, and television sitcoms. By drawing on a number of traditional styles as well as experimenting with modern forms, his plays not only distinguish themselves from traditional theatre but also push modern theatre in new directions. This production from the play's first national tour featured Alec Mapa as Son Liling and Philip Anglim as Rene Gallimard. Directed by John Dexter at the Colonial Theatre in Boston.*

Theatre as a Way of Seeing through Another's Eyes

We all see the world from our own point of view, and most people tend to think that their take on things, as seen through their culture, is the correct view. This phenomenon is called **ethnocentrism**. English philosopher Francis Bacon (1561–1626) called ethnocentrism the "idols of the cave" because we often assume that our own social or cultural group is superior to others, that our sheltered and secluded "cave" is better than someone else's. Most would agree that all cultures should be allowed to express themselves, but what happens when cultures are so different that they come into conflict in their attempt to define a nation's cultural identity?

Several years ago the mayor of New York City, Rudolph Giuliani, threatened to terminate the funding and possibly take over the Brooklyn Museum of Art because it displayed a painting by English artist Chris Ofili called the *Holy*

© Martha Swope

Terrence McNally's Love! Valour! Compassion! *is the story of eight gay men who have come to a house in the country to celebrate summer holidays. Populated with complex characters and energized by witty and passionate dialogue, the play is notable for its straightforward depiction of gay middle-class relationships. This 1995 production featured (l to r) John Glover, Anthony Heald, and Nathan Lane and was directed by Joe Mantello at the Walter Kerr Theatre in New York. Of the thousands of plays written about the gay and lesbian experience,* Love! Valour! Compassion! *is one of the few to be made into a Hollywood film.*

Virgin Mary. The painting depicted a woman representing the Virgin Mary. Attached to the painting were clumps of elephant dung, which prompted some critics to call it sacrilegious and obscene. In fact, a retired schoolteacher found it so offensive that he smuggled a container of latex paint into the museum and threw it on the painting. The painting insulted his culture and he reacted, but he failed to take the time to understand the artist's cultural perspective and intention. Few people did. The public debate over freedom of speech, obscenity, and the painting raged in the national news media for weeks. Yet a closer look at Ofili's background reveals that he is a Roman Catholic of Nigerian descent. Although the elephant dung may shock us in the West, he meant it as an affirmative interpretation of Christianity: Because elephant dung fertilizes the soil of Africa, to Africans it is a symbol of all that is good and nurturing. When cultures come into conflict, it is often a test of how well society as a whole tolerates alternative points of view.

FOR MORE ON

CHRIS OFILI

"Shock for shock's sake? The mayor is still angry. The museum's lifeline is threatened. Now it's finally time to see what the 'Sensation' is all about," *Time,* October 11, 1999

Many plays attempt to open the doors to cultural awareness, including Milcha Sanchez-Scott's (b. 1955) *Roosters* (1987), a play about a generational feud between a proud, headstrong Hispanic father and his equally determined son; Anna Deavere Smith's (b. 1950) series of one-woman plays, *On the Road: A Search for American Character* (1983 to the present), which confronts racial and gender identity issues; and Regina Taylor's (b. 1964) *Watermelon Rinds* (1992), a serio-comic exposé of African American family politics. Currently, perhaps the most famous cultural-awareness play is Tony Kushner's (b. 1956) Pulitzer Prize–winning *Angels in America* (1992), a play in two parts that was adapted for television by HBO in 2003.

Kushner grew up Jewish and homosexual in the turbulent South of the 1960s. He said that he had had "fairly clear memories of being gay" since he was six but he did not come out until after he tried psychotherapy to change his sexual orientation. *Angels in America* tells the interwoven stories of several gay men. One is Prior Walter, a young man dying of AIDS who is visited by a frightening and mysterious angel; another is a Mormon, Joe Pitt, who comes to terms with his homosexuality despite its being forbidden by his religion; and another is Roy Cohn, a powerful attorney who denied his gay lifestyle in public and collaborated with Senator Joseph McCarthy in the 1950s persecution of "un-Americans." *Angels* is a perfect example of a play that challenges an audience to think and calls their values into question. By doing so it transmits knowledge, and with knowledge comes understanding.

Artists who attempt to produce plays that promote cultural awareness sometimes come into conflict with the dominant culture. In 1993 when Terrence McNally's play *Lips Together, Teeth Apart,* which includes positive portrayals of gay men, was produced by a theatre in Cobb County, Georgia, the County Commission attempted to silence any further such productions by establishing a "family values" criterion for funding local art. When that proved to be difficult to defend in court, the commission simply eliminated all art funding for the entire county. A similar incident occurred in 1999 when the theatre department at Kilgore College in Longview, Texas, staged *Angels in America.* On the sold-out opening night the building had to be surrounded by police because there were so many protesters. The play received a standing ovation, but a County Commissioner revoked $50,000 worth of support to the Texas Shakespeare Festival, which was hosted by Kilgore College (but not by the theatre department). The commissioner said that county funds should not be used to support the arts because the "arts are always controversial." The arts are not always controversial, but they can be when they attempt to foster understanding of differing cultures within society. As Tony Kushner put it in a letter to the cast and crew at Kilgore College, "A healthy state needs vigorous, lively, pluralistic debate, not enforced acquiescence to a bullying majority."

People have waged a war against art in the name of decency, in the name of civic stability, in the name of God. But censoring art, even indecent art, isn't decent; it's thuggish, it's unconstitutional, undemocratic, and deeply unwise.

Tony Kushner,
American playwright

FOR MORE ON
THE FUNDING OF CONTROVERSIAL PLAYS

"N.C. county ends arts funding due to plays," Byron Woods, *Back Stage,* April 11, 1997

© L.Mueller/Staff/Charlotte Observer

The controversial subject matter of Tony Kushner's Angels in America has ignited protests since it premiered in 1991. Here, citizens for and against the play protest in 1996 in front of the Charlotte Repertory Theatre in North Carolina. Most recently, Alabama state senator Gerald Allen attempted to ban the Tony Award–winning play and all other literature with homosexual themes and characters from public school textbooks and libraries.

Real and Unreal: *Angels in America*

The breathtaking achievement of theatre that is Tony Kushner's *Angels in America* is, in many respects, hard to imagine as a Hollywood movie. It is a play that is at once odd, poetic, controversial, political, and deeply, genuinely moving—qualities that are not always present in mainstream Hollywood productions. *Angels* follows the stories of two couples, one gay and one straight, and their struggles with sexuality, relationships, politics, religion, and the metaphysical. The play highlights the tensions between the real and the unreal, different worlds existing side by side, historical truth versus magical possibility, and the fact that the fantastical is sometimes arguably more real than the ordinary.

© Joan Marcus

The Angel of America visits Prior in the 1993 Broadway production of Angels in America: Perestroika, *featuring Stephen Spinella as Prior and Ellen McLaughlin as the angel, directed by George C. Wolfe at the Walter Kerr Theatre. Note the sparse set and limitations on the angel's flight.*

Kushner's stage directions call for a "pared-down style of presentation with minimal scenery," giving us a sparse world of people set against an empty, representational backdrop. At the same time, the playwright asks that the play's "moments of magic . . . be fully realized." As such, the stage directions for the arrival of an imposing angel at the end of the first part of this two-part play call for a fantastic array of blinding lights, awesome sound, shaking walls, and collapsing ceilings. It is with these seemingly contradictory directions that we can see the contrast between the everyday and the sublime.

In a stage production, illustrating moments of magic can be a challenge. With a filmed version of a play, it's not such a problem. Technology and special effects make it easy to show characters vanishing into thin air, angels flying, and characters existing in parallel worlds simultaneously. In a theatre, such fantasy has to be carefully managed with clever lighting, wires, trap doors, and techniques such as split staging. For example, one scene in *Angels* shows "PRIOR alone in his apartment, LOUIS alone in the park. Again, a sound of beating wings." Here we have two characters together on a split stage. Yet, both are shown as utterly alone in their own realities; their isolation is palpable. Only the angel, represented by the sound of wings, straddles both worlds. Although we do not see the angel, we get the sense that she sees all.

However, filming *Angels* presented its own challenges. Because audiences are used to seeing realism in movies, film can't get away with minimalist sets. Consequently, the filmmakers risked losing the contrast between the everyday and the sublime. On the other hand, they were able to use the camera's tricks to show us the play's parallel worlds. For example, in the scene with Prior in his apartment and Louis in the park, we see Prior crawl to his bed, fearing the approaching angel. The camera then pans over to the bedroom window and dissolves into the park, as if we, the observers, are airborne. When the scene with Louis is over, the camera cuts back to Prior's apartment, focusing again on the window before panning back to the rest of the room. Thus, like the all-seeing angel, we witness what is happening in the park while Prior is in his bed. The filmed *Angels* is full of these careful manipulations: scene transitions that involve high-angle shots, fades to white, and so on.

Reality may be fully realized in the filmed *Angels* in a way in which Kushner never intended, but the filmed version still stays true to the play's tone and story. In both versions we experience the same people, the same conflicts, the same emotions. In the end, regardless of special effects or theatrical conventions, it is the script, story, and characters that make *Angels* both great theatre and great TV.

Aoise Stratford
Playwright

© Kobal Collection/Picture Desk

The angel visits Prior in the 2003 HBO mini-series Angels in America, *featuring Justin Kirk as Prior and Emma Thompson as the angel, directed by Mike Nichols. Movie special effects enable the filmmakers to open up Prior's apartment and allow the angel to fly.*

Keeping the Theatre of the People Alive

Public opinion polls show broad public support for the arts and artists. The majority of Americans feel that the arts and humanities contribute to the economic health and well-being of society and that they are important to education. Yet today public funding for art that expresses a minority's point of view is sometimes questioned. At the center of this debate has been the National Endowment for the Arts, whose primary purpose has always been to give a voice to all cultures as it "increases the public awareness of our cultural heritage." This policy has put the NEA into conflict with some people who feel that all cultures are not equal. These people seem to believe that Americans must decide which culture is *the* American culture and government policies and funding must reflect that decision. Others feel that the government should stay out of arts funding altogether. Still others feel that without government assistance only those with the loudest voices—representatives of the dominant culture with the most private funding—will be heard.

The U.S. government does have a long history of guaranteeing freedom of speech by financially supporting viewpoints that might otherwise be drowned out. For example, it restricts monopolies by allowing smaller companies access to the marketplace, thereby guaranteeing them a voice. It provides funding for numerous political candidates. It gives tax-exempt status to tens of thousands of organizations, including hundreds of different religions. But should the government simply *allow* for freedom of speech or should it *guarantee* it? And how far should the government go to ensure that all voices are heard? The answers to these questions will continue to be debated as long as what one group calls their culture, another group calls blasphemous or obscene. Richard Bolton says in his book *Culture Wars,* "In the end, censorship of the arts reveals the failure of democratic institutions to articulate and defend the complexity and diversity of the American public. The NEA debate contained many lessons about art's relationship to society, but it also raised many questions about the future of American democracy."

Curtain Call

Today, the East/West Players, El Teatro Campesino, Ujima Theatre Company, Repertorio Español, Puerto Rican Traveling Theatre Company, the Hispanic American Arts Center, Pan Asian Repertory, Teatro de la Esperanza, San Diego Black Ensemble Theatre, and many more culturally specific theatres are opening up opportunities for culturally diverse actors, designers, directors, playwrights, and theatre practitioners. In addition, countless theatres have been formed to highlight gay and lesbian themes, as well as theatre companies that advocate feminist ideas and stories written by women, about women, and for women.

Perhaps the key to protecting the growth of a truly representative theatre of the people is continuing to raise the consciousness of the general audience. Polls have shown that Americans are slowly becoming more aware of the value of diversity and thus more tolerant. A poll published in the *New York Times* in 1999 asked, "If your political party nominated a generally well-qualified person for president who happened to be—Jewish, Catholic, female, black, gay, Mormon, or atheist—would you vote for that person?" The results were then compared to similar polls taken by the *New York Times* in the 1930s. The results are promising:

	1930s	1999
Jewish	46%	92%
Catholic	60%	94%
Female	33%	92%
Black	37%	95%

	1930s	1999
Gay	26%	59%
Mormon	75%	79%
Atheist	18%	49%

Yet the battle over cultural diversity around the world and in the United States continues. Some would agree with the statement in UNESCO's *Universal Declaration on Cultural Diversity:* "Cultural diversity is as necessary for humankind as biodiversity is for nature." Others would agree with William Bennett, the chairman of the National Endowment for the Humanities under President Reagan, who said that to keep a country together, it must share a common culture, which is our "civic glue" and serves as a kind of "immunological system." Without a doubt our cultural differences will continue to be a source of celebration and conflict and the theatre will be part of both. Recently playwright David Henry Hwang wrote, "American theatre is beginning to discover Americans: black theatre, women's theatre, gay theatre, Asian American theatre, Hispanic theatre." American theatre, like its audience, is diverse. The only way to fully appreciate it is to see and study its many forms, not just those that reflect our own culture and beliefs.

© 2000 Don Turner

When Henrik Ibsen's A Doll's House *was first performed in 1879, a protest ensued, similar to those staged against* Angels in America. *Victorian audiences were outraged because the play did not reinforce the family values of the day, which dictated that women stay home to love and amuse their husbands. This play illustrates the need for artists to be free to explore ideas that conflict with mainstream values. This 2000 production at the University of Wyoming featured Aimee Callahan and Michael Childs and was directed by William Missouri Downs.*

Summary

We often think of theatre in terms of stars and spotlights, but theatre of the people, where artists outside the dominant culture express themselves, also thrives. This type of theatre is what Brazilian director Augusto Boal calls "theatre of the oppressed." In its long history the theatre has seldom given a voice to all the people or reflected the many cultures in any society. Instead it has been controlled by the dominant culture through racism, sexism, discrimination, economic power, and social and religious customs. Theatre of the people attempts to give a voice to all members of society as it increases multiculturalism and reduces stereotyping.

There are three types of theatre of the people. Theatre of identity promotes a particular people's cultural identity as it strengthens the bonds of the community. It can also invite members of other cultures to experience that people's joys, problems, history, traditions, and point of view. Theatre of protest objects to the dominant culture's control as it demands that a minority culture's voice and political agenda be heard. Cross-cultural theatre mixes different cultures in an attempt to find understanding or commonality among cultures.

Most people see the world from their own point of view, and they tend to think that their take on things, as seen through the lens of their culture, is the correct view. This ethnocentrism leads to a great deal of conflict between cultures. The theatre of the people attempts to lessen this conflict by raising the cultural consciousness of audiences. Government organizations, such as the National Endowment for the Arts, try to promote cultural understanding by funding art created by non-mainstream cultures and allowing all voices to be heard. These attempts sometimes fail, especially when members of the dominant culture see them as threats to the nation's cultural identity. Yet in order for societies to evolve and progress, artists must be free to voice ideas that challenge mainstream views and values.

THE ART OF THEATRE ONLINE

Use the *Art of Theatre* website at **http://communication.wadsworth.com/downs1** for quick access to the electronic study resources that accompany this chapter, including a digital glossary, a link to InfoTrac College Edition that you can use to find the For More On... InfoTrac College Edition readings listed below, a list of further reading, and a chapter quiz. When you get to the *Art of Theatre* homepage, click on the cover of the book you are using and you will be redirected to the website for your book. Then click on "Student Book Companion Site" in the Resource box, pick a chapter from the pull-down menu at the top of the page, and select an option from the Chapter Resources menu. The *Art of Theatre* website also includes links to interesting and informative theatre websites. Just click on the Theatre on the Web link in the Book Resources menu. The links to these websites are maintained and updated as needed.

Key Terms

blackface / 59
cross-cultural theatre / 66
culture / 52
enculturation / 52
ethnocentrism / 69
Harlem Renaissance / 60
minstrel show / 59
multiculturalism / 55
pop culture / 52
stereotypes / 56
theatre of identity / 56
theatre of protest / 62
theatre of the people / 50
Yiddish Broadway / 57

For More On . . .

InfoTrac College Edition Readings

http://www.infotrac-college.com

Augusto Boal / 52
"The theatre of the oppressed"

Women and theatre / 55
"Women & theatre: The companies they keep"

Multiculturalism and theatre / 56
"The dilemma of multiculturalism in the theatre"

Suzan-Lori Parks / 62
"Whisper to a scream: Digging for Suzan-Lori Parks"

Karen Finley / 66
"Censorship crossroad: High court to hear Finley v. NEA March 31"

Native American theatre / 67
"Jane Lind: Alaskan-born theater artist puts Native American legends on stage"

Chris Ofili / 70
"Shock for shock's sake? The mayor is still angry. The museum's lifeline is threatened. Now it's finally time to see what the 'Sensation' is all about"

The funding of controversial plays / 71
"N.C. county ends arts funding due to plays"

4 The Audience, Criticism, and Free Speech

People go to the theatre for a variety of reasons: Some want to be amused, others desire to be challenged; some want philosophy, others want magic. Theatre can be a vehicle to make us feel, think, and learn, and perhaps even motivate us to take action. To have ample opportunities to do all these things is in our best interest as audience members and as a society. The more options that are available, the less likely are artists' conceptions, themes, and speech to be limited. Similarly, works of art should not be condemned because they challenge opinions or make people think new thoughts. In other words, when we go to the theatre, we should open our minds as we open our programs. When we support playwrights, directors, and actors in expressing themselves, not only do we increase our own awareness, but we also fuel public dialogue, which sometimes can help us change our world.

© Michal Daniel

◀ ***On preceding page:*** Much Ado about Nothing *by William Shakespeare, directed by David Esbjornson at the Delacorte Theater in New York City's Central Park. This play was performed at the New York Shakespeare Festival, hosted by the Joseph Papp Public Theater, in 2004. The New York Shakespeare Festival is held every summer and is free to the public.*

This chapter will explore the dynamics of the audience, what to expect when you go to the theatre, and what is expected of you as an audience member. It will also look at a special kind of audience member, the critic, and explain how to go beyond your own opinion to analyze a play and understand what the theatre artist is trying to convey. Finally, it will explore how the right to freedom of speech applies to the arts and how it affects what audiences see.

The People Who Watch

Theatre is a group activity. Unlike television, which usually is watched alone or with a few family members or friends, theatre is designed to be experienced with a sea of strangers. In fact, unlike television or the movies, without an audience there can be no theatre; there might be a rehearsal without an audience, but not theatre. Remember what the British director Peter Brook said in Chapter 1: At its most basic, theatre requires someone to walk across an empty space while someone else watches. Theatre artists have studied their audiences for thousands of years and have learned to manipulate their feelings, reactions, and even their thoughts. This manipulation is possible primarily because of three factors: group dynamics, the suspension of disbelief, and aesthetic distance.

In a theatre, actors and audience meet each other at the moment of performance; they share the experience and each contributes something towards it. Real actors, acting in the presence of a real audience: This is the essence of theatre.

Stephen Joseph,
British theatre director, producer, and designer, in New Theatre Forms

Group Dynamics

Group dynamics is simply the functioning of humans when they come together into groups. Whether those groups are gangs, families, church congregations, or theatre audiences, studies have shown that people act and react differently when they are in a group than when they are alone. We become less intellectual and more emotional, less reasonable and more irrational, less likely to react as individuals and more likely to react as a group. Perhaps our desire to fit in to a group can be traced back to the prehistoric need to belong to a tribe because there was safety in numbers. Television producers know we like to be part of a group, so most sitcoms include a laugh track; as we sit alone in our living rooms, we hear other people laughing. Because of group dynamics, we have a tendency to join in and laugh. The old saying "laughter is infectious" is true, but only if someone else is laughing. That's why comic movies do not use laugh tracks; they are intended to be viewed with an audience, so there is no need to add the illusion of other viewers.

Theatres take advantage of group dynamics by selling tickets to seat all audience members next to one other. So, even if the play doesn't sell out and the theatre is half empty, the audience will be seated as a group, increasing the chances that they will be influenced by group dynamics. Theatres reason that if the people around you are enjoying the play, there is a good chance you will too. Some theatres even go so far as to **paper the house.** In theatre lingo, *house* is the auditorium, and in this case *paper* means tickets. So to "paper the house" means to give away a lot of free tickets to the families and friends of cast members in order to make it appear as though the performance is well attended. Theatres are most likely to paper the house on opening night when they know a critic is attending. They hope that an audience's positive response to the play will rub off on the critic, who may then write a favorable review. One of the most famous cases of using group dynamics to manipulate an audience happened in 1964 when the Beatles visited the United States for the first time and appeared on *The Ed Sullivan Show.* To sell John, Paul, George, and Ringo to audiences, the show's producers hired young girls to scream and faint during the performance. Soon, young women throughout the country were screaming and fainting for the group.

Suspending Disbelief

When we go to the theatre, or watch a television show or movie for that matter, we must enter into a **willing suspension of disbelief.** We admit that what is happening is not real and so we don't need to rush up and save the actor who is being attacked or call the police to stop the actor playing the criminal. When suspending our disbelief, we put aside our concerns about everyday reality and agree to accept the *play's* particular quasi reality, which communicates some *perception* about everyday reality.

If an artist crosses the line and we don't know if the moment is real or make-believe, it can make for a very powerful performance, but the audience may feel violated. For example, in 1994 performance artist Ron Athey famously broke the audience's willing suspension of disbelief during a performance at the Walker Art Center in Minneapolis. In his piece, which was based on African tribal traditions and was about the spread of AIDS, Athey purposely nicked the skin of another actor—with the actor's permission of course—and blotted the blood onto a paper towel that he then showed to the audience. People get nicks all the time; they cut their skin shaving, cleaning the yard, or playing sports. But because this nick happened in front of a live audience, it sent shock waves through the auditorium and across the country. When Senator Jesse Helms of North Carolina heard about the performance, he sent a letter to the then head of the National Endowment for the Arts, Jane Alexander, accusing her agency of funding a work in which HIV-positive, "blood-soaked towels" were sent "winging" over the audience. None of this was true; the blood was not HIV positive, nor did it come into contact with the audience. The Minnesota Department of Health affirmed that the Walker Center had taken appropriate safety precautions, but that wasn't enough to squelch the commotion. It's interesting to compare the impact of a few droplets of real blood on stage in front of a live audience to the dozens of bloody and severed limbs in summer blockbuster movies. One set off a political firestorm; the other simply seems to sell more tickets. What's the difference between the two? A movie audience knows it isn't real blood.

Athey's performance made a powerful statement about AIDS, but he also blurred the lines between art and life. Theatre artists are always attempting to manipulate the audience's willing suspension of disbelief, sometimes engulfing them in total fantasy and at other times taking them to the edge of reality. Suspension of disbelief allows the audience to laugh at a painful beating during a farce, or come so close to real life that they are moved to tears. For

© Corbis/Sygma

Kobal Collection/Picture Desk

Performance artist Ron Athey (left) famously broke an audience's willing suspension of disbelief when he nicked the skin of another actor and blotted the blood onto a paper towel. His audience was shocked and disturbed because they knew that what was happening onstage was real. In contrast, during this disturbing scene from the World War II saga Saving Private Ryan *(right), audience members did not feel they needed to save the little girl because they willingly suspended their disbelief and understood that what was happening onscreen was not reality. Yet the scene was real enough to allow the audience to feel empathy, give the events serious consideration, and even lose themselves in the story.*

example, the smash Broadway success *Spamalot* (2005), the musical based on the movie *Monty Python and the Holy Grail* (1975), creates a hilarious fantasy world that demands an audience suspend their disbelief in order to find the slapstick violence funny. In contrast, Marsha Norman's play *'night, Mother* (1982) details the last ninety minutes of a woman who has decided to commit suicide. The set of this play features functioning clocks and the actors perform in real time, highlighting the sense of reality for the audience. Yet, because the audience members suspend their disbelief while watching the play, they know the woman is not really going to kill herself and so don't try to stop her.

Distancing Yourself

Closely tied to the suspension of disbelief is **aesthetic distance,** the audience's ability to remove themselves from a work of art just far enough so that they can contemplate it—or even judge it. If we allow ourselves to be immersed in a play, movie, or television show to the point that we forget ourselves, then we have no aesthetic distance. We are simply using the show as a vicarious experience. For example, we want to live a more exciting life, so we go to an action movie or play a video game and feel that we have been on a mini-escapade. But most artists don't want the audience to totally forget them-

© Kevin Berne/Courtesy American Conservatory Theater

The very nature of theatre encourages audiences to maintain a certain aesthetic distance, keeping us from completely losing ourselves in a story. Some plays ask audiences to maintain more distance than others. For example, the character of the Stage Manager in Thornton Wilder's Our Town *acts as an omniscient narrator, interacting with both the audience and the play's characters. Similarly, Mark Hollman and Greg Kotis's* Urinetown, the Musical *(shown here) also features a narrator, Officer Lockstock, who addresses the audience directly. In addition,* Urinetown *spoofs traditional musicals, allowing the audience to laugh at this art form while also enjoying a funny story. This 2003 production was directed by John Rando at San Francisco's American Conservatory Theater.*

selves; they want the audience to distance themselves from the work just enough to be semi-objective but not indifferent. This way, the audience can have a vicarious experience, feel empathy for the characters, and be entertained, yet they can also think about the play's themes and meaning and even its artistic merit.

Some writers and directors go further and challenge or even alienate an audience. The German playwright Bertolt Brecht (1898–1956) believed that an audience's emotional involvement in the characters and story could cloud their grasp of the play's message. He sneered at what he called "culinary theatre," theatre that does not provoke socially meaningful thought but rather feeds us illusion and leaves us feeling content and emotionally satisfied, as we do after a good meal. In his "epic theater" style, he tried to shatter traditional stage illusions and constantly remind the audience that they were sitting in a theatre watching a performance. In this way, Brecht did not allow the audience to lose themselves in the play. Instead he consciously urged them to think about the play's message. (For more on Bertolt Brecht and his plays, see Part III).

© Richard Feldman

Playwright Bertolt Brecht often took pains to remind his audience that what was happening onstage was a performance. During the play he did not want them to lose themselves, but rather to think critically and objectively about the issues raised. In this production of his Mother Courage and Her Children *(1941), the set designer took a Brechtian approach, letting the audience know they were watching a play, not reality, by exposing the lights and using highly stylized set pieces.*

FOR MORE ON
AESTHETIC DISTANCE

"The self-conscious spectator," M. G. Benton, *The British Journal of Aesthetics,* October 1995

| Levels of Participation

Group dynamics, suspension of disbelief, and aesthetic distance also affect the level of audience participation. Audience participation can be divided into two basic levels: active participation, and sitting quietly in the dark. The two types of theatre that correspond to these levels of participation are sometimes called *presentational* and *representational.* **Presentational theatre** makes no attempt to offer a realistic illusion onstage, and the actors openly acknowledge the audience and sometimes even invite members to participate. When Peter Pan begs the audience to clap their hands to help Tinker Bell, that's presentational theatre. In **representational theatre** actors never acknowledge the audience and go about their business as if there were no audience present. Almost all movies and TV shows are representational (an example of an exception is *High Fidelity,* in which the main character often addresses the audience directly), but in the theatre plays are either presentational or representational, and audiences either sit quietly in the dark or are asked to participate. To maximize your and your fellow audience members' theatregoing experience, you need to know what is expected of you for both types of plays and what etiquette you should follow.

> In its essence, a theatre is only an arrangement of seats so grouped and spaced that the actor—the leader—can reach out and touch and hold each member of his audience. Architects of later days have learned how to add conveniences and comforts to this idea. But that is all. The idea itself never changes.
>
> ***Robert Edmond Jones,*** *American theatre set designer*

Sitting Quietly in the Dark

Sitting quietly in the dark to watch a play is relatively new behavior for theatre audiences. It started in the late 1850s but did not become popular until Edison invented the lightbulb. Electric lights allowed designers to control the illumination of the stage and to completely dim the house during performances; before this, the audience were as well lit as the stage. But the major reason for a passive audience was **realism,** a style of theatre that attempts to portray life as accurately as possible. (For more on realism, see Part III.) By the late 1800s, realism had become the dominant form of theatre in the West, and the idea of an actor talking with an audience was considered passé. Asides, prologues, and epilogues were dropped, and the performers began acting as though the audience didn't exist. The actors' "reality" incorporated a **fourth wall,** an imaginary wall between the actors and audience. In this form of theatre, the audience had to sit quietly. In short, the rules of theatre etiquette had changed.

Audience Etiquette

Etiquette is the conventions of behavior prescribed for a particular occasion. Rules of etiquette differ from one type of performance to another. People who talk during a movie will get dirty looks and perhaps a "shh," but in a theatre they will probably get kicked out. In a theatre, people are expected to be on their best behavior and to be considerate of others. Here are some basic rules of etiquette for theatregoers in the United States, especially for plays that require the audience to sit quietly in the dark. (We will cover the exceptions to these rules in the next section.)

These little people are allowed to amuse themselves without anyone troubling to see whether they are behaving well or badly; they are permitted to do as they please; nothing is forbidden them; they laugh when they ought to cry, they cry when they ought to laugh, they talk when they ought to be silent, and they are mute when good manners require them to reply. It is cruelty to allow them to go on living in this way.

Antoine de Courtin,
in The Rules of Civility, *a seventeenth-century manual of etiquette*

1. ***Thou shalt not talk during a play.*** Even whispering can bother other audience members and the actors. At a musical, all talking should end when the lights dim or the conductor enters; the overture is part of the performance. However, vocal responses to the play itself, such as gasping or laughing, are okay.
2. ***Thou shalt not cough.*** If you have a cough, then you should bring cough drops and do everything in your power to suppress the cough until scene changes or the intermission. One cough can obscure a crucial word of dialogue and ruin a scene.
3. ***Thou shalt not eat.*** Food, even candy and gum, is not allowed in most theatres. Cough drops should be unwrapped before the performance begins. The crinkling of cellophane wrappers distracts audience members and actors.
4. ***Thou shalt turn off cell phones and beepers.*** Doctors or others who must for some reason be available during the performance can check their phone or beeper at the box office or coatroom. If the phone should ring or the beeper beep, an usher will come get them.
5. ***Thou shalt be courteous.*** Do not kick the seat in front, fidget, squirm, wiggle in your seat, or put your feet on the chair in front of you. Do not sing or hum along with the music or make any other disruptive noises.

6. ***Thou shalt not block the view of others.*** If you are attending with your sweetheart, do not put your heads together, because that may block the view of the person sitting behind you. If you're wearing a big hat, take it off during the performance so the person behind you can see the stage.
7. ***Thou shalt go easy on the perfume or cologne.*** In the theatre you sit close to other audience members; heavy perfume or cologne may bother them or even trigger an allergic response.
8. ***Thou shalt not be late.*** Latecomers edging down a row to their seats are very distracting. If you arrive late, you will probably have to wait to be seated until a break in the performance. You may be required to stand in the back or sit in a different seat until intermission. Some theatres will not allow you to take your seat until intermission.
9. ***Thou shalt not leave until the intermission or until the end.*** The only reason to leave during a performance is an emergency. Leaving a performance because it bores you or insults you is discourteous and will ruin the play for those who do not find it boring or insulting.
10. ***Thou shalt not take photos or use recording devices.*** Not only is the noise distracting, but the flash can disorient the actors. On occasion actors, blinded by a flash bulb, have actually fallen off the stage. Moreover, taking pictures or recording a performance is a violation of copyright laws. Your ticket allows you to attend the performance once, not to own a copy of it. (For more on copyright, see Chapters 2 and 6.)

Although many of these rules of etiquette apply when you attend a movie, they are even more important when you attend a live theatre performance. Actress Mary-Louise Parker has said, "People think they're watching television. What they don't know is that when you're onstage, one Tic-Tac coming out of the box sounds like an avalanche." If one Tic-Tac sounds like an avalanche, imagine the worst audience behavior of all time, the Astor Place Riot of 1849. (See the Spotlight "Audiences Behaving Badly: The Astor Place Riot.")

Not Sitting Quietly in the Dark

Not all plays require the audience to sit complacently in the dark. For some types of theatre, the audience is supposed to express themselves and even participate in the play. These productions do not allow the audience the safety of the fourth wall, and in some cases the actors embrace or confront the audience during the play. Interactive theatre comes in many forms, from Japanese Kabuki theatre to children's shows to comedies such as *Tony n' Tina's Wedding,* a popular satire of an Italian American wedding in which audience members participate in the ceremony, the champagne toast, and the cutting of the wedding cake. The most extreme example of audience participation may well be in conjunction with the play *Rocky Horror Show* (see the Spotlight on Diversity "Let's Do the Time Warp Again"). In short, when attending the theatre, knowing and obeying the basic etiquette improves the experience for everyone, but you can seldom predict what will be expected of you. Keep an open mind and play along.

Audiences Behaving Badly: The Astor Place Riot

SPOTLIGHT

On the evening of May 10, 1849, demonstrators gathered outside the Astor Place Opera House in Manhattan to protest the appearance of the English actor William Charles Macready (1793–1873). The Astor Place was an opulent theatre with ticket prices of $1 per seat, four times what other theatres in New York charged, and Macready was considered by average Americans to be a symbol of English aristocracy. It had been only thirty years since the English had last invaded, and anti-English feelings in America were still running high. But the demonstrators were protesting more than just Macready's being English; they also didn't like his acting. They preferred the acting style of the American-born Edwin Forrest (1806–1872), who was appearing just a few blocks away in a play about the gladiator Spartacus. Forrest was an "American-style" actor. He was a big presence with a strong voice, and his acting was described as "heroic" and "robust," in contrast to the more restrained and dignified Macready.

A war of words broke out between the two actors. It started when the London critics panned the American when he was acting in England. Forrest blamed his poor reviews on Macready and took revenge by attending Macready's performance of Hamlet and hissing from the audience. When Macready came to New York to play Macbeth, the newspapers reported the charges and countercharges of their war of words. On the night of May 8, 1849, some "shiftless" young men, who had accused the Astor Place theatre of being "elitist" because its patrician dress code required white kid gloves and silk vests, infiltrated the audience. On cue, they began booing Macready. When this didn't stop the play, they pelted the stage with eggs, apples, potatoes, and a bottle of asafetida, a brownish, foul-smelling liquid once used in medicines. Macready's response was mock expressions of fear, which only enraged the young men even more. They threw chairs and wooden shingles at the stage, and Macready finally called off his performance. This was not the first time lower-class Americans had thrown things at him; in Cincinnati someone even pitched half a sheep's carcass on the stage. Only when the owners of the Astor Place promised police protection did Macready agree to return to the stage. But this time it would end in death.

On May 10, the rowdy young men once again managed to get in the theatre, but this time the police were waiting. When they interrupted the performance, they were thrown out. They began pelting the theatre with bricks from a nearby construction site and attracted a crowd, which grew to over fifteen thousand protesters. When the police failed to disperse the crowd, they fired a volley over the crowd's heads, then at their feet, and then into them. When the smoke lifted, twenty-two people lay dead or dying and over one hundred were wounded, all because, as the *New York Tribune* reported, "Two actors had quarreled." The *Philadelphia Public Ledger* concluded, "It leaves behind a feeling to which this community had hitherto been a stranger . . . a feeling that there is now in our country, in New York City, what every good patriot had hitherto considered it his duty to deny—a high and a low class."

© Bettmann/Corbis

One of the bloodiest theatre riots in history took place at Manhattan's Astor Place Opera House in 1849, causing twenty-two deaths and over one hundred injuries—all because "two actors had quarreled."

Let's Do the Time Warp Again

When you go to the theatre, you are not always expected to sit quietly in the dark. With the musical *Rocky Horror Show* (1973) or the movie based on the play, *The Rocky Horror Picture Show* (1975), audience members dance the Time Warp, throw buttered toast, water, rice, and toilet paper at the actors or the screen, and even speak lines of dialogue. You don't go to "see" *Rocky Horror Show;* rather you "experience" it.

Audience interaction is not new to the theatre. In Roman times, audiences at comedies yelled back at the performers and even demanded they change the play or costumes or even remove their costumes. In Shakespeare's day, audiences carried on a lively dialogue with the actors. In Renaissance Italy, audience members often took their servants to the theatre to serve them meals and carry messages to and from others in the audience during the play. In France in the 1750s, audience members could pay to sit on the stage with the actors. In the 1830s, historian Alexis de Tocqueville observed that during plays, American audiences "paid not the slightest attention to the stage, but walked about, drank together, and argued as if nothing else were going on." For most of its existence, theatre has been treated the way we treat television today—we eat, we engage in small talk, we make restroom runs, and sometimes we just treat it as background noise. *Rocky Horror Show* is nothing new in the long history of the theatre; for audience members attending it, sitting quietly is the incorrect etiquette.

© Dave Benett/Getty Images

© AP/Wide World Photos

In the last 150 years, theatre has become an upper-class affair, where the rules of etiquette demand an audience be well behaved, quiet, and passive. But some theatre allows us to bend these rules. During productions of Rocky Horror Show *and showings of its filmed counterpart, the audience are encouraged to participate—and they take full advantage of the invitation, dressing in costume, dancing, singing, and chanting dialogue.*

Going to the Theatre

Going to the theatre in the United States is not always easy: Theatres are few and plans to attend must be made well in advance. Nevertheless, many people consider it an enjoyable experience and are willing to do what it takes. Now that you know how to conduct yourself at the theatre, let's explore what you need to know to find a play you want to see, buy a ticket, choose what to wear, and use the program.

Finding a Play

Unless you live in a small town, finding a play is easy; your local paper probably carries ads, reviews, or a list of local theatres and what is playing. The Internet is also a great resource for information about plays. Most theatres now have websites where you can find a description of what is playing and purchase tickets. Reviews almost always give a bit of the story, which can help you decide whether you are likely to be interested in a play. However, it is also important to take a chance on plays that you suspect might challenge you. They may give you new interests or help you explore your values. It can pay to be adventurous.

Getting Your Tickets

Theatre tickets must almost always be reserved in advance by calling or visiting the box office or buying tickets online. When you buy your tickets by phone or online, the tickets will be mailed if there is enough time or you can pick them up at the box office before the performance. Many theatres have a "Will Call" window for those who are picking up tickets they have already paid for. Be sure to pick them up at least fifteen minutes before **curtain** (the start of the show), or the theatre may assume you are not coming and sell them to someone else.

Once you have purchased your tickets, you usually cannot return or exchange them. Some theatres may offer an exchange of tickets for another performance or play, but most will not. Because you have purchased your seat in advance, the theatre cannot sell it to anyone else and cannot afford to give you a last-minute refund. The same no-refund policy is true if you misplace your ticket or are dissatisfied with the play. Just as with a fishing license, you can't get your money back if you fail to catch any fish.

Saving Money

If you want to save a little money, be sure to ask if student tickets are available. Often theatres sell high school and college students discount tickets if they have a valid student ID. Or you can attend a **preview** performance, for which tickets are usually half price. Previews are performances that are open to the public before the play officially opens. They are common in the professional theatre but rare in college, community, and amateur theatres.

Dress Codes

In the United States you're expected to dress up a little or a lot when you go to the theatre. Unlike movie audiences, theatre audiences are made up of people intending to attend a special event. If you go to the professional theatre, you'll be out of place if you dress the way you do for college classes. Unless you are attending the opera, formal or semi-formal attire is not required, but you will need to reach farther into your closet for something clean and pressed. In other words, the vintage T-shirt and old tennis shoes are inappropriate. But, there are exceptions: If you are attending an outdoor performance of Shakespeare, then dress for the weather. And if you are attending a performance of *Rocky Horror Show,* you might want to dress in costume. (For more on *Rocky Horror Show,* see the Spotlight "Let's Do the Time Warp Again." For more on theatre audiences, see the Spotlight "Who Attends Performing Arts Events?")

Reading the Program

Once you enter the theatre, an usher will give you a program and show you to your seat—unless it's "general seating," in which case you can sit anywhere you like. In the United States programs are free, but in some countries, such

Going to the theatre is considered a special event, in part because of the costs and effort involved—tickets must be purchased in advance, babysitters hired, and transportation arranged. People often dress more formally to attend theatre, and they understand that a higher standard of behavior is involved than that for movie houses.

© Richard Levine

Who Attends Performing Arts Events?

In 2002 the Association of Performing Arts Presenters, with the help of several arts organizations such as the Theatre Communications Group, conducted a survey that asked people how often they attended performing arts events. The survey was conducted in five large cities where performing arts events are easy to find: Austin, Minneapolis–St. Paul, Boston, Sarasota, and Washington. The survey found that approximately 75 percent of respondents had attended at least one professional performing arts event in the past twelve months. Over 50 percent had attended the theatre at least once within the last year. Fourteen percent had attended at least one performing arts event every month. In all five cities, more people had attended a performing arts event in the past year than had attended a professional sporting event.

The survey also found that people who attend performing arts events tend to have higher incomes (18 percent earned at least $100,000 per year) and have more education (22 percent had graduate degrees) than people who don't attend arts events. In addition, the survey revealed that people who attend performing arts events enjoy listening to classical music (63 percent), watching performing arts on television (66 percent), and playing a musical instrument (22 percent). Seventy-five percent of those who had attended an arts event said that they felt that the performing arts were thought-provoking and could help people understand other cultures, and more than 60 percent said that attending performing arts events encouraged them to be more creative. Interestingly, performing arts patrons are also far more likely to do volunteer work than people who don't attend arts events.

as England, programs must be purchased. Try to arrive early enough to spend a few minutes reading the program before the play begins. Programs feature information that will help you better understand the performance, such as the location and time of the scenes and the cast of characters. Some programs also include a **director's note** or a **playwright's note** that explains what he or she intended to accomplish with the play. You might also find historical information about the play, playwright, or style of production. Some larger professional theatres sell **souvenir programs** that have more pictures and information about the cast and production. You don't have to buy one unless you really want a souvenir.

After the Show

As audience members we nearly always evaluate the show we've just seen, whether it was a movie or a play. How often have you walked out of a theatre with your friends, repeating funny lines or discussing how one part was very interesting but another part was way too boring? We also often talk to friends who haven't seen the show to let them know whether it is worth the price of admission. This evaluation, a type of artistic criticism, is what professional movie and theatre critics do for a living. The word *criticism* sometimes has negative connotations, but when it is applied to a work of art, it means an analysis of the work's merits and shortcomings. Let's take a closer look at the role of critics and criticism in the world of theatre.

I Everyone Is a Critic

As a beginning theatre student, you'll probably not only attend plays but also read plays and write about what you've seen and read. To fully appreciate a play and analyze it thoughtfully, it's important to understand the differences between a review, which is an opinion, and criticism, which is a detailed analysis. An opinion tells you what someone else thinks about the play, but educated, thoughtful, and justified criticism will most often lead you to a greater understanding of a play. Let's take a look at what constitutes a review, what constitutes criticism, and how to analyze a play.

Stating Opinions

[The critic's job is to] improve theatrical standards by educating an audience to a level of taste more receptive to ambitious theatre and less tolerant of mediocrity.

Richard Palmer,
American theatre professor, director, and author, in The Critics' Canon

Reviews, sometimes called *notices* in theatre lingo, are evaluations of a play and are often published in newspapers or magazines. They can also be broadcast on television, on the radio, and over the Internet. Reviewers provide a service to their readers and listeners by telling them whether a play is, in their opinion, worth attending. A reviewer assesses the production and gives a thumbs up or thumbs down. Everyone who has ever expressed an opinion about a dramatic performance is, in a sense, a reviewer. Reviewers have been around for a long time. One of the oldest examples dates back to about 1800 BCE. The Egyptian actor Ikhernofret wrote in hieroglyphics his opinions about a ritual play in which he had performed and gave himself a positive review. Today, however, many reviewers' number-one desire is to sell newspapers, so their reviews must above all grab readers' attention. For example, a few years ago, an actor in Denver was mugged and beaten by a gang as he walked home after his performance. The next day, a reviewer wrote in the newspaper that perhaps the gang had seen the actor's performance and were on a mission of revenge.

FOR MORE ON
THEATRE CRITICS

"A critics' summit" [interview with theatre critics Robert Brustein and Frank Rich], Robert Marx, *American Theatre,* May–June 1999

Although some reviews can be insensitive or even as mean-spirited as that example, regularly reading reviews can help you discover which reviewers' tastes you share. And you'll know that when certain reviewers "pan" a play, you'll probably love it. In any case, reviews generally do not provide a deep, scholarly analysis of a play, the artists, or the production—that is left to dramatic criticism.

Offering Interpretation and Analysis

Dramatic criticism, sometimes called *literary criticism* or simply *criticism,* is not meant to draw people to a particular production or warn them away from it, nor is it based solely on opinion. Instead, criticism offers the reader a discriminating, often scholarly interpretation and analysis of a play, an artist's body of work, or a type or period of theatre. Criticism appears in literary quarterlies, in academic books, and in more sophisticated magazines and newspapers. Academics and theatre professionals often study literary criticism when they research a particular play, playwright, historical movement, or genre. Students of theatre find reading criticism often allows them a greater understanding of the plays they read and see.

Criticism comes in many forms. It can examine the structure of a play; it can compare a play with others of its genre; or it can analyze how a play

N E1

THE Arts

MONDAY, APRIL 4, 2005

The New York Times

BOOKS OF THE TIMES

Sealed In a World That's Not As It Seems

By MICHIKO KAKUTANI

The teenagers in Kazuo Ishiguro's bravura new novel seem, at first meeting, like any other group of privileged boarding school students. They are constantly joining and abandoning rival cliques. They support and snipe at one another with petty rage and bantering good humor. They play sports, take art classes and obsess endlessly about sex. Their school, Hailsham, is a hermetic world unto itself — a prettily groomed English Arcadia that boasts a cool sports pavilion, spacious playing fields, a picturesque pond and winding bucolic paths. Their teachers keep telling them that

'Never Let Me Go'
By Kazuo Ishiguro
288 pages. Alfred A. Knopf. $24.

they are "special," that they have an important role to play in later life.

Hidden at the heart of Hailsham, however, is a horrible, dark secret — a secret that the reader only gradually grasps.

As in so many of Mr. Ishiguro's novels, there is no conventional plot here. Instead, a narrator's elliptical reminiscences provide carefully orchestrated clues that the reader must slowly piece together, like a detective, to get a picture of what really happened and why.

Like the author's last novel ("When We Were Orphans"), "Never Let Me Go" is marred by a slapdash, explanatory ending that recalls the stilted, tie-up-all-the loose-ends conclusion of Hitchcock's "Psycho." The remainder of the book, however, is a Gothic tour de force that showcases the same gifts that made Mr. Ishiguro's 1989 novel, "The Remains of the Day," such a cogent performance.

This time, Mr. Ishiguro's art of withholding — his pared-down, Pintereque prose, his masterful narrative control, his virtuosic use of understatement and elision — is put in the service of a far-out science fiction plot involving clones and organ transplants. The result, amazingly enough, is not the lurid thriller the subject matter might suggest. Rather, it's an oblique and elegiac meditation on mortality and lost innocence: a portrait of adolescence as that hinge moment in life when self-knowledge brings intimations of one's destiny, when the shedding of childhood dreams can lead to disillusionment, rebellion, newfound resolve or an ambivalent acceptance of

Continued on Page 8

Photographs by Sara Krulwich/The New York Times

Denzel Washington, left, as Brutus, prepares to stab William Sadler, who plays the title role in "Julius Caesar" at the Belasco Theater.

THEATER REVIEW

A Big-Name Brutus in a Caldron of Chaos

By BEN BRANTLEY

'Julius Caesar'
Belasco Theater

Those cruel forces of history known as the dogs of war are on a rampage at the Belasco Theater, where a carnage-happy new production of Shakespeare's "Julius Caesar" opened last night. Dripping blood and breathing smoke, these specters of martial havoc are chewing up and spitting out everything in their path: friends, Romans, countrymen, blank verse, emotional credibility, a man who would be king and even the noblest movie star of them all, he whom the masses call Denzel.

That's Denzel Washington, the two-time Academy Award winner and the reason that theatergoers are now lining up for a play that hasn't drawn such crowds in New York since Al Pacino gnawed his way through Mark Antony's funeral oration at the Public Theater 17 years ago. Mr. Washington has taken on the quieter but meatier role of Brutus.

As the most important passenger on Daniel Sullivan's fast, bumpy ride of a production, Mr. Washington does not embarrass himself, as leading citizens of Hollywood have been known to do on Broadway. But even brilliantined in the glow of his inescapable fame, he can't help getting lost amid the wandering, mismatched crowd and the heavy topical artillery that have been assembled here.

This is regrettable, since Mr. Washington would appear in many ways an inspired choice for Brutus. Among leading American film actors, he has all but cornered the market on advanced ambivalence. Whether playing unctuously evil ("Training Day") or raggedly heroic ("The Manchurian Candidate"), Mr. Washington exudes the grave, unsettled air of someone who hears the world as a symphony of mixed signals. Casting him as "poor Brutus, with himself at war," a character who anticipates Hamlet in divided feelings about bloody deeds, must have seemed like a no-brainer.

In several shining sequences, Mr. Washington more than justifies his presence in this production, although it's telling that such moments usually occur during monologues, which require little or no interaction with others. In the second-act soliloquy in which Brutus considers the planned assassination of the tyrant Caesar (William Sadler), Mr. Washington is suffused with the uneasiness of a good man struggling against instinct.

He has the self-questioning timber and tired, open face of someone long battered by doubt. The same quality is surprisingly and affectingly carried over into the speech Brutus makes to the frightened mob after Caesar has been slain. You can sense both why the people like Brutus and why they'll soon be putty in the hands of that more flamboyant and assured speechifier Mark Antony (Eamonn Walker).

But in the moment-to-moment dialogue and action that are the bulk of the play, this Brutus seems plagued less by moral and philo-

Continued on Page 7

Rebellion Made Fall Of Muti Inevitable

By JAMES R. OESTREICH

With the attention of the world focused squarely on Rome over the weekend, you may have missed what happened in Milan on Saturday: the culmination of another drama of consuming national interest in Italy.

News Analysis

After weeks of vitriolic public wrangling, the renowned Italian conductor Riccardo Muti, who had been music director of the famous opera house Teatro Alla Scala for 19 years, gave in to the demands of the house's orchestra and workers, and announced his resignation. Though simmering tensions rose to a boil only in mid-February, Mr. Muti's departure had come to seem inevitable. The only real questions were the timing and whether Mr. Muti or the Scala orchestra would finally force the issue.

If Mr. Muti, who continues to turn down requests for interviews, was trying to bury the news, he could hardly have chosen a better moment. But it doesn't seem his style. The 63-year-old Mr. Muti has never shunned the spotlight, whether in triumph or in conflict. It seems more likely, given his intense pride, that he was seizing perhaps the last opportunity to leave more or less on his own terms.

He was scheduled to begin rehearsals today with the Filarmonica Della Scala, the theater's orchestra, for concerts scheduled later this week, and many were convinced, despite assurances to the contrary, that the orchestra would strike, as it has done repeatedly in recent weeks. (Those concerts are now in jeopardy, along with stage productions to have been conducted by Mr. Muti.) He may have chosen to head the orchestra off at the pass.

Then again, the intensely proud Mr. Muti may simply have been worn down by unrelenting attacks in

Continued on Page 7

Andrea Tamoni/La Scala

Riccardo Muti conducting at La Scala before the turmoil.

© The New York Times

Thousands of theatre reviews are published each year, such as this one in the New York Times, *assessing a 2005 production of Shakespeare's* Julius Caesar *starring Denzel Washington. Reviews help audiences decide on the merits or drawbacks of a particular production. Because there is no rating system for the theatre, you have to read reviewers you trust to find out if a play includes adult language, sexual situations, or violence.*

affects an audience. Criticism can judge a play in relation to a particular period or style of theatre. It can challenge or support a play's philosophical or sociological perspective. Or it can chronicle how the play was created and how history and the artist's background and conscious or unconscious motives affected it. Criticism can also attack or endorse other works of scholarly criticism. In short, criticism has less to do with a particular production's effectiveness than with a play's aesthetic effect, history, and dramatic structure.

Being More Than a Reviewer

For beginning theatre students, writing an opinion paper about a production is a lot like writing a review. Often such papers say more about the critic than they do about the play: If you prefer musical theatre, you may not enjoy a tragedy; if you like serious plays, you may not care for farce. Such an essay is a nice exercise, but only when you know the basics of analyzing a play can you take the first steps toward dramatic criticism and analysis. The German romantic playwright, philosopher, and critic Johann Wolfgang von Goethe (1749–1832) offered a simple formula for play analysis that has been used for hundreds of years. He felt that dramatic criticism should answer three essential questions:

1. ***What is the artist trying to do?***
   This question will help determine the direction of your essay. If you understand the intention of the artist, you will understand the reasons for his or her choices. Put aside your opinion of the play and identify the artist's purpose. What is the artist trying to say? What is the artist's goal? Can you explain why the artist chose to bring this particular work into being?
2. ***How well has the artist done it?***
   By answering this question, you judge the degree of success the artist achieves toward the goal you identified in answer to the first question. How do the artist's techniques, methods, and talents help to achieve the goal? How effective is the production in fulfilling the artist's intention?
3. ***Is it worth doing?***
   The final question is whether the finished work of art was worth the artist's and the audience's time and effort. Does the play have new, interesting ideas? Will it help us understand the world, or understand it in a new way? If it didn't communicate to you, did it communicate to anyone else?

Using Goethe's questions can lead to a well-structured, intelligent assessment of a play that is useful to audience members as well as to the artist. Another way to evaluate a play, which can be done separately or combined with Goethe's method, is to break the play into its basic components and analyze the effectiveness of each one. An excellent, time-tested definition of a play's elements is derived from Aristotle's *Poetics.* Twenty-three centuries ago, Greek philosopher Aristotle deconstructed plays into six elements: plot, thought, character, diction, spectacle, and song. (For more on Aristotle and *Poetics,* see Chapters 1, 10, and 11.) Throughout the years, critics have adapted Aristotle's definitions of these elements to plays in their own periods. A clear and cohesive analysis of a play can be written by investigating how each element works by itself and in relation to the others. Here is a brief description of each element followed by questions you might ask when analyzing it.

Plot

Aristotle defined *plot* as a unified "arrangement of the incidents" in which characters, meaning, language, and visual elements come together to comment on a single subject. In other words, plot is the main story of a play. Because Aristotle believed that a story does not copy but, rather, imitates nature, it is not "real life" logic that determines the order of events but, rather, the requirements of the story. The action must be both probable and essential to the story.

1. What plot moments work the best and why?
2. Are any parts of the plot unnecessary and why?
3. Are any parts of the plot unclear and why?

Character

Character is about the personalities of the story. Characters are made up of motivation and action. We are what we do.

1. Are the characters' actions motivated?
2. How does each character advance the play's plot?
3. How does each character advance the play's thought?

Understanding a character's motivations is critical for actors such as Ray Fearon and Zoe Walker, playing Othello and his wife, Desdemona, in this scene from Shakespeare's Othello. Why does Othello believe his wife has been unfaithful? Why is he so enraged that he is willing to kill her for her supposed crime? Why is Desdemona unable to convince Othello of her innocence? To analyze a play effectively, you must ask similar questions. This 2001 Royal Shakespeare Company production was directed by Michael Attenborough at the Barbican Theatre, London.

© Donald Cooper/Photostage Ltd.

- ***Thought***

  Thought is what the play means, the ideas it's trying to communicate. *Plot* is the actions in the play. Thought asks what the actions mean. For some plays, thought is a complicated philosophy; for others, it is simply a question or idea about the universal human condition. Usually the meaning of a play is implied, not stated directly.

  1. What is the play's thought (or thoughts)?
  2. How well does the play communicate its thoughts?
  3. How do the play's thoughts apply to society or to the individual?

- ***Diction***

  Aristotle describes *diction* as "modes of utterance." It is the dialogue used to create the thought, character, and plot. It is the playwright's mode of expression. From beautiful rhyming couplets to guttural grunts, diction comprises the human sounds that communicate the play.

  1. How does the playwright use language to advance the plot and thought?
  2. How does the playwright use language to reveal the characters?
  3. Is any of the language inconsistent with the characters?

- ***Spectacle***

  Spectacle is the performance's set, costumes, and effects—the sensory aspects of the production. Aristotle said that spectacle is the least important element of any play, but he lived long before electric lights, recorded sound effects, and indoor theatres in which the environment could be controlled.

  1. How do the set, lights, sound, and costumes help tell the story?
  2. How do the set, lights, sound, and costumes help set the mood?
  3. Do any elements seem inconsistent with the rest of the play?

- ***Song***

  Portions of ancient tragedies were sung, so Aristotle included *song* as a standard part of any play, but today song is optional. However, if you are analyzing a musical or a drama that incorporates music, you will certainly want to consider song.

  1. How do the songs and music advance the plot, characters, or thoughts of the play?
  2. How do the songs and music help set the mood?
  3. Are all the songs and music necessary? If not, which ones and why not?

Using Goethe's and Aristotle's methods, you can break a play into its elements and specify how and why it does or doesn't work. Analyzing a play can also increase your understanding and open your mind to new points of view and forms of expression in the theatre.

Because plays often appeal to smaller audiences than movies and television do, they are more likely to express ideas outside the mainstream. Consequently, Goethe's last question, "Is it worth doing?" is more often asked in regard to plays. When some group takes a negative response further and insists the play *shouldn't* be done, criticism turns into censorship. The right to freedom of speech affects all of us, but theatre artists and critics are particu-

© Martha Swope

Designer Ming Cho Lee's realistic set design for Patrick Meyers's K-2 dramatized the spectacle of mountain climbers hanging precariously from the side of a mountain. In what ways do you think this set affected the telling and mood of this story about two people injured and stranded on an icy ledge at 27,000 feet? In the theatre, spectacle can be this elaborate and realistic, or it can be simple and stylized. This 1983 production featured Jeffrey DeMunn and Jay Patterson, and was directed by Terry Schreiber at New York's Brooks Atkinson Theatre.

larly concerned about it. Theatre practitioners rarely make a consistent living writing, producing, directing, or acting in plays, so it isn't money that drives them. What motivates many of them is having a forum for expressing ideas they are personally invested in. In the United States, the right to freedom of speech protects that expression.

The Right to Speak: Freedom of Speech and the Arts

We live in a society bristling with consumer warnings. Everything from power tools to children's toys has an inventory of warnings and dangers printed on labels. Even the entertainment industries have been pressured to come up with ratings systems and warning labels that let consumers know what age group the producers think a particular program is suited for and what questionable content is to be expected. And the V-chip allows consumers to block certain programs from their television altogether.

No such warning labels or consumer protections exist in the theatre. A play may be advertised as a children's play or a theatre may choose to warn theatregoers that a particular production is inappropriate for children, but no government institution such as the FCC (Federal Communications Commission) regulates the theatre. Instead, audience members must take responsibility for researching a play if they want to know its content before viewing it. The fact that there is no rating system for theatre can lead to problems regarding the right to express ideas freely. Some members of the public not only want to be warned about the content of a particular play, but they also want to restrict the content of plays so that certain ideas will never be heard, even by those who desire to hear them.

Free speech is most often contested when unpopular or controversial ideas are being expressed. Yet if only popular ideas were protected, there would be no need for the First Amendment, which states, "Congress shall make no law respecting an establishment of religion, or prohibiting the free exercise thereof; or abridging the freedom of speech, or of the press; or the right of the people peaceably to assemble, and to petition the Government for a redress of grievances." **Censorship** is the altering, restricting, or suppressing of information, images, or words circulated within a society. It can take the form of banning or altering books, periodicals, films, television and radio programs, video games, content on the Internet, news reports, theatrical productions, or any other expression of thought that someone finds objectionable or offensive. Even though freedom of speech has been a part of America's tradition since its beginning, some people still call for censorship, particularly in the arts.

You Can't Say That on Stage!

Theatre has been censored for thousands of years. Records of censorship go back to antiquity. In 493 BCE, the playwright Phrynichus presented his tragedy *The Capture of Miletus* at the Theatre of Dionysus in Athens. The play was about the fall of the Greek city Miletus, which had been sacked by the Persians the year before. The government felt that the play reminded the citizens of their misfortunes so it banned the play and fined the playwright. The Roman emperor Caligula ordered actors and playwrights who offended him to be burned alive. In the late Middle Ages and the Renaissance, the church banned or condemned opposing ideas with papal edicts, the Inquisition, and the *Index of Forbidden Books.*

> If the printed word facilitates the working of the imagination, then the staging of dramatic scenes in a public auditorium by presenting these images to our sense in much stronger colors makes a much deeper impression on the spectator and stirs their passion more violently.
>
> ***Czar Nicholas I,***
> *Russian ruler, justifying censorship of the stage*

In 1737, the **Licensing Act** was passed in England. This law placed the censoring of plays under the authority of the Lord Chamberlain, one of the officials of the royal court. Any plays that contained negative comments about the king or queen or unorthodox opinions or were considered heretical or seditious could be censored; the term *legitimate theatre* comes from this period. In 1817 Shakespeare's play *King Lear,* about a king who slowly loses his mind rather than believe that his daughters have betrayed him, was banned for several years in England because officials were afraid the audience might associate it with the madness of King George III. In 1818 Thomas Bowdler published *The Family Shakespeare* in which he had edited out of Shakespeare's plays all words and expressions "which cannot with propriety be read aloud in a family." The result was Shakespeare without the bawdy jokes, playful banter, or any mention of sexuality. This is where the term *bowdlerize* originated. To **bowdlerize** means to remove any possibly vulgar, obscene, or otherwise objectionable material before publication.

Photofest

Although Lucille Ball and Desi Arnaz were married in real life, societal standards dictated that they could not be shown sharing a bed during the run of their 1950s sitcom I Love Lucy. *Even when Lucy was expecting their first child, network officials prohibited the scriptwriters—who had written the birth of the baby into the show—from using the word* pregnant.

In the United States, despite the First Amendment, censorship has been rampant. Early in U.S. history, so many books, plays, and pamphlets were prohibited in Boston because of "obscene" content that the phrase "banned in Boston" became a great selling point in other parts of the country. In 1882, Walt Whitman's book of poems *Leaves of Grass* was banned in Boston because of its sexual content and innovative verse form. For almost eighty-five years the Comstock Act (1873) was used to censor mail in the United States. If Post Office inspectors decided a book, picture, play, or other item was indecent, they would seize all copies and refuse to deliver them. The list of items that could be seized included all information on birth control. James Joyce's novel *Ulysses,* about a day in the life of a fictional Everyman trying to win back his straying wife, was considered obscene and censored in English-speaking countries from its publication in 1922 until 1933. J. D. Salinger's *The Catcher in the Rye* has the distinction of being the most frequently censored book in the United States since its publication in 1951, primarily because the main character, teenager Holden Caulfield, takes the Lord's name in vain 295 times.

Hollywood has also long been a target of censorship. In the 1930s, complaints by religious leaders were so numerous that Hollywood producers "voluntarily" submitted to the Hays Code, which stated, "No picture shall be produced that will lower the moral standards of those who see it." The Hays Code banned any scene that contained homosexuality, adultery, or sex. It even limited the length of a screen kiss to three seconds. The code also banned a long list of words and phrases, including *fairy, goose, madam, pansy, tart, in your hat,* and *nuts.* The Hays Code was in force until 1968, when the modern rating system took over.

The theatre has almost always been the first of the arts to be censored because it can stir emotions, create empathy, hide subliminal messages, and stir groups of people to action. A novel may stir emotions but it does so only one reader at a time—the theatre does it en masse. Another reason the theatre has been heavily censored is the problem of interpretation. The dialogue of a play might appear harmless on the page but it can be interpreted by an actor to have new meanings. Unlike a film or a novel, a play can be changed from one performance to the next. A wink, a change in vocal inflection, or the slightest gesture can change the meaning. In Poland during the Soviet occupation, every theatre performance had to hold seats for censors so that every performance could be monitored.

FOR MORE ON

HISTORY OF CENSORSHIP

"Censors through the ages: Reaching for the red pencil," *The Economist,* December 26, 1992

Although there is no longer a Hays Code restricting what can be said and done in movies, a rating system does exist, and some artists and watchdog groups charge that these ratings result in a form of censorship. For example, top directors are contractually obligated to edit their films to avoid the most restrictive rating, NC-17, and movie theatres located in shopping malls are often contractually prohibited from showing NC-17 films. Some directors even censor themselves to better appeal to family-friendly markets. In the 2002 re-release of the movie E.T., *this scene depicting police officers trying to capture Elliott and E.T. was digitally altered to show the officers with walkie-talkies instead of the guns that appeared in the original movie.*

Photofest

The First Amendment: Rights and Restrictions

The First Amendment protects our right to express ourselves not only with words but also with nonverbal, visual, and symbolic forms of expression. A silent candlelight vigil is protected by the First Amendment as freedom of speech. Symbolic gestures are also protected, such as burning the American flag—as long as the flag is your property and you obey local fire codes. However, freedom of speech is not guaranteed in all situations. Exceptions include defamation; expression that causes a breach of the peace, sedition, or incitement to crime; expression that violates the separation of church and state; and obscenity.

Defamation Freedom of speech does not cover the publication or statement of alleged facts that are false and harm the reputation of another. This exception to freedom of speech is difficult to apply because the expression of an opinion that is false is allowed. In other words, you have the right to express a factually wrong or politically incorrect opinion. Let's say a theatre critic writes a highly negative review about a play and says that the acting is horrible and the playwright is an execrable writer. Even though none of his opinions are accurate, audiences stay away and the producer has to declare bankruptcy. The critic cannot be sued because the review is his opinion and is covered under the First Amendment. But if the critic publishes a false negative statement, such as a made-up quotation from the city inspector saying that the theatre is unsafe, then the producer can sue because a false statement was published as fact.

Breach of the Peace In 1919, Supreme Court Justice Oliver Wendell Holmes wrote, "The most stringent protection of free speech would not protect a man in falsely shouting fire in a theatre and causing a panic." This famous maxim has often been cited to underscore the fact that free speech is not a viable defense when such speech is used to perpetrate a fraud. An example is Orson Welles's *War of the Worlds* radio broadcast. On the night of October 30, 1938, Welles, famous for his movie *Citizen Kane,* broadcast to over one hundred radio stations in the eastern United States a play version of H. G. Wells's novel *War of the Worlds.* In order to make this story of an alien invasion of the earth more realistic, Welles interrupted another show with seemingly real "breaking news" reports about meteors landing on earth and huge mechanical monsters emerging from the debris. Some people who heard the fake bulletins panicked. The newly created FCC (Federal Communications Commission) reprimanded the station and passed rules to prevent such a pseudo-event from happening again.

© Bettmann/Corbis

In 1938, Hollywood writer and director Orson Welles broadcast a dramatization of H. G. Wells's alien invasion story, War of the Worlds. *The program was so realistic that Welles eliminated the audience's aesthetic distance and broke their willing suspension of disbelief. As a result, some radio listeners panicked, believing that an actual Martian invasion was taking place. The broadcast caused such a commotion that the FCC passed rules to prevent future such breaches of peace.*

Sedition and Incitement to Crime The Supreme Court has affirmed that freedom of speech does not cover unlawful conduct against the government or speech that advocates the violent overthrow of the government. This point can be difficult to argue because we all have the right to criticize the government and demand change. You can write a play in which you advocate "throwing the bums out," but you cannot write a play in which you unequivocally urge the audience to assassinate the president.

This exception to freedom of speech also applies to the laws of the land. If your words incite someone to commit a crime, the First Amendment does not protect your words. This exception to freedom of speech has been used for several years in an attempt to silence gangsta rap artists, most notoriously Ice-T and his band, Body Count. Their 1992 track "Cop Killer" was condemned by law enforcement officials, who claimed that the song incited crime against police officers. The same charge has been applied to some movies, such as Oliver Stone's *Natural Born Killers,* a story about a young couple who commits a series of ruthless murders. In the mid-1990s, a family in Ponchatoula, Louisiana, sued Stone and Time Warner Entertainment for damages after a family member was shot by two teenagers. The family claimed that the teenagers' shooting spree was inspired by repeated viewings of Stone's movie. The case was dismissed in 2001 because the family's lawyers couldn't prove that Stone intended to incite violence.

FOR MORE ON

***NATURAL BORN KILLERS* LAWSUIT**

"Court reprieves *Killers,*" *Back Stage,* March 16, 2001

Separation of Church and State The part of the First Amendment that states "Congress shall make no law respecting an establishment of religion" is known as the "establishment clause." It means that the government cannot endorse, or appear to endorse, any religion. This is a sensitive point to many people who view the clause as a violation of their personal freedom of speech. This controversy was highlighted when the National Endowment for the Arts (NEA; see Chapter 2) funded an exhibition of work in 1990 by artist David Wojnarowicz. The exhibition, titled "Tongues of Flame," included a painting that attacked prominent religious and political figures and accused them of being indifferent to the suffering caused by AIDS. A lawyer filed a lawsuit against the NEA, alleging that the exhibition displayed "hostility toward religion" and that the art caused him to suffer "spiritual injury" because it was offensive to his "religious sensibilities." He also charged that, because the art was partly funded by the government through an NEA grant, it violated the establishment clause. The idea was that if the government cannot endorse religion, then it should not be allowed to support art that attacks religion.

The court ruled that there is a difference between spiritual injury and physical or economic injury. Freedom of speech can be suppressed if it causes physical or economic injury but cannot be suppressed if it causes spiritual injury. In other words, you cannot deny someone an opinion just because it makes you feel bad, such as a critic's negative review. But what about the second part of the lawsuit, that the government should not fund art that insults religion? The court ruled that Congress does not directly decide how the NEA funds are to be spent because the NEA is an independent government agency, nor is the NEA simply administering Congress's wishes. Thus the government was not directly attacking religion and the grant did not violate the establishment clause. This decision highlighted a fascinating loophole in the establishment clause: Not only is it legal for the NEA to fund art that criticizes or insults religion, but it can also fund art that promotes an appreciation for religion, which it has done on many occasions.

Obscenity Freedom of speech does not apply to obscenity, but the courts have long struggled to define the word *obscene.* The word means many different things to different people. In 1973 the Supreme Court (*Miller v. California*) established a three-pronged test for obscenity:

1. Whether the average person, applying contemporary community standards, would find that the work, taken as a whole, appeals to the prurient interest
2. Whether the work depicts or describes, in a patently offensive way, sexual conduct specifically defined by the applicable state law
3. Whether the work, taken as a whole, lacks serious literary, artistic, political, or scientific value

These standards remain in effect today but are still surrounded by controversy. The Court basically said that each community could adapt its own idea of what is obscene, but how do we define *community* in the age of the Internet? A web page that may be acceptable to someone in Los Angeles, California, might be grounds for arrest if it were downloaded in Opp, Alabama. And who decides what is of "serious literary, artistic, political, or scientific value"? Many feel that the Court has not solved the problem of defining obscenity but has only made it more complicated, and so obscenity prosecutions are rare.

FOR MORE ON
FREE SPEECH AND THEATRE
"The embattled First Amendment," Anthony Lewis, *American Theatre,* September 1992

Despite these exceptions to the First Amendment, there is much room for freedom of speech in the arts. But there are also many people who still wish to limit speech and control content. For example, in 2005 Ted Stevens, chairman of the Senate Commerce Committee, proposed banning what he considered foul language on cable and satellite television. He was speaking specifi-

© Martha Swope

The rock musical Hair *is considered by some to be a great example of counterculture art, whereas some others consider it obscene because of its use of nudity and its anti-establishment message. Who decides which it really is? Or whether it is neither? Or both? This original Broadway production of* Hair *ran from 1968 to 1972 at New York's Biltmore Theatre. Directed by Tom O'Horgan; book by Gerome Ragni and James Rado; lyrics by Gerome Ragni and James Rado; music by Galt MacDermot.*

cally of the profuse use of "four letter words with participles" in the HBO series *Deadwood,* the story of a rowdy gold-rush mining town in the Dakota Territory in the late 1870s. However, unlike network television, cable and satellite television are not subject to the same FCC standards because they are not broadcast over the public airwaves. In addition, *Deadwood* is probably quite accurate in its portrayal of this slice of American history, obscene language and all.

Today, people who want to censor seldom use the word *censorship.* More often, they hide behind such terms as *speech code, political correctness, decency,* and *morals.* And people who want to restrict speech seldom see themselves as censors; more often they believe that they are protecting basic social institutions and values, such as religion, patriotism, the war effort, or the children. The critical questions remain: Who decides what will be censored and what will not? Is it possible to create a society in which the audience is never offended? And what happens if we succeed? One possibility is that we become less tolerant of other people's opinions and right to express themselves.

Curtain Call

Powerful forces are at work when people join together into a group, and many, including the artists, would like to control those forces. The power of the audience may come from being in a group, but every audience is made up of individuals who must decide if a given work has meaning. Too often today, audience members dismiss a play because it isn't to their liking, but if they knew how to analyze plays beyond simple opinion, they could come to a deeper understanding of the work. Only when audiences learn to analyze and artists are free to create does the theatre become a powerful work of art. As Czechoslovakian playwright Václav Havel said, "[I]f theatre is free conversation, free dialogue, among free people about the mysteries of the world, then it is precisely what will show humankind the way toward tolerance, mutual respect, and respect for the miracle of Being."

Summary

There are as many reasons to attend the theatre as there are audience members. But even though each member of the audience is unique, when they join together in a group, there are forces at work that can change how they feel and react. These forces include group dynamics, the suspension of disbelief, and aesthetic distance.

When you go to the theatre, you never know exactly how much you will be asked to participate. Some plays require you to be active, and others require you to sit quietly in the dark. Depending on what type of play you are seeing, the rules of etiquette change. These rules cover everything from how to behave to what to wear. Attending the theatre is also different than attending a movie; not only are you expected to behave differently, but tickets are harder to get and there are fewer performances to see. Going to the theatre requires more of an effort than going to movies or watching television, so going to the theatre takes a little more planning.

Once you see or read a play, it is important that you think about it and learn to evaluate it with more than a simple "I liked it" or "I didn't like it." In order to become a connoisseur of the theatre, you must learn to justify your critical thoughts by asking these three questions: What is the artist trying to do? How well has the artist done it? Is it worth doing? Plays can also be analyzed in terms of plot, character, thought, diction, spectacle, and sometimes even song.

Who controls what the audience sees and hears? In a few ideal cases the artist controls content, but usually other entities are involved. The government, corporations, religious institutions, or even the audience themselves can demand, legislate, or enforce censorship. Freedom of speech is important because self-expression is at the core of all works of art. However, limitations are placed on artists by the Constitution and the courts, including defamation, breach of the peace, sedition and incitement to crime, separation of church and state, and obscenity.

THE ART OF THEATRE ONLINE

Use the *Art of Theatre* website at **http://communication.wadsworth.com/downs1** for quick access to the electronic study resources that accompany this chapter, including a digital glossary, a link to InfoTrac College Edition that you can use to find the For More On . . . InfoTrac College Edition readings listed below, a list of further reading, and a chapter quiz. When you get to the *Art of Theatre* homepage, click on the cover of the book you are using and you will be redirected to the website for your book. Then click on "Student Book Companion Site" in the Resource box, pick a chapter from the pull-down menu at the top of the page, and select an option from the Chapter Resources menu. The *Art of Theatre* website also includes links to interesting and informative theatre websites. Just click on the Theatre on the Web link in the Book Resources menu. The links to these websites are maintained and updated as needed.

Key Terms

aesthetic distance / 82
bowdlerize / 99
censorship / 98
curtain / 89
director's note / 91
dramatic criticism / 92
fourth wall / 85
group dynamics / 80
Licensing Act of 1737 / 98
paper the house / 80
playwright's note / 91
presentational theatre / 84
preview / 89
realism / 85
representational theatre / 84
reviews / 92
souvenir program / 91
willing suspension of disbelief /81

For More On . . .

InfoTrac College Edition Readings

http://www.infotrac-college.com

Aesthetic distance / 84
"The self-conscious spectator"

Theatre critics / 92
"A critics' summit"

History of censorship / 99
"Censors through the ages: Reaching for the red pencil"

***Natural Born Killers* lawsuit / 101**
"Court reprieves *Killers*"

Free speech and theatre / 102
"The embattled First Amendment"

5 Creativity and the Ensemble

Creativity is at the heart of the theatre. Actors, directors, designers, playwrights—in fact, every member of the ensemble tries to generate creative ideas that will make an evening at the theatre a memorable experience. Yet creativity is hardly limited to artists. We are all capable of being creative, and there is room for creativity in all fields. ***Creativity*** *is a moment of insight. It is the instant we invent or transform something that already exists, thereby adding value to our lives. It is the adrenaline rush and "aha!" that happens when we find the answer to a problem. Creativity can be a flash of enlightenment that changes the world or a solution to a minor problem. From artistically arranging flowers to brighten a room to discovering* $E = mc^2$*, creativity is a moment of insight into just about any subject. The drive to be creative is one of the main reasons we study the theatre, and the lessons we learn can easily be applied to all aspects of our lives.*

© Donald Cooper/Photostage Ltd

◀ ***On preceding page:*** Sunday in the Park with George, *music and lyrics by Stephen Sondheim, book by James Lapine. Directed by Steven Pimlott, Lyttelton Theatre, London, 1990. This musical is about French neo-Impressionist painter Georges Seurat's work, specifically* A Sunday on the La Grande Jatte, *and his relationship with the world.*

It is hard to describe the thrill of creative joy which the artist feels when the conviction seizes her that at last she has caught the very soul of the character she wishes to portray, in the music and action which reveal it.

Maria Jeritza,
Austrian opera singer

In this chapter we will discuss some of the components of creativity and possibly help you learn ways to be more creative. Then we will explore the ensemble, the dozens of creative people who contribute, individually and as a group, to making theatre come alive.

A Creative Life

Playwrights, designers, actors, and directors devote their lives to creating characters, finding new ways to express a play's feeling and mood, digging for new answers to the meaning of life, and solving the thousands of problems that arise while writing, designing, rehearsing and staging a play. Because creative work like this can be mentally challenging and often depends on a certain level of specialized knowledge, some people think that artists must be extremely intelligent people. However, studies have found that an extremely high IQ (intelligence quotient) is not necessarily a great advantage when it comes to being creative. Having an IQ over 120, which is "high-average intelligence" according to the Stanford-Binet Intelligence Scale, doesn't seem to make people more creative. (For more on this subject, see the Spotlight "Identify Your Intelligences and Cultivate Your Creativity.") As a result, an artist of rather average intelligence can often be just as creative as one with a very high IQ. More important to creativity than raw intelligence are technique and talent.

Creativity and Technique

Imagine a talented actor playing the role of Shakespeare's Hamlet. The audience is enthralled, the actor's performance is winning the hearts of the critics, and there is a feeling of magic in the air. But is this actor being creative? Not necessarily—he may be acting with impeccable grace and deep emotion, but what is *creative* about his performance? Is he having any moments of insight into his character, the craft of acting, or the play? More than likely, during a performance, the actor is not being creative but instead is relying on his technique. **Techniques** are procedures that have been proven to work repeatedly. They are methods by which a complex task can be accomplished, such as raising a child, fixing a heart valve, auditing books, or acting in a play.

Let's say that one night during a performance our Shakespearean actor suddenly has an insight into the character and invents a new gesture that allows the audience to better understand Hamlet. *This* is creativity because there was a moment of insight. Actors often experiment with this sort of creativity during the rehearsal process but rarely during a performance because such creative moments might disrupt the flow of the play. If an insight prompted an actor to invent new dialogue or change his entrance in the middle of performance, the other actors would probably be unable to respond in ways that make sense to the audience.

Many of us, just like our Shakespearean actor, depend on technique. In college, students learn techniques that are based on other people's creativity. Only when students master a given subject can they begin to have spontaneous moments of creativity about it. And mastering a subject takes time. In most fields of study, including the theatre, achieving technical expertise can

© Robbie Jack/Corbis

Actors are able to be creative as they explore a character during the rehearsal process. But because they are expected to follow a playwright's direction and dialogue, they are not usually able to be creative during the run of a play. If an actor is not able to be particularly creative during a play, what is it that makes audiences and critics so pleased with her performance? The answer is technique. For example, Nicole Kidman's technique in The Blue Room *won her rave reviews from critics. The play was adapted by David Hare from* La Ronde *by Arthur Schnitzler. The 1998 production also starred Iain Glen and was directed by Sam Mendes at the Donmar Warehouse, London.*

take decades. The French playwright Alexandre Dumas *fils* (1824–1895) once said, "Technique is so important that it sometimes happens that technique is mistaken for art."

> It takes at least five years of rigorous training to be spontaneous.
>
> **Martha Graham,**
> *American dancer and choreographer*

Creativity and Talent

Talent is natural ability. One of the key tests of talent is time. For example, if one hundred people spend ten hours learning to play baseball, all of them would probably understand the game but some would be better players than others because of their superior reflexes, hand-eye coordination, and speed. We would say that these players have a talent for playing baseball. A common question is, are we born with talent or can it be developed? The answer is both.

One of the factors that helps us develop our talents is our environment. Even though we are all born with particular talents, our environment can dictate whether we develop or deny them. For example, many people who play the piano come from a home where at least one parent played the piano or was interested in music. Drew Barrymore, producer and star of the movie *Charlie's Angels,* comes from a family of famous actors going back to her grandfather, John Barrymore. Naturalist Charles Darwin's grandfather was interested in early theories of evolution. Physicist Albert Einstein's father studied math. Our culture, religion, and society as well as our home environment can also affect talent. For example, we may have the talent to be a great dancer, but if we grow up in a cultural environment that forbids dancing, we're less likely to develop that talent.

Identify Your Intelligences and Cultivate Your Creativity

One of the keys to discovering our talents and being more creative is to identify the *types* of intelligences in which we excel. In recent years, the theory of multiple intelligences has become popular among educators because it allows us to account for an expanded range of human potential. Formulated by Howard Gardner, professor at the Harvard Graduate School of Education, the theory states that we all possess different types of intelligence, not just the kind measured with a standard IQ test. It is our unique combination of these intelligences that makes up our talents.

We've all heard stories of geniuses who had trouble with tasks that seem elementary to the rest of us. British playwright, critic, and essayist George Bernard Shaw could write great stories, unforgettable characters, and powerful criticism but he had trouble spelling. Similarly, American statesman, inventor, and philosopher Benjamin Franklin had trouble with simple math. Because we all possess different degrees of the various kinds of intelligences, we all have areas in which we struggle and ones in which we shine. Often we are unaware of our particular gifts—our talents just seem natural to us. The first step in discovering and cultivating our talents is to find out which types of intelligence are our strengths. In his book *Frames of Mind: The Theory of Multiple Intelligences,* Gardner identifies six forms of intelligence: linguistic, musical, logical-mathematical, spatial, bodily-kinesthetic, and personal.

- **Linguistic intelligence.** This kind of intelligence is the understanding of how language works and the ability to use language to convince others and express ideas. According to Gardner, "In the poet's struggle over the wording of a line or stanza, one sees at work some central aspects of linguistic intelligence." Not only poets but also playwrights, writers, political leaders, actors, and legal experts possess a high level of linguistic intelligence. Its characteristic is a great technical facility with words and language.
- **Musical intelligence.** This is the ability to recognize, remember, and organize tones and musical patterns. The musical mind is concerned with pitch, melody, rhythm, and harmonic elements of sound. We say of these people that they have a "gifted ear." Gardner notes, "Of all the gifts with which individuals may be endowed, none emerges earlier than musical talent." People who have a strong musical intelligence are often also gifted in math. People who possess a high degree of musical intelligence include composers, musicians, singers, music critics, and recording engineers.
- **Logical-mathematical intelligence.** This is the ability to order and unify structures and to perceive patterns and causal relationships. This ability can be related to material objects but it more often takes an

Different talents develop at different ages. Musical, mathematical, and acting talent can appear at an early age, but talent for playwriting, philosophy, and poetry seldom emerge until people are in their mid or even late twenties. However, even child prodigies can improve upon their natural talent by gaining technique through practice. For example, Austrian composer Wolfgang Amadeus Mozart began studying music at the age of four and wrote his first symphony at the age of eight. But only 12 percent of his compositions were written in the first ten years of his career and few of them are popular today. Yes, Mozart was a child prodigy and he had natural talent, but he needed to develop his technique. This is true of almost all creative people. In his book *Creativity: Genius and Other Myths*, Robert Weisberg points out that only three major composers produced masterworks before they had at least ten years of musical practice and preparation. Talent is an important part of creativity, but one must develop technique for talent to be fully revealed.

While the intelligent person arrives at the correct answer more or less quickly, the creative individual is more likely to be fluent, to come up with many plausible answers and, perhaps, even with some answers of striking originality.

Howard Gardner and Constance Wolf,
in "The Fruits of Asynchrony: A Psychological Examination of Creativity"

abstract form as with mathematics. People with a high degree of this type of intelligence look for order in what may appear to be chaos. They can perceive and define the relationship between parts of a whole. Philosophers, scientists, and mathematicians often possess a high level of logical-mathematical intelligence.

- **Spatial intelligence.** This is the ability to sense and retain visual images and to mentally manipulate them. It includes the abilities to transform two-dimensional images into three-dimensional objects and to make mental models, which are the key to understanding many scientific concepts. Sculptors, architects, football coaches, and theatre directors all must have a high degree of this type of intelligence. It is also important to anyone who must read maps or create diagrams.
- **Bodily-kinesthetic intelligence.** At first the idea of body movements being a form of intelligence may seem strange. But our brain monitors our body's activity and allows us to judge the timing, force, and extent of our movements. When certain parts of the brain are injured, motor movements can be impaired even though the muscles are fully capable. This type of intelligence also includes eye–hand coordination and fine motor movements. Athletes, dancers, pianists, and actors need a high level of bodily-kinesthetic intelligence.
- **Personal intelligences.** Intrapersonal intelligence is the ability to understand one's own feelings. This talent can also be turned outward in the form of interpersonal intelligence, or the ability to understand the moods, motivations, and intentions of others. Those who need this ability to "read" other people include political and religious leaders, parents, teachers, therapists, counselors, doctors, nurses, and social workers.

To illustrate these various intelligences, Gardner points out that "Sigmund Freud was the exemplar of intrapersonal intelligence; Albert Einstein represented logical-mathematical intelligence; Pablo Picasso, spatial intelligence; Igor Stravinsky, musical intelligence; T. S. Eliot, linguistic intelligence; Martha Graham, bodily-kinesthetic intelligence; and Mahatma Gandhi, interpersonal intelligence." However, most activities require more than one form of intelligence. Dancers combine bodily-kinesthetic, spatial, and musical intelligences. Journalists use interpersonal and linguistic intelligences. Portrait photographers combine spatial and personal intelligences to fully capture their clientele. Engineers need spatial and logical-mathematical intelligence to create their products and linguistic intelligence to explain them. Our unique combination of intelligences forms the building blocks of our talents, and when we discover our unique talents, we are better able to cultivate our creativity.

I Creative People

FOR MORE ON
MIHALY CSIKSZENTMIHALYI'S THOUGHTS ON CREATIVITY
"How to find flow," *Free Inquiry*, Summer 1998 (interview with Csikszentmihalyi)

Talent and technique are essential to creativity, but creative people also share certain characteristics. Many researchers, including David Perkins of Harvard University, Mihaly Csikszentmihalyi (pronounced "Chick-sent-me-high-ee") of Claremont Graduate University, John Dacey of Boston College, and Kathleen Lennon of Framingham State College, have attempted to define these common traits. They have found that creative people have a hopeful outlook when facing complex or difficult tasks, are resourceful when unusual circumstances arise, are less afraid of their own impulses, and enjoy being playful. Creativity and play often go hand in hand. (See the Spotlight on Diversity "Playfulness: The First Quality of Genius.") Researchers have also found that creative people are exceptionally curious, able to concentrate, able to find order and options, and willing to take risks. Many of these characteristics describe theatre people, but they also describe creative people in all walks of life.

A Burning Curiosity

Creative people have a deep desire to know. They marvel at the world, and they want to know how it works. They desire to understand and overcome their own prejudices. As a result, they are open to new experiences and are seldom satisfied with the status quo. As children, when they got a new toy, they probably not only played with it but also tore it apart in order to find out how it worked. For creative people, playing is not enough; it is combined with a deep curiosity, for only when we study cause-and-effect relationships can we invent new causes and effects.

The Power of Concentration

Creativity is seldom as spontaneous as it looks. It comes only after days, months, or years of hard work. But creative people have the ability to concentrate for long hours because they love what they do. Thomas Edison, undoubtedly the most creative and prolific inventor of the modern era, said that creativity was "99 percent perspiration"; he conducted 2,004 experiments before he found the filament that enabled him to invent the electric light. Creative people often have a single-mindedness about them—a single-mindedness that sometimes makes for social errors such as forgetting names or appointments.

The Ability to Find Order

Creative people find order where others see chaos. Finding order can take several forms: making analogies and metaphors, seeing similarities, and finding or inventing structures. Creative people can cut through chaos and find simplicity. Someone once asked Einstein why he used hand soap for shaving instead of shaving cream. He answered, "Two soaps? That's too complicated." Playwrights and storytellers turn the chaotic elements of life into stories that have a beginning, a middle, and an end. Life is fluid, yet creative minds have the ability to find the underlying structures and reveal meaning.

© Sara Krulwich/NYT Photos

Failure is an important part of the creative process—it can move you closer to finding a solution to a problem and can help you assess your strengths and weaknesses. Creative people often take risks, knowing they could fail. For example, filmmaker Quentin Tarantino enjoyed great success with such movies as Pulp Fiction *(1994) and* Jackie Brown *(1997), but he received terrible reviews when he took his quirky acting style to the stage, starring as a criminal mastermind in Frederick Knott's* Wait Until Dark. *Despite this setback, he went on to create more critically acclaimed movies such as* Kill Bill: Volume 1 *(2003) and* Kill Bill: Volume 2 *(2004).* Wait Until Dark *featured (l to r) Juan Carlos Hernandez, Quentin Tarantino, Stephen Lang, and Marisa Tomei. Directed by Leonard Foglia, Brooks Atkinson Theater, New York.*

Mental Agility and the Ability to Find Options

Creative people have the ability to let their minds roam as they search for new perspectives and new approaches to problems. They use both convergent and divergent thinking. **Convergent thinking** is measured by IQ and involves well-defined rational problems that have only one correct answer. **Divergent thinking** involves fluency and the ability to generate a multitude of ideas from numerous perspectives. In short, creative people have both the ability to find logical options and the mental agility to explore outside the norm.

The Willingness to Take Risks and Accept Failure

It is not enough to have a good idea; creative people test their ideas. They seek criticism and they accept failure. Failure is the difference between what we expect and what we get. For many of us, failure is not an option in our jobs or in our lives. But if failure is not an option, then creativity is not an option, because the vast majority of creative work ends in failure. If Thomas Edison conducted 2,004 experiments before he found the right filament for the electric light, that means he had 2,003 failures before he got it right. Pablo Picasso may have produced 20,000 works of art but many of them were mediocre. Ludwig van Beethoven's musical sketchbooks contain over 5,000 pages of music that failed to make it into his symphonies. Playwrights write

Playfulness: The First Quality of Genius

Playfulness has long been associated with creativity. As Donald Newlove says in his book *Invented Voices,* "Playfulness is the first quality of genius—without it we're earthbound." Not only is playfulness an important part of creativity, but many studies have shown that art can foster creativity in young people and can also improve their ability to succeed in school. A study by the Arts Education Partnership found that students with high levels of arts participation outperform "arts-poor" students by virtually every measure. A study reported in *Parade* magazine found that children who study the arts in school get higher SAT scores than children who do not. Shirley Brice Heath of the Carnegie Foundation for the Advancement of Teaching found that disadvantaged youth involved in after-school arts programs do better in school than those who spend their time in after-school sports or community involvement programs. The National Research Center on the Gifted and Talented at the University of Connecticut found that students involved in the arts have greater motivation to learn; instead of just studying to get the right answer, they enjoy learning for the experience itself. Finally, researchers at Harvard University's Project Zero, an educational research group headed by Howard Gardner, found that students whose education includes art often become passionately engaged by subjects that students with less arts education find "boring," such as classical works and Shakespeare.

Theatre is a great way to expose children to the arts because it often includes many different art forms, such as instrumental music, singing, storytelling, dance, and art. Unlike television, children's theatre does not allow children to watch passively; instead they must often join in. The first children's theatre in the United States was founded in 1901. Today, there are hundreds of children's theatre companies across the United States that recognize the connection between children, the arts, and creativity. Many of them have theatre-arts training classes in which children gain greater concentration, coordination, communication skills, and self-confidence, as well as increase their creativity and intelligence. Theatre classes can also enhance children's literacy, develop their storytelling abilities, expand their imaginations, and broaden their cultural and individual identities as it opens their minds to alternative perspectives.

© Rob Levine/Courtesy The Children's Theatre Company, Minneapolis

Children's theatre provides kids with a fun opportunity to express their creativity. In this production of Dr. Seuss' The 500 Hats of Bartholomew Cubbins, *kids learned about acting, singing, dancing, and working with older, more experienced actors. This play, based on a book by Dr. Seuss, featured J. P. Fitzgibbons as King Derwin of Didd and Ryan Howell as Bartholomew Cubbins. It was adapted for the stage by Timothy Mason and was directed and choreographed by Matthew Howe.*

dozens of drafts before they have a finished script, and actors and directors rehearse for hundreds of hours before a play opens. Creative people have the ability not only to learn from their failures but also to accept failure as an important part of the creative process. They know that the odds of finding a creative answer to a problem are directly related to the number of attempts.

FOR MORE ON

THE CREATIVE PERSONALITY

"The creative personality," Mihaly Csikszentmihalyi, *Psychology Today*, July–August 1996

I Enhancing Your Creativity

Too often we think of creativity as happening by chance. For example, in 1901, Wilhelm Conrad Roentgen (1845–1923), a German physicist, discovered X-rays as he was trying to find out why his photographic plates were being ruined. Or we assume that creativity is something people either have or they don't. Certainly, luck is involved with being in the right place at the right time, and talent does make it possible to take advantage of opportunities, but as scientist Louis Pasteur (1822–1895) said, "Chance favors the prepared mind." Or as the lawyer Johnnie Cochran (1937–2005) put it a century later, "Luck is the residue of preparation." In other words, with appropriate techniques and developed talents, we all have the potential to be creative. Let's look at a few basic ways to increase creativity.

Ever tried. Ever failed. No matter. Try again. Fail again. Fail better.

Samuel Beckett,

Irish playwright and novelist, in Nohow On: Company, Ill Seen Ill Said, Worstward Ho

Get Enough Exercise and Sleep

One of the best ways to enhance creativity is to get regular exercise and plenty of sleep. Pulling all-nighters is not a good way to come up with creative answers. Scientists have shown that people whose lives or jobs make too many demands on their sleep are generally less creative than people who get their full eight hours. After getting that full night of sleep, according to neuroscientist Candace Pert of the National Institute of Mental Health, the body can release more endorphins. Endorphins are chemicals that control the brain's perception of and response to pain and stress and can help promote a feeling of well-being. And a feeling of well-being is more conducive to creativity than the state of feeling stressed out. One way to release endorphins in the brain is through exercise. When you exercise, you put yourself into an "endorphinergic state" that can last for hours or days and can increase creativity.

Consider Your Environment

Greece in the fifth century BCE, Florence in the fifteenth century, and Paris in the nineteenth century were all centers of creative activity. The mingling of different lifestyles and beliefs and the freedom to express them encouraged people in each of these places to exchange ideas and solve problems in new ways. But there have been many more times in history when the environment limited creativity. Conformist cultures and rigid regimes are not as likely to produce creativity as are those where new voices and ideas can be heard and appreciated. Nor is creativity likely in societies or groups where adherence to tradition limits new ideas. If you seek out places where creativity is allowed, arrange your life to allow for creativity, and spend time with people who value creative ideas, you will begin to find that elusive creative environment.

© Donald Cooper/Photostage Ltd.

It's possible to be creative in almost any environment, but some environments are more conducive to creativity than others. Throughout history, certain parts of the world exploded as centers of creative thought and activity. Examples include ancient Egypt and Greece, Renaissance Europe, and Harlem's "heyday years" from the 1930s to the 1970s. Sometimes works of art celebrate and explore these creative centers, such as John Van Druten's Cabaret, *a play centered around the club scene of pre–World War II Berlin. This 1993 revival starred Alan Cummings as the Emcee. Staged at the Donmar Warehouse, London.*

Make the Time

Creativity takes time. People whose lives are totally booked with family and work obligations—dashing from school to soccer practice to piano lessons to a part-time job—seldom have much time to be creative. This is true of many Americans. According to a recent report of the International Labor Organization, the United States has overtaken Japan as the nation whose workers put in the most hours in the advanced industrial world. The average American works eight weeks more per year than the average Western European. All this work can be good for personal wealth, the company, or the country, but it can be dangerous for creativity, especially if it is mindless, follow-the-rules work. Creativity requires idle time, time for the brain to work without interruptions or time limits.

Assess Your Motivation

Experts have found that the reason for wanting to be creative can affect the extent of creativity. If a person's primary motivation is a goal outside the creative act itself, he or she will generally be less creative. For example, Konstantin Stanislavsky (1863–1938), the Russian acting teacher and director, observed that actors' creativity is significantly stifled if they are thinking of the audience rather than concentrating on the artistic task. He said that an actor must be able to develop a "circle of his own attention" where other motivations such as wealth, critical praise, or success are unimportant. Beginning artists who dream of making it big tend to drop out of art if they are not immediately successful. On the other hand, beginning artists who focus only on the creative process tend to stick with it for years and have more opportunities to be creative. The same is true in all fields. If the product is more important than the process, you will be generally less creative.

Temper Your Criticism

Creative people are always interested in criticism and feedback, but one roadblock to creativity is allowing yourself to be too critical of your new ideas. People are often more creative when they imagine as many solutions as possible

© Bureau L.A. Collection/Corbis

Many creative people express their creativity in more than one area. In the arts, filmmaker Kitano Takeshi is also a poet and a painter, playwright Samuel Beckett was also a novelist, actor Juliette Lewis is also a musician, and actor Viggo Mortensen is also a photographer. Renowned playwright Sam Shepard, shown here filming his 1994 movie Silent Tongue, *also acts, directs, and once made his living as a musician. If you'd like to make the most of your creative abilities, consider the tips discussed in this chapter. No matter what you're interested in, there's room in your life for a little creativity.*

It hinders the creative work of the mind if the intellect examines too closely the ideas as they pour in.
Friedrich Schiller,
German playwright, poet, and historian

The principal goal of education in the schools should be creating men and women who are capable of doing new things, not simply repeating what other generations have done; men and women who are creative, inventive, and discoverers, who can be critical and verify, and not accept, everything they are offered.
Jean Piaget,
Swiss psychologist

and hold off critical judgment until later. (This process is called *brainstorming* and will be discussed more in the next section.) One study placed a group of scientists in a closed conference room with a problem to solve. They were told that they should all analytically judge every suggestion as soon as it was offered. After a day of thinking and judging, they failed to solve the problem. The next day they were given an equally difficult problem to solve, but this time they spent the morning pitching possible solutions without judging them or even considering plausibility. That afternoon, the scientists were asked to critically judge each possible solution. It worked—one of their morning pitches solved the problem. By withholding criticism, they succeeded in increasing creativity. In short, if you constantly censor your ideas, you will stifle your creativity. The next time you have a problem to solve, write down every solution that comes to mind, without censoring any of them. Soon you'll have a list of possible and improbable solutions. Later, come back to the list and evaluate each solution. In other words, use critical thinking, and you'll have a better chance of solving the problem. Nothing is more detrimental to the creative process than censoring every idea you have the moment it's created; this only causes creative gridlock.

Creative Solutions

Without the ability to solve problems, your creativity will be limited. In order to solve a problem, you must first detect a problem. Mihaly Csikszentmihalyi says, "Many creative individuals have pointed out that in their work the formulation of the problem is more important than its solution and that real advances in science and in art tend to come when new questions are asked or old problems are viewed from a new angle." Once you perceive a problem, you need to look for a creative solution.

Inability to solve a problem is often due to trying to solve too many problems at once. For example, when actors rehearse a play, they stop, go back, and try it again, over and over, in order to solve one little problem at a time; they don't take on the entire play all at once. Another reason for failure to solve a problem is not knowing basic problem solving techniques. Here are steps that artists as well as scientists often use when trying to solve a problem.

- **Specify the problem.** The first step in problem solving is to identify the problem in specific terms. In his book *People in Quandaries,* Wendell Johnson recalls a psychiatrist who was often sent patients who had been diagnosed as seriously maladjusted. He noticed they weren't necessarily more maladjusted than the average patient, but they all had one thing in common: "They were unable to tell him clearly what was the matter." They had not been able to tell their doctors what the problem was, so their doctors had been unable to suggest solutions. Johnson goes on to say, "By far the most important step toward the solution of the laboratory problem lies in stating the problem in such a way as to suggest a fruitful attack on it. Once that is accomplished, any ordinary assistant can usually turn the cranks and read the dials. . . . There cannot be a precise answer to a vague question."

- **Break the problem into manageable components.** Most problems are made up of dozens of smaller problems. We need to unravel the strands of the problem to begin to analyze it. Break the problem into manageable components, and there is a good chance you can solve them one at a time.
- **Brainstorm possible solutions.** Once you have identified the problem and broken it into manageable components, you can start being creative. This part of problem solving is often called *brainstorming.* Solutions that are offered before the problem is specifically defined or broken into manageable components will usually be only wild guesses. Recall the example from the previous section about the scientists pitching out solutions to a problem. Their brainstorming helped stimulate their creativity, which resulted in a number of good ideas for an effective solution. Sometimes brainstorming yields ideas about how to solve a problem by using existing techniques. In these cases, it may seem that brainstorming didn't stimulate any creativity because it did not result in a brand-new technique. However, it did generate a moment of insight into the fact that an appropriate technique to solve the problem already exists.

Every production presents a number of problems that must be solved to ensure a smooth performance. Here, actors from Los Angeles's East-West Players theatre company receive notes from their director. It is the director's job to help identify problems and brainstorm possible solutions with the cast and crew. These solutions can then be tested during rehearsals.

© Michael S. Yamashita/Corbis

- **Test the solution to see if it works.** Here is where you use critical thinking skills to see if the first three steps have in fact provided a solution. Testing the answer is often the longest step, particularly in the sciences, where collecting data can take years. Testing the solution in the theatre also requires data. For example, most new plays are "workshopped," or read in front of an audience numerous times before the official premiere; the playwright evaluates audience reaction to new scenes as the work continues to evolve through development.

At the end of the process, if the most likely solution fails, it's time to start over with step one—did you clearly specify the problem?

If these steps sound similar to scientific method, they should. In many ways, art and science are closely related. They both rely on experimentation, research, free speech, curiosity, originality, intellectual examination, and creativity. And so the next time you attend a jazz concert, watch a ballet, or go to the theatre, think of all the problems the artists had to solve in order to create an evening of entertainment and art. As they express themselves, they realize that art is about more than expressing emotions; it is also about finding those moments of insight that make a live performance communicate ideas and provide a magical experience. However, to complicate things, theatre artists must find those moments of insight while working with an ensemble.

FOR MORE ON

THE CREATIVITY OF PROBLEM SOLVING

"Brain power: People can be trained to use their brains more effectively for creativity, problem solving, and other thinking," Karl Albrecht, *T&D,* November 2002

I Theatre Is Teamwork

When theatre, or almost any work of art for that matter, is at its best, it appears to be almost effortless. The creativity flows; the technique is polished; the entire production is so well coordinated that it seems as if it were the product of a single mind. In the theatre, this effortlessness is an illusion. More often than not, the **ensemble** consists of crews of technicians, dozens of assistants, and numerous artists, including actors, directors, speech coaches, playwrights, and designers, who are using a wide variety of art forms including painting, drawing, writing, and acting, as well as set, lighting, and costume design. The same is true for films; the credits after a movie can go on for several minutes and include hundreds of names. In the theatre the ensemble is so important that some theatre companies—such as the West Coast Ensemble Theatre and the Ensemble Theatre of Cincinnati—include the word in their name.

With so many people and talents involved in a single play, there is a danger that it could become a production created by committee. And, as we all know, committees are infamous for breakdowns in communication, mediocrity, and power struggles. These weaknesses can be just as big a problem for small theatre productions, in which only a few individuals are involved, as they are for large ones. The key to a good production is an organized ensemble with a clear power structure that allows for unfettered communication and a well-thought-out delineation of duties that enables each member of the ensemble to contribute to the final product. Productions succeed by using a complicated command structure (see Figure 5.1) that, when it works, allows

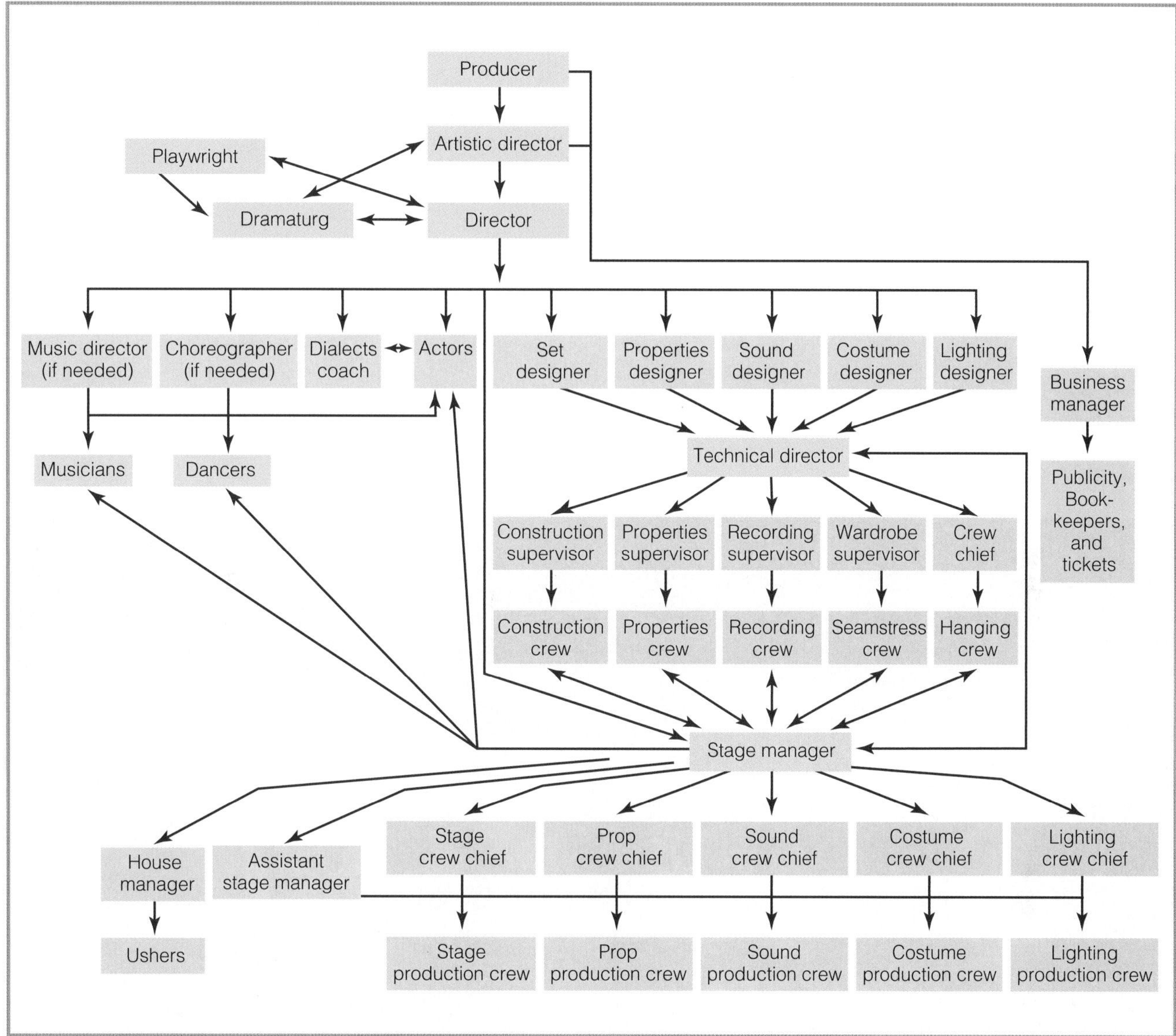

Fig. 5.1 *The production organization*

each member of the ensemble freedom to create and yet ensures that all the artists, technicians, and crew members share the same artistic vision.

A theatre's ensemble is divided into four categories: administrative, creative, construction, and production. The administrative team includes accountants, box-office staff, secretaries, fund-raisers, grant writers, publicity personnel, the artistic director, and producer(s) who run the business aspects of any theatre. The creative team includes the playwright(s), the director(s), actors, designers, and to some extent the producer(s) who work together to create the action, words, style, and theme of the production. The construction team includes the technical director(s) and crew chief(s) who supervise a company of seamstresses, contractors, and laborers, who hang the lights, build the sets, fabricate the props, and stitch the costumes. The production team includes stage manager(s), house manager(s), and ushers, as well as the lighting, set, and costume crews who work behind the scenes during the performances. Let's look a bit closer at each of these teams.

Administrative Team

The administrative team includes the people who are involved with the money, from the person who sells you your ticket to the people financing the production. One of the key members of the administrative team is the producer.

One of the most important members of the administrative team is the producer. Producers put up their own money or manage other people's money in order to fund a production. The musical The Producers *satirized the financial aspects of theatre, providing a protagonist, Max Bialystock, who charms elderly women out of their money so he can fund his awful plays. In reality, producing plays is a serious business. The 2001 production of* The Producers *featured Nathan Lane as Bialystock. Book by Mel Brooks and Thomas Meehan. Music and lyrics by Mel Brooks. Directed by Susan Stroman at New York's St. James Theatre.*

© Paul Kolnik

Producers may be individuals who put up their own money or control an investor's money to finance a production, or an institution such as a university, a church, a community organization, or a theatre company that controls the business side of the production. Depending on the size of the production, the financial responsibilities can be rather small or involve millions of dollars. If the theatre is nonprofit, the producers must manage all the aspects of the theatre's budget to meet government regulations for nonprofit organizations. If a play is performed for profit, the producer assumes financial responsibility for any losses but also pockets any profit. Because money is involved, the producer or producing organization is one of the most powerful positions in the theatre. It is the producer's responsibility to raise money, negotiate contracts, write grants, do publicity, sell tickets, keep financial records, pay taxes, maintain a safe working environment, and hire the creative, production, and construction teams.

The word *producer* has different meanings depending on where it is used. For a Hollywood movie as for a play, the producer is the person in charge of the business, managerial, and overall artistic aspects of the production. For a television sitcom or hour-length drama, the producer is usually a staff writer who may have a title such as "Associate Producer," "Producer," or "Executive Producer." However, for other kinds of television shows, the word *producer* means the same as it does in the movies and in the theatre. Just to make the definition even more confusing, in England the word *producer* is often used to denote the person who directs a play.

FOR MORE ON

BEING A PRODUCER

"How I became a Broadway producer," Kathy Levin, *Cosmopolitan,* November 1996

I'd say one of the most common failures of able people is a lack of nerve. They'll play safe games. . . . In innovations, you have to play a less safe game if it's going to be interesting. It's not predictable that it'll go well.

George Stigler,
American economist and Nobel Prize winner

Creative Team

The creative team is the artists who invent the play and stage the production. The main members are the playwright, the director, the actors, and the designers. The team can also include assistant directors, musical directors, conductors, vocal coaches, understudies, dancers, and choreographers. Sometimes the playwright is called the **primary artist** for conceiving the original idea, creating the characters, and building the story. The rest of the creative team, including directors, actors, and designers, are sometimes referred to as **interpretive artists** because they turn the playwright's thoughts into a play. As director Terry McCabe says in *Mis-directing the Play,* "Strictly speaking, there is only one creative artist in the theatre. It is the playwright, the one who makes something out of nothing. The rest of us—directors, designers, actors—are interpretive artists. We take what the playwright has created and demonstrate to the audience what we think the playwright's creation looks and sounds like."

From the playwright's original idea to the opening night of a production can take years—sometimes even decades. First the playwright must write and rewrite the play. Months before rehearsals begin, the director and designers will brainstorm, research, and experiment with different set, costume, and lighting designs. There will be dozens of concept meetings in which the director synchronizes the many aesthetic elements and talents needed to make theatre. The director, much like a musical conductor, coordinates the primary and interpretive artists. Every aspect must be calculated to achieve the intended effect. (For more on playwriting, directing, and design, see Chapters 6, 8, and 9.) Once the designs are ready, the construction crews enter the picture and begin building the set and costumes.

Construction Crews

In many small theatres, the designers build their own designs; in larger professional theatres, the designers turn over their designs to a technical director who is in charge of all the shop supervisors and construction crews. The technical staff turns the designers' scale drawings, paintings, blueprints, models, and sketches into fully realized sets, lights, and costumes. Depending on the size of the production, the construction crew can have a few members or dozens. The technical side of theatre can include painters, carpenters, electricians, seamstresses, wigmakers, and riggers. Property acquisition crews purchase or build props (*prop* is short for "property" and refers to any object actors use onstage). Lighting crews hang and focus the lights; costume construction (or "wardrobe") crews sew, pull from stock, or rent the costumes; and set construction crews erect the sets.

The **technical director,** often called the TD, stands above all the crew chiefs and answers only to the director, the designers, and the budget office. TDs coordinate, schedule, and engineer the technical elements of the production. They make sure that all the plans are carried out by the different shops, supervise technical rehearsals, and in some theatres also act as the shop manager who maintains equipment and orders supplies.

Production Crews

During the performance of a play, still more crews are involved. There are crews that make sure that the costumes are mended, laundered, and pressed between each performance; dressers who help actors make quick costume changes; grips who help assemble and shift scenery; riggers, also called "flymen," who mount and operate all curtains, sets, and anything else that must be flown in via the fly system above the stage; prop masters and property running crew members who are responsible for placement of all props before, during, and after the show; lightboard operators who run the computer lightboards; and soundboard operators who play the sound cues. Large productions can have far more people behind the scenes than on stage. For example, the Broadway musical *Titanic* needed thirteen carpenters, seven prop people, one lightboard operator, three follow-spot operators, two computer operators, three riggers, and four stage managers working backstage during every performance. It also took five wig dressers to care for the show's seventy-one wigs and fourteen wardrobe people to repair, wash, starch, and press the 180 costumes between performances. In all, over 275 hours a week were spent on costume maintenance alone!

FOR MORE ON

THE LIFE OF A STAGE MANAGER

"Calling the cues: Understanding the behind-the-scenes art of the stage manager," Christopher Hoile, *Opera Canada,* Winter 2003

Once a play is up and running, the director usually leaves and the most important member of the production crew, the stage manager, takes over. The **stage manager,** often with the help of several assistant stage managers, conducts technical rehearsals, fills out rehearsal reports, authorizes the opening of the house to let the audience in, authorizes when an understudy goes on,

© Paul Kolnik

Long before a play opens, costume, set, light, and prop designers and crews labor for months under tight deadlines to make it all happen. During the performance, it often takes dozens of offstage crews to run the lightboard, move the sets between scenes, dress the actors, and wash and press the costumes. In fact, during some productions, such as 2002's smash Broadway musical Hairspray, *there are more people working behind the scenes than appear onstage.* Hairspray *is based on the film by John Waters. Book by Mark O'Donnell and Thomas Meehan, music by Marc Shaiman, and lyrics by Scott Wittman and Marc Shaiman.*

times the length of the show, and calls for brush-up rehearsals. The stage manager keeps a **prompt book** in which all the play's sound and light cues, blocking, and other notes are recorded (see Chapter 8). The stage manager also calls all the cues during the performance, including light, sound, and scene shifts.

For a photo essay that illustrates some key points in the process of creating and staging a play, see the Spotlight "The Process of Putting On a Play."

From inception to fruition, theatre takes thousands of hours and the talents of many trained, creative, and hard-working individuals. At every step, creativity is critical. When theatre succeeds, it does so because the director has designed an ensemble where every member understands his or her duties yet is also allowed to solve problems, express opinions, use the techniques of his or her trade, and be creative. The director who micromanages a production, just like the corporate executive who micromanages a company, will limit the potential for creativity and in the end produce a well-controlled but sterile product. As director Terry McCabe says, a good director sees the creative team "as valuable colleagues precisely because they might enlarge the director's own sense of the play."

The Process of Putting on a Play

Writing, designing, rehearsing, and producing a play can take years and involve dozens of creative people. Let's take a look at some of the work the University of Wyoming's theatre department had to do as they prepared for a 2005 production of Shakespeare's *Love's Labour's Lost.*

© Don Turner

Working long hours for weeks before a play opens, costume shop designers, stitchers, and cutters prepare all the clothes the actors will wear. Here, stitcher Billie Kay Gross and designer Lee Hodgson race to meet the opening night deadline.

© Don Turner

Often, actors rehearse onstage only a few days before the opening of a play. Here director Leigh Selting takes actors Jesse Cohen, Stephen Post, Brandon Taylor, John Hill, and Chris Will through their paces. In the background, stage managers Senda Dimock-Perry and Jessi Sundell take notes that they will later use to help the actors improve their performances.

© Don Turner

During the rehearsal process, fittings, adjustments, and alterations are made to costumes so that they fit well and look right. Here designer Lee Hodgson makes a final modification to actress Ellen Soderberg's costume.

© Don Turner

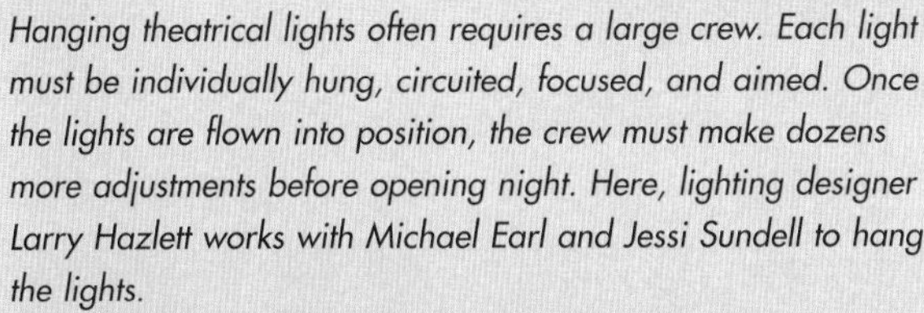

Hanging theatrical lights often requires a large crew. Each light must be individually hung, circuited, focused, and aimed. Once the lights are flown into position, the crew must make dozens more adjustments before opening night. Here, lighting designer Larry Hazlett works with Michael Earl and Jessi Sundell to hang the lights.

© Don Turner

Modern computer-operated lightboards can control hundreds, if not thousands, of lights and generate an incredible variety of effects with a touch of a button. However, every cue must be painstakingly loaded into the computer. Here, a lighting technician tests to make sure the lights are ready for opening night.

© Don Turner

Building the set is a labor-intensive process that can take weeks to complete. Crews must have carpentry and painting skills, and they must be able to follow the set designer's directions to create the set the designer has envisioned. Here, Larry Hazlett, Thomas Stroppel, and Rocky Hopson work on the set's background.

Putting Offstage Action Onscreen: *The Crucible*

The Crucible, Arthur Miller's intense and disturbing play based on the 1692 witch trials in Salem, Massachusetts, is a perfect candidate for adaptation to the big screen. It has a big cast of larger-than-life characters who love and hate with a passion; the story is intriguing and mysterious; and there's a lot of action. In fact, the play is almost an action adventure: People dance naked in the woods and conjure spirits, get stabbed by needles, see flying demons, get hauled off to court in chains, fall into and come out of comas, and of course hang by the neck until dead. But what is really remarkable about *The Crucible* is that although each of these events occurs as the story unfolds, we see hardly *any* of them. Because of the physical limitations of a stage, it is difficult, if not impossible, to portray this kind of action literally. Consequently, drama has long relied on what is called "reported action": onstage discussions about what has already happened offstage.

In contrast, film can show us just about anything. It is no surprise then that the 1996 filmed version of *The Crucible* starts with a sequence in which one of

© Robbie Jack/Corbis

In this 1990 National Theatre production of Arthur Miller's The Crucible, *a sparse set frames the "bewitched" girls, who fake possession so that their lies are not exposed.*

the main characters, Abigail Williams (Winona Ryder), and her girlfriends race off into the woods at night to dance, brew charms, and conjure spirits around a fire—all taboos in their extremely religious Puritan community. As they dance, the girls are seen by Reverend Parris (Bruce Davison), one of the town's ministers. This is the inciting incident, or first major event of the story, that sets in motion the ghastly chain of events making up the plot of *The Crucible*. In the play, we learn about this event only when one of the girls has fallen into a "coma," prompting a series of conversations that reveal the inciting incident in words rather than action. The film, however, continues to show us all the locations we only hear about in the play and to depict almost all the reported action.

The Crucible remains one of the great works of American drama. It is gripping, upsetting, and richly complicated. Although the film fails to convey some of the complexity and ambiguity of the characters, so haunting in the play, it makes up for it by giving us a stunning visual feast of one of the most disturbing periods of American history.

Aoise Stratford
Playwright

Kobal Collection/Picture Desk

In the 1996 movie The Crucible, *Daniel Day-Lewis's character, John Proctor, is tormented by officers of the Salem court. The movie version of the play shows much of the action that on stage is only reported.*

Curtain Call

Creativity is not exclusive to the arts; it is useful in all professions and fields of study. Yes, some of us choose our field for economic reasons (that is, how much we can expect to earn) and not necessarily because we feel that our talent and ability to be creative lie in that field. Yet most people who go into the theatre do not do it for the money but rather the hope of living a creative life. Many factors lead to creativity, but most people who work in creative fields would probably agree that the best way to live a creative life is to just do it. As Anne Bogart writes in her book *A Director Prepares,*

> Do not assume that you have to have some prescribed condition to do your best work. Do not wait. Do not wait for enough time or money to accomplish what you think you have in mind. Work with what you have RIGHT NOW. Work with the people around you RIGHT NOW. . . . Do not wait for what you assume is the appropriate stress-free environment in which to generate expression. Do not wait for maturity or insight or wisdom. Do not wait till you are sure that you know what you are doing. Do not wait until you have enough technique. What you do now, what you make of your present circumstances will determine the quality and scope of your future endeavors. And at the same time be patient.

Summary

Creativity can be defined as a moment of insight. Closely tied to creativity are technique and talent. Technique is composed of the lessons learned from creativity, and talent can often be developed or denied by our environment. To be more creative, it is important to examine the traits of creative people. Creative people have a burning curiosity, strong concentration, and a mental agility that allows them to find order where others see only chaos. They also have the ability to accept failure, because more often than not creative solutions fail. IQ is a factor in creativity, but studies have found that an extremely high IQ does not make people more creative. The key is to find the kinds of intelligence in which you excel. Howard Gardner's theory of multiple intelligences identifies linguistic, musical, logical-mathematical, spatial, bodily-kinesthetic, and personal intelligences.

In order to enhance your creativity, you need adequate amounts of exercise and sleep as well as an environment that nourishes creativity and allows time to be creative. It is also important to examine the reason you want to be creative; if your motivation is too far removed from the creative act itself, you will probably not be very creative. Another important aspect of being creative is to generate ideas without immediately censoring them. One of the best ways to enhance your creativity is to learn to solve problems. The steps of problem solving include specifically defining the problem, breaking the problem into manageable components, brainstorming possible solutions, and testing to see if the most likely solution works.

In the theatre, as in many other professions, creativity often occurs within an ensemble. Theatre's creative ensemble includes four categories: administrative, creative, construction, and production. The key to working within an ensemble is to ensure that all the members of the group are allowed to be creative but also share the same artistic vision.

The Art of Theatre Online

Use the *Art of Theatre* website at **http://communication.wadsworth.com/downs1** for quick access to the electronic study resources that accompany this chapter, including a digital glossary, a link to InfoTrac College Edition that you can use to find the For More On . . . InfoTrac College Edition readings listed below, a list of further reading, and a chapter quiz. When you get to the *Art of Theatre* homepage, click on the cover of the book you are using and you will be redirected to the website for your book. Then click on "Student Book Companion Site" in the Resource box, pick a chapter from the pull-down menu at the top of the page, and select an option from the Chapter Resources menu. The *Art of Theatre* website also includes links to interesting and informative theatre websites. Just click on the Theatre on the Web link in the Book Resources menu. The links to these websites are maintained and updated as needed.

Key Terms

convergent thinking / 113
creativity / 106
divergent thinking / 113
ensemble / 120
interpretive artist / 123
primary artist / 123
producer / 123
prompt book / 125
stage manager / 124
talent / 109
technical director / 124
technique / 108

For More On . . .

InfoTrac College Edition Readings

http://www.infotrac-college.com

Mihaly Csikszentmihalyi's thoughts on creativity / 112
"How to find flow"

The creative personality / 115
"The creative personality"

The creativity of problem solving / 120
"Brain power: People can be trained to use their brains more effectively for creativity, problem solving, and other thinking"

Being a producer / 123
"How I became a Broadway producer"

The life of a stage manager / 124
"Calling the cues: Understanding the behind-the-scenes art of the stage manager"

6 The Playwright and the Script

Theatre begins with the playwright, the artist who conceives the theme, the characters, the dialogue, and the story. The root word wright *in* playwright *comes from the Middle Ages and means "one who builds." A shipwright was someone who built ships; a wheelwright was someone who built wheels. So it follows that a play-*wright *is someone who builds plays. Playwrights are so important to the process that many theatre professionals call them the "primary artist." Yet when a play is produced, it is unlikely that the director, actors, or designers will ever meet the playwright. In fact, the playwright is the only member of the ensemble of a production who can be long dead.*

In this chapter we will look at the artists who build plays and the techniques they use to express themselves. We will also examine the elements that make up a play

© Donald Cooper/Photostage

◀ ***On preceding page:***
A Raisin in the Sun, *by Lorraine Hansberry. Directed by David Lan, Young Vic Theatre, London, 2001, featuring (l to r) William Chubb (inset), Cecilia Noble, and Lennie James. This play, written in 1959, is the story of conflicts that arise when a black family attempts to move into an all-white neighborhood.*

and how playwrights combine these elements to craft a script. Studying the elements of playwriting will help you better analyze performances and the written words upon which the contributions of all other theatre artists depend.

I The Playwright's Life and Words

Unlike the other artists in the theatre, who usually work within the ensemble, the playwright typically works alone. The exception is for scripts conceived through workshops or improvisations, as was the case with Caryl Churchill's *Cloud Nine* (1978), a dark comedy about gender roles and sexuality. Churchill wrote the script but she participated in workshops with actors who improvised some of the dialogue. Similarly, the play *Tracers* (1980), which recounts eight veterans' tour of duty in Vietnam, was created by a group of actors, directors, and writers who contributed lines and ideas. More recently, director and playwright Moisés Kaufman and fellow members of the Tectonic Theater Project collaborated on *The Laramie Project* (2001), about the 1998 murder of Matthew Shepard, through workshops and interviews with the residents of Laramie, Wyoming. But as a rule the playwright labors alone for months, if not years, to write a play. In fact, playwriting is the most time-consuming of all the arts of the theatre. The combined number of hours it takes the actors to rehearse, the designers to design, and the director to direct does not come close to the amount of time it took the playwright to conceive and write the play. This, along with the fact that playwrights are the primary artists, is why playwrights get top billing in the program, even above the director, in contrast to Hollywood movies, where the director gets top billing.

> We playwrights tend to be a solitary bunch. We sit in our little cubbyholes alone, staring out the window (if the cubbyhole has one), talking aloud to ourselves, often in funny voices.
>
> **Dan Berkowitz,**
> *American playwright*

As we mentioned in Chapter 2, playwrights do not sell their copyright. Consequently, they retain control of the script and technically no director, actor, designer, producer, or anyone else can change the script without permission from the playwright or the playwright's lawyer, publisher, or estate. We say "technically" because sometimes members of the ensemble do change the script without seeking the playwright's permission. They just slip the changes in and hope that the playwright doesn't find out. But sometimes the playwright does and decides to sue. For example, several years ago a high school in Utah produced the musical *A Chorus Line.* To make it more acceptable to local audiences and the school administration, the director cut the role of the gay man, cleaned up the language, and rewrote some of the songs. In doing so, he violated U.S. copyright laws. When the writers of *A Chorus Line* found out, they got a restraining order and closed the production. To change the play legally, the director would have had to wait until the play was in the public domain, which occurs seventy years after the death of the writers. (For more on copyright, see "Ownership: Copyrights and Cash" in Chapter 2).

Owning the copyright means that playwrights retain a lot of power over their plays, but they do not necessarily make a lot of money from them. One of the reasons they don't make much money is that they are not employees of the theater and so are not allowed to form closed-shop unions and strike for better compensation. A **closed-shop union,** sometimes called a union shop, is a union to which all employees *must* belong and which the employer formally

© Richard Termine

French playwright Edmond Rostand wrote Cyrano de Bergerac *in 1898. Today the script is in the public domain, so anyone can produce it without paying a royalty to Rostand's estate. (However, if a recent translation is used, a royalty might be owed to the translator.) In addition, plays in the public domain can be freely varied.* The Truth about Cats & Dogs *(1996) with Janeane Garofalo and Uma Thurman,* Roxanne *(1987) with Steve Martin and Daryl Hannah, and the teen comedy* Whatever It Takes *(2000) are all recent movies based on Rostand's play. This 2004 production featured Geraint Wyn Davies as Cyrano (right). Directed by Michael Kahn, the Shakespeare Theatre, Washington, DC.*

recognizes as their sole collective bargaining agent. The advantage to closed-shop unions is that the employees can call a strike if their demands go unmet. Television and screen writers have a powerful closed-shop union called the **Writers Guild of America (WGA).** As a result, staff writers on television shows can earn $5,000–$10,000 or more a week, and a single screenplay can sell for hundreds of thousands if not millions of dollars. In fact, according to *Written By,* the Writers Guild magazine, Hollywood producers pay screen and television writers about $1 billion a year to write, rewrite, and develop new scripts. Screen and television writers are allowed to form a closed-shop union because they sell their copyright, giving up their power to control the script, the production, or the final product. This makes them "writers for hire," or "employees." The only exceptions are screenwriters who direct their own work or who make independent films and have full control of the creative process.

Playwrights, because they retain the copyright, are not "writers for hire." Instead, they are considered "management," and U.S. law does not allow managers to form closed-shop unions. Playwrights' only option is a weak **open-shop union.** In an open shop, membership is optional, so meaningful strikes are impossible. The playwrights' union, the **Dramatists Guild of America (DGA),** can champion the rights of playwrights but it can do little to demand higher pay. The Dramatists Guild is trying to change the situation with a bill that has been making its way through Congress since June 2004. The Playwrights Licensing Antitrust Initiative would give playwrights the right to bargain collectively while retaining their copyright.

Rather than sell their scripts, playwrights rent them to theatres and are paid a royalty when the play is produced. These royalties can amount to a few dollars per performance for a small theatre to several thousand dollars a week for a professional regional, Off-Broadway, or Broadway production—though big money in playwriting is rare. Perhaps fewer than one hundred playwrights in the United States earn a full living from their plays; the majority of playwrights must find second jobs in order to make ends meet. In 2004 Arthur Miller, one of America's most successful playwrights, told the Senate Judiciary Committee when it was considering the Playwrights Licensing Antitrust Initiative, "The American theatre risks losing the next generation of playwrights to other media and opportunities" if playwrights are not allowed to negotiate better economic conditions. Even famous playwrights often turn to more commercial work. For example, Sam Shepard (b. 1943), famous for writing such plays as *Curse of the Starving Class* (1978), *Buried Child* (1979), *True West* (1980), *Fool for Love* (1982) and *Simpatico* (1995), has also written screenplays and teleplays and has acted in over forty movies, including *The Right Stuff* (1983) and *Black Hawk Down* (2001). Similarly, playwright David Mamet (b. 1949), famous for such plays as *American Buffalo* (1976), *Glengarry Glen Ross* (1984), and *Oleanna* (1992), has also written several screenplays, including *The Verdict* (1982), *The Untouchables* (1987), *Wag the Dog* (1998), and *Hannibal* (2001).

FOR MORE ON

PLAYWRIGHTS WORKING IN OTHER FIELDS

"Not-so-simple Sara: Sara Finney-Johnson may have made a name writing for TV, but she feels her playwriting brings her even greater opportunities," Lori Talley, *Back Stage West,* January 22, 2004

The reward for low pay and long hours is that playwrights, unlike most screenwriters, see their work presented as written. Their unique voices remain

Photofest

Playwright Sam Shepard starred with Kim Basinger in a 1985 screen version of his play Fool for Love *(1983). A few famous playwrights such as Sam Shepard, David Mamet, and Anna Deavere Smith are able to make a living from their writing, but most playwrights struggle to make ends meet. Often they must turn to television writing, screenwriting, novelizing—or even waiting tables—to pay the bills.*

pure and their ideas about how the world is or should be are communicated to audiences without alteration. When it comes down to it, all that playwrights have are their words, and to playwrights, their words far more valuable than any paycheck. Playwright Tom Stoppard wrote in his play *The Real Thing* (1982) that words build bridges across incomprehension and chaos. Words, he said, "deserve respect. If you get the right ones in the right order, you can nudge the world a little." And all playwrights, rich or poor, want to nudge the world. (For more on a playwright's life, see the Spotlight on Diversity box "The Life of a Playwright: Rebecca Gilman.")

> I'm better at writing than I am at organizing [political action]. [My play] *Slaughter City* is my small contribution. If it gives people a voice, it is worth something.
>
> ***Naomi Wallace,***
> *American playwright*

The Art of Playwriting

Playwriting is a limited form of storytelling because all a playwright can write is what the audience sees and hears. A play script is limited to dialogue, stage directions, and an occasional parenthetical. **Dialogue** is the spoken text of the play, the words the characters say. Playwrights write everything the actors say, including fillers such as "ah," "so," and "uh-huh." Finding the right words for each character takes many rewrites and an acute sensitivity to how people express themselves. The playwright also writes the **stage directions,** which are notes that indicate the physical movements of the characters. The director and actors decide the majority of the movements, so a playwright usually limits the stage directions to short notes such as "with a smile" or "closing the door." ("Exit, pursued by a bear" from Shakespeare's *The Winter's Tale* is perhaps the most famous stage direction ever written because it seems to require a bear.) Not all the stage directions in a published play were necessarily written by the playwright. Occasionally a publisher includes stage directions taken from a stage manager's notes in order to help amateur companies with the staging of a play. **Parentheticals** are short descriptions such as *(loving), (angry),* or *(terrified)* to help the actor or the reader interpret a particular line of dialogue. To distinguish them from dialogue, parentheticals are enclosed in parentheses and usually italicized. Within these script parameters, a playwright builds a play using the basic tools of playwriting including theme, characters, conflict, language, and plot.

What Does It Mean? The Theme

Playwrights are philosophers in that they search for meaning in the world and attempt to understand human nature. Their search results in a statement about life, a central idea, or a moral; this is the play's **theme.** For example, the theme of David Henry Hwang's play *M. Butterfly* is the blinding effects of racial stereotyping. The theme of a play is more often implied than directly stated because playwrights rarely sit down to write a play about a particular theme. Instead, the theme usually reveals itself during the writing process. American playwright Arthur Miller said that he often didn't know what his plays were about until the second or third draft. Even then, playwrights rarely state the theme, because themes that are explicitly stated are less powerful than those that are revealed through action. In other words, the playwright tries to make the theme clear without spelling it out. Consequently, the theme is often open to interpretation by audiences and readers.

> All my fiction—short stories, novels, or plays—began as personal experiences. I wrote those works because something happened to me, because I met someone or read something that became an important experience for me. I am not always aware of . . . why an experience gradually becomes a source of encouragement to invent or fantasize about.
>
> ***Mario Vargas Llosa,***
> *Peruvian playwright and novelist*

The Life of a Playwright: Rebecca Gilman

Rebecca Gilman attended the MFA playwriting program at the University of Iowa. After graduation she moved to Chicago, where she worked as a clerk in an accounting office during the day and wrote plays at night. "I was writing," Gilman said, "because it was cheaper than therapy. I never thought I would ever make any money off these things—that never seemed even a possibility for me." Her first big success came with *Spinning into Butter* (1999), a play about the secret prejudices of "respectable" white people and the vocabularies we all invent to hide our prejudices. The play transformed her from a struggling Chicago writer into one of America's most talked-about and sought-after playwrights. Soon she was the winner of the Goodman Theatre's Scott McPherson Award and the American Theatre Critics Association's Osborn Award, and her plays were being performed in such theatres as the Goodman in Chicago, Lincoln Center in New York, and the Royal Court Theatre in London.

Spinning into Butter is about a young white dean in a liberal arts college in New England. When a black student starts receiving racially motivated threats, the white students and staff form committees to organize public meetings against racism. Only the dean thinks that they should investigate the charge first. She says, "All you do is talk about racism, and then you heave this collective sigh of white guilt, and then everyone feels better, and then they drive downtown in their Saabs and buy sweaters." At the end of the play, however, the dean admits that she also has racist thoughts. *Spinning into Butter* is about political correctness. "While the concept of political correctness has made us more sensitive to how we perceive each other," Gilman says, "there's also a danger that the rhetoric will be allowed to mask some of our really angry feelings. People are now often afraid to articulate what they actually feel about each other."

Like most playwrights, Gilman was inspired by events in her own life. Born in Alabama, she did her undergrad work in Vermont at a school with few black students. "People I didn't know would hear I was from Alabama and come knocking on my door and say: 'Tell me about racism in the south.' I'd say: 'Tell me about racism in the North.' It was as though they didn't think racism was their problem." Citing a survey of Americans in which 80 percent said they knew a racist but only 5 percent admitted to being racist, Gilman said, "The figures just didn't add up. Someone wasn't being honest."

Gilman has gone on to write other important plays including *Boy Gets Girl* (2000), a play about a blind date who turns into a stalker; *The Sweetest Swing in Baseball* (2004), the story of a celebrated artist who adopts the persona of the troubled baseball legend Darryl Strawberry; and an adaptation of Ibsen's *A Doll's House* (2005).

© Courtesy Magic Theatre, San Francisco

Playwright Rebecca Gilman

Characters in Action

Playwrights love to study people. As a matter of fact, all plays are about human beings and their emotions and actions. Even children's plays about lions, tigers, or bears or the Broadway musical *Cats* are not about animals but about human emotions and thoughts imposed upon animal characters. Playwrights build all their characters from what they know about people via their own experience or through observation and intuition. A playwright's ability to write good characters is based on an ability to examine and understand people's motivations and emotions. For this reason, playwrights often write about people they know and understand, including themselves.

Yet not all characters are good material for the stage. Stage characters are different from those written for novels, poems, or short stories because they must be able to express themselves and take action. For thousands of years playwrights have used the word *action* to define character and story. In a broad sense, **action** means simply "a thing that is done." Actions are the characters' deeds, their responses to circumstances, which in turn affect the course of the story. In other words, characters in plays come to life not when they *feel* and *think* but when they *say* and *do*.

© Carol Rosegg

Stage characters, such as Sophocles' Oedipus, are different from ordinary people in that they are willing to take action even at the risk of dire consequences. In this 2001 production, Avery Brooks played the doomed Oedipus, and Aleah Windham and Mercedez Tashamba Mitchell played his daughters Ismene and Antigone. Directed by Michael Kahn, the Shakespeare Theatre, Washington, DC.

In real life, most people rarely take action. We receive an unjust parking ticket and we pay it rather than fight it in court; our boss treats us unfairly and we bear it rather than file a complaint; a huge corporation or the government cheats us and we accept it rather than deal with the red tape. Most people in real life would make horrible characters in a play because dramatic characters must be willing to take action. Romeo must be willing to endanger his life to proclaim his love; Oedipus must be willing to seek the king's killer even though there may be dire consequences; and Lena (Mama) Younger in *A Raisin in the Sun* must be willing to take a stand to change her family's lives. If these characters were not willing to take action, there would be no story and no play. Once playwrights know the action, they must next find what is standing in the characters' way, for every play is full of roadblocks and obstacles called *conflict*.

Conflict as Catalyst

Unfortunately, conflict is one of the constants of human existence. Hardly a day goes by that we are not involved in some major or minor conflict with ourselves or each other; this is true for individuals, families, societies, and nations. Historians Will and Ariel Durant write in their book *The Lessons of History* (1968) that in the last 3,420 or so years of recorded history, only 268 have seen no war. And in all those thousands of years, there has never been *one single day* without conflicts among individuals, families, and societies. A play is essentially the history of a particular conflict. Plays are not about people who have idyllic lives; they're about people who have unfulfilled needs and desires and the obstacles or opponents preventing them from obtaining what they want. The result is conflict. It's a simple equation: desire + obstacle × lack of compromise = conflict.

Drama cannot deal with people whose wills are atrophied, who are unable to make decisions which have even temporary meaning, who adopt no conscious attitude toward events, who make no effort to control their environment.

John Howard Lawson,
American playwright, screenwriter, and author

Here are some examples:

Desire: Romeo loves Juliet and Juliet loves Romeo.
Obstacle: Their families will not allow them to see each other, let alone marry.
Reason compromise is not an option: They can't live without each other.

Desire: Oedipus wants to find the killer of the King of Thebes.
Obstacle: He is blind to his own shortcomings.
Reason compromise is not an option: A terrible plague haunts the city of Athens. Oracles have said that if the killer is not found, many more will die.

Desire: Lena Younger wants to give her family a better home.
Obstacle: The white homeowners association will not allow a black family to live in its neighborhood.
Reason compromise is not an option: If she does not move her family, they will lose their dreams and fall into depression and self-doubt.

© Donald Cooper/Photostage

"O Romeo, Romeo! wherefore art thou Romeo? / Deny thy father and refuse thy name; / Or, if thou wilt not, be but sworn my love, / And I'll no longer be a Capulet." These lines by Shakespeare give voice to Juliet's willingness to enter into the conflict that drives the story of Romeo and Juliet. *In order to drive the story forward, playwrights must use language to let audiences know what characters think, feel, want, and intend. This 2004 production featured Tom Burke as Romeo and Kananu Kirimi as Juliet. Directed by Tim Carroll, Shakespeare's Globe, London.*

Notice that the third element, the reason compromise is not an option, is what makes the story possible. The playwright can write a play because the characters are not willing to compromise and must take action. In the process, they cause conflict. Once playwrights know what the conflict is and why the characters must take action, they must write characters who express themselves with language. Language helps audiences comprehend what characters are thinking, feeling, wanting, or intending to do. Characters use language as action or to promote or enhance action. They use language to drive the story forward.

The Art of Language

Words are the playwright's paint. When mixed properly, they can glance or glaze, collide or clip to reveal the heart of a character. Yet dialogue does not begin with words; it begins with the need to talk. We talk because we want. If we want nothing, we say nothing. Even small talk about nothing in particular can be traced to our need for companionship. As infants, we cry when we want to be fed or changed. As we grow, our needs become more complicated and we learn language in order to communicate. The need for a bottle or a fresh diaper is replaced by the needs for friendship, for justice, and for protection of our ego. As we mature, our strategies to get what we want through speech become more complicated. We learn to manipulate language in order to provoke, settle scores, find love, defeat enemies, and satisfy our wants without announcing them directly. Sometimes, when our deepest wants go unfulfilled, they seep into our subconscious, coloring our speech with secondary meanings and concealed desires. Dialogue is a combination of what the character needs to say and what the character is compelled to say. It's simple communication colored by the character's environment, history, emotions, and situation. Let's look at a few of the tools playwrights use to write dialogue: subtext, listening, imagery, rhythm, tempo, and sound.

Subtext A line of dialogue has two levels: what the character says (the text) and what the character consciously or subconsciously means (the subtext). **Subtext** is the hidden meaning behind the words, the real reason a character chooses to speak. In other words, dialogue is like an iceberg; only part of the meaning can be seen above the waterline. For example, when a playwright adds subtext the simple line "I hate you" can take on any of hundreds of possible meanings, from "I love you" to "I miss you" to "I wish I were you." When King Lear speaks the famous line "Blow, winds, and crack your cheeks. Rage, blow!" he is not talking about the weather but about his own troubled life and madness. The subtext makes the line memorable.

Listening Playwrights are psychologists in that they are constantly analyzing the human character. One way to understand a character, or another person for that matter, is to understand *how* they hear, because what is said and what is heard can be very different. More often than not, people filter what they hear through their own needs, emotions, and prejudices. People ignore, misinterpret, or read special meanings into just about everything. We project our own thoughts and emotions onto other people. For example, look at a simple exchange between two people:

BETH: Honey, where's the coffee?
SHANE: In the cabinet near the fridge.
BETH: And the sugar?
SHANE: Right beside it, on the left.

This is boring dialogue because both characters hear each other perfectly and respond obviously. But look what happens when the characters hear something different from what the other is saying. In this next example, simple questions are heard but misinterpreted, adding depth and subtext to an otherwise mundane exchange.

BETH: Honey, where's the coffee?
SHANE: You don't think I know, do you?
BETH: And the sugar?
SHANE: Are you testing me?

Obviously, what Shane hears is quite different from what Beth is saying, so we learn something about Shane's psychological makeup. Playwrights know that how someone listens and responds reveals a lot about who they are and what they are thinking.

Imagery In a movie it's easy to show images. What the screen can show is almost limitless, so screenwriters love to write scenes that let the audience see all manner of things firsthand. Playwrights, on the other hand, are limited by the confined space of the stage and small budgets. So they must be more like poets and write dialogue that allows the audience to see things in the mind's eye. They do this by writing dialogue full of imagery, picture-making words that allow the audience to see into their imaginations. A classic example comes from Eugene O'Neill's *Long Day's Journey into Night* when the character Edmund recounts his days at sea.

EDMUND: I was on the Squarehead square rigger, bound for Buenos Aires. Full moon in the trades. The old hooker driving fourteen knots. I lay on the bowsprit, facing astern, with the water foaming into spume under me, the masts with every sail white in the moonlight, towering high above me. I became drunk with the beauty and singing rhythm of it, and for a moment I lost myself—actually lost my life. I was set free! I dissolved in the sea, became white sails and flying spray, became beauty and rhythm, became moonlight and the ship and the high dim-starred sky! I belonged, without past or future, within peace and unity and a wild joy, within something greater than my own life, or the life of Man, to Life itself! To God, if you want to put it that way. Then another time, on the American Line, when I was lookout on the crow's nest in the dawn watch. A calm sea, that time. Only a lazy ground swell and a slow drowsy roll of the ship. The passengers asleep and none of the crew in sight. No sound of man. Black smoke pouring from the funnels behind and beneath me. Dreaming, not keeping lookout, feeling alone, and above,

> and apart, watching the dawn creep like a painted dream over the sky and sea which slept together. Then the moment of ecstatic freedom came. The peace, the end of the quest, the last harbor, the joy of belonging to a fulfillment beyond men's lousy, pitiful, greedy fears and hopes and dreams!

If this were a scene from a movie, the scriptwriter could take us to the crow's nest and show us the flying spray and the black smoke. One shot might be enough to convey the thoughts and feelings of the character. But the playwright is limited by the stage and must verbally communicate the thoughts and images critical to the story. Shakespeare often used verbal scene-painting in which the characters describe their environment so that elaborate (and expensive) sets were unnecessary. (For more on set design, see Chapter 9.)

A play is as personal and individual a form of self-expression as a poem or a picture.

Oscar Wilde,
Irish poet and playwright

© Joan Marcus

In contrast to movies, plays create imagery with words rather than photography, special effects, or action sequences, so playwrights work hard to find the right words for each character and scene. For example, in Eugene O'Neill's classic Long Day's Journey into Night, *Edmund's monologue about his days at sea is necessarily as powerful as any movie scene. This 2003 production featured Robert Sean Leonard and Brian Dennehy. Directed by Robert Falls, Plymouth Theatre, New York.*

Rhythm, Tempo, and Sound Playwrights love the music of language; they write dialogue that has a particular rhythm, tempo, and sound. By not only choosing the character's words carefully but also adjusting the sounds, a playwright can reveal a character's feelings. For example, in Tennessee Williams's *Cat on a Hot Tin Roof* (1955), Maggie describes her sister-in-law, her rival for Big Daddy's money, as a former "Cotton Carnival Queen." The hard sound of each of the first letters gives the character a chance to show jealousy and contempt without being too obvious. Sounds are combined to create "rhythm." As in music, *rhythm* in dialogue is a variation of sounds that creates a pattern, which prompts an emotional response. The characters each have their own rhythm, which manifests itself in the dialogue. The rhythm of dialogue is much more subtle than the rhythm of poetry. It's a gentle adjusting of the lines' sounds and stresses. Given the needs of the moment, dialogue should pulsate or flow, jingle or swing, oscillate or tranquilize. To understand rhythm, look at the following line:

The right word in the right place.

Its rhythm comes from the repetition of the *r* sound juxtaposed with the soft ending word, *place.* Now compare the following lines, which have the same meaning but different rhythms:

The perfect word perfectly placed.
An accurate word in its correct location.
A proper expression placed with perfection.

Playwrights understand that how each of us speaks tells others a lot about who we are, what we believe, and how we think. They use different characteristics of speech to reveal information about characters and set the tone of a play. In his play Glengarry Glen Ross, *David Mamet uses staccato rhythms and repetition to suggest confusion, intensity, dominance, and tension. This 2005 production featured Alan Alda as Shelly Levene, the desperate salesman, and Frederick Weller as John Williamson, the office manager. Directed by Joe Mantello, Jacobs Theatre, New York.*

© Scott Landis

Rhythms and sounds convey particular *tones* and evoke particular character types. The first line, "The perfect word perfectly placed," is dominated by the percussive sound of the *p*'s but also contains the soft consonants *th* and *w*. This gives the line what some might call a comfortable sound—perhaps we see a young woman laughing in her lover's arms. "An accurate word in its correct location" is more formal and harder sounding with the *c*'s and *t*'s; it might bring to mind a business executive praising a subordinate. "A proper expression placed with perfection" is dominated by a rhythmic pattern of soft *p*'s; we might envision a retired English professor describing a favorite line of poetry. No two people talk the same way or use the same rhythms. A playwright adjusts each line so that the words reveal each character's inner rhythm.

Dialogue is also designed to be spoken at a particular speed, or *tempo*. A good line of dialogue has an internal clock that makes the tempo unmistakable to the reader or actor. For example, Shakespeare masterfully uses Leontes' tempo and rhythm to expose Leontes' true nature in *The Winter's Tale*:

> Is whispering nothing?
> Is leaning cheek to cheek? Is meeting noses?
> Kissing with inside lip? stopping the career
> Of laughter with a sigh? (a note infallible
> Of breaking honesty). Horsing foot on foot?
> Skulking in corners? Wishing clocks more swift,
> Hours minutes, noon, midnight? And all eyes
> Blind with the pin and web but theirs; theirs only
> That would unseen be wicked? Is this nothing?

Here, Shakespeare gives the usually even-tempered King Leontes a fervent, fanatical tempo as he wonders whether his wife has committed adultery. The many short, almost half-asked questions reveal thoughts tumbling out at breakneck speed, suggesting a jealous temper.

FOR MORE ON

HOW TO WRITE A PLAY

"August Wilson on playwriting: An interview," Elisabeth J. Heard, *African American Review*, Spring 2001

Plotting the Story

Playwrights are always trying to plot the stories of life. Although we often use the words *plot* and *story* interchangeably, there is a difference between the two. *Story* is everything that happens, and *plot* is how it all fits together. The plot gives the story a particular focus. For example, "the king died and the queen died" is a very basic story. But "the king died, and the queen died of grief" is plot. This example comes from novelist and critic E. M. Forster, who, in his book *Aspects of the Novel* (1927), said that *story* is the chronological sequence of events and **plot** is the causal and logical structure that connects events. A play generally has only one story but may have a main plot and a subplot or a multitude of plots. Playwrights may start developing a play with the characters and the conflict, but soon they must get down to plotting the story.

Plotting the story means finding its structure. Real life is raw and disorganized; a play structures life into a unified whole. **Plot-structure,** as it is sometimes called, is the playwright's selection of events to create a logical sequence and as a result to distill meaning from the chaos of life. Even a play written to argue that life is meaningless must be logically structured. Plotting the structure of a story is not easy because thousands of factors can change the

FOR MORE ON

PLOTTING A STORY

"Three writers on plot: Dennis Lehane, Gaffe Lynds, and Stuart Woods tell you how to create a great plot," Jillian Abbott, *The Writer*, May 2004

Genre

Playwrights often write plays of a particular genre, or type of stories. The most common genres are comedy and tragedy. Other genres include melodrama, realism, romanticism, expressionism, and absurdism. Each genre may also have subgenres. For example, a subgenre of comedy is sentimental comedy, which takes an entertaining look at the troubles of everyday people. *The Dining Room* (1982) by A. R. Gurney and *The Man Who Came to Dinner* (1939) by Moss Hart and George Kaufman are examples of sentimental comedies. Another subgenre of comedy is farce, such as *Noises Off* (1982) by Michael Frayn, in which the characters are caught in a fast-paced story and broadly satirical circumstances. Situation comedy, called "sitcom" on television, is a subgenre that takes a light look at comic situations, such as the TV show *Seinfeld* (1990–1998). Dark comedies, such as *Little Murders* (1966) by Jules Feiffer and the movie *Eternal Sunshine of the Spotless Mind* (2004), allow the audience to laugh at the bleaker or absurd side of life.

Working within a genre means obeying its rules. A playwright who sets out to write a realistic play cannot include supernatural events or dream sequences because such moments would not be realistic. Romantic plays have protagonists who set out against impossible odds simply because they know in their hearts they're right. Expressionist plays use highly stylized methods to show the characters' inner feelings rather than external realities. And absurdist plays have stories that show the world as cruel, unjust, and meaningless. In Part 3 of this book, you will learn more about the many genres and how they came into being.

Sometimes playwrights deliberately mix genres in an attempt to shock the audience, to increase irony or comic effect, or to express ideas that can't be limited to a single genre. For example, in *Macbeth* (1606) Shakespeare follows the tragic scene where Macbeth returns from killing King Duncan with a broadly comical scene by a drunken porter. By juxtaposing a serious scene with a comic scene, he creates ironic moments and powerful dramatic effects. Playwrights may also mix genres to show different points of view. For example, Arthur Miller's *Death of a Salesman* (1949) is a realistic play but switches to expressionism when it enters into the mind of the main character, Willy Loman, thus allowing the audience greater understanding of the troubled salesman.

© Chris Bennion

One of the most popular types of comedy is farce, a fast-paced story in which characters are caught up in improbable situations. Some farces are called "door-slamming farces" because the characters enter and exit so many times. One of the most famous door-slamming farces is Noises Off *by Michael Frayne, a broadly comical look at what goes on backstage during a play. This 2004 production featured Bradford Farwell, Lori Larsen, Mark Chamberlin, Bhama Roget, Michael Patten, and Suzanne Bouchard. Directed by Richard Seyd, Seattle Repertory Theatre.*

sequence of events. The character's deepest motivations must be taken into account, but the playwright must also consider believability, style, and the norms of the particular genre. **Genre** is a category of an artistic work that has a particular form, style, or subject matter. (For more on genre, see the Spotlight "Genre.") Sometimes playwrights create a unique plot-structure; at other times they use a conventional plot-structure.

| Formula Plots

Playwrights don't come up with a new plot every time they tell a story. Sometimes they depend on formula plots. A formula plot is one that follows a blueprint. Today, formula plots prevail in most big Hollywood movies and many plays. Formula is nothing new; it is, in fact, as old as humanity. In his book *The Hero with a Thousand Faces,* Joseph Campbell examines myths and storytelling throughout the ages. He found that most myths have a similar structure no matter what country, culture, or century they come from; they all follow similar formulaic plotlines. Storytellers from ancient Greece to Kenya to China to Hollywood often use the same formula. In fact, the first bedtime story you were told as a child was probably a formula story.

> The very impulse to write, I think, springs from an inner chaos crying for order, for meaning, and that meaning must be discovered in the process of writing or the work lies dead as it is finished.
>
> **Arthur Miller,**
> *American playwright*

To study formula, let's compare the structures of several plays and movies:

- *Marvin's Room* (1992), a play written by Scott McPherson, about estranged sisters, Bessie and Lee, who attempt to heal old wounds when they discover that Bessie has been diagnosed with cancer; the movie version starred Diane Keaton, Meryl Streep, and Leonardo DiCaprio.
- *A Raisin in the Sun* (1959), an award-winning play written by Lorraine Hansberry, which chronicles the struggles of an African American family's fight against poverty and segregation; the most famous movie version starred Sidney Poitier in 1961.
- *Romeo and Juliet* (ca. 1595), the play written by William Shakespeare four hundred years ago, is a classic story of forbidden love.

© Mary Evans Picture Library

A melodrama is an endlessly popular type of story that depends heavily on a formula plot. Many plays, movies, and TV shows follow a melodramatic structure. Examples are prime-time TV soap operas such as The OC *and* Desperate Housewives *and movies such as* Mulan, Terms of Endearment, *and even* Mission Impossible. *Dating from the early nineteenth century, melodramas typically feature over-the-top theatricality and villainous antagonists.*

- *Oedipus Rex* (ca. 431 BCE), a play written by Sophocles in Greece 2,400 years ago about a king who kills his father and mistakenly marries his mother.
- *Star Wars* (1977), the modern sci-fi adventure movie written and directed by George Lucas.

As unlikely as it may seem, these stories share a similar formulaic structure, just as a grand cathedral and a plain box-like office building can share the same skeletal design. First we will identify the basic structural elements and then use a grid to show how each of these works follows the formula.

The basic sections of a formula plot are *beginning, middle,* and *end.* By pinpointing the moment one section of the story ends and the next begins and by defining the components of each section, we can discover the mechanics of a formula plot.

In the Beginning

In the beginning of most plays, the playwright sets up the characters and the basic situation, which includes the time and location, character relationships, and some exposition. **Exposition,** sometimes called **back story,** lets the audience in on what happened to the characters before the play began and what happens between the scenes and offstage. For example, if two characters talk about what happened the night before, that's exposition.

At the beginning of a play, the playwright also introduces the protagonist and antagonist. The **protagonist** is the central character who pushes forward the action of the play. The protagonist can be a hero or a severely flawed soul as long as the audience can identify with, care for, and even root for him or her. The **antagonist** is what the ancient Greeks called the "opposer of action." It's the adversary who stands in the way of the protagonist's goals. An

© David Allen/Courtesy Berkeley Repertory Theatre

The People's Temple *(2005) is about the "Jonestown massacre" of 1978, the mass suicide of over 900 followers of the charismatic preacher Jim Jones. Jones's congregation had followed him to a remote corner of South America, where they hoped to build a utopian community. In this play, the event is the opportunity to create a new world, the disturbance is the social inequity experienced by group members in the United States, and the point of attack is the decision to move to Guyana. This 2005 production featured John McAdams as Jim Jones. Written by Leigh Fondakowski with Greg Pierotti, Stephen Waugh, and Margo Hall. Directed by Leigh Fondakowski, Berkeley Repertory Theatre.*

antagonist may be a one-dimensional villain, a complex character, an element of nature such as a storm or a huge whale, or even an aspect of the protagonist's own character such as alcoholism or self-doubt.

This information about setting and characters is conveyed through the structural components of the beginning of a formula plot: event, disturbance, point of attack, and major dramatic question. (See Table 6.1).

Event Most plays begin with an **event,** an unusual incident, a special occasion, or a crisis in the characters' lives. This unique moment could be a wedding, a funeral, a homecoming, or preparation for a party. With the event, the playwright draws the audience into the play.

Disturbance At the beginning of a play, the basic situation often has equilibrium. In other words, the lives of the characters have achieved a certain stasis, or balance—a balance that must be disturbed if there is to be conflict. The **disturbance** is an inciting incident that upsets the balance and gets the action rolling by creating an opportunity for conflict between protagonists and antagonists.

TABLE 6.1: The beginning of a formula plot

Play	Event	Disturbance	Point of attack (decision)
Marvin's Room	Bessie goes to the doctor because she's not been feeling well.	Bessie discovers she has leukemia.	Bessie decides to communicate with her sister, to whom she hasn't spoken in years.
A Raisin in the Sun	The poor African American family is excited about a large check that's to arrive in the mail.	The check for $10,000 arrives.	Mama decides to trust her son Walter Lee to manage the money.
Romeo and Juliet	Young men from the warring Capulet and Montague families engage in a street brawl.	Romeo, of the house of Montague, and Juliet, of the house of Capulet, fall in love, despite their families' feud.	Romeo and Juliet decide to marry, despite the obstacles they face.
Oedipus Rex	The citizens of Thebes gather at the palace of Oedipus.	Oedipus learns that the plague upon his city will not end until the murderer of King Laius is found and punished.	Oedipus decides to investigate the crime, find the guilty party, and punish him.
Star Wars	Luke Skywalker meets the Jedi master Obi-Wan Kenobi.	Luke's family is killed.	Luke decides to join Obi-Wan, become a Jedi knight, and fight for good.

Point of Attack The disturbance causes the situation to deteriorate to the point where the protagonist must make a major decision that will result in conflict. This moment is called the **point of attack.** It is the moment in the plot when the fuse is lit. This decision defines what the play is about; it states the protagonist's goal. It's the core action of the play, sometimes called the *through line,* for at that moment we know what the play is about.

The disturbance and the point of attack cause a **major dramatic question,** sometimes called MDQ. This is the hook that keeps people in the theatre for two hours because they want to know the answers. It is the major dramatic question, not the theme of the play, that causes curiosity and suspense. For example, if the major dramatic question in *Romeo and Juliet* is "Will love triumph over hate?" then the theme would be a broader statement about the nature of love.

In the Middle

The middle of a formula play consists of conflict and crisis. Until the final climax, there's a string of conflicts or crises. The characters and the story are in a constant state of flux. This instability is governed by **rising action,** which

TABLE 6.2: The middle of a formula plot

Play	Conflict, crises, and complications	Dark moment
Marvin's Room	Bessie must convince her sister, Lee, to stay. She must convince Lee's son, Hank, to have a bone marrow test.	Hank says he won't help Bessie by giving her a bone marrow transplant. He runs away.
A Raisin in the Sun	Walter Lee discovers that his friend is really a con man and has run off with his money.	Walter Lee falls into a deep depression. He thinks that the only way out is to sell his mother's new house back to Karl Lindner, the white homeowners' association representative.
Romeo and Juliet	Tybalt, Juliet's beloved cousin, challenges Romeo to a fight, but Romeo refuses to fight back—until Tybalt kills Romeo's friend. (Tybalt is now Romeo's kin because Romeo and Juliet have secretly married.)	Romeo kills Tybalt and is banished from the city.
Oedipus Rex	Oedipus accuses Creon of being guilty, but he begins to suspect himself.	Oedipus learns that he is in fact the murderer of King Laius.
Star Wars	Luke must join forces with the less-than-trustworthy Han Solo; they are caught by the evil Death Star and wind up facing death again and again, such as when they are nearly crushed by an enormous garbage compactor.	Han Solo refuses to help. As part of the Republic's fighting force, Luke attacks the Death Star. All his fellow fighters are killed. The evil Darth Vader is about to kill Luke.

means that each conflict, crisis, and complication is more dramatic and more serious than the ones before. In other words, the middle of a play follows *the path of most resistance.* Any moments of apparent success always lead to an even greater undoing. As film director Alfred Hitchcock said, "Drama is life with the dull parts left out." The components of the middle are conflicts, crises, and complications, and the dark moment. (See Table 6.2).

Conflicts, Crises, and Complications The middle of a formula play is full of conflicts, crises, and complications, which are the hurdles that the protagonist must clear to achieve the goal. *Conflict* is the struggle of opposing forces in the play; *crises* are events that make it necessary for the characters to take action; and *complications* are roadblocks that stand in the way of success. Conflicts, crises, and complications are what make a story interesting, for no one wants to see a play about what UCLA writing professor Richard Walter calls "the village of the happy people."

The Dark Moment The middle of a formula play ends with the **dark moment,** when the protagonist fails for internal or external reasons, the quest collapses, and the goal seems unattainable.

Where It All Ends

The end of a formula play is usually the shortest part. Here, the playwright adds up the events and comes to some sort of conclusion. Although the ending may not have been predictable at the beginning, by the end, in retrospect, it must appear to have been inevitable. The components of the end are enlightenment, climax, and denouement. (See Table 6.3).

© Warner Brothers/Photofest

In this scene from the 1966 movie version of Edward Albee's Who's Afraid of Virginia Woolf? Martha (Elizabeth Taylor) falls apart as George (Richard Burton), Nick (George Segal), and Honey (Sandy Dennis) respond, respectively, with derision, concern, and shock. George and Martha fight constantly and bitterly throughout the play. Yet in the end, it is the "perfect" young couple, Nick and Honey, who contemplate ending their marriage. Unexpectedly but perhaps inevitably, the cynical and burned-out George and Martha remain together and still in love.

Enlightenment **Enlightenment** occurs when the protagonist comes to understand how to defeat the antagonist. Enlightenment can come in many forms: The protagonist may join forces with someone; a revelation may shed light on the problem; or the protagonist, after falling into an emotional abyss, may now see the error of his or her ways. The enlightenment is often closely tied to the theme of the play, because the manner, the cause, and the type of enlightenment often reveal the playwright's philosophy.

Climax Enlightened, the protagonist is ready to defeat the antagonist. For the first time the protagonist is able to resolve the conflict with the antagonist. The **climax** is the point of the greatest dramatic tension in the play, the moment the antagonist is defeated. The climax doesn't have to be violent or horrible. It can be quiet, even subtle. Whatever its quality, the climax must be a direct result of the protagonist's actions.

TABLE 6.3: The end of a formula plot

Play	Enlightenment	Climax	Denouement
Marvin's Room	Hank returns home and agrees to the bone marrow transplant.	Bessie learns that Hank's bone marrow doesn't match hers. He can't save her life.	The family is reunited. Bessie discovers that she has been lucky because she's had so much love in her life.
A Raisin in the Sun	Walter Lee realizes his family's pride is more important than the money.	Walter Lee throws Karl Lindner, the spokesman for the white community, out of his house.	The family moves out of their flat and into the better neighborhood. There are still hard times ahead, but they are ready.
Romeo and Juliet	Friar Laurence mixes a potion that causes Juliet to fall into a deep sleep. Her parents, thinking she's dead, transport her to the family tomb, where Romeo goes to save her.	Thinking his love dead, Romeo commits suicide. Juliet awakens and, finding her lover dead, also takes her life.	The grief-stricken Montagues and Capulets promise to end their long feud.
Oedipus Rex	Oedipus is proved to be the killer.	Oedipus blinds himself as punishment.	Oedipus is exiled, thus freeing the city of the plague.
Star Wars	Han Solo comes to Luke's rescue.	In another attack on the Death Star, Luke feels the Force and is able to blow the Death Star to pieces.	Princess Leia rewards Luke and Han Solo for their service and bravery.

Denouement The **denouement** is the final outcome of the play, a short final scene that allows the audience to appreciate that the protagonist, because of the preceding events, has learned some great or humble lesson. The scene also often hints at the future for the characters, as balance returns. This new balance enables the protagonist to comprehend why he or she suffered and take charge of or accept destiny. The denouement also allows audience members to feel catharsis, or purging of emotions. They may leave the theatre believing, if only for a moment, that someday their lives too might include a moment of understanding, forgiveness, or triumph.

How Many Acts? How Many Intermissions?

Modern plays can be anywhere from a few seconds to many hours long. Most long plays are divided into sections called *acts,* which are separated by short breaks called *intermissions.* The practice of taking an intermission originated about four hundred years ago during the Italian Renaissance, when indoor theatres were introduced. At the time, theatres were lit with candles; performances had to be halted at regular intervals so that the spent candles could be replaced and lit. For most plays the candles had to be replaced four times, so plays were divided into five acts. When you read a Shakespeare play, you'll notice that they have five acts. Interestingly, the division into acts was added after Shakespeare's day—his plays were performed outdoors during the daytime, so he included no intermissions. Later, as candle technology improved, four-act plays with three intermissions became the norm. Today, indoor theatres are no longer lit by candles, but most long plays still have at least one intermission as a relic of the Italian Renaissance and a chance for audience members to stretch their legs. Most plays today are staged in one of the following formats:

Three-act full-length play: The three-act format is not as common today as it was fifty years ago. The double intermission makes the play longer and more formal. Michael Frayn's *Noises Off* (1982) is an example of a contemporary three-act play.

Two-act full-length play: This is the most common way to divide a full-length play. The intermission is generally taken just after the middle of the story. Most modern plays, such as Caryl Churchill's *Top Girls* (1982), follow this format. However, when directors stage older plays, they often break for only one intermission. For example, today Shakespeare's plays are often staged as two-act plays.

Full-length one-act play: There is no intermission in this type of play, so the beginning, middle, and end flow without interruption, much like a movie. Because people cannot sit for too long without a break, full-length one-act plays are generally shorter than two- or three-act full-length plays (usually between 1 hour 20 minutes and a maximum of 1 hour 35 minutes). *Art* (1996) by Yasmina Reza is an example of a full-length one-act.

Short one-act plays: These plays can be anywhere from several seconds to about an hour long. Often, several short one-acts are produced on a single night with an intermission between each play. Some playwrights even write several short one-act plays as *companion pieces,* designed to be performed on the same night. By doing this, the playwright doesn't have to share the evening with other short one-acts. Companion pieces can have related or unrelated themes and stories. Examples of related one-acts are *Lone Star* (1979) and *Laundry & Bourbon* (1980) by James McLure. Examples of unrelated one-acts are Christopher Durang's *Sister Mary Ignatius Explains It All for You* (1979) and *The Actor's Nightmare* (1981).

Ten-minute plays: Ten-minute plays are a relatively new format and are growing in popularity. Theatres that produce these tiny plays will stage as many as ten in one evening. Often there is no formal intermission between ten-minute plays, but there may be a short pause while the set is changed. The Actors Theatre of Louisville, a major regional theater, is often credited with pioneering this format as a way to introduce new voices in playwriting during their new-play festival each year.

FOR MORE ON
FORMULA
"Is there a right way to write?" Michael Lazan, *Back Stage*, July 20, 2001

Although these works have different characters and stories, they all follow the same basic formulaic structure. The fundamental elements—event; disturbance; point of attack; major dramatic question; conflict, crisis, and complications; dark moment; enlightenment; climax; and denouement—all occur in exactly the same order. This formula can be used in full-length plays or ten-minute plays (see the Spotlight "How Many Acts? How Many Intermissions?") and in big Hollywood action-adventure flicks or small independent films. In fact, formula storytelling is so common that there are even software programs such as *Script Wizard* and *Plots Unlimited* to help writers build formulaic stories. But not all plays or Hollywood movies follow the formula. Sometimes playwrights use nonformulaic structures.

Plots outside the Formula

When playwrights or screenwriters abandon formula, they allow the story to grow naturally from the characters' actions, motivations, and needs. Writers who abandon formula are often trying to look at life the way it *is*, or as they perceive it, rather than trying to fit it into a standard structure. Many writers who create character-driven stories believe that formula plots do the audience a disservice because they don't require them to confront the chaotic and ineffectual parts of life. In real life we seldom defeat our antagonists, confront our problems, risk it all, refuse to compromise, or have enlightening experiences.

When playwrights abandon formula, they allow stories to grow naturally from the characters, often presenting a "slice of life." Marsha Norman's Pulitzer Prize–winning play 'night, Mother *is one such nonformulaic play. This 2004 revival starred Brenda Blethyn and Edie Falco. Directed by Michael Mayer, Royale Theatre, New York.*

© Joan Marcus

A good example of a nonformulaic movie is Quentin Tarantino's *Pulp Fiction* (1994), starring John Travolta and Samuel L. Jackson, which cleverly interweaves the stories of several characters involved in varying degrees of criminal behavior. This movie is unique in the highly fragmented telling of its stories, whose ties are revealed only at the end. An example of a nonformulaic play is Marsha Norman's Pulitzer Prize–winning *'night, Mother* (1982). It is about a woman, Jessie, who explains to her mother, Thelma, why she's decided to kill herself as she goes through the house tying up the loose ends of her life. The play has no clear-cut protagonist or antagonist nor is there an opening event or disturbance. Jessie's decision was made before the play begins and not as a reaction to any event that happens on stage. There is a great deal of crisis and conflict as Thelma tries to talk Jessie out of her decision, but there are few complications and nothing makes Jessie reconsider. The play ends at the point of its greatest dramatic tension; there is no denouement.

Russian playwright Anton Chekhov neatly alluded to the power of nonformulaic plays when he said, "Let everything on the stage be just as complicated and at the same time just as simple as it is in life. People eat their dinner, just eat their dinner, and all the time their happiness is being established or their lives are being broken up." When you attend a nonformulaic play, expect the playwright to take you on a journey that, just like real life, is unpredictable.

Existentialist playwrights are famous for their adherence to nontraditional plot structures. Samuel Beckett's Waiting for Godot *(1953) consists of two clownlike tramps waiting on a barren plain for a mysterious character who never comes. In this funny and disturbing existentialist classic, Vladimir and Estragon are determined* not *to take action. As a result, they never move toward enlightenment. This 1991 production featured Adrian Edmondson and Rik Mayall, Queen's Theatre, London.*

© Robbie Jack/Corbis

> We're one of the last handmade art forms. There's no fast way to make plays. It takes just as long and is just as hard as it was a thousand years ago.
>
> ***Steven Dietz,***
> *American playwright*

Curtain Call

Playwrights are philosophers, psychologists, poets, and storytellers all rolled into one. They write because they have a deep desire to tell stories that change or entertain the world. They are often solitary people who search their life experiences for interesting stories and characters with the hope that they reveal a bit of truth about human nature. They are also opinionated and want to express themselves. So great is their need to communicate their thoughts about how life is or should be that they often accept low pay in order to find an audience. But in return for their low pay and hard work, they can create worlds and can try to find truths about our relationships and our problems as well as our successes. An old saying in the theatre is "Playwrights write to get well." If they are well, so is the world.

FOR MORE ON

THE PROCESS OF WRITING A PLAY

"I ain't sorry for nothin' I done: August Wilson's process of playwriting," Eugene Nesmith, *American Theatre,* April 1999

Summary

The playwright is the artist who conceives the theme, characters, conflict, dialogue, and plot of a play. So important to the theatre are playwrights that they are often called the primary artist. Yet playwrights are often not a part of the theatre ensemble; in fact, most members of an ensemble never meet the playwright whose play they are producing. Playwrights often have trouble making a living because they are self-employed artists. They can join a union that will champion their rights, but because theirs is an open-shop union, they cannot strike to negotiate better compensation. However, because they own the copyright for their work, they are able to control how their plays are presented and they get top billing in the program. A playwright's life may be difficult, but they know the joy that lies at the heart of sole authorship and find great satisfaction in communicating their ideas without alteration.

In a sense, playwriting is a very limited form of writing. Plays consist only of dialogue, stage directions, and parentheticals. But playwrights do have many tools with which to construct a play, including theme, character, conflict, language, and plot. With these tools, playwrights can create stories of dramatic power, full of action and insight.

Playwrights may create unique plots or use formula plots, which are based on myths and stories that have been told for centuries. The basic elements of a formula plot are event; disturbance; point of attack; major dramatic question; conflicts, crises, and complications; dark moment; enlightenment; climax; and denouement. When playwrights create their own structures, the plot grows naturally from the characters' motivations and needs, not from a formula's predetermined requirements.

THE ART OF THEATRE ONLINE

Use the *Art of Theatre* website at **http://communication.wadsworth.com/downs1** for quick access to the electronic study resources that accompany this chapter, including a digital glossary, a link to InfoTrac College Edition that you can use to find the For More On . . . InfoTrac College Edition readings listed below, a list of further reading, and a chapter quiz. When you get to the *Art of Theatre* homepage, click on the cover of the book you are using and you will be redirected to the website for your book. Then click on "Student Book Companion Site" in the Resource box, pick a chapter from the pull-down menu at the top of the page, and select an option from the Chapter Resources menu. The *Art of Theatre* website also includes links to interesting and informative theatre websites. Just click on the Theatre on the Web link in the Book Resources menu. The links to these websites are maintained and updated as needed.

Key Terms

action / 139
antagonist / 148
back story / 148
climax / 152
closed-shop union / 134
dark moment / 151
denouement / 153
dialogue / 137
disturbance / 149
Dramatists Guild of America (DGA) / 135
enlightenment / 152
event / 149
exposition / 148
genre / 147
major dramatic question (MDQ) / 150
open-shop union / 135
parenthetical / 137
plot / 145
plot-structure / 145
point of attack / 150
protagonist / 148
rising action / 150
stage directions / 137
subtext / 141
theme / 137
Writers Guild of America (WGA) / 135

For More On . . .

Infotrac College Edition Readings

http://www.infoTrac-college.com

Playwrights working in other fields / 136
"Not-so-simple Sara: Sara Finney-Johnson may have made a name writing for TV, but she feels her playwriting brings her even greater opportunities"

How to write a play / 145
"August Wilson on playwriting: An interview"

Plotting a story / 145
"Three writers on plot: Dennis Lehane, Gaffe Lynds, and Stuart Woods tell you how to create a great plot"

Formula / 154
"Is there a right way to write?"

The process of writing a play / 156
"I ain't sorry for nothin' I done: August Wilson's process of playwriting"

7 THE ART OF ACTING

The actor is perhaps the most romantic role in the theatre. On the opening night of a new play, the playwright goes unnoticed, nervously pacing the lobby; the director sits unseen in the audience; and backstage dozens of stagehands labor incognito. Unlike these "offstage" members of the theatre ensemble, the actor takes center stage on opening night and is *the play. Who among us hasn't dreamed of being an actor or a movie star? It would be a charmed life, speaking great speeches, commanding the attention of admiring audiences, and winning critics' hearts—in fact even actors dream of such a life. Yet for all its rewards, acting is hard work. The applause comes only after months of rehearsal and years of training. And actors rarely land a role before they have failed tens of dozens of auditions and struggled for months if not years with little or no income. (See the Spotlight box "The Life of an Actor: Don Cheadle.")*

© Donald Cooper/Photostage

◀ ***On preceding page:*** Festen, *by David Eldridge, adapted from a film and a play by Thomas Vinterberg, Mogens Rukov, and Bo hr. Hansen, featuring Jane Asher (standing) and Andrew Maud (far right). (The inset features Luke Mably, Rory Kinnear and Michael Thomas.) Directed by Rufus Norris, Almeida Theatre, London, 2004. This play is about a son who decides to tell a dark family secret at his father's 60th birthday party.*

In this chapter, we will examine the training and life of actors. We'll also look at the techniques actors use to analyze and play characters, especially the techniques that apply to everyday life as well the stage. Basically, acting is performing a part, something we all do. As Shakespeare said, "All the world's a stage and all the men and women merely players." You may never direct or write a play, but at some point in your life you'll need to play a part.

| Training to Be an Actor

Some people just have a natural talent for acting. They have the charisma and stage presence that make them interesting to watch. They can even make the art of acting appear effortless. However, good acting on stage or in film or television requires a lot of training. Yet for most of theatre's history there were no acting schools. The only way to learn acting was by becoming an apprentice at a theatre. Apprentices helped out backstage and sometimes played what are jokingly called "spear-carrier roles." These are the small roles such as servants, attendants, or soldiers and seldom have any lines. After years of service to a theatre, if the apprentice had proven himself, he might be allowed to take a larger role. Today, actors in the United States and Canada usually start their training in a conservatory, university, or college. Undergraduates can earn a BFA (Bachelor of Fine Arts) in acting, and many graduate schools offer an MFA (Master of Fine Arts) in acting. An MFA in acting takes two to three years and includes intense training in voice, dialects, movement, singing, dance, auditioning, characterization, theatre history, dramatic literature, acting styles, and much more. BFAs and MFAs are also available in directing, design, playwriting, and other theatre arts.

FOR MORE ON

THEATRE TRAINING IN COLLEGE

"Theatre training at colleges and universities," *Back Stage,* April 14, 2005

FOR MORE ON

ACTING FOR THE CAMERA VERSUS ACTING ON STAGE

"Theatre in a town of cineplexes," Robert Hofler, *Back Stage,* August 20, 1993

Once an actor leaves academia, it takes determination, imagination, and most of all stamina to live the actor's life, but it is seldom the end of the training. When actors are not struggling to find an acting job or working a second job to make ends meet, they are often taking classes to improve their body, voice, and mind—what actors call their "instruments."

Training the Body

Actors, like athletes and dancers, train for years in order to learn greater physical control. This training can include dance, martial arts, and yoga to enhance movement and relaxation; gymnastics, fencing, and stage combat to prepare for realistic-looking fight scenes; and even circus-arts training such as clowning and juggling to prepare for physically demanding roles in broad comedies. They also learn to reduce body tension as they focus on the physical characteristics, mannerisms, and body language of a character or of a particular style of acting.

Training the Voice

An actor's vocal training can be divided into two broad categories: breathing and speaking. At its most basic, the act of breathing simply ensures an adequate supply of oxygen to the blood. But actors must learn to allow the body to breathe in the most tension-filled moments. No matter what is happening on the stage, the actor must know how to permit the body's air pressure to support the voice so that it can be heard at the far corners of the theatre. To do this without amplification takes training—years of rigorous exercises and techniques designed to allow speech without rigid shoulders, braced knees, a tense back, or any of the other posture problems that can make non-actors appear ill at ease when they speak in front of crowds.

> Acting is simply my way of investigating human nature and having fun at the same time.
>
> **Meryl Streep,**
> *American stage and screen actor*

The Life of an Actor: Don Cheadle

Don Cheadle is perhaps best known for his film performances, including *Hotel Rwanda* (which earned him an Oscar nomination), *Devil in a Blue Dress, Hamburger Hill, Volcano, Boogie Nights, Bulworth, Swordfish, Ocean's Eleven, The United States of Leland,* and the all-digital *Manic.* He also has won several Emmy nominations for his television performances, including one for his portrayal of Sammy Davis, Jr., in HBO's *The Rat Pack.* But Cheadle started in the theatre and still acts on stage.

He was bitten by the acting bug in the fifth grade when he played Templeton the Rat in the children's play *Charlotte's Web.* He went on to study acting at the prestigious California Institute of the Arts. "I loved Cal Arts," said Cheadle. "I knew I would be acting all the time there. You might not get the part you want, but you know you're going to be in twenty-four plays no matter what. Then you get out of school and you get five hundred noes to one yes." One of his first roles after acting school was that of Horatio in *Hamlet,* which was staged in an empty Hollywood parking lot. "We did it on skid row—real guerrilla theater," Cheadle recalled. "It was amazing: We'd look out into the audience and see homeless people saying the words with us."

Soon he became an accomplished stage actor, with roles in such plays as *Leon, Lena and Lenz* at the Guthrie Theater in Minneapolis, *Cymbeline* at The New York Shakespeare Festival, and *'Tis a Pity She's a Whore* at Chicago's Goodman Theater. His most famous role was that of Booth in *Topdog/Underdog* at New York's Public Theater. Suzan-Lori Parks's Pulitzer Prize–winning play *Topdog/Underdog* is a comic drama about two brothers who share a claustrophobic one-room apartment in New York. Named Lincoln and Booth by their father as a joke, they were abandoned by their parents at a young age. The older brother is a hustler and card shark who works at a local arcade as a Lincoln impersonator. Cheadle played Booth, the younger brother who desperately wants Lincoln to teach him how to play three-card monte. Opposites by nature but similar by birthright, the two brothers want a better life but disagree on how to get there.

The immediacy of the stage has always attracted Cheadle. "Plays are so wonderful. There's so much latitude, I think, with that great fourth wall and we're all in here together and people suspend their disbelief. That's one of the troubles with the movies; people are not using their imagination as much."

© Michal Daniel

Don Cheadle as Booth in Suzan-Lori Park's Topdog/Underdog. *Directed by George C. Wolfe, Public Theater, New York, 2002.*

© Michal Daniel

Meryl Streep, who began voice lessons at the age of 12 and continued her training at Yale's School of Drama, is known for her ability to take on almost any accent and apply it convincingly in her film and stage roles. Here she plays the actress Arkadina in Chekhov's The Seagull *in a 2001 production at the Delacorte Theater, Central Park, New York. New version by Tom Stoppard. Directed by Mike Nichols.*

Like singers, actors take years of voice training in order to learn to control their pitch, volume, and resonance. They must also learn to project their voices night after night without becoming hoarse. In addition, actors may learn a variety of dialects so that they can be cast as a character who speaks with a French, Italian, Southern, or other accent on a moment's notice. In order to learn an accent and to speak clearly, actors often use the **International Phonetic Alphabet (IPA).** IPA is a system for transcribing the sounds of speech; it is independent of any particular language but applicable to all languages.

With training an actor can build a flexible, dynamic, articulate voice with which to flesh out a character, focus on the sounds and images of the playwright's words, and sound natural performance after performance while being heard by thousands of people. As one famous voice teacher puts it, "It's simple; it just takes twenty years to do."

An actor lives, weeps, laughs on the stage, but as he weeps and laughs he observes his own tears and mirth. It is this double existence, this balance between life and acting that makes for art.

Konstantin Stanislavsky,
Russian acting teacher and director

Training the Mind

It takes concentration and discipline to perform in the theatre. Actors train their minds to memorize thousands of lines of dialogue in a short period of time as well as to think on their feet. They must be involved with the needs of their characters but never forget that they are acting in imaginary situations. This duality means that actors must have unwavering focus but also be aware of everything going on around them. In fact, acting may be the ultimate multitasking. In order to train their minds, actors use improvisation, game-like acting exercises, and even yoga to help build their self-confidence and ability to concentrate even in the most difficult situations.

FOR MORE ON
THE MIND, BODY, AND ACTING
"Theatrical movement and the mind-body question," Lea Logie, *Theatre Research International,* Autumn 1995

Gurus and Mentors: Acting Teachers

The need for actor training has given birth to countless acting schools and teachers who each expound particular methods for helping actors tap into their creativity and train their body, mind, and voice. Some of the most famous acting teachers are Stella Adler, Sanford Meisner, Uta Hagen, Michael Chekhov, and Lee Strasberg. Some acting teachers have created actor-training methods for the needs of their own styles of theatre; these teachers include Jerzy Grotowski, Bertolt Brecht, and Tadashi Suzuki. Almost all modern actor-training methods trace their heritage, at least in part, to one of the greatest of all acting teachers, Konstantin Stanislavsky (1863–1938). Often called the father of modern acting, Stanislavsky was the co-founder of the world-famous Moscow Art Theatre. He also wrote several books that revolutionized the world of acting, including *An Actor Prepares* (1926) and *Building a Character* (1949). Throughout his life, Stanislavsky advocated many different approaches for training actors. One of his most famous techniques taught actors to be more natural onstage by recalling their own emotions and transferring those feelings to their characters, thereby finding a detailed emotional identification with the characters they played. This individualized, psychological approach to acting became known as the **Stanislavsky system,** or **method acting.**

In January 1923, members of the Moscow Art Theatre arrived in America for a tour. By the time they left in the spring of 1924, they had changed U.S. acting forever: In their productions even the tiniest spear-carrying role was fully thought out and played as a multidimensional individual with deep motivations. Shortly thereafter, Stanislavsky's ideas about acting would revolutionize the American theatre.

American acting gurus such as Stella Adler (1902–1992) and Lee Strasberg (1899–1982) developed Stanislavsky's methods, and new theatres such as the Group Theatre and the Actors Studio, both in New York City, promoted variations of Stanislavsky's methods. Marlon Brando, James Dean, Rod Steiger, Geraldine Page, Dustin Hoffman, Jane Fonda, Robert De Niro, Paul Newman, Jack Nicholson, Christopher Walken, Gene Wilder, Anne Bancroft, and Al Pacino are some of the actors trained in Stanislavsky's methods at the Actors Studio.

Acting teacher Konstantin Stanislavsky is best known for his revolutionary approach to acting, which advocated that actors identify emotionally with their characters rather than simply playing "types."

© Bettmann/Corbis

Even Marilyn Monroe studied there when she got tired of playing the ditzy-blonde roles that had made her famous. Today, Stanislavsky's influence in the United States still predominates; nearly all actors and actor-training programs borrow from his system. (One of the few actor-training methods that does not is the one devised by Tadashi Suzuki. See the Spotlight on Diversity box "Tadashi Suzuki.")

Acting Techniques We All Can Use

> The fact is that acting is inevitable as soon as we walk out our front doors and into society.
>
> **Arthur Miller,** *American playwright*

Acting is not limited to actors. Every day we are confronted with situations that call for acting: The professor looks at us during a lecture and we stifle a yawn and feign interest; we're pulled over for speeding and try to act remorseful; we attend our cousin's wedding and heartily congratulate the bride even though we're convinced she is making a colossal mistake. Although we are told honesty is the best policy, we all learn how to act and hide our emotions at an early age—in fact, acting may even have been one of the reasons for our survival as a species. After all, human beings are woefully unprepared compared to other animals; our strength is meager, our skin thin, our eyesight below average, and our sense of smell is poor. Prehistoric hunters would have gone hungry if they had been honest with their prey. Instead, they used stealth to sneak up on a deer: They moved downwind, wore a costume made of deerskin, and acted as a member of the herd. By the time the deer knew an impostor, an actor, was in their midst, it was too late. So here we're going to look at acting techniques not only from the actor's point of view but also at how non-actors can use these techniques in everyday life.

Tadashi Suzuki

Not all modern actor-training methods trace their heritage to Stanislavsky. One exception is Tadashi Suzuki's actor-training system, which became popular in the United States in the early 1980s. Suzuki was enthralled with the traditional Japanese forms of theatre, Noh and Kabuki. Noh acting and its more popular version, Kabuki, take years of training and discipline to master. In fact, some Japanese Kabuki actors train from childhood. Others learn the art from their fathers, who learned it from their fathers in a process that goes back many generations. Some Kabuki actors in Japan are even declared "national treasures" the way important sites and structures in the United States are put on the National Register of Historic Places. (For more on Noh and Kabuki, see Chapter 10.)

Suzuki decided to form his own theatre that would embody the stamina and concentration of traditional Japanese theatre. He began training actors in techniques ranging from modern Western ballet to Indian Kathakali dancing (a traditional form of folk drama) in order to develop their ability to control their body. Suzuki said that his rigorous training was designed to temper and shape the body so that the actor can bring to the stage a "brilliant liveliness" that takes into account the "tiniest details of movement." He wanted to free the actors to express the character in every way possible.

An example of Suzuki's attention to the details of movement is his work with actors' feet. Traditional Japanese plays are performed in tabi, white divided-toe socks that put a focus on the feet and thus make them an important part of the performance. Suzuki developed complex exercises so that actors could discover how their feet could express character. He even named a chapter in his book *The Way of Acting* "The Grammar of the Feet." By putting so much attention on a part of the body that is often ignored by modern Western actors, he teaches actors that there is more to characterization than just circumstances, objectives, and character analysis. In fact, sometimes the most complex understanding of character comes when actors free their body and thus find power and control.

Courtesy Donald Keene Center of Japanese Culture, Columbia University

Acting coach Tadashi Suzuki

Changing How You Feel: Outside/In and Inside/Out

Actors have known for thousands of years the two basic methods of controlling one's emotions. These methods go by many names, but, for simplicity, we'll label them "outside/in" and "inside/out." If you change yourself physically—in other words, on the outside—you can change how you feel on the inside, and if you change how you feel on the inside, you can change what other people see. The mind and body connection is a two-way street: Change your body and you can affect your emotions; change your emotions and you can cause your body to react. For example, when you get ready to take part in a formal wedding, you clean yourself up, put on a fancy dress or tux and, as a result, feel more confident and attractive. The physical adjustments change how you feel.

© Donald Cooper/Photostage

Costumes, makeup, wigs, and masks can help actors really feel *like the characters they play. Here Alex Jennings, with Claire Price (l) and Imogen Stubbs (r), has certainly dressed the part of the pompous Lord Foppington in John Vanbrugh's* The Relapse *(1696), a Restoration comedy about marital politics. Directed by Trevor Nunn, Royal National Theatre, London, 2001.*

The same principle is true for people who have makeovers on television shows; often participants say that their new look makes them feel more alive, sexy, or in control. In fact, the purpose of makeovers is not to change people's appearance but to change how they feel—in other words, to make them *act* differently. Changing your appearance is an obvious way to change how you feel, but you can also alter how you feel by manipulating the shape of your body or by, say, changing what you hold in your hand. You feel very different cradling a bouquet of flowers than you do when you clutch a gun. Actors have been doing this for thousands of years. In 400 BCE, a Greek actor named Polus performed the title role in Sophocles's *Electra.* (Men played women's roles in ancient Greek theatre. For more on this topic see Part III.) In the play, Electra grieves the death of her brother Orestes. In her hand is an urn, which she believes contains his ashes. In order to feel the true, deep emotions of the character and give a convincing performance, Polus put the ashes of his recently deceased son in the urn and held it on stage.

You may also be able to change how you feel by making a small physical change—try it yourself. The next time you feel upset, tired, or bored, force yourself to smile. It may take a few minutes, but if you're sensitive to it, the forced smiling may make you begin to feel better. The opposite is also true. Sometime when you are feeling good, force yourself to frown. After a few minutes, your emotions may follow the physical cue and you may start feeling a little sad.

This outside/in technique can be quite useful for non-actors. For example, several years ago a newly graduated law student was going to interview with a fancy law firm in Switzerland. The first round of interviews was to be held over the phone, and then the company would fly the three final candidates to Switzerland for face-to-face interviews. The new lawyer desperately wanted the job, or at least the free trip to Switzerland. The lawyer sat there in his in tattered shorts and frayed tee shirt waiting for the phone to ring, but he didn't feel right for the job; even though he passed the bar examination, he didn't feel like a lawyer. So he pulled out his best suit, shirt, and tie. He shaved, showered, and dressed for the interview as if it were to be face-to-face. He made himself feel the part of a capable young law-school graduate. Changing himself physically brought out that part of his personality that was good enough to get the job. During the phone interview, he easily played the part of the competent young lawyer because he felt like one.

Just as changing physicality can engender a mood or feeling, changing the way you feel can alter your physicality. Sadness causes your body to collapse slightly as your shoulders curve in and your head droops. Joy brings your shoulders back and your head up. By simply producing a feeling, you may change your outward appearance. But how does one *control* feelings, or choose which feeling to express? One method is through what Stanislavsky called **emotional memory**—also known as sense memory or affective memory. The idea is to think back over a certain incident and remember it well enough to relive the accompanying emotions. This process occurs all the time in daily life; we can get so caught up in telling a story that we relive the emotions. For example, as we are telling a friend about how our significant other dumped us and get to the moment when "good-bye forever" was said, suddenly the tears start flowing again. Our memory causes us to relive the emotions accompanying the event. Acting from the inside out is no different. We have all fallen in love, felt anger, or suffered the death of someone close. These emotions, if they can be recalled and controlled, allow an actor to make genuine connections with how the character feels and responds.

> Emotional power is maybe the most valuable thing that an actor can have.
>
> **Christopher Walken,** *American stage and screen actor*

Non-actors can also make good use of this inside/out technique. Let's go back to our law school graduate who used the outside/in technique for the phone interview. A few weeks later he found himself in Switzerland awaiting the face-to-face interview. As he looked at the elegant brass and leather decor of the lobby, he was overtaken by a sense of inadequacy. He thought he wasn't good enough to work in such a fancy office. So he searched his emotional memory for a time when he felt confident and recalled his game-saving home run in college. He concentrated on the sights and smells of the ball field. He could almost see the stern look on the pitcher's face and then the fastball and hear the thwack of the bat as he connected. Rounding first, he looked up and saw the ball soar over the fence—the fans were going wild and his teammates were running out from the dugout. As he recalled the details of the event, he felt a sense of confidence come over him; soon his breathing calmed and his shoulders relaxed. During the interview, the trepidation returned a few times, but all he had to do was think "thwack!" and he felt, and therefore acted, confident. Was this job applicant lying to his future employers? No. His confident feelings were real, just as an actor's emotions can be real. He simply chose which emotions he was going to play rather than letting his emotions control him. In short, he was a good actor. By the way, he got the job.

FOR MORE ON
STANISLAVSKY'S METHOD

"The challenges of really understanding Stanislavsky's method," Ira J. Bilowit, *Back Stage*, December 21, 1990

An actor working from the outside in, concentrating on physical details, is often said to be using a **technical approach** to acting. An actor working from the inside out, finding the right memories to relive the needed emotions, is often said to be using method acting. Whichever system is used, and actors often use both, the intended result is feeling the needed emotions rather than being dominated by whatever emotions are naturally occurring. In short, acting isn't always *acting;* it is also *being.*

Acting is more than controlling emotions. It also is the ability to see ourselves in someone else's shoes. One of the highest forms of intelligence is the ability to see life from someone else's point of view. Art lets us see someone else's point of view. An actor playing a part must not only control emotions but also needs to understand life. Sometimes this means seeing life from the point of view of a character that has very different values and perceptions. Two methods actors often use to achieve this empathy are the "magic *if*" and substitution.

© Sara Krulwich/The New York Times

Finding an emotional identification with a character takes training, research, understanding, preparation, and emotional honesty. Here Natasha Richardson's expression reveals the weariness of her character, Blanche, an emotionally exhausted Southern woman in Tennessee William's A Streetcar Named Desire *(1947). This production was directed by Edward Hall, Studio 54, New York, 2005.*

Empathy and the Magic If: Sympathy Transformed

Sympathy is concern for another person, but empathy is more. **Empathy** is the ability to understand and identify with another's situation, feelings, and motives so completely that you feel you are experiencing that situation and those emotions. In other words, when you feel empathy, you're feeling yourself in the place of another. Empathy is as close as people can come to a shared experience. Many believe that actors cannot truly know a character without empathy. But this doesn't mean that actors must have experienced the death of a loved one before they can understand a character who is in mourning, or face death to understand how a terminal patient feels, or commit a murder in order to know the inner thoughts of a killer. Empathy is also possible when an actor vicariously stands in the shoes of another, builds a vivid image of the situation, and reacts.

Stanislavsky used a technique that he called the **magic *if*** to stimulate the imagination toward empathy. This technique is based on one question: "What would I do *if* I were this character in these circumstances?" The magic *if* is a springboard to the imagination; it allows actors to find similarities between themselves and the character and to explore the resulting emotions and thoughts. Of course, in order for the magic *if* to work, actors must spend many hours researching a character's motivation, situation, and back story. Empathy and the magic *if* can lead to a deep personal understanding or to a flash of tolerance that can be mined for greater insight into the character. Stanislavsky said, "We must study other people and get as close to them emotionally as we can, until sympathy for them is transformed into feelings of our own." In other words, the actor must study the character until the actor has empathy. Needless to say, here is a great lesson that many non-actors—as well as many countries, races, and cultures—could stand to learn.

All art in the theatre should be not descriptive, but evocative. Not a description, but an evocation. A bad actor describes a character; he explains it. He expounds it. A good actor evokes a character. He summons it up. He reveals it.

Robert Edmond Jones,
American theatre set designer

Substitution: It's All Yiddish to Me

Of course, no actor has the personal experience and understanding to quickly slip into every role. Occasionally, a play demands a character with which the actor has no experience or emotional bond. The solution is sometimes the actor's technique of **substitution.** When actors have little or no emotional bond with a character, they replace the character's emotions with unrelated but personal emotions of their own.

Robert Lewis tells a wonderful story about substitution in his book *Method—Or Madness.* Many years ago, an actor named Ben-Ami was in a Yiddish play in New York City. In one scene Ben-Ami's character had to attempt suicide. He stood at the edge of the stage staring into audience with a revolver to his head. During every performance, sweat would break out on his face and his eyes would seem to pop out of his head. Ben-Ami could keep the audience on the edge of their seats for well over a minute without saying a word and hardly moving, as he debated whether he should pull the trigger. Finally he would say, "Ikh ken nit!" (I can't do it!), and the audience would bring down the house with cries of relief and applause. Night after night, he created such an emotional reality that soon he became the hit of Yiddish theatre. A young actor in the play asked him how he did it, but Ben-Ami said, "It's better for people not to know. . . . It'll spoil the show." On the closing night, Ben-Ami finally told the young actor how he pulled it off—he used substitution. Here is his explanation:

> My problem with this scene was that I personally could never blow my brains out. I am just not suicidal, and I can't imagine ending my life. So I could never really know how that man was feeling, and I could never play such a person authentically. For weeks I went around trying to think of some parallel in my own life that I could draw on. What situation could I be in where, first of all, I am standing up, I am alone, I am looking straight ahead, and something I feel I must do is making me absolutely terrified, and finally that whatever it is I can't do it?. . . I finally realized that the one thing I hate worse than anything is washing in cold water. So what I'm really doing with that gun to my head is trying to get myself to step into an ice-cold shower.

Ben-Ami found an emotional parallel that worked for him, one that allowed him to play the moment and to some extent find empathy. Through the use of the empathy, the magic *if*, and substitution, it is possible to understand the emotions of another, even a character who is quite unlike yourself.

© Carol Rosegg

Occasionally, actors have the opportunity to play a character beyond their emotional knowledge and life experience. In this situation, they rely on the technique of substitution, replacing the character's emotions with unrelated emotions of their own. Here, David Morse and Mary-Louise Parker have most likely used that technique to play victim and victimizer in Paula Vogel's How I Learned to Drive *(1997), a play about the repercussions of sexual abuse.*

Confinement, Close-Ups, and Clues: Alfred Hitchcock's *Rope*

Alfred Hitchcock often based his films on books—*Rebecca, The Birds,* and *Strangers on a Train* are all examples. Fiction and film have enough in common structurally that it is usually hard to tell whether a movie is based on a book. But *Rope,* Hitchcock's 1948 film about two men who murder a friend, shove him into a trunk in their living room, and then throw a dinner party over his dead body, looks very much as if it was originally written for the theatre—and it was. The play *Rope* was written by Patrick Hamilton and was first performed at the Strand Theatre in London in 1929.

Several aspects of the movie show us that this story originated as a play. For one thing, it has few silent scenes. Dialogue is constant throughout the film, and what people say contributes much of the tension as guests talk unwittingly about the murdered man while the villains trade word games, dropping clues like breadcrumbs. But more obviously, all the action of the story takes place in one apartment in continuous time. A single location is very common in plays but is rare in film, a medium known for visual variety. In addition, Hitchcock chose to use the play's stage directions. For example, as guests arrive at the dinner party, we might expect to see at least some of the characters parking their car, ringing the doorbell, or entering the apartment. Instead, we see the characters "enter" from the side of the "stage," just as they would in a play. Why does Hitchcock choose to forgo a movie's visual freedoms and instead present

© Donald Cooper/Photostage

The dinner guests don't suspect a thing in this 1994 production of Rope. *Directed by Keith Baxter, Wyndham's, London.*

FROM STAGE TO SCREEN

Kobal Collection/Picture Desk

In Alfred Hitchcock's film version of Rope, *the murderers' former teacher, played by James Stewart, lets on that he knows what they've done.*

what is essentially a stage play on film? Because the single location and continuous time help focus the film's suspense. The camera doesn't let us see the outside world until the final scene (one of Hitchcock's most masterful endings), so we are trapped in that apartment along with the murderers—and the corpse.

Rope is filmed in just eleven shots, each three to nine minutes long, creating a suspenseful sense of real time. In each shot the camera serves almost as a witness, coming in close and focusing on clues. In the microcosm of the apartment, small details take on huge significance, and with lingering close-ups, Hitchcock repeatedly brings our attention back to a murder that is practically out in the open. These close-ups create a great tension because we know the importance of objects and actions that the unsuspecting dinner guests do not:

- They set things down on the trunk.
- The end of the rope used to strangle the murder victim dangles out of the trunk.
- Guests walk by the trunk carrying books tied with rope.
- The housekeeper methodically clears the top of the trunk while the guests talk offscreen.
- The murderers' former teacher, who begins to suspect them, holds the dead man's hat.

We ask ourselves how the guests could possibly miss the trunk in the middle of the room, the one with the dead body in it! The murderers are playing a dangerous game, and we wait, with mixed feelings of dread and delight, for them to be discovered. Hitchcock's *Rope* is a great example of how filmmakers can use the limits imposed on time and space by theatrical conventions.

Aoise Stratford
Playwright

Understanding a Character

Centuries before the invention of psychology, actors were studying people's mental states and the motivations behind their behavior; playing a convincing character requires the ability to analyze personality. One key to analyzing stage characters is to treat them as if they were real people. Understanding character can also be of great help to non-actors; compassion can make our jobs and relationships more fulfilling. One way to start analyzing a character is to make a list of the character's traits by answering a series of questions about general, physical, sociological, and psychological traits (see Table 7.1).

This list of questions could go on for pages but every single aspect of a character is too much for an actor, or a psychologist for that matter, to totally comprehend. A simpler method is to look at basic elements such as these: circumstances and objectives, public and personal sides, internal conflicts and character flaws, and motivation.

TABLE 7.1 Questions to help analyze a character

General Information	Sociological Traits
• What is the character's education? • What is the character's career or occupation? • What is the character's financial situation? • What are the character's talents? • What are the character's hobbies? • What are the character's tastes?	• What is the character's nationality? • What is the character's religion? • What is the character's class or status? • What are the character's family relationships? • What are the character's political views?
Physical Traits	**Psychological Traits**
• What is the character's age and sex? • What is the character's appearance? • What does the character wear? • What is the character's health status, including medical problems? • What are the character's mannerisms?	• What is the character's temperament? • What kind of childhood did the character have? • What are the character's hopes and ambitions? • What are the character's disappointments? • What are the character's fears and phobias? • What are the character's inhibitions? • What are the character's obsessions? • What are the character's superstitions? • What are the character's morals and philosophy of life?

Circumstances and Objectives

When trying to analyze characters, or people for that matter, a good place to start is with the circumstances of their life: their situation, their problems, and the limits life has placed on them. Actors often call this approach to character analysis the **given circumstances.** It can include broad topics such as upbringing, religion, and social standing, but it can also include what happened to the character the moment before he or she entered the stage. For example, if the character has been fighting with a spouse, that particular given circumstance will certainly affect the character's emotional state and behaviors, such as tone of voice.

Next, it is important to understand the character's objective: What does he or she desire? Because characters may desire many things during the course of a play, a good actor often singles out the most important want, or the driving force that governs the character's actions throughout the entire play. This driving force is called the character's **superobjective.** For example, the character of Hamlet has many objectives during the course of Shakespeare's great tragedy—he wants to find his father's killer, he wants justice—but his superobjective, at least according to Stanislavsky, is to find God. Knowing the superobjective and given circumstances can take you a long way to understanding a stage character, another person, or even yourself.

Fully understanding a character such as Richard III requires understanding his circumstances and objectives. What are his given circumstances? Born with a deformity that affects others' perceptions of him, he has learned to manipulate others to gain their sympathy; he is in line for the throne of England, but many are before him. What is his superobjective? He feels he deserves power—and the love that comes with it—as a reward for the bad hand that life has dealt him. This 2004 production of Shakespeare's Richard III *features Peter Dinklage. Directed by Peter DuBois, Public Theater, New York.*

© Michal Daniel

Public and Personal Images

There are two ways to view a character—or a person. One is from the public side, or what other people see. The second is from the personal side, or how we see ourselves. For example, from the outside, or the public image, a character might be described as

- Irritating
- Perfectionist
- Hypercritical
- Anxious
- Work-centered
- Domineering
- Fault-finding

You may recognize this description. It's the classic definition of an obsessive-compulsive. Here is another description:

- Fears disapproval
- Self-doubting
- Anticipates catastrophe
- Wants to be admired for ability
- Feels wounded when others don't value helpful hints
- Feels there is a right way and a wrong way
- Rarely feels support

Although this sounds completely different, it is also a description of an obsessive-compulsive, but viewed from the inside, the personal image. To develop a strong, unique character, an actor must always look from both the public and personal images. How people or characters perceive themselves and how others perceive them is seldom harmonious and often results in conflict. This discrepancy between the personal and public views happens because stage characters, like people, have limited self-awareness. To make this point, playwright Arthur Miller used the story of *Oedipus,* the ancient Greek tragedy about a king who gouges out his eyes when he discovers he has unknowingly killed his father and married his mother (for more on *Oedipus* see Part III). If Oedipus had had more self-awareness, he would have seen that "he was not really to blame for having cohabited with his mother, since neither he nor anyone else knew she was his mother. He would have decided to divorce her, provide for their children, firmly resolve to investigate the family background of his next wife, and thus deprive us of a very fine play." Because Oedipus doesn't have clear, perfect knowledge of himself, discovery, growth, and a great tragedy are all possible. Limited self-awareness often causes some sort of flaw, vice, error in judgment, or internal conflict.

FOR MORE ON

UNDERSTANDING CHARACTER

"Creating an original role: Eleven actors discuss the process," *Back Stage,* January 17, 2003

Inner Conflicts and Character Flaws

Another way to understand a character is to identify internal conflicts and character flaws. Powerful characters are often in conflict not only with others but also with themselves. This **inner conflict** can be a ghost from the past or some sort of unfinished business that is so compelling that it handicaps the character until it is confronted. In *Hamlet,* there is a literal ghost—the ghost of Hamlet's father. But Hamlet is also torn by the conflicts between his desire to seek revenge, his gentle nature, and his need to find an elusive God. A character's inner conflict can be an unresolved disagreement, a lost opportunity, a sense of inadequacy, or some other debilitating factor that preoccupies the character over the course of the play until he or she is able to put it to rest.

If this inner conflict is powerful enough to affect the character's good judgment and cause the character to make unfortunate choices, then it's a **character flaw,** sometimes called a **fatal flaw** or **tragic flaw.** This personality imperfection cripples the character and prevents him from achieving his superobjective. Knowing a character's inner conflicts and flaws, as well as the given circumstances, superobjective, and public and personal images will take you a long way to understanding one of the most defining elements of character: motivation.

© Ron Scherl

Plays are often about imperfect characters whose unfulfilled desires lead to inner conflict. In August Wilson's Fences *(1987), patriarch Troy Maxson feels he has been "fenced in" by discrimination. He once had a shot at playing major-league baseball, but now he toils at a dead-end job. He still dreams of being a ballplayer, but he is well past his prime. His broken dream colors every interaction with his family. In this photo from the original Broadway production, James Earl Jones plays Troy Maxson. Directed by Lloyd Richards, 46th Street Theatre, New York.*

Motivation: Thinking in Positives

Motivation is the reason a character takes a particular action. It is embodied in the character's conscious or subconscious personality. It can come from some dark part of the character's past or simply be the desire to do the right thing. Wherever they come from, the motivations of characters are seldom complicated; the character may be complicated and the motivation may be hidden, but once it appears, it can usually be stated in a single sentence. For example, Juliet's motivation is that she is in love with Romeo and will do anything to be with him.

The key to understanding a character's motivation is to look at it from the character's point of view. A well-drawn character is always attempting to change negatives into positives—from his or her perspective. Characters, like people, may be misguided, even totally wrong, but they seldom see their motivations or the resulting actions as negative or evil. For example, if an actor studying the character of a father who abandons his child concludes that the father is "hateful" and "uncaring," he is not doing his homework. "Hateful" and "uncaring" are negative ideas coming from an external image and lead to a shallow interpretation of the father's motivations. Instead, the actor must find the positive motivation, the character's own reasons, for doing such a terrible thing as abandoning a child. After deeper analysis, the actor may discover that the father must think his actions are best for the child—perhaps he cannot provide for the child or he sees himself as too emotionally unbalanced to care for him or her. These would be reasons for thinking that abandoning the child would be best for the child; they are examples of positive motivations. A character can commit an evil act based on a strong "positive" motive. To truly understand a character, or another human being, you must find their positive motivations. Using your own morals or values to judge a character or a person seldom leads to true understanding.

> Actors are responsible to the people we play. I don't label or judge. I just play them as honestly and expressively and creatively as I can, in the hope that people who ordinarily turn their heads in disgust instead think, "What I thought I'd feel about that guy, I don't totally feel right now."
>
> ***Philip Seymour Hoffman,***
> *American stage and screen actor*

> I think very few people are interested in the craft of acting, which is actually to demask, to reveal what it is to be human.
>
> ***Cate Blanchett,***
> *Australian stage and screen actor*

These are just a few ways that actors analyze a character in order to gain a greater understanding. Good acting is far more than simple imitation. It is the ability to understand why characters think what they think, feel what they feel, and do what they do. Only when an actor can see life from someone else's point of view can he or she play a life on stage convincingly.

The Actor's Life

Like professional sports, acting is a business and, like athletes, actors need agents to help them find jobs, promote their careers, and negotiate contracts. There are also several labor unions that fight for actors' rights, including fair wages and safe working conditions. The union that represents stage actors is the **Actors' Equity Association,** often shortened to "Actors' Equity" or simply "Equity." The **Screen Actors Guild** (SAG) represents movie and television actors, and the **American Federation of Television and Radio Artists** (AFTRA), which is affiliated with the AFL-CIO, represents talk-show hosts as well as announcers, singers, disc jockeys, newscasters, sportscasters, and even stuntpeople. Many actors join all three unions because they never know which medium their next job may come from.

An actor's life can be romantic, but most of their days are full of hard work, because finding an acting job is not easy. Whether they are looking for

© Mike Segar/Reuters/Landov

In 2000 cable advertising reportedly brought in $13.5 billion in revenue, but the actors who made those commercials received only a tiny fraction. Such inequities prompt actors' unions to fight hard to ensure that their members receive a fair share of the money made from their labor. Here, highly paid movie stars Richard Dreyfuss, Paul Newman, and Susan Sarandon support their less well-paid colleagues in a strike called by SAG-AFTRA in 2000 to demand fair wages and safe working conditions.

work on the stage or in movies, commercials, or television, the competition is fierce and paying jobs are rare. At every audition dozens if not hundreds of actors are battling for the same part. In fact, acting jobs are so scarce that Actors' Equity has created the **Equity waiver,** a loophole that allows its members to work for free in small productions. Equity-waiver productions have to meet many qualifications. For example, the theatre must be fully insured, the play cannot run for more than twelve performances, and the theatre must have fewer than one hundred seats. As a result, many Equity-waiver theatres have ninety-nine seats.

When actors are lucky enough or talented enough to land a job, it seldom lasts long. They spend a few weeks in rehearsal and then perhaps a few months acting, but they are eventually back on the streets, without a paycheck and looking for new auditions. At least stage actors have one big advantage: Unlike movie actors, they are indispensable to the art. (See the Spotlight box "Synthespians versus a 'Poor Theatre'.")

Synthespians versus a "Poor Theatre"

SPOTLIGHT

One of the first movies to use computer-generated or enhanced actors was Disney's *Tron* (1982). Today, computers make it possible for movies to convincingly re-create ancient Rome and simulate the attack on Pearl Harbor, but they can also be used to change an actor's performance. For example, in the movie *Contact,* director Robert Zemeckis wanted a long, emotional close-up of Jodie Foster gazing at the stars. But in the shot he wanted to use, there was a tiny twitch in one of Foster's eyebrows, so he had the twitch digitally eliminated. Removing a twitch is one thing, but computer animators now have the technology to create convincing digital actors called **synthespians.** Synthespians have appeared in *Spider-Man,* the *Lord of the Rings* trilogy, and *I Robot,* and they were the subject of the film *Simone.* Synthespians are really digital slaves because they will do the director's bidding without demanding a salary, coffee breaks, or creative input. "I am very troubled by it," said actor Tom Hanks. "But it's coming down, man. It's going to happen. And I'm not sure what actors can do about it."

In addition, film and television actors often have to act in synthesized scenes. With the blue-screen technique, actors perform in front of a blank blue backdrop, and digital backgrounds and characters are added in post-production. The resulting shots are so seamless that actors seem to be standing on the flight deck of an anthropomorphic spaceship or running away from fast-approaching dinosaurs. This technique has been used in any number of movies, including *Jurassic Park* (1993), *Men in Black* (1997), *Sky Captain and the World of Tomorrow* (2004), and the second *Star Wars* trilogy (1999–2005). The actors are shot against a blue screen because human skin has very little blue in it, so a computer can more easily determine where the actor ends and the background should begin. Sometimes green or orange screens are used instead, depending on the colors of an actor's skin, makeup, and costume. Blue-screen acting requires actors to react to characters and things they cannot see and to work with few, if any, props. Often the actors don't know until the film is released if the acting techniques they used really worked. Blue-screen acting is so difficult that some film schools offer classes on the subject.

There are no synthespians or blue screens in the theatre because theatre is always live. Some theatre directors and acting teachers have gone out of their way to emphasize this. One of the most famous was Jerzy Gro-

> I was told to avoid the business altogether because of the rejection. People would say to me, "Don't you want to have a normal job and a normal family?" I guess that would be good advice for some people, but I wanted to act.
>
> ***Jennifer Aniston,***
> *American screen actor*

Pursuing the Part: Perpetual Auditions

There are as many types of auditions as there are plays, theatres, and directors. A common type of audition is the **cattle call,** also known as the "open call." *Call* is theatre lingo for "audition." During a cattle call, actors are generally given only about one minute to strut their stuff. If the director is impressed, the actor's name is placed on a **callback list** and allowed to come back for a second and perhaps a third and fourth audition as each callback narrows the field of candidates. Other auditions consist of **cold readings** of a script; in other words, the actors are not given a chance to prepare. For other auditions, actors can bring prepared scenes or monologues, or they might be asked to improvise, dance, or sing. The director can take the actors through a myriad of tests to look for vocal clarity, energy, stage presence, talent, and personal chemistry. Auditions are so important that some actors take more classes on how to audition than on how to act.

towski (1933–1999), a Stanislavsky-trained actor and director who worked in Poland, the United States, and Italy. In his book *Towards a Poor Theatre* (1968), he declared that theatre should not try to compete against the visual spectacle of film. Instead, theatre should concentrate on what makes it unique—the fact that it is live. So Grotowski stripped theatre down to its essence and created bare-bones plays that had no set, few props, no makeup, no special lights, not even a stage. He called this a "poor theatre" because it had none of what he called the superfluous elements. He felt that to act without a set, costumes, makeup, or computers that eliminate twitches—what he called "clutter" and "gimmicks"—actors require years of training. He wanted the actors' performances to be so real that they would make the audience uncomfortable. And so Grotowskian actors train for years so that their body and voice are all that is needed to make great theatre.

© Warner Brothers Pictures/Photofest

Tom Hanks and his synthespian counterpart in The Polar Express *(2004).*

Perfecting the Part: Rehearsals

Once the actors are cast in a play, they begin rehearsal. Normally rehearsal lasts from three to five weeks, but there are exceptions. Rehearsals for complex or experimental plays can last much longer—Stanislavsky once rehearsed a play for nearly a year—whereas rehearsal for a simple summer-stock play might be crammed into one week. However long the rehearsal process is, actors seldom rehearse on the stage until just a few days before a play opens. Most rehearsals take place in a rehearsal hall, which is an empty room approximately the same size as the stage. In the rehearsal hall, actors must use their creative imaginations because there is no finished set. They have to use simple rehearsal furniture and props. A plain folding chair can represent a grand throne, or a simple piece of wood may stand in for a king's jeweled staff. Costumes aren't generally ready until just a few days before the play opens.

I trained as a theatre actor, and you had a bare stage and you had to pretend. One prop and you are in the middle of Eighth Avenue and traffic is just going by.

Benicio Del Toro,
American independent-film actor

Here is an approximately chronological list of the kinds of rehearsals:

- **Table work:** Some directors start rehearsals by having the cast read aloud through the play while seated around a table. After the reading, the director and actors discuss their thoughts about the characters and motivations and about the play in general. Sometimes the director invites the designers to the first table reading to make presentations about what the set, lights, and costumes will look like.
- **Blocking rehearsals:** This is a series of rehearsals during which the director and actors work out the basic movements, a process that is called "blocking."
- **General working rehearsals:** During these rehearsals the director and actors work on individual scenes and concentrate on understanding the characters' motivation, emotions, and personality.
- **Special rehearsals:** If a play has fight scenes, musical numbers, or dance numbers, or the characters have dialects, the director can call special rehearsals for each.
- **Off-book rehearsal:** During this rehearsal, the actors must have their lines memorized. It's called "off book" because the actors no longer have the script, or the "book," on stage with them.
- **Run-throughs:** During these rehearsals, the actors go through the entire play from beginning to end with as few interruptions as possible. A run-through gives the actors a feel for how the play works as a whole.
- **Tech rehearsals:** By this point, rehearsals have moved from the rehearsal hall to the stage. During tech (short for "technical") rehearsals, the lights, sounds, props, and set are added.
- **Dress rehearsals:** These are the final rehearsals, only a few days before the play opens, when the costumes and makeup are added.
- **Final dress rehearsal:** This is the last rehearsal before an audience is invited. Ideally, the play is run as if it were a real performance.

Playing the Part: Performances

After the opening night, the actors settle in for the run of the play. A short run can be just a few performances, as is often the case with smaller theatres and university and community theatres; a long run can last for months or even years as is the case in big Broadway theatres. In the professional theatre, plays are traditionally performed six nights a week. Actors may also have one or two matinee performances a week; on those days, they face the exhausting task of performing the play twice in one day. Mondays are typically **dark nights,** when the theatre is closed.

Depending on how complicated their costumes and makeup are, actors usually arrive an hour or so before the performance. Traditionally, actors enter and exit the theatre via the **stage door,** a back door located behind or to side of the theatre. They spend the time before the performance warming up their body and voice, putting on makeup, and dressing. Once the play begins, the actors wait to make their entrances in the **green room,** a small waiting room located just off the stage where the audience cannot overhear their chitchat and last-minute warm-ups. There are many theories about why it is called a green room. The most likely comes from England where, many years ago, the waiting room for the actors was often painted green because the color was thought to be soothing and help the actors relax before their entrances. Today, in spite of the name, green rooms are painted every color of the rainbow. However, they almost all have speakers so that the actors can hear what's happening on stage and the audience's reaction; some theatres also have speakers in the dressing rooms and bathrooms so that actors will never miss their cues. Some theatres even have closed-circuit television monitors so that actors waiting backstage can watch the play.

FOR MORE ON

ACTING AND THE STATE OF THE CRAFT

"Roundtable: Acting out: Top professionals with an eye on acting discuss the state of the craft," Chris Koseluk, *Hollywood Reporter*, January 5, 2002

I Curtain Call

The general public often assumes that actors are highly paid. This certainly can be true for big screen and television stars. For example, on the last season of his hit sitcom, comedian Jerry Seinfeld earned $2 million per episode, and Tom Hanks was reportedly paid over $30 million to star in the movie *Saving Private Ryan*. But these fat paychecks are the exception; the vast majority of actors take home very little money for their efforts. In fact, according to the U.S. Department of Labor, the median annual income of actors in the United States is $23,470, yet the average income of Screen Actor's Guild members is less than $5,000 a year. The explanation for the difference between these two figures is that the majority of actors do something besides acting in order to make ends meet—they are waiters, secretaries, and deliverypeople. They take jobs that allow for a flexible schedule so they can attend acting classes and go

William Missouri Downs

© Brian Seed

At left: *Moments before curtain, director Wolf Sherrill sits in the green room with nervous actors Mariah Everman, Andrew Franks-Ongoy, Keith Hull, and Brandon Taylor. Behind them, a stage manager goes over the final cues in the script. Most green rooms are located just off the stage, are plainly furnished, but are rarely painted green.* ***At right:*** *Joan Allen (front) and fellow actors review a script during a table reading.*

to auditions. They quit once they find what they really want: an acting job. It is a tough life, but actors who continue in the craft are willing to suffer while pursuing the joys of a creative life.

Summary

It may look easy, but becoming an actor takes dedication and years of training. That training usually begins at a conservatory, a university, or a college, but most actors go on to train for years after that in order to perfect their voice, body, and mind, or what they call their "instrument." The need for actor training has led to many acting schools and teachers who teach various acting systems. Most of these systems trace their heritage to the father of modern acting, Konstantin Stanislavsky, the founder of the Moscow Art Theatre and the Stanislavsky System or what is often called method acting. Stanislavsky taught his actors to recall their emotions and then transfer those feelings to their characters in order to find a detailed emotional identification with them.

Actors use many techniques that can be useful to non-actors. These include outside/in acting, or changing physically in order to change emotions, and inside/out acting, or changing emotions in order to change physically. Outside/in acting is often referred to as the technical approach. Inside/out acting is often referred to as method acting. Other techniques actors use are empathy, the magic *if,* and substitution. In order to understand the characters they play, actors study the character's physical, sociological, and psychological traits. They also examine the character's public and personal images and the character's inner conflicts, flaws, and motivation.

An actor's life can be full of auditions, rehearsals, and performance. But it is also full of unemployment because paying acting jobs are scarce. The vast majority of actors work second jobs to make ends meet. Even when they find a job, they aren't always well paid. In order to protect their interests, performers have formed three unions to help win fair wages and safe working conditions: Actors' Equity, the Screen Actors Guild (SAG), and the American Federation of Television and Radio Artists (AFTRA).

THE ART OF THEATRE ONLINE

Use the *Art of Theatre* website at **http://communication.wadsworth.com/downs1** for quick access to the electronic study resources that accompany this chapter, including a digital glossary, a link to InfoTrac College Edition that you can use to find the For More On . . . InfoTrac College Edition readings listed below, a list of further reading, and a chapter quiz. When you get to the *Art of Theatre* homepage, click on the cover of the book you are using and you will be redirected to the website for your book. Then click on "Student Book Companion Site" in the Resource box, pick a chapter from the pull-down menu at the top of the page, and select an option from the Chapter Resources menu. The *Art of Theatre* website also includes links to interesting and informative theatre websites. Just click on the Theatre on the Web link in the Book Resources menu. The links to these websites are maintained and updated as needed.

Key Terms

Actors' Equity Association / 176
American Federation of Television and Radio Artists (AFTRA) / 176
blocking rehearsals / 180
callback list / 178
cattle call / 178
character flaw / 175
cold reading / 178
dark night / 180
dress rehearsal / 180
emotional memory / 167
empathy / 168
Equity waiver / 177
fatal flaw / 175
final dress rehearsal / 180
general working rehearsals / 180
given circumstances / 173
green room / 180
inner conflict / 175
International Phonetic Alphabet (IPA) / 162
magic *if* / 168
method acting / 163
motivation / 176
off-book rehearsal / 180
run-through / 180
Screen Actors Guild (SAG) / 176
special rehearsal / 180
stage door / 180
Stanislavsky system / 163
substitution / 169
superobjective / 173
synthespian / 178
table work / 180
technical approach / 168
tech rehearsals / 180
tragic flaw / 175

For More On . . .

Infotrac College Edition Readings

http://www.infoTrac-college.com

Theatre training in college / 160
"Theatre training at colleges and universities"

Acting for the camera versus acting on stage / 160
"Theatre in a town of cineplexes"

The mind, body, and acting / 163
"Theatrical movement and the mind-body question"

Stanislavsky's method / 167
"The challenges of really understanding Stanislavsky's method"

Understanding character / 174
"Creating an original role: Eleven actors discuss the process"

Acting and the state of the craft / 181
"Roundtable: Acting out: Top professionals with an eye on acting discuss the state of the craft"

8 The Art of Directing

American playwright Tennessee Williams said that a play script is only the "shadow of a play and not even a clear shadow of it. . . . The printed script is hardly more than an architect's blueprint of a house not yet built." The ***director*** *turns the printed script, the blueprint, into a production. To do this, the director must have the artistic vision and the talent to coordinate dozens of theatre artists, technicians, and other personnel to work toward that vision with a singleness of purpose. This coordination allows a production to speak with the unique voice of an individual artist. The director also represents the audience members, because the director frames each moment of the play by deciding exactly what the audience will see. In order to turn these decisions into reality, the director must guide and persuade every member of the theatre ensemble and oversee all the artistic and technical aspects of the production. The director must synthesize the*

© Sara Krulwich/The New York Times

◀ ***On preceding page:*** Twelve Angry Men, *by Reginald Rose. Directed by Scott Ellis, American Airlines Theatre, New York, 2004–2005. This play, about a jury struggling to decide a capital murder case, provides a director with interesting opportunities for placing actors on a stage for maximum effect.*

work of the playwright, the designers, and the performers into a unique theatrical event.

Although many major universities offer a Master of Fine Arts (MFA) in directing, most directors start their theatre career as an actor, designer, playwright, choreographer, or critic. For example, one of America's most renowned directors, Elia Kazan, who directed the first production of Arthur Miller's *Death of a Salesman* as well as such great films as *On the Waterfront,* was an actor long before he started directing. Similarly, Robert Brustein, director of the Yale Repertory and American Repertory Theatres, started as a drama critic; Harold Prince, director of such Broadway productions as *The Kiss of the Spider Woman* and *The Phantom of the Opera,* was a producer; and Susan Stroman, director of the Broadway smash *The Producers* since it opened in 2001, began as a choreographer. Directors come from these many backgrounds because directing takes many talents. Directors must know how to inspire and coach actors, they must know how to communicate complex aesthetic ideas to designers, and they must understand the playwriting process. Directors must also know how to create a cohesive, pleasant working environment. Moreover, an effective director must have the ability not only to lead but also to inspire everyone involved with the play to be creative, to make decisions, and to add their talents to the production. The director must have the sensitivity of an

The Life of a Director: Tisa Chang

Born in China, Tisa Chang grew up in New York City, where as a child she learned to play piano and perform traditional Chinese dances and ballet. She attended the High School of Performing Arts and Barnard College at Columbia University. Soon she was dancing and acting in successful Broadway plays including *Pacific Overtures, The Basic Training of Pavlo Hummel,* and *Lovely Ladies.*

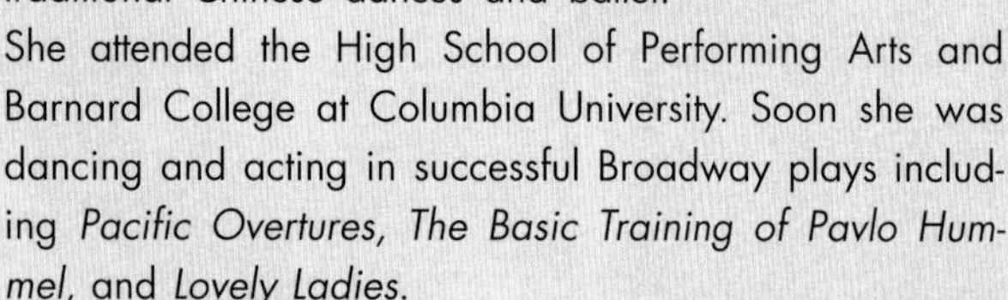

In 1977 she founded the Pan Asian Repertory Theatre in New York City. The goals of the Pan Asian Rep are to celebrate professional Asian American artists and to present "Asian American masterpieces, adaptations of American classics, and . . . new work by Asian American writers, which reflect the evolution of Asians in America." The Pan Asian Rep fast became one of the most influential Asian American theatres.

Chang has directed intercultural productions such as *Return of the Phoenix,* which was adapted from the Peking Opera; she has also directed Cambodian and Tibetan plays. She has staged Asian adaptations of Shakespeare including an intercultural, bilingual version of *A Midsummer Night's Dream* in Mandarin and English, as well as a Shogun *Macbeth.* "Beyond language and playwriting as the source . . . our theatrical production relies a great deal on the articulation. . . . We're talking about incorporating direction and design [that can] absolutely alter a script," says Chang. "I think that I would probably never direct a two-person play where people are sitting on chairs and talk to each other and expound. . . . I really love the magic and the latitude that we can have with direction and design and music and poetry."

About her directing style Chang says, "I don't like directors who over-impose or superimpose things onto a play. I just think all we [as directors] are doing is making the play clear and engaging." One of Chang's latest projects was to direct Elizabeth Wong's *China Doll,* a play that tells the life story of Anna May Wong (1905–1961), a Chinese American actress who starred artist, the fortitude of a good teacher, and the skills of an efficiency expert. (For more on the life of a director, see the Spotlight box "The Life of a Director: Tisa Chang."). And yet, as important as directors are to the process today, they are relatively new to the history of the theatre.

It's our job to create an atmosphere of creativity that will stimulate the best work from the actor, to be a mirror, tell them what they are doing and what we see. Both for the playwright and for the actor, the director is the surrogate audience until the actual audience arrives.

Marshall Mason,
American director

The Birth of Directors

For thousands of years, the role of director was not filled by a single person. The director's functions were simply tacked on to the duties of playwrights and actors. In ancient Greece, around 400 BCE, playwrights staged the plays they wrote. The term for these playwright-directors was **didaskalos,** or "teacher," because they not only wrote the play but also instructed the performers and advised the designers and technicians. Two thousand years later, in Shakespeare's day, directing was quite simple, at least compared with today. Elizabethan plays were staged outdoors in the midday sun, so there was no need for a lighting designer. The actors wore costumes appropriate to their character's station and profession, but no one took into account the overall look or historical accuracy, so there was little need for a costume designer. And the stage set was virtually the same for every play, so there was no need

FOR MORE ON
HOW DIRECTORS UNLEASH CREATIVITY

"Directors and actors discuss directing's primary function: Unleashing the creative instincts of actors," Dennis Embry, *Back Stage,* June 21, 1985

in such early Hollywood movies as *The Thief of Bagdad* with Douglas Fairbanks, Sr., and *Shanghai Express* with Marlene Dietrich. Wong acted in Hollywood at a time when the vast majority of Asian roles were played by white stars in "yellowface." She spent her life trying to achieve stardom as she fought against Hollywood stereotypes. Chang, whose own work is often geared toward challenging stereotypes, has said, "I think the best theater has a cohesive concept and a solid ensemble, and speaks to people on many different levels. And hopefully, the audience members leave the theatre thinking about what they saw."

Director Tisa Chang

Courtesy of the Pan Asian Repertory Theatre

Scene from Elizabeth Wong's China Doll, *about Hollywood's first Asian American movie star, Anna May Wong. With Rosanne Ma as Anna May Wong, directed by Tisa Chang, Pan Asian Repertory Theatre, 2005.*

© Corky Lee. Courtesy of the Pan Asian Repertory Theatre

for a set designer. Consequently, there was little need for a director to coordinate the designs. Playwright Ben Jonson, Shakespeare's contemporary, complained that directing a play was an exhausting job for which one did little more than prompt actors and yell at musicians. The job was so trivial that programs of the day have no mention of the position. When the first indoor theatres were built, they were lit with candles. The lighting was so inadequate that the actors would just try to find the brightest spot to stand in when the time came to speak their lines. Most of the directing at that time was done by an actor-manager, often the play's star, who told the other actors where to stand so that he could be seen in the best light.

The modern concept of a director did not come about until the nineteenth century, when a new genre of theatre called realism became popular. Realism called for psychologically complex characters, honest acting, and natural-looking sets. Realism also played off the worldwide scientific, social, and philosophical movements of the day. At the end of the century came the invention of electric lights, which made sophisticated lighting effects possible. Theatre was becoming a complex illusion, so there was a need for one person, a master coordinator, to oversee the various elements of production.

George II, the Duke of Saxe-Meiningen (1826–1914), the ruler of a small German state, is often credited as the first modern director. Being a wealthy monarch gave him the freedom and the resources to construct his own theatre and to organize and direct a resident company of actors and other artists. He was in a total leadership position, for he was the actors' literal ruler as well as their director—a power, no doubt, some modern directors wish they had. Duke George organized his actors, his subjects, into an ensemble in which there were no stars. He insisted on long rehearsal periods and ordered his actors to explore every psychological aspect of their characters. He also made many advances in staging. His crowd scenes were famous for looking like paintings, and his costumes, scenery, and props were fully integrated and authentic. Once he even used a real stuffed horse on stage in order to make a battle scene waged among fallen horses seem more real. One critic said that his production of Shakespeare's *Julius Caesar* was so real and so well directed that "one could believe that one was actually present at the beginning of the revolution."

From 1874 to 1890, the duke and his acting company toured Europe and gave over 2,600 performances of forty-one plays. In the audience for one of these productions was Russian acting teacher Konstantin Stanislavsky (see Chapter 7). So impressed was Stanislavsky by the duke's staging that he used many of his directing techniques at the new **Moscow Art Theatre.** When Stanislavsky directed, he, like the duke, was concerned with every detail of the production, from the accuracy of props to the timing of special effects such as birdcalls and cricket chirps. He made copious notes about the characters, as well as detailed diagrams of the actors' movements. He also insisted on a rehearsal process that lasted for months rather than days or weeks, which was the norm for most theatre in that day. Like the duke, he spent a long time in rehearsals for even the smallest bit parts. (The Moscow Art Theatre is the source of the saying "There are no small parts, only small actors," meaning that every role is worthy of study and rehearsal.) Stanislavsky also felt that the director should lead the actors through a process of discovery rather than command them or treat them as his puppets.

© akg-images, London

Few directors have had as much power as George II, the Duke of Saxe-Meiningen, whose actors were also his subjects. Often called the first modern director, he was famous for meticulous blocking, picturesque staging, and realistic crowd scenes. The Duke forbade the "star" system in his company—in some plays his actors played the leads, but in others they played background parts with no dialogue.

However, for Stanislavsky the new job of director was constantly evolving. After a lifetime of directing he wrote, "I used to think that the director was like a chef, whose job it was to mix the correct ingredients in the correct proportions; then I thought that the director was rather more like a midwife; and now I am not quite sure at all what a director is." Even though the specifics of their job were constantly changing, these early directors created the modern idea of the director as the person who interprets, organizes, and coordinates all the elements of a play into a meaningful, integrated whole.

Today, directors are an indispensable part of the theatre ensemble. They receive top credit in the program—only the playwright is listed higher. And in Hollywood, movie directors have become so important that theirs is always the final name in the credits before the movie begins.

I Before Rehearsals Begin

The director's job can be split in two phases: pre-rehearsal and rehearsal. Pre-rehearsal might be called the "paper phase" of the job because everything is on paper: designs drawn on paper, scripts written on paper, research in books, and notations in notebooks. During the paper phase, the director must discover what the play means and how the theatre ensemble might convey that meaning to the audience. The paper phase often lasts longer than the rehearsal phase. The paper phase includes script analysis, structural analysis, concept meetings, production meetings, and casting.

It All Starts with a Script: Script Analysis

The director's pre-rehearsal preparation begins with **script analysis.** Although studying a play can be as simple as using Goethe's play-analysis formula (see Chapter 4), in order to direct a play, every character and every word of the script must be scrutinized. The director's analysis might include working with the playwright (if the playwright is alive and available) as well as spending countless hours rereading the script, combing newspaper archives, and researching the history and criticism of the play. The director's intensive analysis includes finding the script's strengths and weaknesses. For example, if a particular character is underdeveloped, the director may note that a particularly strong actor is needed to flesh out that part. The director must understand each character's motivations, desires, and given circumstances (see Chapter 7) as well as the play's mood and atmosphere and the moral and philosophical statements made by the playwright.

However, a director's analysis does not end with the script. In order to have a comprehensive understanding, a director must research previous productions—for it is a good idea to know how other directors have staged the play—and what the critics said about them. The director may also study the playwright's life. Often playwrights write about personal events and emotions, so knowing about the playwright can lead to a greater understanding of the play. The play's location, period, and historical background must also be carefully investigated, including the political trends and the social and moral codes that were in effect when the play was written.

Not doing this research can lead directors to mistaken interpretations of the characters. For example, a director who has not done the historical research might assume that Hedda in Henrik Ibsen's *Hedda Gabler* (1890) is a bit of a spinster. After all, she is in her mid- to late-twenties and only recently married. But research would reveal that twenty-five was the average age of marriage for women in 1890 Norway. Without the research, the director might read into the character something the playwright never intended. This little bit of investigation could change the director's concept of Hedda, which in turn would affect the director's casting and staging decisions.

FOR MORE ON
THE DRAMATURG
"The literary guy: Defining the dramaturg," Robert Simonson, *Back Stage*, December 8, 1995

All this script analysis and research can be very time consuming. For example, when Konstantin Stanislavsky directed Anton Chekhov's *The Seagull*, he spent a month and a half alone in a tower in the Ukraine studying. For help with the research process, some directors work with a **dramaturg,** a literary advisor and theatre-history expert. Dramaturgs can assist a director or the-

© Michael Brosilow. Courtesy of the Goodman Theatre

Script analysis is a crucial aspect of the director's job. Understanding the playwright's thoughts, philosophy, and opinions about a play is invaluable. Here, Robert Falls (right), artistic director of the Goodman Theatre in Chicago, is fortunate enough to be able to discuss a 2004 production of Arthur Miller's Finishing the Picture *with the playwright himself.*

atre company in many ways. They can aid with the selection of plays, work with the playwright to help fully realize the script, and research the historical or literary background of a play in order to help directors, designers, and actors better understand the text. Armed with a strong background in theatre history, literature, and criticism, the dramaturg can serve as an information resource or as an integral part of the director's decision making. The dramaturg can make sure that the director's concepts and style stay within the standards of the theatre or are consistent with the ideas a theatre company wishes to express in a particular season of plays. Although common in other parts of the world, dramaturgs are still rather rare in U.S. theatre. Some directors feel that dramaturgs are an important part of the process, but others feel that what dramaturgs do is really part of the director's job.

Studying Even the Smallest Elements: Structural Analysis

While accumulating social, historical, and critical knowledge of the play, the director also studies the script's structure. This analysis often includes all the elements covered in Chapter 6, such as theme, characters, language, and plot, but it can also lead to the study of the smallest structural units within a play: french scenes and beats.

A **french scene** begins whenever a character enters or exits and continues until the next entrance or exit. For example, let's say a father and daughter are arguing and then Mom enters. Mom's entrance marks the beginning of a new french scene. If the father or mother or daughter exits, a new french scene begins. The length of each french scene varies, as does the number of french scenes within a play, act, or scene. A fast-paced farce may have dozens, but a play with no entrances or exits has only one. The idea of french scenes originated in, of course, France when the printing press was still a novelty and quite expensive. To cut costs, actors were given only the pages on which they had lines rather than the full script. The most cost-efficient way of dividing a play was from one entrance or exit to the next entrance or exit. Although this did little to help the actors with character analysis and continuity, it did save a few precious pages. If you ever read a French neoclassical tragedy such as *Phaedra*, you'll notice that the script is split into french scenes. However, this antiquated method of dividing a play would have been long forgotten had it not been such a help in playwriting and directing. Because a french scene deals with only certain characters at a particular point in the play, it divides a play into small, workable units. The director treats each french scene as a mini-play that has the structural elements of a full play: beginning, middle, and end. With each entrance or exit, the play changes, the characters' attitudes shift, and the story moves forward.

A **beat** is the next smaller structural unit; it is a single unit of thought. It's a section of dialogue about a particular subject or idea. A change in subject or idea means the beginning of a new beat. A beat can be anywhere from a single word to several pages long. Beats are similar to paragraphs in other kinds of writing, but they are not signaled by indentations or any other typographical device. As an illustration, the following scene is divided into beats—but remember, beats are never indicated in a real script. This scene, which has four beats, is about a woman who has returned home to take her elderly father to the hospital for what she thinks is a hernia operation.

BEAT ONE

DARLA: We gotta go. Where is she?

HENRY: Moonpie? She's out.

DARLA: Wish you wouldn't do that. Cats that wander don't live as long. How long she been missin'?

HENRY: She's not missin'. She killed a warbler two hours ago. Feathers everywhere.

DARLA *(yelling out the window)*: Moonpie! Moonpiiiie!

HENRY: Absolute carnage. Apocalypse in the backyard. So she can't be far.

DARLA: M. P! M. Peeee!

HENRY: If the cat don't know its name, what the hell makes you think it'd know its initials?

BEAT TWO

DARLA: You're feelin' better.

HENRY: Me? I feel terrible.

DARLA: Where the blazes is a double hernia anyway?

HENRY: I'd show you, but I'd be arrested.
DARLA: Are you sure it's a hernia?
HENRY: What do I know; pain is pain.

BEAT THREE
HENRY: I cancelled the papers and I'm havin' my mail forwarded to you.
DARLA: Why can't Mom pick up your mail?
HENRY: Your mother'll just lose it. Besides I think she sneaks over here and opens my mail. Tries to find out if I got a lover. I can't prove anything, but my Sears bill is missin'.
DARLA: I can only stay two days. I think it'd be better if she picked up your mail. She could read it to you in the hospital.

© Craig Schwartz

One of the most memorable ends to a french scene is surely "Exit, pursued by a bear" from Shakespeare's The Winter's Tale. *In this play, King Leontes jealously suspects that the baby his wife has just given birth to is not his. He orders his courtier Antigonus to abandon the newborn girl. Antigonus reluctantly takes the baby to a desolate spot. As he is leaving, a bear chases him offstage. Because it's impractical to use a real bear as a prop, designers and artistic directors have had to be creative. Solutions have included shadows, growling sounds, and stylized props such as the one shown here.*

BEAT FOUR

HENRY: She can't read my mail.

DARLA: Why not?

HENRY: She had her cataract surgery.

DARLA: What? When? *(dialing the phone)* Why didn't you tell me?!

HENRY: I told her not to dilly dally. Told her, one eye at a time. Did she listen? Course not.

DARLA: She never lets it ring more than twice.

HENRY: Waited too long, so she had to get both eyes done at once. Got some nurse with her twenty-four hours a day.

DARLA: Did you send flowers?

HENRY: Why should I? She can't see 'em.

DARLA: Daddy, you should've told me.

HENRY: She's fine. Blind but fine. Got two huge silver patches on her face. Makes her look like some kinda massive gnat.

The word *beat* is misleading. It usually refers to a rhythmical unit. So why do theatre people use the word *beat* instead of *unit* or *section*? The explanation dates from the time when the disciples of Stanislavsky came to the United States to teach. Americans were supposedly confused by the Russians' thick accents, so they mistook the word *bit* for *beat*. If you say, "First you must split the play into little bits" with a Russian accent, you'll find some truth to this theory. Whether it's true or not, looking at "beats" as "bits" makes sense. A director, as well as actors and playwrights, divides dialogue into bits/beats to understand moment-by-moment changes in the characters' actions, conflicts, and motivations. This process is seldom as obvious as shown in Table 8.1, because directors often go through this process subconsciously, but the table illustrates how each beat reveals the moment's action, conflict, and motivation. Try it yourself—take a scene or a french scene from your favorite play and break it into beats. In doing so, you will find a deeper understanding of how the play was constructed and learn how the scene works moment by moment, just as a director does.

Meetings and More Meetings: Realizing the Production Concept

After spending weeks and even months researching and analyzing a script, the director gains a deep understanding of all the elements of the play. The next step is to devise a **production concept.** This is the metaphor, thematic idea, symbol, or allegory that will be central to the whole production. A director without a production concept is like a driver without a road map. However, for all the work that goes into it, the production concept is usually quite simple. For example, a director working on Ibsen's *A Doll's House*, a play about a woman who breaks free of her domineering husband, could envision the lead character, Nora, as a woman trapped in a beautiful birdcage. During the course of the play, Nora could come to see this birdcage as terrible dungeon. With this concept, the director would be making a statement about how we allow ourselves to be trapped by our lives, seldom questioning our premises, rarely realizing that we are entangled by our own limited point of view. Once the director has a concept, it must be communicated to the designers through

Table 8.1 Action, conflict, and motivation beat by beat

Beat	Action	Conflict	Motivation
1	Darla must find the cat before she locks up the house and takes her father to the hospital.	Her elderly father doesn't seem to care about the cat or the hospital.	Darla's parents are divorced, so she feels she must take care of them, including little details like the cat.
2	Darla asks her father about why he's going into the hospital.	He doesn't want to tell her the truth about his medical condition. He's dying.	Henry feels that a real man doesn't complain. Darla feels that real men are too secretive.
3	Darla and Henry disagree about who will pick up his mail.	Darla wants her parents to get back together and will do anything to make them have contact. Henry doesn't want to talk about his medical condition, so he changes the subject.	Darla feels that her parents are lonely and need each other. Besides, she wants some time for herself. Henry knows he has cancer and doesn't want anyone to know.
4	Darla learns that her mother is also in the hospital.	Darla must find out about her mother. She feels guilty because she hasn't called her in a few days. Henry is thrilled that the attention is off him.	Darla loves her mother, perhaps more than she loves her father. Henry wants Darla to know that there is no chance of his getting back together with her mother.

a series of **production meetings.** During these meetings the designers and director also discuss the play's philosophy, interpretation, theme, physical demands, history, and style. Between meetings, the designers attempt to realize the director's production concept by drawing sketches of possible sets, costumes, and other designs. There can be dozens of production meetings held over a period of weeks, even months, before final designs are agreed upon. Only after the homework and production meetings are done is the director ready to cast the play and begin rehearsals. (For more on production concepts and meetings, see Chapter 9.)

FOR MORE ON

BEING A DIRECTOR

"Can I do that? The *Herald-Tribune*'s theater critic crosses the footlights to try his hand at directing a play," *Sarasota Herald-Tribune,* July 18, 2004

Don't Call Us; We'll Call You: Casting the Right Actors

Casting the right actors is critical for the success of a play. A common theatre adage is that 90 percent of directing is casting. In fact casting is so important that some directors hire **casting directors,** who specialize in finding the right actor to fit the part—a practice that is common with Hollywood movies.

Actors are usually hired because they are stars and can draw an audience or because they have the talent to play the role, or a combination of the two. There is no fairness-in-casting law. Directors have the right to cast whomever they feel is the best person for the job; they don't have to give everyone a fair chance.

> What does the director do? He bears to the preparation of a play much the same relation as an orchestra conductor to the rehearsal of a symphony. But the symphony is performed by the conductor with each member of the orchestra playing under his leadership. He does not play the leading part. He does more. He interprets, shapes, guides, inspires the entire performance.
>
> ***Tyrone Guthrie,***
> *British director*

Directors can **cast to type,** or hire an actor who physically matches the role. In other words, if they are looking for a seventy-year-old Italian mother, they cast someone who looks just like, or is, a seventy-year-old Italian mother. Casting to type can also mean finding an actor who has a deep understanding of the character's emotions and motivations. Directors can also **cast against type,** or deliberately cast actors who are the exact opposite of, or very different from, what is expected. For example, the director might choose to cast an older-than-usual pair as the lovers in *Romeo and Juliet*, thereby making a statement about how love is right for all people, not just the young and beautiful. Directors also sometimes use **gender-neutral casting,** or casting without regard for the character's gender, and **cross-gender casting,** or intentionally casting men to play women's roles and women to play men's in order to study societal perceptions of gender identity. One of the most controversial forms of casting is **color-blind casting,** or choosing actors without regard for their race or ethnic background. (For more on color-blind casting, see the Spotlight on Diversity box, "Color-Blind Casting.")

The Director's Role during Rehearsals

Once the paper phase is over, the director is ready to begin rehearsals. The first few days of rehearsal are critical because this is when the director must unite all the actors into an ensemble with a common goal. No two actors are alike; they have different methods and personalities. Some actors need reassurance, while others need a firm foundation. Some actors approach their roles through intellectual analysis, while others thrive on nothing but inspiration. Early in the rehearsal process the director must present to all the actors a game plan and clear goal. Initial rehearsals may be taken up with reading and analyzing the script, as well as improvisation. Then the director, with the help of the actors, begins blocking. **Blocking** is the movement of the actors on stage. At its most basic, blocking is simply making sure the actors don't bump into each other or the furniture, but it quickly becomes a complex set of movements that express the characters' emotions, thoughts, and relationships. Blocking is also how the director achieves focus and "picturization."

> When I create something, I usually have it completely created in pre-production. But then I go in and I feed off of the actors also, because that ultimately gives me the best result.
>
> ***Susan Stroman,***
> *American director and choreographer*

Directing the Audience's Eyes

Achieving **focus** in a movie is easy. Directors can simply point the camera at whatever they want the audience to look at. Close-ups and lingering camera angles can emphasize a tiny drop of incriminating blood on a killer's hand or a character's fleeting glance of guilt. On stage, focus is much more difficult because the audience is free to look wherever they like. The stage director must gain the audience's attention and direct their gaze to a particular spot or actor. This can be accomplished through lighting, costumes, scenery, voice, and movements. Focus can be gained by simply putting a spotlight on one actor, by having one actor in red and everyone else in gray, or by having one

Color-Blind Casting

The opposite of ethnic-specific casting, color-blind casting ignores race and awards roles solely on the talent of the actor. This can lead to unexpected and illogical combinations of characters that the playwright never intended. Color-blind casting is often necessary at colleges and universities if few plays match the ethnic makeup of the theatre-major population. But it is also used in the professional theatre and in movies. For example, Denzel Washington was cast as Don Pedro in Kenneth Branagh's film version of Shakespeare's *Much Ado about Nothing*. He is black, but his brother in the play, played by Keanu Reeves, is white.

At a recent symposium sponsored by the Non-Traditional Casting Project, actors of a multitude of races presented roles traditionally played by white actors. For example, Hispanic actors performed a scene from Molière's *Imaginary Invalid*, a seventeenth-century French comedy. A black woman played Hedda in scenes from Ibsen's *Hedda Gabler*, a nineteenth-century Norwegian play.

During the symposium, several directors advocated color-blind casting as a way to ensure that all actors, regardless of skin color, have an equal chance of being cast, but others felt that trying to ignore skin color only makes for unbelievable interpretations and fundamental changes in the text and denies the racial conflicts in our society. Several audience members pointed out that 90 percent of all plays in the United States are written for white characters and that the way to ensure more roles for Hispanics, blacks, and Asian Americans is not color-blind casting but the creation of a library of new works by and for Americans of color. August Wilson, one of America's most respected playwrights, agrees. In his view, color-blind casting is not a substitute for plays about the black experience. Needless to say, the controversy over color-blind casting is not over. In the meantime, if you should see a play where the racial makeup of the cast doesn't correspond to the script, know that you are watching a play with color-blind casting and you are expected to accept it and devote yourself to the drama rather than being preoccupied by the race of the actors. (For more, check out the Non-Traditional Casting Project on the web at http://www.ntcp.org/.)

© Joan Marcus

The choice of Whoopi Goldberg to play Prologus, a Greek actor, in a 1997 Broadway revival of A Funny Thing Happened on the Way to the Forum *is an example of color-blind (as well as gender-blind) casting. This practice has generated much controversy although it is gaining popularity. Some feel it a fair way to ensure all actors are considered equally for a role, and others feel it masks the scarcity of roles for people of color in U.S. theatre.*

actor move while the others remain still. All these techniques will quickly draw the audience's attention to the actor whom the director wants to be in focus. There are also more subtle ways to lead the audience's eyes and pull focus. A few of these are body position, stage area, level, contrast, and triangulation.

One of the most basic ways a director achieves focus is through actors' body positions. For example, in Figure 8.1 (A) the actors are **sharing focus.** They both have a shoulder thrown back (a position sometimes called "one-quarter" because the actors are turned a quarter away from the audience). Because the audience can see the actors equally, this position is used when what both actors are saying is of equal importance. In (B) the actor on the right takes focus because the actor on the left is standing in **profile,** or "half" away from the audience. The audience's eyes naturally go to the actor on the right because he is in the most "open" position. Perhaps at this moment in the play the character on the right is talking about how he knows his wife is cheating on him. The director feels that this speech is very important to the story and doesn't want the audience to miss a word of it, so she has the actor on the left "close" himself by standing in profile. In (C) the actor on the right is standing in "three quarters," an even more closed position than profile, so the actor on the left naturally demands a great deal of focus. Perhaps the character on the left is having an affair with the other character's "loyal" wife and the director wants the audience to see his guilty reaction, so the actor on the right gives the focus to the actor on the left.

Of course, all movements must be justified and fit into the action of the play. Actors mechanically turning to give and take focus would look silly, so motivated reasons for each individual movement must be found. During rehearsals actors are often asked to "open" themselves, to "share focus," to "give focus" or to "close" themselves in order to fit the focal demands of the moment. Actors who take focus when they aren't supposed to are said to be **stealing focus** or **upstaging** the other actors.

A director can also achieve focus by using different **stage areas** (see Figure 8.2). Each area is labeled from the actors' point of view as they face the audience; for example, "stage right" is the audience's left. Using these labels, directors can easily ask the actors to move to a particular part of the stage or look in a particular direction. An actor who is center stage or downstage tends to draw the audience's attention more than actors in other areas.

Focus can also be achieved through level (see Figure 8.3). An actor who is at a different level than the other actors tends to pull focus. The director can also use contrasting positions. An actor who is separated from the other actors always pulls the audience's focus. A contrast in movement also directs the audience's focus. The actor who is moving when the others are still or who is moving in a different direction will attract the audience's attention. Finally, one of the most common methods of drawing focus is **triangulation.** When

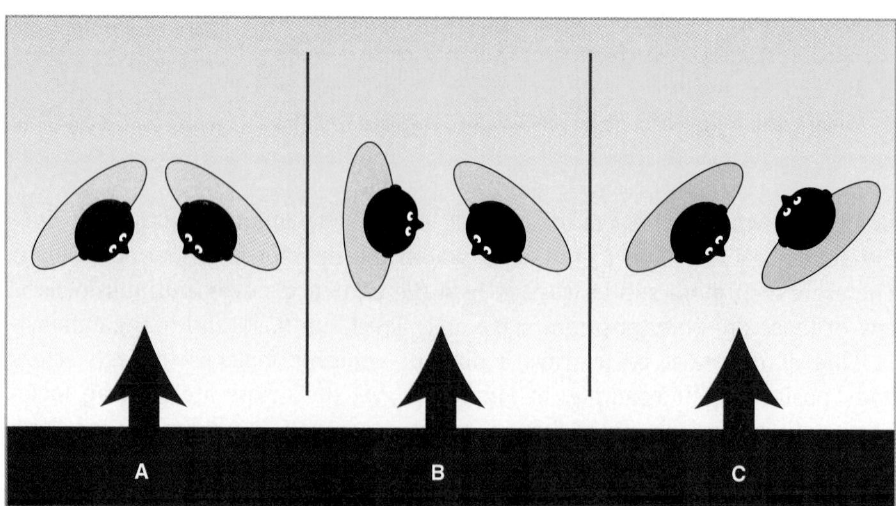

Figure 8.1 *Achieving focus through the actors' body positions.*

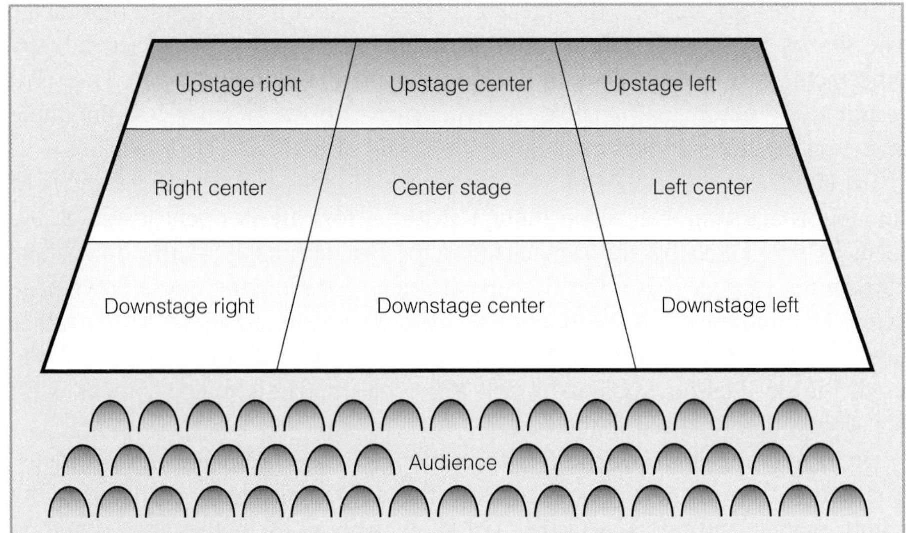

Figure 8.2 Stage areas *To help with blocking, the stage is split into a grid and each area is labeled. Using these labels, directors can easily ask the actors to move to a particular place or look in a particular direction.*

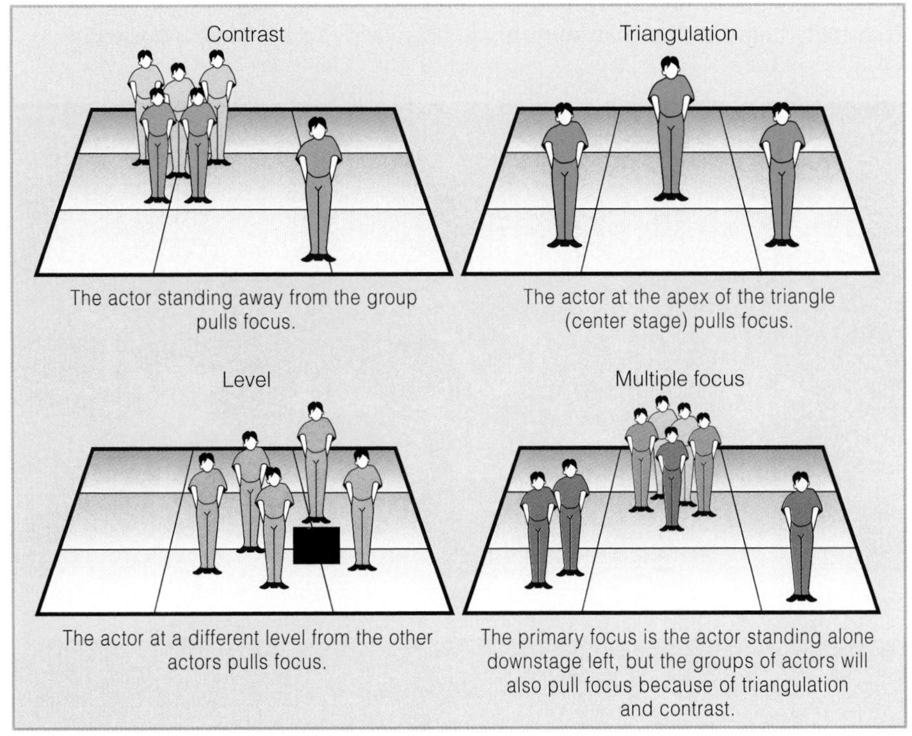

Figure 8.3 *Achieving focus through contrast, triangulation and level.*

there are three actors, or groups of actors on stage, whoever is at the upstage or downstage apex of the triangle generally takes the focus.

To understand focus, study the pairs of production photos in Figures 8.4–8.9. The best way is to close your eyes and then open them on one of the photos. The first millisecond after you open your eyes, your focus will fall on a random spot on the picture, but then your eyes will move to the most dominant character in the picture, the main focal point. Don't force your gaze or think about where to look; just let it happen. Once you have picked the point of focus, read the caption and see how the director made you look at that particular spot.

In Figures 8.4 and 8.5, the director is using several techniques to pull focus. The first is level: Only one actor is standing, so he pulls focus. Second, the other actors are giving focus by looking toward the standing actor. The third technique is contrast: The three seated actors are leaning back at the same angle, giving the standing actor focus by virtue of his contrasting position.

In Figures 8.6 and 8.7, the director is using a triangle to pull the focus to the downstage character. Even though all the actors are in open positions, the focus is still taken by the downstage actor because he is at the downstage apex of the triangle. Also, the two upstage actors are looking at the downstage actor. The audience has a tendency to look where the actors look. It's rather like the chain reaction created by a person on a crowded street corner looking up at the sky—curious passersby will also look up. The secondary focus is on the woman because she is the best lit.

The director must be the master of theatrical action, as the dramatist is the master of the written concept.

Harold Clurman,
American director and theatre critic

In Figures 8.8 and 8.9, there is a double focus, perhaps even a triple focus. The two actors on the right are the first focus. The secondary focus is on the young woman sitting stage right, and then focus goes to the actor standing with his arms around the young women. Notice that if you look to whom any actor is looking at and then to whom that actor is looking and so on, all eyes eventually come to the man with his hand raised, so he takes main focus.

Figure 8.4

Source: University of Wyoming photo archives

Figure 8.5 *Drawing focus with level, gaze, and contrast. From a University of Wyoming production of Edward Albee's* Who's Afraid of Virginia Woolf? *directed by Rebecca Hilliker.*

Source: University of Wyoming photo archives

Figure 8.6

SOURCE: University of Wyoming photo archives

Figure 8.7 *Drawing focus with triangulation. From a University of Wyoming production of Henrik Ibsen's* A Doll's House *directed by William Downs.*

SOURCE: University of Wyoming photo archives

Figure 8.8

SOURCE: University of Wyoming photo archives

Figure 8.9 *An example of double or triple focus. From a University of Wyoming production of Arthur Miller's* Death of a Salesman *directed by William Downs.*

SOURCE: University of Wyoming photo archives

Reinforcing the Story with Pictures

> The director builds a bridge from the spectator to the actor. Following the dictates of the author, and introducing onto the stage friends, enemies, or lovers, the director with movements and postures must present a certain image which will aid the spectator not only to hear the words, but to guess the inner, concealed feelings.
>
> ***V. E. Meyerhold,***
> *Russian director and designer*

Words are a fine method of storytelling, but directors often go a step farther by composing pictures with the actors that reinforce the story. This technique is called **picturization.** It uses many of the visual-art principles of painting and photography in order to express the characters' relationships, psychological situations, and moods at a glance. In real life people move without regard for where others are around them, groups of people seldom arrange themselves to tell a story, and there is randomness to crowds. For example, from a random photo of a bankruptcy auction on a farm in Iowa, we could probably tell that an auction was being held. The auctioneer might be in focus and around him would be dozens of farmers, but we'd know little else about the people or the situation. If the same scene were being shown on stage, the director would create pictures to help tell the story. From a single stage picture, we would be able to identify the members of the unlucky farm family. We'd know that this person is the mother, this is the father, and here stands the best friend. If a picture is well staged, we should even be able to tell what the characters' relationships are. We would know which of the farmers in the crowd had a vested interest in the proceedings and who were merely onlookers. We would also understand the mood of the moment, the sense of loss, and how the auction is the end of a way of life. A director arranging the actors to make these pictures is concerned not just with which characters are in focus but also with telling the story.

If it is well staged, showing the purpose of the scene, the characters' objectives, and the mood of the moment, the picture can be given a title, like the title of a painting. One moment might be titled "True Love," the next moment "The Betrayal," and the next moment "The Confession." This title identifies the moment's main thrust or principal purpose. For example, in Figure 8.10, a scene from a production of Shakespeare's *Macbeth*, the placement of the actors creates a picture that tells a story. Without knowing any of the dialogue we could write a title such as "The Promotion" or "The Ruling." Most of the time, the audience is unaware that they are seeing a succession of deliberate images. Yet when these stage compositions are well done, the audience might be able understand the play even if the dialogue was in a foreign language.

Figure 8.10 *Well-placed actors create a composition that tells a story. From a University of Wyoming production of William Shakespeare's* Macbeth *directed by Lou Anne Wright.*

SOURCE: University of Wyoming photo archives

The Director's Collaboration with Others

As rehearsals progress, directors work with the actors on motivations, emotions, performance, and clarity. They also continue to meet with the designers until the full production is realized. So complex is the director's job that several assistants are often required to help with paperwork and organization. For example, in a large production with a huge cast, the director may have an **assistant director** to lend a hand with the staging. But all productions, large or small, have a stage manager. The **stage manager** is not only responsible for running the show during the performance, but also helps the director during the rehearsal process by taking notes, recording blocking, scheduling rehearsals, assisting during auditions, and enforcing safety rules. The stage manager also keeps a prompt book, which is a copy of the full script with notes on blocking, cues, and other important information about the production. The stage manager may even need an **assistant stage manager** to help with the workload. The director can also be joined in rehearsals by different types of acting coaches. For example, if a production calls for particular style of movement, a **movement coach** can be hired to work with the actors. A production might also need a **voice and dialect coach** to help the actors with speech clarity, volume, and accents. A **fight director** can help choreograph realistic-looking but faked fistfights and swordplay. For musicals there must also be a **musical director** and a **choreographer** to work with the musicians and teach the actors the songs and the dance numbers.

FOR MORE ON
THE STAGE MANAGER
"Stage managers: The power behind the throne," Warren Kliewer, *Back Stage,* June 21, 1991

Different Types of Directors

Today, there are as many styles of directing as there are directors. Some directors are authoritarian leaders who micromanage every aspect of the play. Others are more like creative coaches who guide and inspire as they orchestrate the play in a democratic style. Every director has unique philosophies and methodologies about this highly individual process. But when it comes to working with an existing script, directors all fall somewhere in the spectrum between interpretive and creative.

Interpretive Directors

Interpretive directors attempt to translate the play from the page to the stage as accurately and faithfully as possible. They are not slaves to the playwright, but they make every attempt to realize the playwright's words and actions in a style that is true to the script. Directors inevitably impose their individual style on a production, but interpretive directors attempt to stage the play in a manner that they feel would please the playwright. Of course, an exact translation from page to stage is impossible—every line an actor speaks is an interpretation of the playwright's words, every movement an actor makes is an interpretation of the script, and every design is an interpretation of the playwright's wishes. French director and critic Jacques Copeau was describing the interpretive approach when he stated in his manifesto that the director's job is to faithfully translate the playwright's script into the "poetry of the theatre."

© Michael Broslow. Courtesy of the Goodman Theatre

Interpretive directors set out to stage a play as the playwright envisioned it. Some playwrights won't allow anyone but interpretive directors to produce their plays. One such playwright is Edward Albee, who collaborated with director Robert Falls on a 2003 production of his The Goat, or Who Is Sylvia? *a play about a man whose interspecies relationship threatens to ruin his marriage. This production featured (l to r) Patrick Clear, Michael Stahl-David, and Barbara Robertson.*

Creative Directors

Creative directors often add concepts, designs, or interpretations atop the playwright's words that were never intended by the playwright. Their plays are sometimes called **concept productions,** because the director's artistic vision, or concept, dominates. In 1937, American director Orson Welles (1915–1985), famous for writing, directing, and starring in the movie *Citizen Kane*, directed one of the most celebrated concept productions. For a production of Shakespeare's *Julius Caesar,* he placed the action in pre–World War II Rome. He made the character of Caesar into the dictator Benito Mussolini and replaced the Shakespearean music with the anthem of Mussolini's fascist regime, thereby making a statement about the politics of the day. English director Peter Brook staged another famous concept production in 1970 when he turned Shakespeare's *A Midsummer Night's Dream* into a circus, with magic tricks, trapeze artists, and actors spinning plates on sticks. Brook and his designer, Sally Jacobs, set the play within a roofless white box with ladders, swings, and catwalks. The result was an athletic, acrobatic performance that did not look like anything Shakespeare originally intended. Today, concept productions are common, with directors staging *Hamlet* in Chicago during the gangland wars of Prohibition and *The Taming of the Shrew* in the Wild West. Creative directors stage concept productions in order to capture the spirit of the play, modernize the play, or simply create a unique evening of theatre.

Some creative directors go so far as to almost discard the playwright's words, using the script as only a loose outline. These directors believe that the script should mutate to fit the needs of an individual director or production. Of course, the main problem for these directors is the small number of plays they can direct, because playwrights own the copyright to their plays and have the right to deny production to any director who does not properly follow the script. Directors who wish to alter a playwright's intention must gain the playwright's permission or wait until the play is in public domain, as are Shakespeare's plays. (For more on copyright and public domain, see Chapter 2.) There have been several famous battles between playwrights and directors over who controls a play. One of the most famous took place in 1984 during a production of Samuel Beckett's *Endgame* at the American Repertory Theatre. (See the Spotlight box "Playwright versus Director.")

FOR MORE ON

THE RIGHTS OF DIRECTORS

"Protecting the [intellectual property rights of the] director," Ted Pappas, *American Theatre*, February 1999

Contemporary Trends

Traditionally, theatre artists were divided into *creative artists,* the playwrights who create the scripts, and *interpretive artists,* the directors, actors, and designers who work within the parameters the playwright has set. This dividing line between creative and interpretive artists is now being questioned by

© Max Waldman, 1970. All Rights Reserved

For concept productions, creative directors take the play in directions that the playwright never intended. If the play is under copyright, the playwright can refuse permission for it to be altered. As a result, creative directors frequently rely on scripts in the public domain—this is why concept productions of Shakespeare plays are common. A famous example is director Peter Brook's version of Shakespeare's A Midsummer's Night Dream, *which incorporated an all-white background, trapeze swings, and magic tricks.*

Playwright versus Director

In 1984, JoAnne Akalaitis directed Samuel Beckett's *Endgame* at the American Repertory Theatre. Samuel Beckett is one of the world's most famous absurdist playwrights. *Endgame* is the story of two clown-like characters, Hamm and Clov, one of whom is partially paralyzed and the other acts as his servant. Other characters are Hamm's parents, who live in trash cans. Beckett's stage directions state that the play takes place in a room with two windows and little else. But Akalaitis saw the play differently. She set the action in a New York City subway station after a nuclear holocaust, which changed the meaning of the play. When Beckett heard about the production, he went to court to shut it down. In the end, they settled out of court. The production was allowed to go forward, but the program included a note, written by Beckett, condemning the production. The note says that the American Repertory Theatre's production is a "complete parody" of his work, and that anyone who cares for the play can't help but be "disgusted" by what Akalaitis did to it. The theatre's artistic director responded in a program note that reads in part, "To insist on strict adherence to each parenthesis of the published text not only robs collaborating artists of their interpretive freedom but threatens to turn the theatre into a waxworks."

This exchange defined one of the greatest problems of the relationship between the director and the playwright: Who has the power? Is the play set in stone when the playwright writes it, or can it be adjusted to fit the director's artistic vision? Some playwrights and directors have attempted to solve the problem by making the playwright in charge of the words and the director in charge of staging, but this division of labor doesn't totally solve the problem because playwrights write stage directions that describe the physical aspects of the play, and they are copyrighted along with the dialogue. With Hollywood films, screenwriters have lost this battle. Writers for movies are secondary characters whose vision is seldom realized. In the theatre, the battle has just begun. However, unlike screenwriters, playwrights have a powerful advantage because they own the copyright, so they may not be so quickly defeated. As the character Howard Roark says in Ayn Rand's novel *The Fountainhead,* "No work is ever done collectively, by a majority decision. Every creative job is achieved under the guidance of a single individual thought." This is true in the theatre—the guidance comes from the playwright—but how closely the rest of the ensemble follow that "single individual thought" will be hotly debated for many years to come.

© Richard Feldman

In recent years, playwrights have sometimes threatened legal action to stop directors from altering their work. Examples include a production of Edward Albee's Who's Afraid of Virginia Woolf? *in which a man in drag was cast as Martha and a play by an experimental theatre company that incorporated a portion of Arthur Miller's play* The Crucible. *One of the most famous cases of a playwright intervening to stop a production of one of his plays involved JoAnne Akalaitis's 1984 production of Samuel Beckett's* Endgame *(pictured here).*

many directors as well as playwrights and actors. They are blurring the traditional assignments and creating and staging plays that allow all the members of the ensemble to be creative artists and share in the development of the play. Plays have always been developed; seldom does a playwright labor in total isolation and then suddenly put forth a finished script. Most plays go through an extensive process of readings and workshop productions that help the playwright rewrite. But now many directors and actors are getting involved in the development process much earlier, even at the moment of conception. So instead of the production being an interpretation of the playwright's script, the production is the creation of an ensemble of playwright, designers, actors, and director.

Playwright Caryl Churchill often workshops her plays using a communal method of development that allows actors to help create the script through improvisation and the director to co-determine the direction of the final script. Such was the case with Churchill's play *Cloud Nine,* the story of several generations of a family and how they are governed by class, race, and gender—a play, by the way, that features cross-gender casting. Instead of writing in a secluded study, she spent several weeks working with the director on the idea and setting for the play. Then actors were brought in to improvise as they jointly workshopped the idea. Churchill took what she learned and wrote a tentative script with rudimentary dialogue. This first script was again workshopped with the director and actors to refine the dialogue, and this collaboration resulted in the final production. Another famous example of this new method of directing is Moisés Kaufman's play *The Laramie Project,* a docudrama about the murder of a gay university student. The play was researched by a company of actors who conducted personal interviews with people who lived in the town in which the student was murdered. Kaufman acted as both director and playwright as he worked with the actors to develop the final production.

FOR MORE ON

NEW DIRECTIONS FOR DIRECTORS

"Directing: New directions for directors," Holly Hildebrand, *Back Stage,* February 11, 2000

Curtain Call

In the end, all directors are judged by process and product. The process is everything that leads up to opening night; the product is opening night and beyond. A good process doesn't always lead to a good product, but occasionally a good product is born of bad process. The acid test for the process is if all the members of the ensemble have clearly seen and added to the production. Did the environment allow meaningful creativity for all the members? The acid test for the product is far more subjective, because more people are involved, including the audience and critics. But, as director Peter Brook says in *The Empty Space*:

> I know of one acid test in the theatre. It is literally an acid test. When the performance is over, what remains? Fun can be forgotten, powerful emotions also disappear and good arguments lose their thread. When emotion and arguments are harnessed to a wish from the audience to see more clearly into itself—then something in the mind burns. The event scorches onto the memory an outline, a taste, a trace, a smell—a picture. It is the play's central image that remains, its silhouette, and if the elements are rightly blended this silhouette will be its meaning, this shape will be the essence of what it has to say.[1]

So the acid test for a production is whether its meaning stays with the audience. The playwright's words will be forgotten or paraphrased, the actors' names will disappear, the designer's colors will fade, and the set will be discarded, but the director knows that the production was successful if the thought remains.

[1] Peter Brook, *The Empty Space* (New York: Atheneum, 1968), 123–124.

Summary

In order for a production to succeed, dozens of artists, technicians, and other personnel must work together with a singleness of purpose seldom found outside the theatre. The director is the leader and coordinator who takes the playwright's words and frames them into a production. The job requires many skills: The director must know how to work with and inspire actors, designers, and playwrights, and how to coordinate all the elements that make up a production. Yet the director is one of the newest positions in the theatre. For thousands of years, playwrights and actors essentially functioned as directors. It wasn't until about 150 years ago, when realism became popular, that the duties of the director were separated into a single job. Two early directors who helped define the position were the Duke of Saxe-Meiningen and Konstantin Stanislavsky.

The director's job can be split in two parts: pre-rehearsal and rehearsal. Pre-rehearsal is spent evaluating and researching the script, conceiving a production concept, and working with designers. To analyze a play, a director often breaks it into french scenes and beats. Dividing the play into these small units helps the director discover the structure and understand the play moment by moment. Once the director has done careful analysis and research, it is time for meetings with the designers in order to find a production concept, or central metaphor, that unites all the elements of the production. Only after weeks or months of work does the director finally cast the play.

The director has many casting options, including casting to type, casting against type, gender-neutral casting, cross-gender casting, and color-blind casting. During rehearsals the director blocks the play to lead the audience's eyes and achieve focus. The methods the director can use to pull focus include body position, stage area, level, contrast, and triangulation. Directors also use picturization to tell the play's story.

The director's job is so complex that it often requires several assistants, such as an assistant director and a stage manager. Some productions also need a movement coach, a voice and dialect coach, and a fight director. Musicals need a musical director and a choreographer to work with the musicians and teach the actors the songs and dance numbers.

No two directors have the same working methods. But they can be divided into two broad, nonexclusive categories: interpretive directors who are loyal to the playwright's intentions, and creative directors who often impose upon the script their own concept that is independent of the playwright's intentions. Some directors are now challenging traditional ideas by staging plays that allow actors, playwrights, and directors to work on a play from its inception to the opening night.

The Art of Theatre Online

Use the *Art of Theatre* website at **http://communication.wadsworth.com/downs1** for quick access to the electronic study resources that accompany this chapter, including a digital glossary, a link to InfoTrac College Edition that you can use to find the For More On... InfoTrac College Edition readings listed below, a list of further reading, and a chapter quiz. When you get to the *Art of Theatre* homepage, click on the cover of the book you are using and you will be redirected to the website for your book. Then click on "Student Book Companion Site" in the Resource box, pick a chapter from the pull-down menu at the top of the page, and select an option from the Chapter Resources menu. The *Art of Theatre* website also includes links to interesting and informative theatre websites. Just click on the Theatre on the Web link in the Book Resources menu. The links to these websites are maintained and updated as needed.

Key Terms

For More On . . .

Infotrac College Edition Readings

http://www.infoTrac-college.com

How directors unleash creativity / 187
"Directors and actors discuss directing's primary function: Unleashing the creative instincts of actors"

The dramaturg / 190
"The literary guy: Defining the dramaturg"

Being a director / 195
"Can I do that? The *Herald-Tribune*'s theater critic crosses the footlights to try his hand at directing a play"

The stage manager / 203
"Stage managers: The power behind the throne"

The rights of directors / 205
"Protecting the [intellectual property rights of the] director"

New directions for directors / 207
"Directing: New directions for directors"

9 The Art of Design

The house lights dim, the curtain rises, and we see a solitary actor standing in the center of a bare stage. There is almost nothing to support the actor—simple work lights, no costume, no set, nothing but a blankly lit empty space. Could this be theatre? Absolutely. Yet theatre also often uses designers to assist the actors, playwright, and director by setting the stage. When sets, lights, sounds, and costumes are added, the audience is immersed in the world of the play even before the first line is spoken. Theatre is intended to be experienced by our eyes, our ears, our mind, our whole being, so theatre has always had designers in one form or another to help create the experience.

Today, most plays have set, lighting, and costume designers, but some also have sound and makeup designers. All these artists must work together to create the visual effects of a dramatic production—in other words, the play's environment. Environment is integral to any story. Every plot,

© Craig Schwartz. Courtesy of the Mark Taper Forum

◀ ***On preceding page:*** *Traveler in the Dark, by Marsha Norman. Directed by Gordon Davidson, Mark Taper Forum, Los Angeles, 1985. Set designed by Ming Cho Lee, costumes designed by Susan Denison, and lighting designed by Marilyn Rennagel. This play is about a surgeon who, coping with guilt over the death of his childhood sweetheart, seeks to renew his relationship with his long-estranged father.*

Design is an act of transformation. Working with a director, a designer transforms words into a world within which actors are engaged in human action. It might be a metaphoric world, an emotional world or an architectural world, but it is a process of bringing design ideas into a place where they can be executed.

Ming Cho Lee,
American theatre designer

conflict, and character would change if they were moved to new surroundings. Imagine the Christmas movie *Miracle on 34th Street* transported to the steamy South or the chilly moral fable *Fargo* set in sunny Hawaii. Their stories, characters, and possibly themes would be transformed. Even the most well-known plays by Shakespeare seem new and different when they are set in unexpected periods and locations. The feud between families in the early Renaissance Italy of *Romeo and Juliet* is transformed into a contemporary gang war in the Leonardo DiCaprio movie version. The plots and most of the dialogue are unchanged, but the shift in environment drastically alters the tone and the characters. Whether the set is complicated or simple, familiar or novel, the designer's duty is to create a virtual environment that will remind the audience who the players are and where they're supposed to be. Design can communicate to the audience the spirit and soul of the play.

From Page to Stage

There are as many methods of designing a virtual environment as there are designers and productions, so this will be only a sweeping look at what might be called a typical design process: taking the play from the page to the stage. "My approach, after reading the script," says Ming Cho Lee, one of the United States' premier set designers, "is to question the director about an overall production scheme, discussing choices: Should it be realistic or abstract? Should it be period or not? Should the material be metal, wood, granite? Then I do a rough sketch for the director to find out if I'm going in the right direction. Then I make a one-half-inch scale model and paint it up. All this takes time." In fact, the process can take so much time that designers must begin their work many months before the actors arrive on the scene.

Doing the Homework

Long before the rehearsals begin, the designers begin work by studying the script. The playwright has created the blueprint for a production; in order for the play to exist, the words on the page must be transformed into action and environment on the stage. The designer's analysis of the script is as detailed and comprehensive as any director's or actor's is. A complete understanding of the characters is essential because the characters define the environment and the environment reveals the characters, especially their personal surroundings—their home, office, or room. Characters' tastes, lifestyles, incomes, jobs, educations, and temperaments are reflected in the environment they've created, just as the décor of your dorm room and how you dress reflect your character.

Understanding the characters and script, however, is only the beginning. In order to create an accurate virtual environment, set, lighting, sound, costume, and makeup designers must often do detailed investigations into the location and historical period. They may need to study the architecture, the color schemes, and the styles. They might also study the customs, manners, and cultures. This research helps the designers answer dozens of critical questions, including the following ones:

- How does the play's environment affect and reflect the story and characters?
- How do the story and characters affect and reflect the environment?

© Michal Daniel

To create an environment that accurately reflects the mood and content of a play, theatre designers research the time and place in which the play's story happens. For example, the historically accurate set and costumes of Caroline, or Change, *about an African American maid and the Jewish family she works for, depict the racial and economic politics of 1963 Louisiana. This 2003 production featured Tonya Pinkins as Caroline and, shown here, Harrison Chad and Veanne Cox. Book and lyrics by Tony Kushner, music by Jeanine Tesori, sets by Riccardo Hernández, costumes by Paul Tazewell, and lighting by Jules Fisher and Peggy Eisenhauer. Directed by George C. Wolfe at the Public Theater, New York.*

- What significant details of the environment will define and individualize the characters?
- How do the characters feel about their environment?
- How does the environment relate to the play's theme?
- Is the personal environment in or out of harmony with the characters?

There are also historical considerations:

- What is the time period of the play?
- What was the religious, social, and political climate of that period?
- What was the religious, social, and political climate when the play was written?

Designers also consider practical questions, such as these:

- What are the mechanical requirements, such as the number of doors needed for exits?
- What are the budgetary limitations?
- What are the deadlines?
- What are the physical limitations of the stage?
- What are the physical dimensions of theatre in which the play will be performed? Like baseball parks, no two theatres are exactly the same. The

Theatre Spaces

Environment begins with the theatre itself. Theatre can take place just about anywhere, from stages to street corners. For much of its history, theatre has not been performed in theatre buildings but in what are called **found,** or **created, spaces.** Typically, these have been parks, churches, and town squares, but they can also be basements, warehouses, gymnasiums, jails, or subway stations. Theatre can take place just about anywhere an audience can gather. Set designer Robert Edmond Jones said, "In its essence, a theatre is only an arrangement of seats so grouped and spaced that the actor—the leader—can reach out and touch and hold each member of his audience. Architects of later days have learned how to add conveniences and comforts to this idea. But that is all. The idea itself never changes." The standard types of theatre today are proscenium arch, thrust, arena, and black box.

The most common type is the **proscenium arch.** The word *proscenium* comes from the ancient Latin word for "stage." The proscenium arch originated in Italy in the 1500s. (For more on the history of the proscenium arch and perspective scenery, see Part III.) Proscenium arch theatres are a little more formal than the other types because the audience is separated from the actors. As in a movie theatre, the audience sits safely in the dark, looking through a picture frame at the actors on the other side. In fact, proscenium arch theatres are sometimes called "picture frame" theatres. In some theatres, the separation between actors and audience is made even greater with the addition of an orchestra pit between the audience and stage. However, in modern proscenium arches the actors can come closer to the audience on what is called a **lip** or **apron,** a part of the stage that extends into the audience's side of the picture frame. Some aprons are on a hydraulic or manual elevator and can be raised and lowered; at stage level they are an extension of the stage, and when lowered they become the orchestra pit. Above the stage, a traditional proscenium arch hides an elaborate network of pulleys, riggings, and counterweights called a **fly system** that raises scenic pieces out of the audience's sight. Fly systems can tower 80–100 feet above the stage and are usually manually operated, although some modern proscenium arch theatres have computerized fly systems. At the sides of a proscenium arch stage are the **wings.** Out of the audience's sight, the wings are areas from which actors make their entrances and where set pieces can be stored or moved onto the stage.

A **thrust stage** has a lip (apron) that protrudes so far into the auditorium that the audience must sit on three sides of the stage. This "peninsula" or "runway" type of stage reduces the distance between the actors and audience. Even from the back rows, the distance is small. This allows for a more intimate style of acting. Occasionally size, seating arrangement, and layout can directly affect the design. (For more on types of theatres, see the Spotlight box "Theatre Spaces.")

In order to answer all these questions, designers must have well-rounded educations in history, dramatic structure, art, art history, and criticism. Many universities offer an MFA (Master of Fine Arts) degree in set, costume, light, and sound design. Designers must also have a great deal of imagination, because, in the words of Robert Edmund Jones (1887–1954), one of the United States' foremost set designers, they need to "immerse themselves in [the play]" and even "be baptized by it." Only then can they begin their work on the design.

FOR MORE ON
DESIGNING WOMEN
"Designing women," Tish Dace, *Back Stage,* March 20, 1998

Courtesy of The Stratford Festival of Canada

Proscenium arch theatres are sometimes called "picture frame" theatres because the arch resembles the frame of a picture. Today proscenium stages, like this one in Canada's Avon Theatre, are the most common type of stage in North America, but they originated in Italy during the Renaissance.

Courtesy of The Stratford Festival of Canada

Thrust stages, like that of the Festival Theatre in Canada, protrude into the auditorium so that the audience sits on three sides. Like the proscenium arch, thrust theatres have been around for hundreds of years. In fact, William Shakespeare's plays were first performed on a thrust stage.

called "three-quarters-round," many thrust theatres have passageways or tunnels called **vomitories,** or "voms," that run into and under the audience to allow actors quick access to the stage. Vomitories are just like the stadium tunnel a football team disappears into at halftime. Historically, it is unclear how the word *vomitory* came to be used for a theatre space, but the word comes from the Latin verb *vomere,* which means to "spew out"; literally, actors are "spewed out" from the stage down these tunnel-like exits.

The thrust stage is much older than the proscenium arch theatre. Twenty-five hundred years ago, ancient Greek tragedies were performed on a version of the thrust stage. Four hundred years ago, Shakespeare's plays were first performed on a thrust stage.

Arena theatres are far less common than proscenium arch or thrust theatres. Often called "theatres-in-the-round," arenas have the stage in the center, like an island, surrounded on all sides by audience. Arena theatres resemble sports stadiums, boxing arenas, and circus rings. Like thrust theatres, arenas have vomitories to allow actors easy access to the stage as well as a close relationship with the audience. Arena productions may cost the least to stage because elaborate scenery is not possible. Walls, doors, and large furniture pieces would only block the audience's view, so sets are kept simple. Although this keeps expenses low, it limits the number of plays that can be effectively produced. The major challenge for productions on arena stages is the audience's **sight lines,** because there are few places the actors can stand or sit without blocking someone's view. To solve this problem, actors often try to keep their backs to the vomitories so they are open to a majority of audience members. Another solution is to keep moving. Some directors make the actors move, shift, or turn every thirty seconds or so to ensure that no one audience member's view is blocked for too long. Arena stages are probably the oldest type of theatre, for whenever people gather for an outdoor event, whether a tribal ceremony, a sporting event, or a rally, a circle seems to be our natural method of gathering.

Most **black box theatres** seat fewer than a hundred people. The audience sits close to the actors, making these theatres ideal for small, intimate plays. Sometimes called "studio," "flexible," or "experimental" theatres, most black boxes have no permanent seating arrangement. They are bare spaces that allow seats to be arranged differently for every production. The space can be set up as a proscenium arch, a thrust, or an arena, or it may be configured in some experimental, nontraditional actor/audience arrangement. In some black box productions, audience members have sat on stage with the actors or followed the actors from location to location or looked down into a pit where the action was taking place. Black box theatres are often in found spaces, such as converted warehouses or storefronts. They are called "black boxes" because the walls are usually painted black to de-emphasize them, and the space is often square. However, no two black box theatres are exactly alike.

Design Team Meetings

Once the designers have researched and studied the play, they are ready for the artistic and production meetings. The director, stage manager, and designers begin by reviewing practical issues: the physical limits of the theatre, safety concerns, budget limitations, and scheduling. But soon they get down to finding, understanding, and communicating the production concept. As you read in Chapter 8, the production concept is the master symbol or allegory that the director, playwright, and designers conceive as the central metaphor. The director and designers use this metaphor to physically express the mood, tone, theme, and philosophy of the script.

A central design metaphor expressed through physical symbols is an important aspect of the theatre. Art is often symbolic because the human brain is attracted to symbols that evoke complex thoughts and emotions. Designers can externalize these symbols so that they evoke similar thoughts and feelings

In arena theatres, or theatres-in-the-round, the audience surrounds the stage, as in a sports arena. Performing on an arena stage can be a challenge because actors must often shift positions to remain open to the audience. This example is the Fichandler Stage of Arena Stage in Washington, DC.

Black box theatres, such as the National Theatre's Cottesloe in London, are also known as studio, flexible-space, or experimental theatres and they come in all shapes and sizes. They are called black box theatres because their walls are almost always painted black and they often have a boxlike shape.

in others. Some symbols are familiar: red symbolizes fire, bars symbolize confinement, the capital letter *I* symbolizes self. But symbols can also be elaborate allegories representing our deepest emotions; these symbols communicate on conscious and subconscious levels. Designers in the theatre communicate the production concept—the central metaphor of the play—through lights, sound, sets, and costumes. They make a play's ideas more clear and complete than they would be in real life. Nothing on stage is arbitrary. Everything, from a costume's button to the color of the light to the angle of a door is chosen to communicate the production concept.

It can take many meetings for the director and designers to agree on a production concept. During these meetings they talk about how they see the play, how they feel about each scene, and how they hope to affect the audience. The director may tell personal stories that connect to the play's theme or discuss reasons for staging the play. Some directors use models, sketches, photos, paintings, and even music as well as words to communicate their ideas about the production concept. "Designing is something that you don't approach in a linear way like you approach climbing a ladder, one step at a time," says set designer Ming Cho Lee. "It's actually a constant exploring of ideas. It's about how you connect with a play, how you live the life of the play." During these meetings the director and designers talk about mood, pace, atmosphere, and colors as well as character and story. The director also talks about the production's style—perhaps realism or expressionism or some combination of "isms." (For more on style, see the Spotlight box "Theatrical Styles.")

After the director and designers determine the production concept, there are meetings to discuss every detail of the production. The designers' opinions

Theatrical Styles

SPOTLIGHT

All plays have a style. *Style* is the way in which a work is expressed or performed. Some plays, like most television shows, are lifelike imitations of nature. This is a style known as **realism.** To design realistic sets, lights, makeup, and costumes, designers pay close attention to details that will make everything appear to be a genuine duplication of real life, whatever the period. For example, if a scene is about a 1950s housewife in her kitchen, then the designers would use historically accurate faucets, running water, and a working refrigerator from the postwar era. They would also design natural-looking light that seems to be coming from a source onstage, such as a ceiling fixture or sunlight flowing in through the window and bouncing off the 1950s flowered wallpaper and linoleum floors. The housewife's costume would be genuine to the period, as if it came off a department-store rack, and the dinette set would look as if it came from the time Eisenhower was president. The only difference from real life would be that one wall of the kitchen is missing so that the audience can peek in on the action.

For some plays, **simplified,** or **suggested, realism** is appropriate. For this style, designers *suggest* rather than duplicate the look of a period. What the audience sees is not a carbon copy but a suggestion of a 1950s kitchen, whose details they must fill in with their imagination. This style is sometimes called **selective realism** because some design elements appear authentic, but other elements are stylized. For example, our 1950s kitchen might appear real, but the lights may express the mood rather than seem to come from a source on stage. Or our housewife's costume might be authentic, but the set more symbolic.

Once designers step away from realism, they are set free to create virtual worlds with their own logic and rules. They can pursue a metaphorical, symbolic, or stylized look. Stylization can take several forms; one of the most common is **expressionism.** With expressionism, the

Billy Rose Theatre Collection, The New York Public Library for the Performing Arts, Astor, Lenox and Tilden Foundations

Selective realism gets its name from the selected elements of reality designers choose to highlight. With this style, some aspects of a play's environment are presented realistically whereas others are merely suggested and allowed to take less focus. In this set designed by Jo Mielziner for a 1949 production of Arthur Miller's Death of a Salesman*, the furniture looks quite real but is placed within a skeletal framework of a house.*

may change the entire look of the play. For example, when Julie Taymor designed the costumes for the Broadway hit *The Lion King: The Musical,* she wanted race to be an important part of the story. "What I love about *The Lion King,*" says Taymor, "is that this is a show with a predominantly nonwhite cast that is not about race. On the other hand, it's all about race—and that should be acknowledged, because there are very powerful traditions . . . and that fact shouldn't be ignored." The producers, on the other hand, did not think the theme of race was particularly important, but Taymor persisted. During a production meeting, she convinced them to agree to the design for African-inspired clothes. The result was a change in the whole production concept.

audience sees the story through the mind of one character. Settings may be distorted by the character's conscious or subconscious phobias, prejudices, or psychoses. Instead of photographic reality, the audience sees the character's inner reality. With an expressionistic style, our 1950s kitchen might have slanted walls leaning in on our housewife showing her feelings of claustrophobia and being trapped in her marriage. The TV shows *Ally McBeal* and *That 70s Show* have used expressionism to illustrate the mindset of a character, such as someone literally drowning in a cup of coffee or the walls closing in on an office worker.

When stylization is taken to an extreme, little or no attempt is made to re-create reality; instead, oversized symbols and fantastic dreamlike or nightmarish images dominate the stage. With **surrealism,** the subconscious of the characters is emphasized in the design—now our 1950s kitchen is located in Hell. With **symbolism,** a certain piece of scenery, a costume, or light may represent the essence of the entire environment: Our 1950s kitchen might have huge faucets that torture the housewife with their incessant dripping.

Finally, some sets contain little that looks real. The purpose of these sets is to remind the audience that they're watching a play. Now our 1950s kitchen has only a sink, and no walls. Instead, advertising posters are hung around the stage with smiling 1950s housewives looking down on our character and extolling the marvels of a modern kitchen.

Few designs have only one style. Designers often mix styles to fulfill their aesthetic goals for an environment that fits the production concept and the needs of the play.

© R. Finkelstein

Whereas realism aims for authenticity, expressionism attempts to re-create the world as the characters see and feel it—subjectively, with their emotions and unconscious thoughts made visible. This 2001 production of Elmer Rice's expressionist play The Adding Machine *at the University of Colorado, Denver, featured a set by Richard Finkelstein, lights by Scott Hay, and costumes by Jane Nelson-Rudd.*

© Robbie Jack

Inspired by psychoanalysis and the workings of the human mind, surrealist playwrights attempted to break down the barriers between the conscious and the unconscious. In this 2005 production of August Strindberg's A Dream Play, *adapted by Caryl Churchill, we see inside the mind of the main character as he dreams of his past. Directed by Katie Mitchell and designed by Vicki Mortimer, National Theatre, Cottesloe, London.*

Filling the Empty Space

Once the designers understand the production concept, they need to make the leap from words to images. They create drawings, renderings, thumbnail sketches, models, and plans of the sets, costumes, makeup, and lights. After each production meeting, the designers combine the play's needs, their research, the style, and the concept, and let them "bake." Designers may contemplate these issues for weeks to allow their training and their creative mind to conceive ideas that will express the production concept. No two designers work the same way. But they all must take into account the demands of the play and the limitations of the theatre while transforming abstract ideas into concrete designs that convey the central metaphor of the play. They use the basic elements of design.

The basic elements of design are line, dimension, balance, movement, harmony, color, and texture. For example, if the master symbol of the play is the need to get back to nature, the designers might choose earth tones, the colors of growing plants, and natural textures. If the master concept is to glorify humankind's great achievements as represented in our cities, then straight lines and massive forms that reflect the sun might be used. If the master concept is to show a world out of balance, then the designers might use odd-shaped masses that seem to teeter unsteadily or defy the laws of gravity. The designer's choices are limitless because there are infinite possibilities that could meet a play's production needs. To understand more about the design process, let's look at each of the major design categories: set, lights, sound, costume, and makeup.

Designing the Set

Twenty-five hundred years ago in ancient Greece, designers painted screens, sewed costumes, and built masks to help create the characters and suggest the play's virtual environment. During the Italian Renaissance, designers constructed elaborate stage settings using two-dimensional flats that were painstakingly painted to appear as if they were three-dimensional throne rooms, landscapes, and dungeons. At other times in theatre's long history, the set design has been simple. For example, for hundreds of years Chinese opera was performed outdoors on bare platforms. Instead of complex designs, settings were indicated with simple symbolic gestures of the actors or with minimal set pieces. If the story required a character to climb a tall mountain, the actor would pantomime it using only a small stepladder; a plain wooden stool could represent a grand golden throne. This worked for the Chinese opera because the audience knew they had to use their imagination to "see" the set.

> I'm looking for a connection with the world we live in, a passion for seeing that [connection] translated in visual terms. What I'm trying to train [students] is the ability to translate text or music into meaningful images.
>
> ***Ursula Belden,***
> *American theatre designer and professor*

Whether the set is complicated or simple, real or suggested, there is always a designer. All set designers have a strong background in interior design, architecture, and art history, as well as theatrical conventions of various periods. They must know how to paint, draw, and draft. Each preliminary drawing must take into account not only the needs of the script but also the budget of the theatre. If the theatre owns scenery pieces that will work, new ones will not have to be built from scratch. Budget is always a concern, as are the physical needs of the play and the limitations of the theatre. The set designer makes numerous thumbnail sketches in an attempt to realize the production concept, taking into account the locations, environment, and historical background of the script. This doodling can be done in pencil, pen, or charcoal. Figure 9.1 shows an early drawing by designer Michael Earl for a production of *My Fair Lady.* After this rough sketch, he decided that that set had to be more open, so he eliminated the pillar on the right and showed more of the city's skyline in the background (Figure 9.2).

Once the director approves the thumbnail drawings, which may take several meetings and trips back to the drawing board, the designer makes a final full-color rendering of the set. This color rendering (Figure 9.3) shows the set as the designer wants the audience to see it. It will be used by the director to stage the play and by the other designers to coordinate the lights, costumes, and other design elements. This rendering also gives the actors an idea of what the set will look like long before it's built.

When the set design has been finalized, the designer draws dozens of detailed blueprints. These blueprints used to be done by hand, but today designers often use **computer-aided design (CAD)** programs to produce the final drawings. Just like architectural drawings for a building, these blueprints

Figure 9.1 *Early rough sketch of a set from a University of Wyoming production of Alan Jay Lerner and Frederick Loewe's* My Fair Lady, *drawn by designer Michael Earl.*

SOURCE: Michael Earl

Figure 9.2 *The later rough sketch.*

SOURCE: Michael Earl

include scale drawings of every part of the set. The view from above is called the **floor plan;** the views from front and back are called the **elevations** (see Figure 9.4). These drawings must be rendered exactly to scale and show the placement of every door, window, and platform, as well as furniture, light switches, and even the baseboards. Everything must be drawn to exact scale so that the set-construction crew can make measurements. While making these detailed drawings, the designer must take into account durability, budget, and safety, as well as the length of time available for construction. Along with the blueprints, the designer will make painter's elevations, which include the color and wallpaper patterns, shading, and texture.

Once the blueprints are completed, the set-construction crew gets to work. The complete process from production meeting to final design often takes months. Figure 9.5 shows the final set for the production of *My Fair Lady,* generated from the sketches shown in Figures 9.1, 9.2, and 9.3.

Figure 9.3 *The final color rendering.*

Source: Michael Earl

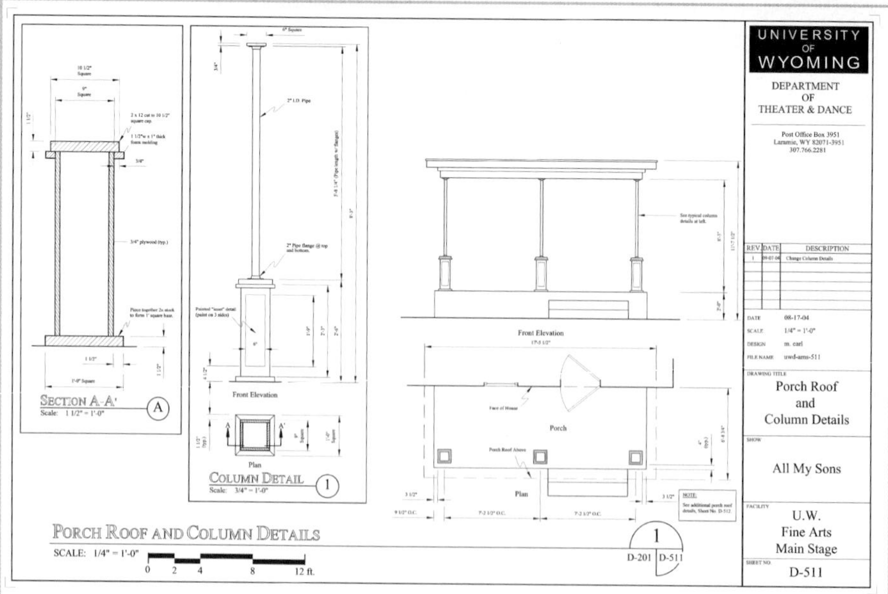

Figure 9.4 *Elevation of a set from a University of Wyoming production of Arthur Miller's All My Sons, drawn by designer.*

Source: Michael Earl

Figure 9.5 *The final set for* My Fair Lady *at the Struthers Theatre in Warren, Pennsylvania.*

SOURCE: Michael Earl.

Figure 9.6 *A white model from a production of* All My Sons, *prepared by designer Michael Earl.*

Source: Michael Earl

Sometimes the designer also builds three-dimensional scale models of the setting. The preliminary model is called the "white model" because it is made of heavy white paper and foam board and is only a foot across (Figure 9.6). After the director and designer study the white model and agree on changes, the designer now makes a second, more detailed color model. The second model includes every aspect of the set in detail (Figure 9.7). Figure 9.8 shows the final set for a production of *All My Sons,* generated from the models shown in Figures 9.6 and 9.7.

For more on set design, see Spotlight on Diversity box "The Life of a Designer: Ming Cho Lee."

Designing the Lights

For thousands of years, theatre was performed outdoors, so the sun provided the light. Many of these pre-electricity civilizations built their theatres so that the afternoon sunshine would hit the stage. The first indoor theatres were built about five hundred years ago and used chandeliers filled with sputtering candles to illuminate the stage. In 1545, Sebastiano Serlio (1475–1554) published *Architettura,* a book on Italian set design, in which he described how to change the color of the light by placing reflectors behind the candles and

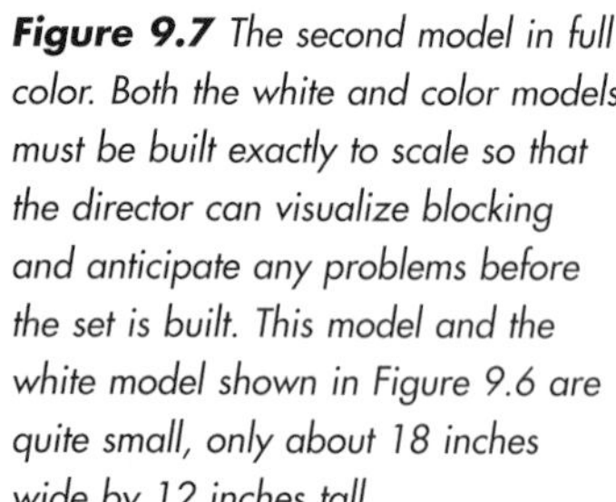

Figure 9.7 *The second model in full color. Both the white and color models must be built exactly to scale so that the director can visualize blocking and anticipate any problems before the set is built. This model and the white model shown in Figure 9.6 are quite small, only about 18 inches wide by 12 inches tall.*

SOURCE: Michael Earl

Figure 9.8 *The final set for* All My Sons.

SOURCE: University of Wyoming photo archives

The Life of a Designer: Ming Cho Lee

Ming Cho Lee has been called the "dean" of American scene design. Born in Shanghai, Lee's parents divorced when he was six and, as was common in China at the time, he lived with his father. "I had weekend visits with my mother, and those were the great moments of my life," he recalled. His mother took him to the theatre, movies, and Chinese opera. She also allowed him to study drawing and watercolor painting. In 1949 he came to the United States and studied art, design, and theatre at Occidental College and UCLA before moving to New York City, where he became principal designer for the New York Shakespeare Company, the Juilliard Opera Theatre, and Peabody Arts Theatre in Baltimore.

Lee became known for his minimalist sets that used basic colors and geometric shapes to create "environments" rather than realistic-looking settings. He did not, however, limit himself to minimalism. One of his most famous sets was for Patrick Meyers' play *K2.* Although he made the rocky face of the world's tallest mountain from sculpted Styrofoam covered with layers of tissue and paint, the audience could believe that the actors were really hanging hundreds of feet in the air. For *K2* Lee won the 1983 Tony Award for best set design. Other famous shows he has designed include the original production of the rock musical *Hair,* a revival of Arthur Miller's *The Crucible,* Ntozake Shange's *For Colored Girls Who Have Considered Suicide/When the Rainbow Is Enuf,* and Michael Cristofer's *The Shadow Box.*

In 1969, Lee became professor of design at Yale School of Drama, where he trained many of today's important set designers including John Lee Beatty, Heidi Landesman, Michael Yeargan, Marjorie Bradley Kellogg, Adrianne Lobel, and Douglas Schmidt. "Teaching," says Lee, "forces a teacher to always go through a process of self-evaluation." And self-evaluation is at the heart of all art.

Lee is a strong supporter of multiculturalism and laments the lack of it in U.S. design today. He believes its absence is "linked to the lack of visibility of designers and production people. A black child can see black actors and say, 'I want to do that.' He or she can read about black directors. But if that child sees a set or a lighting design, there's no sense of who is responsible for it. It's almost as if it came into being completely on its own somehow." Lee feels the only way to combat the problem is for designers of color to become more visible. "We must let young people know, and I mean young Asian, black, Latino, and Native American boys and girls, that this kind of expression is available to them, that they can survive in this field, and they don't have to give up who they are to do so."

© Hsu Ping. Courtesy of the Yale University School of Drama, Department of Design

Theatre designer Ming Cho Lee

© Michal Daniel

This set design by Ming Cho Lee for Eugene O'Neill's Ah! Wilderness *illustrates his characteristically spare use of color and shapes to suggest a more substantial environment. This 2001–2002 production by the Guthrie Theater was directed by Douglas C. Wager.*

globes of colored water in front. A hundred years later, Nicola Sabbattini (ca.1574–1654) published the *Manual for Constructing Theatrical Scenes and Machines,* which told how oil lights could be dimmed by lowering tin cylinders over the flames. But these early lighting design techniques were complicated and their effects modest. Because the light in the theatre was so dim, the auditorium and audience had to be lit as well as the stage. The actors resorted to painting their faces with cosmetics so that their expressions could be seen.

> Light is the most important medium on the stage. . . . Without its unifying power, our eyes would be able to perceive what objects were but not what they expressed. . . . What can give us this sublime unity which is capable of uplifting us: . . . Light!"
>
> ***Adolphe Appia,***
> *Swiss lighting designer*

By the 1840s, gas-lit theatres were common. There were even gas-powered spotlights, in which jets of hydrogen and oxygen were ignited with small bits of lime; this is the source of the word **limelight** and the phrase "to be in the limelight." Needless to say, all that gas made theatres prone to fire. For example, the Paris Opéra used 28 miles of tubing to carry the highly flammable gas to all its lights. In 1856, the magazine *The Builder* stated that it was the fate of all theatres to eventually burn down. Their fate changed in 1881 with the advent of electric lights. For the first time in theatre's history, lighting designers could adequately light the stage and allow the audience to sit in the dark. Soon there were master lighting designers, such as Adolphe Appia (1862–1928), who used light, shadows, and color to create complex lighting effects. Today, theatrical lighting has become a refined art. Designers have a wide range of instruments and effects at their disposal, and new inventions continue to improve the art. For example, in the last few decades, computer-controlled lightboards have become common and make it possible to store an entire show's lighting design, including hundreds of exact levels and cues, on a small disk or a keychain hard drive. With the touch of a button, these lightboards can automatically fade hundreds of lights at a preprogrammed speed.

Stage lighting can be divided into two categories: motivated and nonmotivated. **Motivated light** comes from an identifiable source such as a candle, a table lamp, or the sun. **Nonmotivated light** reinforces the mood of a scene but doesn't necessarily come from an identifiable or onstage source. Nonmotivated light can be obvious or faint, and the lighting designer can change the light's direction, balance, and color in order to create cool shadows or warm highlights. These shadows and highlights establish a scene's mood, space, and environment. For every light cue the audience is aware of, dozens of other more subtle light changes affect the audience subconsciously.

Unlike the other designers, lighting designers cannot easily make renderings or models to demonstrate the look of the final lighting design. Some lighting designers make drawings in an attempt to show the director the proposed effect, but usually, the lighting designer just draws a **lighting plot.** This detailed drawing shows the location of each lighting instrument on the hanging grid and where its light will be focused. The lighting plot also shows the type of lighting instrument, the circuitry necessary, the wattage, and the colors. Colored lights are achieved by filtering the light through **gels,** or sheets of colored plastic attached to the front of lighting instruments. (They are called *gels* because they were once made of gelatin.) Gels come in thousands of colors, giving the lighting designer an almost limitless palette. Patterns, such as sunlight coming through the leaves of a tree, can be projected on the stage with metal cutouts, called **gobos,** placed in front of the light. Other more sophisticated devices make it possible to project moving clouds, flickering fire, or twinkling stars.

FOR MORE ON
LIGHTING DESIGNERS

"Lighting designer [The life of a theatrical lighting designer]," Michael Stanton, *Occupational Outlook Quarterly,* Winter 1988

Figure 9.9 *Lighting can create a mood, imitate natural light, illuminate important aspects of a stage, and direct the audience's focus. In this University of Wyoming production of a play by William Missouri Downs about the 1925 Scopes "monkey trial," the lighting designer Larry Hazlett puts the focus on the center of the courtroom, de-emphasizing the courtroom audience at either side. In addition, the U.S. flag and photos of the actual trial are illuminated, giving them a visual presence that helps tell the play's story.*

SOURCE: University of Wyoming photo archives

Although set designers can turn their blueprints and models over to crews for construction, lighting designers must often act as their own crew chief and supervise the hanging and focusing of each light. The reason is that the only way to design lights is with light. Once each light is circuited to the main lightboard, the lighting designer programs the computer and builds hundreds of cues, setting the length and intensity of each cue. The lights are almost always the last design element to be added to any production. They are often not completed until hours before the opening night performance.

Modern lighting designers have the technology to make light an instrument of expression, "like a paintbrush, or a sculptor's chisel, or a phrase of music," Robert Edmond Jones said. "At rare moments, in the long quiet hours of light-rehearsals a strange thing happens. We are overcome by a realization of the *livingness* of light. As we gradually bring a scene out of the shadows, sending long rays slanting across a column, touching an outline with color, animating the scene moment by moment until it seems to breathe, our work becomes an incantation. We feel the presence of elemental energies." (See Figure 9.9.)

Designing the Sound

The ancient Greeks used simple implements to imitate wind, rain, and thunder. The Romans went further and built copper-lined thunder tunnels in the floors of their theatres. Stagehands dropped boulders down these tunnels to create the sound of distant thunder or, if the boulders were large enough, an earthquake effect. Some fifteen hundred years later, Shakespeare's plays included the sound effects of trumpet fanfares and cannon fire to thrill the audience and help set the scene. In fact, one of these sound effects was the reason that Shakespeare's theatre burned to the ground in 1613: A spark from one of the cannons lit the roof on fire. In minutes the wooden theatre was engulfed in flames, creating a special effect a little more spectacular than the one Shakespeare intended. Many forms of non-Western theatre also use sound effects. For example, Japanese Kabuki theatre uses special floor resonators to amplify the sounds of the actors' feet as they dance.

Today's sound designers can record, mix, filter, reverberate, modulate, amplify, and cue up sound effects exactly when they are needed. They record sounds from real life, and they use sounds from vast sound libraries that contain everything from distant foghorns to birds singing in the morning, and from crickets chirping on a calm night to deadly gunfire. Sound designers in the theatre and in film can also digitally sculpt sounds in order to get the right ring of a doorbell, and they can synthesize sounds for the exact tone needed to convey a particular emotion or meaning. Sound designers may take extraordinary steps to get the perfect sound. The sound of Luke Skywalker's land speeder in *Star Wars* (1977) was made by recording Los Angeles freeway traffic through a vacuum-cleaner tube. The sounds of torpedoes firing in *The Hunt for Red October* (1990) were layered with animal growls, a Ferrari engine, and a screeching screen-door spring. Theatrical sound designers, like their film counterparts, spend hours trying to record or synthesize the exact sounds needed, for the right sound can often express things that words cannot.

Designing the Costumes

Throughout theatre's history, actors and designers have tried to find the right costumes to reveal the character and play. In precolonial African theatre, masks and costumes were an integral part of the performance. In Shakespeare's day, wealthy lords and ladies donated their worn gowns and leggings to the local theatre so that actors might have a variety of costumes. Today's costume designer is in charge of designing all aspects of the production's costumes, including hats and accessories, such as jewelry, wallets, purses, shoes, and watches.

FOR MORE ON

COSTUME DESIGNERS

"Dressing up the voices: The role of the costume designer is a very visible (and sometimes risible) mix of creativity and craft," Robert Jordan, *Opera Canada,* Summer 2002

Many factors go into a costume design, for each costume must reflect and establish the character's social and economic status, lifestyle, age, country, occupation, education, and geographical origin. The costume designer must also take into account the historical period, season, and even the time of day. Further, costumes have to fit the needs of the script, the budget of the theatre, the style of the set, the color of lights, and the production concept. In other words, the costume designer must be a visual artist, fashion designer, historian, and psychoanalyst.

Like all other designers, the costume designer is an expert at play analysis, especially character analysis. A costume is the most personal expression of a character, so the costume designer must understand the purposes of clothing. Beyond the basic need for protection from the elements, dress is a form of body ornamentation that says a lot about who we are. True, we dress in what we can afford, but we also dress to impress others, to attract a mate, to intimidate, to celebrate, to imitate, to be comfortable, to be in style, and to rebel. There is no such thing as a generic costume; every color, fold, and cut is a reflection of character. As designer Robert Edmund Jones said, a costume is "not just for a character in a scene in a play, but for *that* character, in *that* scene, in *that* play." Because costume is so closely related to character, the costume designer often designs the actors' hairstyles and sometimes the makeup.

Like all other designers, costume designers attend production meetings and use drawings to communicate what the designs will look like. The first costume renderings are tentative sketches, which can go through many variations before the final design is agreed upon. Costume designers use all the standard design elements—line, mass, balance, harmony, composition, color, movement, and texture—but they must also take into account how the costume will fit. In addition, different fabrics move differently—some are flowing and others stiff—and can create various effects.

Once the designs are agreed upon, the costume designer paints detailed **costume plates** that the costume construction crew will use to assemble the costumes. These sketches indicate how each costume is shaped, where seams and folds are, how the costume flows, and what fabrics are to be used—some designers even attach fabric swatches to the plates. (See Figures 9.10–9.13.)

FOR MORE ON

SET AND COSTUME DESIGN FOR THE MUSICAL *TITANIC*

"Godspeed, Titanic," David Barbour, Ellen Lampert-Greaux, and David Johnson, *TCI (Theatre Crafts International)*, August–September 1997

Figure 9.10 **Figure 9.11**

Costume renderings give the director and designers a sense of how the costumes will look and move. They are also invaluable guides for the cutters and stitchers who build the costumes. Figures 9.10 and 9.12 show designer Lee Hodgson's renderings for a University of Wyoming production of William Shakespeare's Love's Labour's Lost. *Notice how exactly the finished costumes in Figures 9.11 and 9.13 match the renderings.*

SOURCE: © Lee Hodgson (illustration) and University of Wyoming photo archives

Figure 9.12

SOURCE: © Lee Hodgson (illustration) and University of Wyoming Photo Archives

Figure 9.13

At smaller theatres the costume designer sometimes doubles as head of the costume-construction crew. But at larger and professional theatres the designer leaves the constructing of the costumes to patternmakers, cutters, tailors and fitters. Depending on the size and type of show, the building of the costumes can take weeks. Once the costumes are done, a **dress parade** is held. The actors try on their costumes and parade in front of the costume designer and director, who confer on changes needed before opening night.

Preparing Makeup, Wigs, and False Noses

Around the world and over the centuries, actors have used makeup to disguise and to exaggerate their features. Japanese Kabuki theatre is known for its striking, stylized makeup that exaggerates the actors' features. In the West there are two categories of makeup. **Straight makeup** does not change the actors' looks but makes their faces look more three-dimensional and therefore more visible to the audience because the bright theatrical lights wash out their facial features. Actors also wear makeup so they will look more like the character they are playing and less like themselves. **Character makeup** is an attempt to transform the way actors look—for example, by adding gray hair, wrinkles, and shadows to a youthful actor who must play an old man. The type and the amount of makeup actors need changes with every production. For a realistic play in a small theatre, the actors might wear no makeup. For a realistic play in a large theatre, the actors might wear lots of powder and rouge to add shadows and highlights so that they can be seen from the back row. For a nonrealistic or highly stylized play, they may have to come in many

© Reuters/Corbis

Makeup design is often the responsibility of the costume designer, but makeup artists are hired for complicated makeup designs, as in the musical Cats. *Makeup effects can be achieved by painting the face with color, shadows, and highlights or by using three-dimensional pieces such as beards, wigs, false noses, scars, or, in this case, whiskers.*

hours before curtain so that an artist can apply layers of special makeup. Actors who are playing a character much older, younger, or different from themselves might also need to wear a beard or a wig. These are often designed by the costume designer and constructed by a specialized wigmaker.

If the play requires only straight makeup, the actors often do it themselves. All actor-training programs include classes in how to create and apply a makeup scheme. But more complicated makeup often requires a makeup designer. The musicals *Cats* and *Beauty and the Beast* needed a makeup designer to design exactly how each character should look and to make renderings of the design much like those of costume and set designers. If a special prosthetic piece, such as a scar, a false nose, or a wart, is needed, the makeup designer makes a plaster cast of the actor's face and casts the prosthesis in synthetic rubber. An exact fit allows the prosthesis to be held on with just a dab of nontoxic theatrical glue.

A Mad, Mad World Inside and Out: Louis Nowra's *Cosi*

Australian playwright Louis Nowra has written some of the darkest and funniest plays in Australian theatre, and *Cosi* (1992) is one of his best known and most comedic works. *Cosi* is about Lewis, a young director attempting to mount a production of Mozart's Italian opera *Cosi Fan Tutte* as drama therapy for the patients at a Melbourne mental hospital. In the process of trying to pull together an opera with a cast of drug addicts, pyromaniacs, manic-depressives, and obsessive-compulsives who can't sing and can't speak Italian, Lewis battles his feelings of alienation and fear to become part of the group. *Cosi* is set in the charred remains of a theatre, which is a wonderful metaphor for this absurd, magical event in the patients' scorched lives.

The events and tone of the 1996 film version of *Cosi* are mostly faithful to the play, although there are a few key differences. The film has a larger cast of characters, including hospital workers, extras, and a variety of patients who audition in a scene

Courtesy Ocean Theatre Company

This 2004 stage version of Louis Nowra's Cosi, performed by the Ocean Theatre Company and directed by Andrew Miller, highlights the intimacy of a makeshift theatre.

FROM STAGE TO SCREEN

© Miramax/Photofest

In the 1996 film version of Cosi*, director Mark Joffe was able to move some of the action outside the theatre.*

that rivals *American Idol* outtakes. The film also omits Lewis's monologue at the end of the play that tells us what happened to various patients. Overall, the film is more upbeat, the violence more slapstick, and the madness toned down.

However, the most noticeable difference between the play and the film is the setting. A theatre is a perfect setting for a play about a play, and *Cosi* makes good use of it, creating a sense that the inhabitants of this strange world are locked in, literally. However, an entire feature film shot in a single interior location can be monotonous, so the filmmakers widened the scope of *Cosi,* adding other locations, such as Lewis's house and the hospital's grounds, mental ward, and dining room. And for even more visual interest, the movie features a scene in which the theatre burns down and the opera rehearsals are moved to an old laundry building.

In the next few movies you watch, try to notice how many times the filmmaker moves from inside to outside to create visual variety and control the pace. Based on the variety of locations, try to guess whether the movie was made from a play. Conversely, the next time you read or watch a play, think of how you might film it to provide scenic variety without changing the story too much or compromising its tone.

Aoise Stratford
Playwright

Now It's Got to Be Built

Once the designs are finished, they are turned over to the technical director (or TD in theatre lingo). The TD turns the designers' drawings, paintings, blueprints, models, and sketches into fully realized sets, lights, and costumes. The TD usually presides over large construction crews who build the set, stitch the costumes, and hang the lights. (Although lighting designers often hang and focus the lights, the TD usually helps. If the designer is not available to hang lights, then it is the TD's responsibility.) For a small or simple production, these crews may consist of only a few people, but most plays have dozens of crew members and they almost always outnumber the actors. (For more on the ensemble that makes theatre work, see Chapter 5.) A theatre usually needs a well-equipped **scene shop** with a variety of metalworking and woodworking tools; a **costume shop** with sewing machines, laundry facilities, fabric-cutting tables, and fitting rooms; an **electric shop** with equipment to maintain, repair, and hang lights; a **paint shop,** where paint is stored and mixed; and a **sound booth,** where sound effects and music cues can be edited and prepared. Theatres also often have a **property shop,** where the props are designed, built, and stored. **Props** (theatre lingo for "properties") include **set props,** or anything that sits on the set including sofas, chairs, and beds, and **hand props,** or any objects actors handle while on stage, such as pens, fans, cigars, money, and umbrellas.

> Scenery and costumes can sometimes evolve in rehearsal at the same time as the rest of the performance, but often practical considerations of building and dressmaking force the designer to have his work cut and dried before the first rehearsal.
>
> ***Peter Brook,***
> *British theatre director*

Theatres often save time and money by reusing basic set units. The standard unit for walls is called a **flat.** Flats are made of wooden frames covered with canvas, muslin, or thin plywood that can be painted to fit the design. Most flats are from twelve to sixteen feet tall and one to six feet wide. Some flats are plain wall units, while others are built to accommodate doors, windows, and fireplaces. Other scenery units are platforms, steps and staircases, fake fireplaces, doors, and window frames.

Most theatres also have a variety of curtains that can be used to frame the set and conceal offstage spaces. The curtains used on the sides are called **legs,** and those that frame the top of the stage are referred to as **teasers. Scrims,** open-mesh gauze curtains, can be transparent or translucent depending on whether the light hits from the front or behind. The **cyclorama,** often shortened to "cyc," is a large, stretched curtain suspended from a U-shaped rod. It makes a background that curves around the back of the stage setting. Cycloramas are usually neutral in color, but lighting designers can turn them into almost anything, from a symbolic collage of colors to a starry sky.

A production acquires its costumes in several ways. The theatre may already have appropriate costumes in storage, or the costumes can be rented, bought, borrowed, or built. Renting costumes is always a compromise, because what the costume rental companies have in stock is unlikely to exactly fit the production concept. Renting saves time but not that much money, because the rental, insurance, cleaning, and shipping fees add up to a substantial amount. Another option is to "pull" a show, or take the costumes from the theatre's storage vaults. Most college and professional theatre companies have huge costume vaults where they store thousands of costumes of various styles, sizes, and historical periods that were created for other productions, donated, or purchased. Pulling a show can save the theatre a great deal of time and money, but unless the vaults contain exactly what the play or director demands, numerous alterations must be made.

A theatre needs lots of storage space for all the costumes, props, wood, platforms, flats, and the rest of the theatrical inventory. The Denver Center for the Performing Arts uses a four-story building to store just its props. Sometimes the storage areas can be housed within the theatre building; if not, the theatre may have to rent storage space.

FOR MORE ON

TALES FROM STAGE DESIGNERS

"Tales from the designers' side; stage designers discuss violations of their rights," Tish Dace, *Back Stage,* July 8, 1994

Curtain Call

In the end, just days before the play opens, everything comes together with the technical rehearsals. The first tech rehearsals combine sound and lights with the set. These rehearsals are often called so that the crews can ensure they have everything covered. Next come the dress rehearsals when the actors get to rehearse in costumes for the first time. The night before the play opens is the final dress rehearsal. At this point, the only thing missing is the audience—even the curtain call is run to a mostly empty house and the only people sitting in the dark are the designers. (For more on the various types of rehearsals, see Chapter 7.) Although the designers aren't part of the curtain call, their work is onstage for all to applaud.

In the last analysis the designing of stage scenery is not the problem of an architect or a painter or a sculptor or even a musician, but of a poet.

Robert Edmond Jones,
American theatre designer

About the challenges of being a designer, Robert Edmond Jones said:

> The designer is forced to work and think in a hundred different ways—now as an architect, now as a house-painter, now as an electrician, now as a dressmaker, now as a sculptor, now as a jeweler. He must make idols and palaces and necklaces and frescoes and caparisons. As he works, he may be all too well aware of the outward limitations of the play he is to decorate and the actors he is to clothe. But in his mind's eye he must see the high original intention of the dramatist and follow it.

The only limitations—for today's designers—are imagination and budget.

Summary

Designers have been a part of the theatre for thousands of years. Whether plain or complex, their job is to remind the audience of where the characters are supposed to be—in other words, to create the play's environment. To do this, designers must do a lot of homework. They must research and analyze the play's dramatic structure, period, history, location, mood, characters, and theme. They must also take into account the budget and the physical configuration and size of the theatre: proscenium arch, thrust, arena, or black box.

All designers work with a director to create the production concept, which is devised from the master symbol or allegory and becomes the central metaphor for the production. The director and designers must also decide what style the play will reflect: naturalism, realism, selective realism, expressionism, surrealism, or symbolism.

Once they have a production concept, the designers make numerous drawings, renderings, thumbnail sketches, models, and plans of the sets, costumes, and lights. Many, if not most, designers have a strong background in art and history as well as interior design, architecture, and theatre. They must know how to paint, draw, and draft. The process of designing a set can take months as the designers move from thumbnail drawings, rough drawings, and final drawings to models and blueprints. Once the designs are done, the technical director and construction crews turn them into fully realized sets, lights, and costumes.

THE ART OF THEATRE ONLINE

Use the *Art of Theatre* website at **http://communication.wadsworth.com/downs1** for quick access to the electronic study resources that accompany this chapter, including a digital glossary, a link to InfoTrac College Edition that you can use to find the For More On . . . InfoTrac College Edition readings listed below, a list of further reading, and a chapter quiz. When you get to the *Art of Theatre* homepage, click on the cover of the book you are using and you will be redirected to the website for your book. Then click on "Student Book Companion Site" in the Resource box, pick a chapter from the pull-down menu at the top of the page, and select an option from the Chapter Resources menu. The *Art of Theatre* website also includes links to interesting and informative theatre websites. Just click on the Theatre on the Web link in the Book Resources menu. The links to these websites are maintained and updated as needed.

Key Terms

apron / 214
arena theatre / 216
black box theatre / 216
character makeup / 230
computer-aided design (CAD) / 221
costume plate / 229
costume shop / 234
cyclorama / 234
dress parade / 230
electric shop / 234
elevations / 222
expressionism / 218
flat / 234
floor plan / 222
fly system / 214
found, or created, space / 214
gel / 226
gobo / 226
hand props / 234
legs / 234
lighting plot / 226
limelight / 226
lip / 214
motivated light / 226
nonmotivated light / 226
paint shop / 234
property shop / 234
props / 234
proscenium arch / 214
realism / 218
scene shop / 234
scrims / 234
selective realism / 218
set props / 234
sight lines / 216
simplified, or suggested, realism / 218
sound booth / 234
straight makeup / 230
surrealism / 219
symbolism / 219
teasers / 234
thrust stage / 214
vomitories / 216
wings / 214

For More On . . .

Infotrac College Edition Readings

http://www.infoTrac-college.com

Designing women / 215
"Designing women"

Lighting designers / 226
"Lighting designer [The life of a theatrical lighting designer]"

Costume designers / 228
"Dressing up the voices: The role of the costume designer is a very visible (and sometimes risible) mix of creativity and craft"

Set and costume design for the musical *Titanic* / 229
"Godspeed, Titanic"

Tales from stage designers / 235
"Tales from the designers' side; stage designers discuss violations of their rights"

10 Theatre's Beginnings

Most of theatre's early history was unrecorded or was lost, so there is a great deal of speculation about its origins. Where did theatre come from? What spark created it? The most common theory is that theatre grew out of religious ritual and myth. Many thousands of years ago people used rituals to help them understand and deal with their environment. Because they did not have scientific methods with which to grasp the causes of plagues, floods, droughts, earthquakes, volcanic eruptions, and eclipses, they developed ceremonies to try to influence the intangible forces that they believed controlled the cosmos. The idea behind these rituals was not simply to perform ceremonial acts but to achieve a desired effect: adequate rainfall, an end to sickness, a bountiful harvest, a successful hunt, victory in battle, or favor from supernatural powers or gods. Rituals were also a means to pass on

© Donald Cooper/Photostage

◀ ***On preceding page:*** Oresteia *by Aeschylus. Directed by Gordon Davidson, National Theatre, Olivier, London, 1981. This trilogy about a family vendetta comprises* Agamemnon, Libation Bearers, *and* Eumenides. *This production is notable for its effective use of striking masks.*

traditions and knowledge of a society's history and heroes; thus the sophisticated storylines called myths were born. Soon people discovered that these rituals could also be entertaining.

Today, ritual still plays an important part in our lives. We have religious rituals such as baptism, communion, bar and bat mitzvahs, and last rites. We have legal rituals such as marriage and divorce; governmental rituals such as presidential inaugurations; rites of passage such as graduation ceremonies; and historical rituals such as fireworks on the Fourth of July. But at what point do these acts cease to be rituals and become theatre? Scholars have debated this question for decades. Some divide the answer into three stages: ritual, ritual theatre, and theatre. **Ritual theatre** uses the theatrical techniques of song, dance, and characterization, but it is still firmly rooted in religion. This three-stage approach makes sense because there probably wasn't one defining moment when ritual turned into theatre. The transformation probably took thousands of years.

Many scholars agree on two traits that distinguish theatre from ritual. First, theatre has an actor who plays a character, a person who takes on a role portraying another human being or even an object, animal, or embodied idea. A priest doing what a priest does may be theatrical, and the religious ritual may be dramatic, but it is not theatre. (The words *theatrical* and *dramatic* are often used to describe things that are not really theatre or drama.) Theatre is artifi-

© Erich Lessing/Art Resource, NY

Historian Will Durant theorized that ritual music, song, and dance merged at some point to create drama: "When rhythm disappeared from these performances, the dance passed into the drama and one of the greatest of art-forms [theatre] was born." In this Egyptian wall painting (ca. 1350 BCE), musicians and dancers entertain guests. Could this have been the birth of theatre?

cial. To paraphrase Aristotle, a play is an imitation of an action, not the action itself. Second, theatre usually has a story with a conflict. Conflict is the key to all drama. Few religious or social rituals contain scripted conflict. (*Scripted* doesn't necessarily refer to a written play; it can also refer to a simple outline, scenario, or improvisation.) Many rituals have a prescribed order of events, but they do not act out a story that contains conflict. When these two traits are present—actors who play characters and stories with conflict—we have theatre. Looking at theatre this way, we can see that a play can be a ritual (ritual theatre) but not all rituals are plays.

When was the transition from ritual to theatre complete? No one knows, of course, but historical clues allow us to make an educated guess that theatre has existed for thousands of years. In Africa, long before the development of written alphabets, ritual plays were passed down through generations. In India during the Bronze Age (4000 BCE–1500 BCE), there were mythological dramas full of song and dance, and the Indus Valley civilization (2700–1500 BCE) even had a god, named Nataraja, of actors and dancers. There are records of ritual performances with singing, dancing, and impersonators in China during the Zhou dynasty (1122–256 BCE). And there are records in hieroglyphics of what may have been theatrical activity in Egypt during the Early Dynastic Period (3100–2686 BCE). Later in Egypt, around 1800 BCE, a man named Ikhernofret wrote of his participation in a ritual play in Abydos about the death and resurrection of Osiris, the Egyptian god of fertility and of the underworld. He describes how he put on costume, or "regalia," and ceremonially "overthrew the enemies of Osiris" and of "conflict." But we do not know if this was a play or a traditional ritual. The first unambiguous evidence of theatre as we know it today, including written artifacts and physical remains of theatres, is about 2,600 years old and comes from Greece.

FOR MORE ON

AFRICAN THEATRE

"The strange and the familiar: Intercultural exchange between African and Caribbean theatre," Osita Okagbue, *Theatre Research International,* Summer 1997

Wine and Fertility: The Birth of Tragedy

Around 500 BCE, Greece was made up of independent city-states; the main ones were Sparta, Corinth, Thebes, and Athens. They seldom united except against foreign invaders. In the early years of the fifth century BCE, they joined to fight two massive invasions by the Persians, who ruled over the largest empire of the day. As the Greeks basked in the glory of their underdog victory, the great age of the city-state of Athens began. The next ninety years were ones of remarkable literary, philosophical, and artistic accomplishments. This was a period of power and prosperity known as the golden age of Greek theatre.

Although there are many theories about how theatre began in Athens, many scholars accept Aristotle's claim that theatre grew out of a ritual called the **dithyramb.** The dithyramb was a hymn sung at the altar of the god **Dionysus,** the god of wine and fertility, and it was accompanied by dancing, singing, and perhaps improvisations by a chorus that may have numbered as many as fifty men. A similar god of wine and fertility had been honored in many different regions of the ancient world for well over a thousand years. Depending on the locality and period, the celebration took different forms. In some countries naked women spent a day running wild in the hills surrounding the town. A fresco from the Roman province of Pompeii depicts ritual flogging, heavy drinking, and wild dancing in celebration of Dionysus. The Athenian festivals included a rowdy procession, which today would be rated NC-17 because some of the participants carried huge phalluses. The parade was followed by a competition of dithyrambs. All-male dithyrambic choruses often competed for prizes and awards for the best presentation at the **City Dionysia,** one of two religious festivals held in Athens each year to honor Dionysus. Although we are uncertain how dithyrambs evolved into plays, we do know that by the sixth century BCE the dithyrambic competition had been replaced by a play competition. In 534 BCE, an actor named **Thespis** wrote and acted in a play that won the competition. According to tradition, Thespis created theatre by stepping from a dithyramb chorus and playing an individual role. In other words, he moved from being one of a group of men performing a ritual to an individual performing a character. (The word *thespian,* meaning "actor," derives from Thespis's name.) Early Greek plays, like the dithyrambs before them, were performed with all-male casts; women were not allowed to perform, and men played women's roles.

Our city is an education to Greece. . . . Future ages will wonder at us, as the present age wonders at us now.

Pericles,
Athenian statesman responsible for building the Parthenon

Built into the side of a hill below the Parthenon in Athens, the **Theatre of Dionysus,** the largest of the Greek theatres, could seat as many as 17,000 people. The main features of ancient Greek theatres were a circular playing area called the **orchestra,** or "dancing place," and a seating area called the **theatron,** or "seeing place." This is the source of the word *theatre.* There was also a building behind the orchestra called the **skene.** The skene held dressing rooms and storage spaces, and its front façade was used as a backdrop for productions (the word *skene* is the source of the words *scene* and *scenery*). At first, the skene was most likely a simple tent put up for performances (*skene* comes from the Greek word for "tent"). Later it became a wooden structure and then a permanent stone building.

Tragedies That Weren't All That Tragic

Today the word *tragedy* means an unfortunate or disastrous turn of events. To the Greeks, however, the subject of a tragic play was serious but not necessarily sad or disastrous. In fact, *tragedy* comes from the ancient Greek word *tragōidia,* which means "goat song," and may refer to the fertility rites from which the Dionysian festivals grew; the Greeks considered the goat a sexually potent animal. For the ancient Greeks, tragedies were about the meaning of life and were designed to help the audience understand the reasons for the suffering and daily dilemmas they faced. These plays ask powerful questions:

William Missouri Downs

William Missouri Downs

The Theatre of Dionysus (left) was built into the natural hollow of the southern slope of the Acropolis in Athens, Greece, and it remained in use for over a thousand years. The plays of Aeschylus, Sophocles, Euripides, and Aristophanes were first performed here. Today, the circular orchestra and theatron are clearly visible, but the skene building no longer stands. The theatre of the Asklepieion of Epidaurus (right) was built as part of a larger complex that housed monuments dedicated to Asklepios, a healer god of antiquity. Notice the size of the people—imagine how helpful theatre masks must have been to audience members in the top rows!

What is humankind's purpose? Are we at the mercy of fate or can we rise above our destiny? Which moral code is more important, honoring our family or obeying the state? Can we recognize our character flaws before they destroy us? The purpose of these plays was not to make the audience feel somber but rather to enable them to experience an intense, twofold feeling of pity and fear known as **catharsis.** Catharsis occurs when one truly encounters life and confronts its many riddles.

Modern Western plays have a simple framework of acts and intermissions. Ancient Greek plays have a slightly more complicated framework consisting of five elements. They begin with a **prologue,** a short introductory speech or scene. That is followed by the **parodos,** or parade, when the chorus enters the orchestra. The parodos contains many songs and dances as the chorus tells the audience who they are in the play and provides background information. The parodos is followed by the first **episode,** when actors step from the skene building and play a scene. Next comes the **stasimon,** which contains more songs and dances by the chorus as it comments on the events in the play. Additional episodes alternate with stasimons—until the **exodos,** which is a summation by the chorus on the theme and wisdom of the play. The play ends in a processional song as the chorus leaves the orchestra. (For an example of this framework applied to a play that is still performed today, see the Spotlight box "*Oedipus Rex.*")

Tragic Trilogies and Satyr Plays

Tragedies were presented in trilogies. During the Festival of Dionysus, playwrights presented three plays that might have related themes. The *Oresteia* (458 BCE), written by Aeschylus, is the only extant trilogy, so it gives us an idea of how the plays within a trilogy were connected. The three plays are

© Archivo Iconografico, S.A./Corbis

This mosaic from the first century CE shows actors, surrounded by their masks, getting ready to rehearse a comic satyr play. Satyr plays provided comic relief after the heaviness of trilogies. The only satyr play that has survived from antiquity is Cyclops by Euripides, which parodies the story of the Odyssey.

Oedipus Rex

Oedipus Rex was first presented in the Theatre of Dionysus around 430 BCE. Written by the playwright Sophocles, it, like most Greek tragedies, is based on a myth. This myth starts with Laius and Jocasta, the childless king and queen of Thebes, an ancient city-state in central Greece. Wanting an heir, the king seeks the advice of the oracle of Apollo at Delphi. In Greek society, oracles housed mediums (also known as *oracles*), considered people of wise counsel who could foretell the future, and priests who interpreted their words. The oracle tells the king that if he has an heir, his son will grow up to murder him and marry his own mother. Naturally, the king is upset when the queen announces she is pregnant.

When his son is born, the king gives the infant to a shepherd with the order to leave it on the slopes of Mt. Cithaeron. (In those days, exposure to the elements was a common way to get rid of an unwanted child.) But the shepherd takes pity on the baby and gives him to some passersby who happen to be servants of King Polybus and Queen Merope of Corinth. The king and queen adopt the boy and rear him as their own. When the child, Oedipus, is about eighteen, a drunken guest informs him of his adoption. Oedipus travels to the oracle at Delphi to ask about his identity. Instead of revealing his lineage, the priest simply repeats the grim prophecy given to Laius about a son who kills his father and marries his mother. Overwhelmed by the prediction, Oedipus vows to get as far away from Corinth as possible, determined to prevent the prophecy from coming true.

At a crossroads near the city-state of Thebes, Oedipus argues with a man in a chariot about who has the right of way. The war of words escalates, and the young Oedipus kills the man in self-defense. When Oedipus approaches Thebes, he finds that a Sphinx—a monster usually depicted as a winged lion with a woman's head—is terrorizing the city. Sitting atop a cliff over the road into the city, she asks each passerby a riddle and kills those who fail to answer correctly. The Sphinx asks, "What walks on four legs in the morning, two legs in the afternoon, and three legs in the evening?" Oedipus, confident in his wisdom, answers, "Man, for when he is born, he crawls on all fours; as he grows older, he stands on two feet; and at the end of his life, he uses a cane as a third leg." The Sphinx is furious that Oedipus has the correct answer, and she plunges off the cliff to her death. Oedipus is rewarded by being crowned king of Thebes, and he marries the queen Jocasta, whose husband has just been murdered. Everything is going well for Oedipus until a plague strikes the city.

This is the place in the myth where Sophocles begins his play. Greek tragedies usually deal with only the climactic final part of the myth on which they are based. Here is how Sophocles' play unfolds.

Agamemnon, The Libation Bearers, and *The Eumenides.* In the first play, Agamemnon, king of Argos, returns home after winning the Trojan War. His wife, Queen Clytemnestra, welcomes him, but during the years that he has been away she has taken a lover. She had grown bitter toward Agamemnon because he had sacrificed their daughter to the gods so that his fleet would have favorable winds as they sailed to Troy. To make matters worse, Agamemnon returns accompanied by his concubine. Seeking revenge, Clytemnestra lures Agamemnon into the palace, where she stabs him to death.

In the second play, *The Libation Bearers,* Orestes, the son of Agamemnon and Clytemnestra, is ordered by the god Apollo to avenge his father's death or face terrible consequences. Orestes murders his mother and her lover, but now the Furies—terrible, winged goddesses of vengeance with serpentine hair—

The prologue: King Oedipus learns of the plague and how an oracle has foretold that it will not end until the murderer of former King Laius is found and punished.

The parodos: The chorus enters. It represents a crowd of elderly men who pray that the gods will end the horrible disease.

First episode: King Oedipus proclaims that he will investigate the murder, find the person responsible, and punish him. He prays that the murderer's life be "consumed in evil and wretchedness." Oedipus sends for a blind prophet to help find the murderer, but when the old man refuses to help, Oedipus accuses him of conspiring with Creon (Jocasta's brother) in the murder. The prophet professes ignorance, but suggests that Oedipus is the guilty party, which sends Oedipus into a rage.

First stasimon: This choral song expresses great doubt about Oedipus having anything to do with the murder.

Second episode: Creon defends himself against the charges, but Oedipus still wants him executed for treason. Jocasta tells Oedipus to ignore the oracle because this same oracle predicted that Laius would be killed by his son, yet he was reportedly killed at a crossroads by thieves. Oedipus begins to doubt himself.

Second stasimon: The choral song expresses doubts about Oedipus's innocence and condemns his hubris, or pride, arrogance, and vanity. The chorus is beginning to turn against Oedipus as it warns the audience members to remember their place and to accept their fate.

Third episode: A messenger arrives with the news that the king of Corinth has died of natural causes. Jocasta is thrilled because this means that the oracle was wrong, that life is governed by chance, not destiny. But then the messenger, in an attempt to add some good news, announces that the king of Corinth was not Oedipus's father but that Oedipus was adopted.

Third stasimon: The chorus warns that any human who has the audacity to question the powers of the gods will be tangled in a web of pain.

Fourth episode: Fearing the worst, Oedipus sends for the shepherd who had found him on Mt. Cithaeron and forces him to tell the story of what happened, so many years ago, when he was ordered to expose the baby. Learning the truth, Oedipus rushes into the palace (the skene).

Fourth stasimon: The choral song bemoans the downfall of Oedipus.

Final episode and exodos: A messenger reveals Jocasta has hanged herself and that Oedipus removed a pin from her dress and has stabbed himself in the eyes. Blind, Oedipus begs Creon to forgive him and asks to be let out of the city to wander until the end of his days.

attack the grief-stricken Orestes. The final play of the trilogy, *The Eumenides,* questions the idea of revenge killing. Orestes' fate is taken away from the gods, and the final judgment is given to a court of citizens who find Orestes not guilty. This third play makes a statement about how human reason must replace the unyielding rule of the gods. The *Oresteia* is also an endorsement of the Athenian inventions of democratic government and trial by jury.

Trilogies were followed by a short comic-relief play called a **satyr play.** Often burlesque, these plays parodied the myths, gods, heroes, and characters in the tragedies. Satyrs were filled with wild dancing, indecent language, and obscene gestures and were named for the half-beast, half-human creatures who were said to be companions of the god Dionysus. The word *satire* is derived from satyr plays.

FOR MORE ON

GREEK TRAGEDY

"The Aristotelian theatrical paradigm as cultural-historical construct," Ronald Vince, *Theatre Research International,* Spring 1997

© Richard Termine

Euripides is famous for writing some of the most powerful female characters of Greek tragedy, including Electra, Medea, and Hecuba. Hecuba (ca. 425 BCE) is the story of the former queen of Troy, now a prisoner of war, who takes revenge for the sacrificial death of her daughter. This play provides a timeless examination of the psychology of the victor and the victim in time of war. This 2005 production starred Vanessa Redgrave and was staged by the Royal Shakespeare Company performing at the Brooklyn Academy of Music.

Playwrights of the Golden Age

Dozens of Greek playwrights wrote plays during the fourth and fifth centuries BCE, but the majority of their scripts have been lost. Of the scripts remaining, only three tragic playwrights are represented: Aeschylus, Sophocles, and Euripides. Fortunately, these three were considered the best playwrights of the age.

Aeschylus (ca. 525–456 BCE) is the earliest writer of Greek tragedy whose plays still exist. Often called the father of tragedy, he was born into a prominent family near Athens and fought in the battles of Marathon and Salamis, which crushed the Persians. His first play was produced at the Theatre Dionysus in 499 BCE, and during the next forty years he wrote some ninety plays, of which six, or perhaps seven, have survived. Aeschylus is often considered the most "theatrical" of the ancient playwrights because his plays have huge casts, lavish costumes, and lots of special effects. Ancient critics said that the special effect used at the entrance of the Furies in his play *The Libation Bearers* was so powerful that pregnant women in the audience miscarried.

Sophocles (ca. 496–406 BCE), the son of a wealthy merchant, was well educated and became a highly respected citizen of Athens. He served as the city's treasurer and was appointed to important government committees. As a playwright, his first victory at the Theatre Dionysus occurred in 463 BCE, when he defeated Aeschylus. He went on to write more than 120 plays, of which seven have survived. He won the City Dionysia twenty-four times, and he never came in less than second. His plays are known for their complex characterization, harmonious lyrics, and effective dialogue. Sophocles' dramas often depict human beings trapped by fate. Fate, he said, is not predetermined by the gods but is rather a result of our inflexible personalities (see the Spotlight box "*Oedipus Rex*").

Euripides (ca. 480–406 BCE) was never afraid to speak his mind and often took on the government and society. He filled his plays with stinging indictments against war and the savagery of Athenian warriors. In *The Trojan*

Women (415 BCE), he questions the use of the army. During the **Peloponnesian War** between Athens and Sparta and their allies, the Athenian army demanded that the people of the island of Melos, who were neutral in the war, surrender. When they did not, the Athenian army murdered all the men of military age and sold the women and children into slavery. In *The Trojan Women,* Euripides dramatizes a similar event and points out that such events are not caused by the gods, or natural right, but rather by human cruelty. Because of his political views, Euripides seldom won popularity contests such as the City Dionysia. In fact, he did not win that contest until he was in his forties and took the top honor only four times. Of the ninety-some plays he is said to have written, nineteen have survived, and he is now the most often produced of the ancient Greek tragic playwrights.

When good men die their goodness does not perish,
But lives though they are gone.
As for the bad,
All that was theirs dies and is buried with them.

Euripides,
Greek playwright

Greek Comedies: Political Satire and Dirty Jokes

The last day of the City Dionysia was devoted to comedies, at least after 486 BCE. These comic plays had a loose structure that directly or indirectly lampooned society or the political landscape of the day—much as a *Saturday Night Live* skit satirizes government figures and current events. But ancient Greek comedies went even further. Not only were they full of sight gags, obscene humor, and outrageous political banter, but the actors also wore thickly padded costumes, grotesque masks, and abnormally large leather phalluses that hung down between their legs and mocked the male genitalia. Scholars now called these early comic plays **Old Comedy** because they were written before the end of the Peloponnesian War, when there was a relatively high degree of freedom of speech in Athens.

Of all the plays of Old Comedy, only one playwright's work has survived. Fortunately, by all accounts, he was the best comic writer of his day. His name was Aristophanes (ca. 448–380 BCE). Of the forty comedies he wrote, eleven have survived. Aristophanes was famous for caricatures of Greek leaders and stinging attacks on society. He was daring enough to lampoon politicians, generals, and other celebrities sitting in the audience. In *The Clouds* (423 BCE)

William Missouri Downs

The comedies of Aristophanes are popular with modern audiences, despite having been written more than 2,400 years ago. In particular, Lysistrata, *his anti-war sex comedy, seems to resonate with twentieth-century audiences. Four modern musical adaptations have been staged on Broadway since 1925, and many other versions of the story have appeared on stages all over the world. This 2004 update by Sean Keogh, called* Good Morning Athens, *was directed by William Missouri Downs at the Kennedy Center for the Performing Arts.*

FOR MORE ON
LYSISTRATA
"Let's make love, not war (*Lysistrata*)," Gersh Kuntzman, *Newsweek International*, March 17, 2003

Aristophanes mocked the great philosopher Socrates, and in *The Wasps* (422 BCE) he made fun of lawyers. Aristophanes' most famous work is the anti-war comedy *Lysistrata* (411 BCE). Written in the twenty-first year of the Peloponnesian War, it is about a woman named Lysistrata who organizes the women of Athens and Sparta into staging a sex strike; the women lock themselves in the Acropolis and deny their husbands sex until the men stop the war. This bawdy comedy, like his others, is full of sexual innuendo and overtly crude references. In his plays, Aristophanes used over seventy different words, modifiers, and metaphors to describe male genitalia and over seventy others to describe their female counterpart.

I Aristotle, Alexander, and the Spread of Greek Theatre

Ancient Athens is often called the "cradle of Western Civilization" because so much of modern Western democracy, art, and philosophy originated there. But in 404 BCE the period of relative liberalism and innovation came to a close when Athens surrendered to Sparta, ending the Peloponnesian War. Athens's city walls were torn down and its navy burned. The 140-year-old Athenian democracy was over, but the city itself was spared. The generals of Sparta, as they conquered Athens, were reportedly so moved by a chorus singing from one of Euripides' plays that they decided not to burn down the city. However, the Athenians were forced to give up democracy and adopt Sparta's more autocratic form of government. Sparta was ruled by a supreme magistrate and a council of elders. There was an assembly of the people, but it could only rubber-stamp the magistrates' decisions. Any assembly member who proposed a new law had to wear a noose around his neck; if the law failed to pass, he would be hanged. Sparta was a much more inhibited society than Athens, and it had no great love for art or theatre.

During this turbulent period, political issues became too dangerous to discuss openly, civil liberties disappeared, and freedom of speech was strictly

William Missouri Downs

The influence of ancient Greek culture can still be seen throughout the Mediterranean. The Theatre of Marcellus, which used elements of Greek architecture, was completed in Rome in 11 BCE and held approximately 14,000 people. The theatre was abandoned around 300 CE after the Christians came to power. During the Middle Ages it was used as a fort, and in the sixteenth century a private home was built atop it. Today, only the lower columns of the theatre exist. It is the only one of the four major theatres of ancient Rome that still stands.

controlled. This was the period when the philosopher and teacher Socrates was put on trial, found guilty of "corrupting the youth," and forced to drink poisonous hemlock. Denied freedom of speech, comic playwrights turned from personal and political satire to what scholars now call **New Comedy.** Its safe themes and mundane subject matter steered clear of insulting those in power. The subjects included young lovers, meddling mothers-in-law, and marital misunderstandings—themes shared by many modern sitcoms. One of the most popular playwrights of New Comedy was Menander (342–292 BCE), who wrote more than one hundred plays. Like those of other comic writers of the day, his plots featured humorous situations and never questioned the political structure or troubled the audience to think too much. The title of his only extant play gives an idea of the sorts of topics his plays addressed: *The Curmudgeon.* Menander's comedies were popular for seven hundred years and were often imitated.

Fifty years after Athens was defeated in the Peloponnesian War, Greek tragedy also lost its brilliance. The plays were shallow; the writers lacked the talent or the freedom to write great scripts; and performances were seldom noteworthy. The philosopher, educator, and scientist Aristotle (384–322 BCE) called the playwrights of his day "hacks." In an attempt to remind playwrights how to construct a proper tragedy and to rebut Plato's condemnation of theatre in *The Republic* (ca. 378 BCE), Aristotle wrote ***Poetics,*** the first known treatise about how a dramatic story is constructed. He called the work *poetics* because playwrights were known as *poets* in ancient Greece. (Aristotle also wrote a treatise on comedy, but it has been lost.) With typical Greek rationalism, Aristotle approached dramatic storytelling as a science. He sought the universal guidelines that characterize a dramatic story. When *Poetics* was rediscovered during the Renaissance, these guidelines became hard-and-fast rules. Today, many consider *Poetics* to be the single most influential work in all literary criticism. It is used as a how-to book in many playwriting and screenwriting classes. In fact, it is required reading at every major film school in the United States. (For more on *Poetics,* see Chapters 1, 4, and 11).

Musée du Louvre/ The Bridgeman Art Library

This statue of the Muse Melpomene (ca. 50 BCE), featuring a Greek-influenced theatre mask, is all that remains of the Theatre of Pompey, the largest of the Roman theatres. Built in 55 BCE, the theatre stood just north of Rome's center, near the spacious lawns of the Campus Martius (the Field of Mars). In a disturbing show of Roman spectacle, a massive event staged at the theatre's inauguration included the slaughter of exotic creatures from all over the Roman Empire.

Had it not been for Aristotle's most famous pupil, Alexander the Great (356–323 BCE), Greek theatre might have been a footnote to history. At the age of eighteen, Alexander became king of Macedonia in northern Greece. By the time of his death, at the age of 32, he was one of the greatest military generals in history and controlled an empire that encompassed modern-day Greece, Turkey, Iran, Iraq, Pakistan, Afghanistan, and Northern Africa, including Egypt. It was here that Alexander championed the **Library of Alexandria**—one of the first universities. This is where Euclid (325 BCE–ca. 65 BCE) wrote *Elements,* his treatise on geometry and algebra; Archimedes (ca. 287–212 BCE) discovered pi; and Eratosthenes (275–194 BCE) calculated the distance around the earth to within fifty miles of its true circumference. And it was here that much of the world learned of the great Greek playwrights. The original manuscripts of Euripides, Aeschylus, and Sophocles were first owned by the city of Athens, which was reluctant to lend them to the Library of Alexandria. As insurance, library officials paid an enormous cash deposit. Athens sent the manuscripts, but once the library received them, it forfeited the deposit, kept the originals and, to the dismay of Athenians, returned only copies.

As Alexander built his empire, he spread Greek culture, including art, philosophy, science, and theatre to its far corners. The two centuries between his death in 323 BCE and the Roman conquest of Greece in 146 BCE became known as the **Hellenistic period,** from the Greek word meaning "to imitate the Greeks." Greek culture, including theatre, was exported into many societies and civilizations around the Mediterranean and beyond. So great was the reach of Hellenism that Greek theatre may have influenced theatre in India.

I Classical Theatre of India: The Believable and the Unbelievable

India has one of the oldest civilizations in the world and some of the oldest theatre traditions. Some scholars believe that theatre in India began when the army of Alexander the Great staged Greek-style plays during its invasion in 326 BCE. Other scholars argue that theatre in India existed well before Alexander's invasion and that the Greeks only influenced it. Whether theatre existed in India before the Greek invasion or not, there is evidence that Indian theatre was at the very least affected by ancient Greece. For example, when a curtain was used in an ancient Indian play, it was called "the Greek."

The oldest known form of theatre in India is **Sanskrit theatre,** named for the ancient Indian language in which the plays are performed. For over a thousand years, professional touring companies performed Sanskrit drama in courts, temples, palaces, or temporary theatres on special occasions. These plays combine the natural and the supernatural, the believable and the unbelievable. They touched on comic and serious themes; depicted fables; incorporated poetry, love stories, and political topics; featured heroic, mythological characters; and rewarded virtue and the righteous.

One of the most famous Sanskrit plays is *Shakuntala,* a love story in seven acts written by the playwright Kalidasa (373?–415 CE). The play opens with a

© Image Entertainment, Inc./Photofest

In Sanskrit drama, the natural and the supernatural blend to create a fantastic universe. A particularly ambitious Western retelling of a Sanskrit story was Peter Brook's 1985 production of The Mahabharata. *This cycle of three plays about an epic battle between two sets of cousins in an ancient Indian dynasty took twelve hours to stage and featured performers from all over the world. In this scene from the 1989 filmed version of the play, the Hindu god Ganesh communes with the poet Vyasa, the mythic composer of the* Mahabharata. *Directed by Peter Brook and adapted by Jean-Claude Carrière.*

prologue in which the audience is invited to enjoy the beauty of nature. The setting is a forest, where a hermit lives with his adopted daughter Shakuntala. Their peaceful existence is interrupted by King Dushyanta, who arrives in a chariot. King Dushyanta instantly falls in love with Shakuntala and marries her, but after consummating the marriage, he is called back to court. He gives Shakuntala a ring and assures her that he will return to her as soon as possible. Soon Shakuntala discovers she is pregnant, so, having heard nothing from the king, she decides to travel to court to find him. A holy man tells Shakuntala that the king will remember her only as long as she keeps the royal ring he gave her. She loses the ring while bathing in a river during her journey, and when she arrives in court, indeed the King does not recognize her. A despondent Shakuntala is lifted into the air and carried off to a forest, where she gives birth. Meanwhile, in another part of the wood, a fisherman finds the king's ring in the belly of a fish. Before he can explain how he came to have it, he is charged with stealing it. He is taken before the king, and when the king sees the ring, his memory of Shakuntala is restored. Stricken with remorse, he

© Hideo Haga/HAGA/The Image Works

Kathakali is one of the oldest types of theatre in the world. A form of Indian folk drama that traces its traditions back to Sanskrit theatre, it features dramatized versions of the Hindu epic poems Ramayana *and* Mahabharata. *Kathakali is notable for its elaborate makeup, extraordinary costumes, and highly stylized dance and gestures.*

sets out to find her. He flies over the Himalayas, where he discovers her and their son. He begs forgiveness, wins her heart, and everyone lives happily ever after.

Sanskrit plays always end happily and never deal with death or violence. The scenery is scant, but the costumes and makeup are elaborate. The performances are always accompanied by music from tambourines, lutes, flutes, and zithers. Sanskrit plays have magical imagery and fantastic stories in which animals and trees can speak. They are longer than Western plays, taking up to six hours to perform.

Roman Entertainment: Obscene Spectacle

By the first century CE, Rome had become an entertainment nexus, a sort of Las Vegas of the ancient world. There were chariot races at the Circus Maximus, gladiator fights in various stadiums, and plenty of spaces for theatre. Rome alone had four huge theatres, and nearly a hundred others were built throughout the empire—in what today are Italy, Spain, France, England, North Africa, Greece, and Asia Minor. The attitude of Roman audiences toward theatre was much like our attitude toward television; if a show was not to their liking, they did the equivalent of changing channels by simply walking out. As a result, the theatres tried hard to amuse the audience, including using lots of special effects. Some theatres were equipped with copper-lined tunnels cut beneath the seats so that boulders could be rolled through them to create an "earthquake" that would shake the entire theatre. On other occasions, theatre engineers flooded the orchestra so that sea battles, complete with miniature warships and slaves fighting to the death, could be staged.

Roman Mimes

One of the most popular forms of entertainment was that of the mimes, whose shows were filled with jugglers, acrobats, comic skits, and plenty of vulgar language, buffoonery, and nudity. Needless to say, these plays had little literary value. Their stories were about drunkenness, greed, adultery, and sex; for example, one popular play was *Grandpa Takes a Wife.* Women were allowed onstage but usually only as scantily dressed sex objects. According to some historical accounts, when audiences grew bored with a performance, they sometimes demanded that the players stop the play, take off their clothes, and perform sex acts onstage; most mime troupes were happy to oblige. Originally, mime performers were not silent—unlike Marcel Marceau and other modern pantomimes—but had spoken lines and plenty of improvised ad-libs. As empire grew and the population of Rome became more diverse with many native languages, the mimes became wordless and depended more on music, action, gesture, dance, and mimicry.

By the Late Empire, the obscene mimes were the most popular form of theatre in Rome—they were number one at the box office. Mime performances sometimes contained satire, even though satire was against the law in Rome. To play it safe, the actors set most of their skits in Greece and made fun of Greek characters and customs, cloaking their jokes in double entendres. Once in a while a mime attempted a joke about the emperor, but this was risky. Emperor Caligula ordered one actor burned alive on stage for making an insulting jibe. However, the mime troupes' audacity seemed undiminished, for later that same year another troupe mocked the murdered actor's death by staging a play with a performer pretending to be a charred cadaver.

However, not everyone was entertained, particularly the new religious group known as Christians. At the time, thousands of different deities were worshipped in Rome. Never before had there been such a variety of religious beliefs concentrated in one place. Soon Rome became the center of religious diversity and tolerance. The only catch was a law that required all religions to include in their rituals some brief homage to the emperor's "genius." This is where the Christians got into trouble; they, unlike the other religions, refused to proclaim their loyalty to the state. They also voiced moral objections to the Roman entertainments of gladiator contests and the theatre. The earliest record of Christian writing against the theatre comes from Tatian (ca. 160 CE), who denounced theatre as "a chronicler of adultery" and "a storehouse of madness." The reaction of the Roman mimes was typical: They made the Christians one of their favorite targets for parody—a choice that did little to win favor from the Christians when they took power a few hundred years later.

2,000-Year-Old Sitcoms

Roman playwrights never reached the level of sophistication achieved by the ancient Greeks. In fact, most Roman plays were translations loosely based on Greek comedies. One of the most popular playwrights during the Roman Republic was Plautus (254–184 BCE). His plays gave Roman audiences just what they wanted: pure entertainment full of gags, rollicking puns, improbable coincidences, love stories, and slapstick. Plautus was so popular that many theatre managers replaced other playwrights' names with his in order to increase attendance. Over a thousand years later, Shakespeare (1564–1616) used Plautus's play *The Twin Menaechmi,* a farce about identical twins, as the basis for his play *Comedy of Errors* (1591). Plautus's play *The Pot of Gold* (ca. 194 BCE), about a man who is driven berserk by an elusive buried treasure, was the basis for Molière's comedy *The Miser* (1669). Even today his plays and characters are still being recycled. Stephen Sondheim's musical *A Funny Thing Happened on the Way to the Forum* (1966) is based on the comedies of Plautus.

© Robbie Jack/Corbis

Roman playwright Plautus filled his plays with boisterous indecencies, seductions, and cheap gags. Like many Roman playwrights, he populated these plays with Greek characters, thus limiting the chance that any Roman would take offense. His stories have retained their popularity throughout history. This scene from the musical A Funny Thing Happened on the Way to the Forum, *which is based on the comedies of Plautus, illustrates the bawdy silliness that marked his work. This 2004 production featured Desmond Barrit as Pseudolus, a slave trying to buy freedom from his owner. Music and lyrics by Stephen Sondheim, book by Burt Shevelove and Larry Gelbart. Directed by Edward Hall, National Theatre, London.*

Theatre's Beginnings through the Middle Ages

	3500 BCE	2500	1500	1000	900
Theatrical events and plays		• Ritual plays performed in Egypt (ca. 2500–550 BCE)	• Ikhernofret writes about participation in a ritual play in Egypt (ca. 1850 BCE)		
Historical / cultural events	• Early Dynastic Period in Egypt (3100–2686 BCE)	• Indus Valley civilization thrives (2700–1500 BCE)	• Shang Dynasty in China (ca. 1500–1027 BCE)	• Zhou Dynasty in China (1122–256 BCE)	

	50	1 CE	50	100	150
Theatrical events and plays	• Nero, great supporter of Roman theatre, overthrown (68) • Coliseum constructed in Rome (ca. 80)	• Lucius Annaeus Seneca (ca. 4 BCE–65 CE)	• First permanent theatre in Rome, built by Pompey (55 BCE) • Theatre of Marcellus built in Rome (11 BCE)		• Terence (195–159 BCE)
Historical / cultural events	• Fire destroys Rome (64) • Romans crush rebellion in Jerusalem (70) • Pompeii destroyed by Mount Vesuvius (79)	• Traditional year for Jesus' birth (1 CE)	• Julian calendar instituted (46 BCE) • Caesar killed at Pompey's theatre (44 BCE)	• Ptolemy (ca. 90–168 BCE)	

	100	200	300	400	450
Theatrical events and plays	• Shadow theatre starts in China (ca. 100)	• Tertullian writes that Christians should have nothing to do with theatre (ca. 200)	• Kalidasa, Sanskrit playwright (ca. 373–415) • Theatregoers excommunicated by the Church (401)	• *Shakuntala*, Kalidasa (ca. 400)	
Historical / cultural events			• Constantine converts to Christianity (312) • Constantinople, capital of eastern Roman Empire, founded (330)		• Fall of Rome (476)

	1300
Theatrical events and plays	• Cycle plays begin (ca. 1300)

THEATRICAL EVENTS AND PLAYS

HISTORICAL / CULTURAL EVENTS

800	700	600	500	450
	• Early forms of ritual theatre in China (ca. 700 BCE)	• First dithyrambs in Athens (ca. 625 BCE) • Thespis wins play contest at City Dionysia (534 BCE) • Aeschylus (ca. 525–456 BCE)	• Sophocles (ca. 496–406 BCE) • Comedy added to City Dionysia (486 BCE) • Euripides (ca. 480–406 BCE) • *Oresteia*, Aeschylus (458 BCE)	• Aristophanes (ca. 448–380 BCE) • *Medea*, Euripides (431 BCE) • *Oedipus the King*, Sophocles (430 BCE) • *Lysistrata*, Aristophanes (411 BCE)
• First Olympic games (776 BCE) • Legendary founding of Rome (753 BCE)			• Founding of the Roman Republic (509 BCE) • Battle of Marathon (490 BCE)	• The Peloponnesian War (431–404 BCE) • Plato (427–347 BCE)

200	250	300	350	400
• *Natyasastra*, classic treatise on Sanskrit drama (ca. 200 BCE–ca. 200 CE)	• Plautus (254–184 BCE)	• Livius Andronicus (284–204 BCE)	• Menander (ca. 342–292 BCE) • *Poetics*, Aristotle (ca. 330 BCE)	• Aristotle (384–322 BCE) • Plato condemns theatre in *Republic* (ca. 373 BCE) • First theatrical performance in Rome (ca. 364 BCE)
	• Construction of Great Wall of China begins (214 BCE)	• *Elements*, Euclid (ca. 300 BCE)	• Alexander the Great (356–323 BCE)	• Socrates tried and executed (399 BCE)

500	550	600	650	700
• Last known theatre performance in Rome (533) • Theatre is all but extinct in medieval Europe (533–900)		• First theatre in China is built (610)		• Pear Garden theatricals of Emperor Ming Huang of China (714)
• Plato's Academy is closed (529)	• Buddhism introduced to Japan (ca. 552) • Mohammed (ca. 570–632)	• Block printing introduced in China (ca. 600)	• Muslims conquer Syria, Persia, and Egypt (636–651)	• Muslims conquer Spain (711)

1200	1100	1000	900	800
• Sanskrit drama ceases (1206) • Pope Innocent III bans plays in religious services (1210) • The Church allows plays during Feast of Corpus Christi (1264) • Flowering of theatre in China (1280–1368)	• Simple plays in religious services are popular in Europe (ca. 1150)		• Sanskrit drama begins to decline (900) • Liturgical playlets incorporated into Easter Mass (923) • Hroswitha (ca. 935–ca. 1001)	
• Muslims conquer central and north India (1206) • Magna Carta drafted (1215) • St. Thomas Aquinas (1225–1274) • Inquisition begins (1231) • Yuan (Mongol) dynasty in China (1280–1368)		• Reconquest of Spain begins (1000) • Crusades (1095–1270)		

Terence (ca. 195–159 BCE) was another popular Roman comic playwright. His full name was Publius Terentius Afer; "Afer" most likely indicates that he was from Africa and was black. One of his most famous plays was *The Self-Tormentor* (163 BCE), a comedy about a son who marries a girl his father has forbidden him to wed. Unlike Plautus, whose plays were essentially translations of Greek comedies, Terence adapted the stories and added his own perceptions. His scripts had the refined sentiment lacking in most popular Roman plays, which were elaborate spectacles interspersed with crude jokes.

The Singing, Acting Emperor

> I come home more greedy, more cruel and inhuman, because I have been among human beings. By chance I attended a midday exhibition, expecting some fun, wit, and relaxation. . . . But it was quite the contrary. . . . In the morning they throw men to the lions; at noon they throw them to the spectators. The crowd demands that the victor who has slain his opponent shall face the man who will slay him in turn; and the last conqueror is reserved for another butchering. . . . Man, a sacred thing to man, is killed for sport and merriment.
>
> ***Seneca,***
> *Roman playwright—on gladiators*

In 48 CE, Emperor Claudius made Lucius Annaeus Seneca (ca. 4 BCE–65 CE) the tutor to his 11-year-old adopted son Nero (37–68 CE). Seneca was perhaps Rome's greatest tragic playwright. His dramas reflected the Stoic belief that disaster results when passion overtakes reason; he believed it was important to detach ourselves from everything we do not have the power to control. Claudius's choice of tutors was logical because Seneca was not only a playwright but a scientist: His book *Quaestiones Naturales* was a popular science text well into the Middle Ages.

Seneca taught the young Nero about theatre, and by the time he became emperor, he saw himself as a talented poet, singer, and actor and often performed in Roman theatres. By most accounts, however, he was a terrible actor who allowed no one to leave the theatre for any reason while he was on the stage. It was reported that some audience members faked their deaths so that they could be carried out of the theatre without offending Nero. As a singer, Nero went on what was perhaps the first concert tour, performing all over the Mediterranean.

Nero fancied himself such a friend of the arts that he required his troops to take at least one wagon packed with musical instruments and theatrical effects whenever they left for war. In the end, Nero suspected many people, including his old tutor, of plotting against him. He ordered Seneca to kill himself. Seneca protested but was compelled by his Stoic beliefs to obey. Three years later Nero was overthrown and fled Rome; when troops closed in on him, he took his own life. His last words were reported to have been "Oh, what an artist dies with me!" Today, Nero is often thought of as terrible emperor, largely because of his callous persecution of Christians after the great fire of Rome. Many believe that this persecution was not due to religious differences but to the common suspicion that Christians had started the fire. Whatever the truth about these events, it still can be said that Nero was one of the greatest supporters of art and theatre in Western history.

The Rise of Christianity

The Roman Empire fell apart about four hundred years after Nero and Seneca. During those centuries, there were civil wars, plagues, and a series of devastating invasions. Many Romans were convinced that the empire's problems were due to their traditional gods being neglected. Whenever there was a famine, flood, or war, the Christians were often blamed. They were singled out because they scorned the Roman gods, refused to show patriotism to the state, including serving in the military, and were endlessly prophesying the destruction of Rome. Many emperors saw Christianity as a radical movement whose aim was to overthrow the government.

With the help of Christian emperors, starting with Constantine (ca. 280–337 CE), the Christians eventually took control of the Roman Empire and set about creating a state that persecuted their former persecutors—anyone not a member of the Christian religion. Pagan temples and statues were destroyed throughout the Roman Empire, and pagan rituals were forbidden under punishment of death. In the fourth century CE, Christian mobs attacked a subsidiary branch of the Library at Alexandria, burning its books and murdering the librarians. Its manuscripts on science, mathematics, astronomy, art, philosophy, and medicine were viewed as worthless pagan gibberish. In about 500 CE, the Parthenon in Rome was turned into a Christian church. In 529 CE, the Academy, Plato's school of philosophy in Athens, was ordered closed. It had been in existence for over 900 years but the Christians, now in power, considered it a pathway to paganism. In 530 Emperor Justinian decreed that anyone who was not baptized would not have right to own goods or property. The Church became all-powerful; in effect the Pope became the new caesar, and Christian theology reigned as "the queen of the sciences."

As the Christians attained power, they stepped up their attacks on the one institution they felt was not only obscene but also insulted their beliefs: the theatre. Saint John Chrysostom (ca. 347–ca. 407 CE) called theatre a "plague" and preached its destruction. In 401 CE, the fifth Council of Carthage decreed excommunication for all who attended the theatre rather than church on holy days. Later, actors were forbidden from taking the sacraments unless they left their profession. And in 438 CE, the Theodosian Code, an update of all Roman law at the time, included a stipulation that deprived actors of all rights, even the right to salvation. Soon the theatre was forced out of existence. The last known reference to theatre in Rome is in a letter written in 533 CE; after that, the historical record goes dark.

Returning home from the theatre, your house seems to you to be too simple, your wife ceases to be attractive, since she is not as beautiful as the actress whom you applauded, and you take out your ill humor on your immediate family.

Saint John Chrysostom,
Early Church Father

© DreamWorks/Kobal Collection

In the movie Gladiator (2000), Roman warrior Maximus, played by Russell Crowe, fought wild animals and other gladiators to the death in the Colosseum. Dedicated in 80 CE, the Colosseum was also used to stage short plays with deadly outcomes. The Christians found these sorts of human "entertainments" morally reprehensible, and when they came to power, they put a stop to them. However, fights between wild animals and other public events continued in the Colosseum until 523 CE.

Roman theatres fell into decay as the memories of the classical world faded. The empty ruins of the ancient Greek and Roman theatres, closed for hundreds of years, dotted the European landscape; some were looted for their marble, others were devastated by erosion and earthquakes. However, companies of jugglers, storytellers, dancers, acrobats, and musicians traveled from town to town. These theatrical descendants of the Roman mimes performed slightly sanitized versions of their unruly skits. Theatre had gone underground, and its players had become shady vagabonds performing wherever they could drum up an audience or whenever the religious authorities blinked.

I Peking Opera Is Not Opera

© Robbie Jack/Corbis

Peking opera, like many forms of traditional Asian theatre, is highly stylized. The makeup and costumes are symbolic, and actors train for years to master the music, dance, gestures, and acrobatics associated with their characters. Traditional string and percussion instruments provide a strong rhythmic accompaniment to the acting. The sets and props are simple and suggestive—audiences understand that they must use their imaginations to fill out the scenery. For example, a simple chair can represent a grand throne, and an actor waving a blue flag can represent an angry sea.

While the theatre had gone dark in Christian lands, theatre in other parts of the world was alive and well. Theatre in China grew out of regional rituals related to Confucianism, Taoism, and Buddhism and to ritual dances performed during the Shang dynasty (ca. 1500–1027 BCE). The first theatre building in China was constructed in 610 CE, although Chinese actors traditionally date their drama to 714 CE, when Emperor Ming Huang (712–755) created a school of the arts. Theatre was well established in China by the reign of Chen Tsung (998–1022), but it did not really blossom until the Yuan dynasty (1280–1368), which was established by Kublai Khan and his Mongol warriors. During this period, as many as five hundred playwrights were turning out hundreds of plays. After the Mongols were defeated, the Ming dynasty (1368–1644 CE) introduced more literary forms of theatre that were designed for the elite members of society. Then in the Qing dynasty, Emperor Ch'ien-lung (1736–1795 CE) brought to Beijing the best performers from all over China and created the *ching-hsi,* or "opera of the capital"—what Westerners call the Peking, or Beijing, opera.

Peking opera is a synthesis of music, dance, acting, and acrobatics. It was first performed by strolling players in markets, temples, courtyards, and the streets. Although it is called *opera,* all it has in common with Western-style opera is singing and musical accompaniment. Because they originally performed outdoors, Peking opera actors developed a piercing style of singing their lines in order to be heard over boisterous crowds. The orchestra—made up of gongs, cymbals, lutes, rattles, drums, castanets, and a two-string violin—also had to turn up the volume. The sets had to be simple so that the stage could be quickly set up and struck. Because there was little scenery, audience members had to use their imaginations. Scenes could be changed quickly because they were indicated by a song, dance, pantomime, or symbolic movement. For example, by circling the stage, an actor signified that he was on a long journey; by running across the stage holding a piece of flowing cloth, the actor showed that it was windy; if the story required the character to enter on horseback, the actor pantomimed a stylized gallop while swinging a riding whip.

The two types of plays of the Peking opera were based on history, mythology, folklore, and tales of romance. Civil plays feature plots about imperial

© Liu Liqun/Corbis

The makeup in Peking opera is symbolic and specific to categories of characters. Here, a Jing, or painted face, actor applies black for brusqueness, red for good, white for treachery, and blue for wildness. Jing actors play swaggering, extroverted characters such as army generals, warriors, or state officials.

concubines, conniving palace eunuchs, chivalry, and romance. The military plays often take place during the Three Kingdoms period (220–265 CE), when China was divided into three rival kingdoms. Although this was a period of great turmoil, the Chinese regarded it as a time that exemplified the highest ideals of chivalry and honor. An example of a military play is *Yang Ping Pass,* the story of two warlord-emperors. Emperor Cao Cao seeks revenge on rival Emperor Liu Bei for the death of one of his generals. Cao Cao's troops are poised to attack at Yang Ping Pass. Discovering the planned attack, one of Liu Bei's chief staff officers wants someone to burn Cao Cao's store of grain to force him to withdraw. An old general agrees to set the fire although the other officers feel it's a suicide mission. Undaunted, the old general succeeds in burning the grain, but he is then surrounded by Cao Cao's troops. The old general seems doomed, but at the last moment, Liu Bei's troops come to his aid. A chorus of actors stages a glorious battle, using swords, javelins, and spears as they fill the stage with acrobatic, swashbuckling action, deafening percussion, and triumphal tableaus. In the end, the old general is rescued.

The Japanese Say Yes to Theatre

> When the components of art are dominated by restraint, the result is very moving.
>
> ***Chikamatsu Monzaemon,*** *Japanese playwright*

In Japan, theatre was greatly influenced by Buddhism and Shinto, an indigenous religion. Shinto does not divide existence into a physical world and a supernatural world. Instead, Shintoists worship the life force in rivers, rocks, trees, and other elements of nature from which they believe creativity, healing, and even disease originate. In the sixth century, Buddhism, a religion that stresses spiritual enlightenment through meditation, proper conduct, and wisdom that releases one from desire and suffering, merged with Shinto. These belief systems had a tremendous influence on Japanese society.

Japanese theatre, like that of most other cultures, can be traced to ritual. Over a thousand years ago Buddhist and Shinto festivals included dancelike dramas intended to drive away demons, bring health, celebrate the harvest, and deliver prosperity. Japanese theatre began when Buddhist priests added choral songs to these ritual dances. Like the Japanese tea ceremony, Japanese drama emphasizes mood, serenity, contemplation, and simplified movements. To fully appreciate the Japanese theatre, one must prepare to receive the dreams, poetic vision, and beauty that are derived from simplicity and restraint. There are two types of traditional Japanese theatre: Noh drama and Kabuki.

Noh

Japanese Noh drama developed during the 1300s from the dance-prayers of Buddhist priests, who danced, sang, and prayed at religious shrines. It is said that in 1374 a shogun named Yoshimitsu saw one of these dance-prayers and was so impressed that he invited the performers to his court; there he set about joining poetry, acting, singing, and dance into a new form of theatre called **Noh,** which means "talent." By the middle of the fifteenth century, Noh was the favorite theatre of the shoguns and their aristocratic patrons. Noh performances, like the Japanese tea ceremony and sumi paintings, were understated and refined. Everything redundant was pruned. The actors—men only—moved in a stately manner with a deliberate tempo that allowed every step, gesture, and word to be dignified and fully contemplated. The great Noh actor Zenchiku (1405–1470) described Noh as "the inexpressible beauty of doing nothing." The stage was a simple raised platform with a floor of highly polished wood that reflected the actors' brightly embroidered kimonos and expressive masks (see the Spotlight box "Masks and Theatre"). Under the floor were special resonators that amplified the sounds of the actors' feet when they danced. Painted on the back wall of the stage was a pine tree symbolizing eternal life.

Noh stories had five possible subjects: the deities; the deeds of heroic samurais; women (these were known as "wig plays" because men who played women wore a wig); insanity; and famous legends. An evening of Noh drama often included several plays with small farces in between them. Some of these farces parodied the serious plays on the same program, much as the ancient

© Koichi Kamoshida/Getty Images

Noh plays are performed on a bare stage whose only adornment is the kagami-ita, *a painting of a pine tree at the back of the stage. The tree symbolizes eternal life, a meaning that may derive from Shinto ritual—according to myth, deities descended to earth via the pine tree. To the left of the Noh stage is the* Hashigakari, *a narrow bridge that the principal actors use to make their entrances.*

© Morton Beebe/Corbis

In contrast to the sparse stage, Noh masks are highly expressive and the actors' costumes are sumptuous. The main focus is on the actors, who move slowly and gracefully, and who chant poetic texts that follow the seven-five rhythm used for haiku poems.

Greek satyr plays parodied the tragedies performed the same day. The similarities between Noh and ancient Greek drama has led some scholars to speculate that Alexander the Great and Hellenistic theatre may have a more far-reaching effect on world theatre than is generally believed, but others conclude that the only relationship between the two is the human tendency to develop theatre from ritual.

Masks and Theatre

Although actors today in the West rarely wear them, masks have been important in ritual, religion, and theatre for thousands of years. Archeologists have found twenty-thousand-year-old cave paintings depicting people wearing masks. There is evidence of masked rituals in prehistoric Africa, Europe, Asia, and the Americas from the Andes to Alaska. Masks can help wearers enter an altered state or at least allow them anonymity as they take on the qualities of a different person, an animal, or a mythical being. On Halloween, children and adults who might otherwise feel inhibited put on masks and in doing so assume the qualities of the mask. Children suddenly become little devils or princesses, and adults do things that they would never consider if they were not masked: Once you change your face, you can change who you are. In fact, the word *person* derives from the Greek word for "mask." Your face is a mask that embodies how you feel, what you are thinking, and who you are.

In the theatre, masks have been used for many reasons; some are decorative, but others provide complex symbolic meanings. Masks can help actors play characters, and they can help the spectators identify the characters. In some countries masks are considered a higher form of characterization than an actor's facial expressions, because a mask embodies a character in its purest form. When masks are regarded this way, they are seen as amplifying expressions rather than hiding them. For example, in traditional African theatre, the mask allows the wearer to identify with and assume the spirit of mythical ancestors or supernatural beings. In Japanese Noh drama, the masks are so important that they have been handed down from father to son for centuries. Noh masks have even been declared national treasures. In ancient Greek drama, masks that covered the entire head not only helped actors play different characters but may also have helped them be heard, for some had large mouth openings that served as megaphones.

Today in Indonesia, India, China, Japan, and Africa, masked theatre is still regularly performed. Masks encourage and empower us to transform ourselves as they permit us to replace our reality—if only temporarily—with that of another one. Masks are as old as theatre itself and as modern as *The Lion King*.

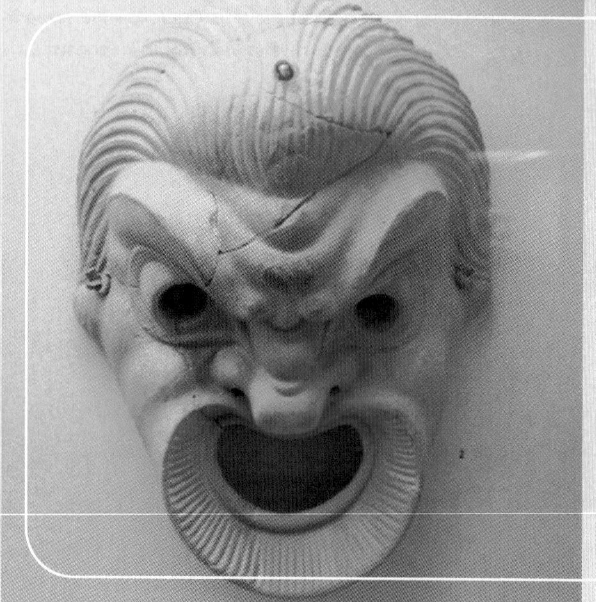

Courtesy Museum of the Ancient Agora, Athens

© Joan Marcus

Throughout history, masks have played an important role in theatre. In ancient Greece, actors used masks like the terracotta mask shown at left so that all audience members could easily see which character they played. This large opening at the mouth of this comic mask may have acted as a megaphone to project the actor's voice. Masks are still common in theatre. Designer Julie Taymor is well known for her innovative use of masks, such as the wooden one shown at right, designed for Juan Darién: A Carnival Mass, *the story of a jaguar turned into a boy.*

Kabuki

Noh drama was designed for aristocrats and shoguns; there were few performances for the general public. But by the seventeenth century, a robust and spectacular version of Noh was created for the masses. It was called **Kabuki,** from the characters for "song" (*ka*), "dance" (*bu*), and "skill" (*ki*). A woman named Okuni, the owner of a brothel, began doing Noh theatre imitations in front of her shop in order to drum up more business. Her female Kabuki players were a sensation; after each performance men lined up to purchase the ladies' services. But when the samurais began fighting duels over the women, they were no longer allowed to perform Kabuki. This left Kabuki theatre to male actors, as it remains today (see the Spotlight on Diversity box "Women on Stage").

Over the centuries, Kabuki has become a popular form of mass entertainment. Although it borrowed a great deal from Noh, Kabuki is decidedly less restrained. It has a greater variety of characters, contains more battle scenes,

Kabuki theatre began in the early 1600s as a popular form of Noh drama. Kabuki is known for stylized movements, singsong speech, and elaborate makeup. Over the years, Kabuki has gone in and out of fashion in Japan; it was briefly banned by occupying U.S. forces after World War II, but today it is the most popular form of traditional theatre. It has long influenced Western theatre artists, and today is often melded with Greek drama to great effect. This is a Kabuki version of Euripides' Medea *(shown here with her sons). Directed by Yukio Ninagawa, Olivier Theatre/National Theatre in London, 1987.*

© Donald Cooper/Photostage

Women on Stage

Theatre's religious origins have often meant that women were barred from performing, as many religions have historically been dominated by men. This was certainly the case in Western theatre. The women of ancient Greece were not allowed to act in plays, and in Rome there were only a few female performers. Not until the 1500s did women begin appearing on stage in the West, and they didn't become commonplace until the 1600s. Today, men still occasionally play female characters—Dustin Hoffman and Robin Williams each played a woman in the movies *Tootsie* and *Mrs. Doubtfire.*

Outside the West, women actors have fared better. Women have been performing in Chinese theatre for thousands of years. They were briefly banned from the stage in the late eighteenth century by a decree of Emperor Ch'ien-lung (1736–1795). When the Qing dynasty was overthrown, they began acting again, although men playing female characters remained popular. For example, in 1924 Mei Lanfang, what Westerners would call a female impersonator, was voted the best actor in China. In India, women have always been part of the theatre, and in African countries, the participation of women has varied from one country to another.

Today, prohibitions against women on stage are rare. One holdout is Japan's Kabuki theatre, where women have been banned for over 350 years. In the Meiji period (1868–1912), the suggestion that women be allowed to act in Kabuki plays was quickly rejected, because many felt that women playing female characters would be too real. Today, although the ban has been lifted, there are still no female Kabuki actors in Japan. The men who play female roles are called **onnagata.** Like all Kabuki actors, they train from childhood. Onnagata performers take their study of female characters very seriously. In fact, in the first half of the nineteenth century, they often lived as women offstage in an attempt to perfect female movements and manners. Even today no onnagata is considered to be at the peak of his abilities until he has been playing women's roles for at least twenty years. After a lifetime of studying and imitating women, according to Kabuki expert Shutaro Miyake, onnagata often feel they know women better than women know themselves. As they see it, only a man can *objectively* understand a woman. Of course, many in the West would argue this point.

© 20th Century Fox/Kobal Collection

© Monika Graff/The Image Works

Men have played women's roles in theatre for thousands of years, often because of social or religious restrictions placed on women in public. In Kabuki theatre, men played women until fairly recently, training for many years to act, dance, and move like women. Today in Western theatre and entertainment, men play women mostly for comic effect, as Robin Williams did in the title role of the movie Mrs. Doubtfire.

and enacts many melodramatic moments. Kabuki actors wear the colorfully embroidered, gold-lined kimonos and elaborate makeup and wigs of Noh theatre, but Kabuki adds spectacular scenery, including revolving stages, trapdoors, and breathtaking special effects. Even Noh's pine tree painted on the back wall of the stage is exaggerated. Another notable difference is the audiences. Unlike Noh theatregoers, Kabuki audience members are expected to be active participants. They call out an actor's name if they like a particular moment, or if they don't like an actor, they might cry out "*Daikon,*" or "radish," the Japanese equivalent of calling an actor a "ham."

FOR MORE ON

KABUKI AND NOH

"Noh and Kabuki: The beauty of form," Masao Yamaguchi, *UNESCO Courier,* April 1983

I Meanwhile, Back in Medieval Europe

During the Middle Ages, the thousand years between the fall of Rome and the start of the Renaissance, Europe experienced economic recovery, stronger governments, and longer periods of peace. The Church grew more powerful, yet in many ways it remained mired in the past. Mass was given in Latin even though most Europeans neither spoke nor understood it. The copies of the Bible that did exist were handwritten and locked away in monasteries, and few ordinary citizens were literate enough to read them. The Vatican (papal government), sensing that it was losing the common people, began to allow theatrical elements into the Mass, but only for the purpose of "fortifying" the faith of the general populace. In the early tenth century, priests were permitted to act as "living impersonators" of biblical figures in short plays on religious topics. These living impersonations were special because they were acted in the vernacular, not in Latin. By the late 1100s, these modest church plays were becoming popular throughout Europe.

However, the church plays began to interfere with worship, and some in the Church questioned the propriety of clergy dressing up and acting. Exodus 20:4 states, "Thou shall not make unto thee any graven images, or any likeness of anything that is in heaven above, or that is in the earth beneath, or that is in the water under the earth." Some took this verse to mean that acting like someone else was an affront to God. Yet the popularity of the plays could not be denied. To the dismay of Church leaders but to audiences' delight, some bawdy bits were working their way into the performances. Soon the Mass became a sideshow to the main event: a play.

In 1210, Pope Innocent III decreed that plays should be moved outside the church and townspeople should be encouraged to take over the acting. A new method of staging was needed. The answer was horse-drawn wagons, called **pageant wagons,** which were pulled up in front of the audience in the town square and used as the stage for performances of short religious plays. Some of these wagons were quite complicated. Reports of the day describe wagons that were two stories tall and had trapdoors, cranes from which God and angels could descend, and hell-mouths that opened to belch clouds of smoke as they swallowed up townspeople acting out the fate of the damned.

Three types of plays became popular: mystery, miracle, and morality. The word *mystery* here has nothing to do with the modern meaning of "enigma" or "puzzle," but comes from the Anglo-French word for occupation, *mesterie,* because these liturgical plays were often performed by guilds, the labor unions of the day. For example, the shipwrights might stage a play about Noah's ark, the goldsmiths might stage the story of the Magi, and the bakers might stage

Northwind Picture Archives

During the Middle Ages, traveling pageant wagons were commonly used to stage plays. Strict limitations were imposed on the players by the Church. Only stories and themes from the Bible could be depicted, and individual interpretation of stories or characters was not allowed—in contrast to the variety of interpretations of myths by playwrights of the golden age of Greek theatre. In this scene staged on an English pageant wagon, players act out the story of Christ appearing before Pilate.

the Last Supper. When a number of mystery plays were performed in biblical chronological sequence from Creation to the Day of Judgment, the result was called a **mystery cycle** and was often named for the town where the performances took place. For example, the Wakefield Cycle had thirty-two mystery plays, including *The Fall of Lucifer, The Anti-Christ,* and *Doomsday.* The writers of these religious plays seldom put their names on the scripts because that would show pride, one of the seven deadly sins.

The one element almost all mystery plays shared was comic relief. Audiences in the Middle Ages, just as today, wanted to be entertained. However, the Bible provides little light entertainment, so comedy had to be added to the plays. However, tampering with stories from the Bible could lead to charges of blasphemy, and so the players got around the rules by filling in the blanks of biblical stories with comic scenes. For example, the Bible says that Noah got on the ark with his wife, but it doesn't specify the particulars; so boarding the ark becomes a comic episode in which Noah's wife at first refuses to budge unless she can take along her "gossips." Another example of comedy added to a biblical story is in *The Second Shepherd's Play.* This play asks what the three shepherds in the field were doing before the angel came to tell them that Christ had been born. As one might guess, they were involved in a comic farce.

FOR MORE ON

MYSTERY PLAYS

"Giving voice to women: Teaching feminist approaches to the mystery plays," Katie Normington, *College Literature,* Spring 2001

The popularity of these dramatizations of scripture led to the development of other types of religious drama. **Miracle plays** told stories about the lives of the saints, and **morality plays** were about how we should conduct our life. The emphasis was now on created characters facing moral choices between vice and virtue. Some of these plays had simple points, such as the attack on poor hygiene and gluttony in *Condamnation de Banquet* (1509). Other morality plays are *Money Is the Root of All Evil* and *Everyman.* Today, some churches stage morality plays on Halloween in what are called "Hell Houses." The rooms contain scenarios that are supposed to lead to Hell, such as drunk driving, abortion, drugs, AIDS, and the occult—each showing a battle between angels and demons. These plays are no different in theme from the morality plays of five hundred years ago.

Theatre in the Shadows

Unlike Christianity, which took more than three centuries to become a viable force, Islam spread rapidly. It was founded around 610 by the prophet Muhammad (ca. 570–632 CE). Over the next century, Islam spread east from Mecca to the border of China and southwest through Upper Egypt. By 711 CE, Islam had spread from North Africa into Spain. North African Muslims (Moors) occupied Spain for nearly seven hundred years and built great cities such as Granada and Córdoba, which had over seventy libraries and became an intellectual center of Europe.

The Muslim view excluded theatre as a viable social entity, so plays were not an important part of the early Islamic world. The Koran, Islam's holy book, contains a warning about "graven images" similar to the one in the Bible. This prohibition included dolls, statues, portraits, and people playing a character. It is upheld by some Muslims today; in 2001, Taliban leaders in Afghanistan ordered massive 2,000-year-old statues of Buddha to be blown up. In many parts of the Muslim world, theatre, as we know it in the West, was slow to arrive. But the impulse for the theatrical is universal, and to get around the ban on actors, shadow plays became popular in many Islamic countries.

Shadow theatre, which probably originated in China around 100 BCE, is created by lighting two-dimensional figures and casting their shadows on a screen. The audience watches the silhouettes while a narrator tells a story, a little like a primitive television set. The first records of shadow theatre in Arab lands come in the seventh century, but it wasn't always accepted. One of the

Storytellers got around Islamic laws forbidding "graven images," including acting, by staging shadow plays with puppets. The puppets were generally made from the hides of camels or cows and were brightly painted. A puppeteer manipulated the puppets behind a transparent white curtain; lit from behind with candlelight, the shadows of the puppets were thrown onto the curtain. In this picture Karagöz and Hacivat, two of the most famous characters of Turkish shadow theatre, exchange clever dialogue.

Courtesy of University of Exeter Library, Bill Douglas Centre

first shadow-theatre artists was a man named Batruni. During one performance in a mosque, Batruni showed the South Arabian king riding on a horse. The image so frightened the audience that Batruni was accused of being a magician and executed. By the eleventh century, shadow plays were popular in Islamic Spain, and by the thirteenth century they had spread throughout North Africa and into what today is Turkey. Shadow plays include stories about Allah and his prophets as well as stories about historical events.

Curtain Call

Around the year 1000, Spain's Christian neighbors, spurred on by the Pope, began the *reconquista,* or the attempt to re-take Spain from the Muslims. The attacks continued intermittently, until 1492, the year Ferdinand and Isabella sent Columbus exploring, when the great Muslim city of Granada was sacked. During the "reconquest," many Muslim libraries in Spain were burned but a few survived. These conquered libraries drew scholars from all over Europe. As they read the Arabic translations of ancient Greek texts, they were staggered by what they found. Here were stacks of forgotten knowledge: books on science, medicine, and astronomy, as well as Aristotle's *Poetics*.

In 1453, after a six-week siege, Constantinople, the center of the Eastern Roman Empire, had fallen to the Ottoman Turks. As the Turks ransacked the city, they burned Constantinople's libraries. Housed in these burning buildings were thousands of documents and manuscripts from classical Greece. Countless texts were lost, but once again, a few were saved by fleeing scholars. On their modest wagons, among their meager belongings, they salvaged a few of the plays of Aeschylus, Euripides, and Sophocles. This was the dawn of the Renaissance. Europe stood at the cusp of a new classical age and some Europeans seemed to know it. The Italian poet Francesco Petrarch (1304–1374) knew that a change was coming. He wrote: "We must awake or die!"

Summary

No one knows for certain where theatre and drama originated, but many scholars believe that it grew out of religious rituals, ceremonies, and storytelling. Theatre is different from ritual in that it has actors who play roles, not themselves. Theatre is artificial. A play is an imitation of an action, not the action itself. When and where theatre and drama separated from ritual is not known, but it must have existed for thousands of years before the Greeks.

From the Greeks we have the first firm evidence of theatre in the West. Greek theatre grew out of religious rituals that celebrated the god Dionysus. Five hundred years before the birth of Christ, the Greeks built enormous theatres and performed tragedies and comedies. Through their drama, they were searching for the meaning of life and asking powerful questions about humankind's purpose. The most famous of tragic playwrights were Aeschylus, Sophocles, and Euripides. Aristophanes is the only Greek comic playwright whose plays have survived.

In 404 BCE, the Peloponnesian War ended the golden age of Greek theatre. As liberties decreased and freedom of speech was limited, Greek theatre faded. Aristotle wrote *Poetics* in an attempt to teach the playwrights of his day how to construct a proper tragedy. His most important student was Alexander the Great, who began the Hellenistic Age by spreading Greek culture and theatre throughout the Mediterranean and beyond on the point of his sword. Hellenism may have affected theatre as far away as India.

The expanding Roman Empire consumed the Hellenistic empire and appropriated Greek culture and theatre. As time went by, Roman theatre became less associated with religious ceremony and more about amusement, and Rome became the entertainment capital of the ancient world. One of the most popular forms of theatre in Rome was mime. Its actors packed the theatres with obscene plays, vulgar language, and buffoonery. With the fall of the Roman Empire, Christians took control. Christians despised the theatre and eventually had it banned.

Theatre may have been outlawed in Europe, but in India Sanskrit drama had been popular for centuries. In China theatre was getting its official start at the time actors in Europe were being forced to become vagabonds; after a millennia, the music and dance of the Peking opera was being performed in markets, temples, courtyards, and the streets throughout the country. In Japan,

Noh drama, which had developed from the dance-prayers of Buddhist priests and which would spawn Kabuki plays, was becoming popular at about the same time that Europeans were rediscovering the theatre. In the middle of the Middle Ages, theatre was reintroduced in Europe but allowed only if it fortified the unlearned people in their faith. Soon mystery, miracle, and morality plays became popular and were produced by common people and trade guilds.

The Art of Theatre Online

Use the *Art of Theatre* website at **http://communication.wadsworth.com/downs1** for quick access to the electronic study resources that accompany this chapter, including a digital glossary, a link to InfoTrac College Edition that you can use to find the For More On... InfoTrac College Edition readings listed below, a list of further reading, and a chapter quiz. When you get to the *Art of Theatre* homepage, click on the cover of the book you are using and you will be redirected to the website for your book. Then click on "Student Book Companion Site" in the Resource box, pick a chapter from the pull-down menu at the top of the page, and select an option from the Chapter Resources menu. The *Art of Theatre* website also includes links to interesting and informative theatre websites. Just click on the Theatre on the Web link in the Book Resources menu. The links to these websites are maintained and updated as needed.

Key Terms

catharsis / 243
City Dionysia / 242
Dionysus / 241
dithyramb / 241
episode / 243
exodos / 243
Hellenistic Period / 250
Kabuki / 263
Library of Alexandria / 249
miracle play / 267
morality play / 267
mystery cycle / 266
New Comedy / 249
Noh / 260
Old Comedy / 247
onnagata / 246
orchestra / 242
pageant wagon / 265
parodos / 243
Peking opera / 258
Peloponnesian War / 247
Poetics / 249
prologue / 243
ritual theatre / 240
Sanskrit theatre / 250
satyr play / 245
shadow theatre / 267
skene / 242
stasimon / 243
Theatre of Dionysus / 242
theatron / 242
Thespis / 242

For More On . . .

Infotrac College Edition Readings

http://www.infoTrac-college.com

African theatre / 241
"The strange and the familiar: Intercultural exchange between African and Caribbean theatre"

Greek tragedy / 245
"The Aristotelian theatrical paradigm as cultural-historical construct"

Lysistrata / 248
"Let's make love, not war (*Lysistrata*)"

Kabuki and Noh / 265
"Noh and Kabuki: The beauty of form"

Mystery plays / 267
"Giving voice to women: Teaching feminist approaches to the mystery plays"

11 Theatre's Revival in Europe

By the late 1400s, mystery, miracle, and morality plays still dominated theatre in Europe, but secular plays were becoming popular at royal courts and at universities. These plays were called **interludes** *because they were performed between other forms of entertainment, such as musical concerts. From a historical perspective,* interludes *is the perfect name for these plays because they represent the transition between medieval plays, whose only purpose was to moralize and teach biblical lessons, and the wholly secular plays of such soon-to-be-born playwrights as William Shakespeare.*

By the 1500s the trickle of ancient knowledge flowing from Spain and Constantinople had become a flood, and the plays of Roman and Greek playwrights were widely translated into the vernacular and imitated. Yet much had been lost. Of the 123 plays of Sophocles once housed in the Library of Alexandria, only seven survived. Of Aristotle's

© Erich Lessing/Art Resource, NY
© Bernard Gotfryd/Getty Images (inset)

◀ ***On preceding page:*** Le tombeau de Maître André *(1717), a painting by Claude Gillot, depicts Renaissance commedia dell'arte actors. While the other characters fight over a bottle of wine, Harlequin (seated) drinks the wine.* ***Inset:*** *Bill Irwin as Harlequin in a modern commedia dell'arte performance.*

two books on playwriting, only one remained. Of the thousands of books on science, philosophy, astronomy, and medicine, only a fraction had escaped destruction. Nonetheless, enough knowledge was passed down to spur three of the most fruitful eras in Europe's history: the Renaissance, the Enlightenment, and the Romantic age.

I The Renaissance, the Reformation, and the Return of Secular Theatre

The Renaissance (ca 1350–1650) was an extraordinary period in European history. In many ways, it was a time of rebellion and rebirth—in fact, the word *renaissance* means "rebirth." During the Middle Ages, the overwhelming concerns had been God, redemption, and life after death. In contrast, the foremost concerns of the Renaissance were humankind, ancient wisdom, and life in the present. Renaissance values of individualism and creativity led to the emergence of such great artists as Michelangelo and Leonardo da Vinci. In the theatre, the liturgical drama of the Middle Ages declined and secular theatre once again became popular.

One of the defining moments of the Renaissance came at noon on October 31, 1517, when a monk named Martin Luther (1483–1546) used the front door of All Saint's Church at Wittenberg as his personal complaint box by nailing up a list of ninety-five complaints against the Roman Catholic Church. His action might have gone down in history as an isolated act of defiance, but within a month, the newly invented printing presses in three German towns were rolling out copy after copy of his declaration. This heralded the end of a unified Christendom and the beginning of the Protestant Reformation. Warring religious factions made the next century one of the most violent in history. There were sieges, assassinations, massacres, and seesaw battles as Christian sects fought over alternative interpretations of the Bible and the boundaries of the empires and kingdoms of Europe. By 1648, the end of the Thirty Years' War between Protestants and Catholics, one writer counted over 180 different denominations of Christianity.

The mystery, miracle, and morality plays that defined drama in the Middle Ages began to cause conflict because of differences depending on which denomination produced them. In the end, the divisions within Christianity would bring an end to liturgical drama. In 1539, the Roman Catholic Church decreed that church officials could produce no liturgical drama without prior approval. In Protestant countries, religious plays were often viewed as a relic of Catholicism and their performance was forbidden. Soon, monarchs all over Europe were curbing liturgical plays.

As liturgical drama became less popular, the theatre of the common people morphed into simple comedies that were actually loose imitations of Plautus, Terence, and the Roman mimes (see Chapter 10). Traveling companies searched for crossroads, squares, and fairs where they could set up a makeshift platform and attract an audience. The most successful form of this theatre was the **commedia dell'arte.** Commedia dell'arte originated in Italy in the 1500s and became popular throughout Europe between 1550 and 1750. These wandering players were not the amateur actors of the mysteries but professional actors who performed impromptu farces. It is from the commedia

FOR MORE ON
COMMEDIA DELL'ARTE

"Actor-authors of the commedia dell'arte: The dramatic writings of Flaminio Scala and Giambattista Andreini," Cesare Molinari and M. A. Katritzky, *Theatre Research International,* Summer 1998

© ArenaPAL/Topham/The Image Works

Like many Renaissance playwrights, Jean Racine was heavily influenced by the theatre of ancient Greece. His most famous work, Phaedra *(1677), was based on the tragedy* Hippolytus *(428 BCE) by Euripides. Phaedra, the wife of the king of Athens, is in love with her stepson, Hippolytus. When word arrives that her long-absent husband has died, she reveals her deep, forbidden love. Then she finds out that her husband is not really dead, and she attempts to cover her transgression by accusing her stepson of rape. This 2003 production highlights the classical Greek roots of the play. Directed by Patrice Chéreau, Théâtre de l'Odéon, Ateliers Berthier, Paris.*

dell'arte that we get the word *slapstick,* which is comedy that stresses farce and horseplay. In commedia dell'arte, a slapstick is a device made of two pieces of wood hinged together so that they "slap." When the slapstick is applied to an actor's behind, it makes a loud crack, as if the actor really were getting a painful licking; in fact the victim is in no pain.

Common subjects of commedia dell'arte plays were slaves tricking their masters, misunderstandings between lovers, and peasants who were smarter than aristocrats. There were no scripts, so the players improvised on basic scenarios, and no two performances were exactly the same. During parts of the performance, the actors may have improvised scenes based on suggestions from the audience, much like Drew Carey's televised comedy contest *Whose Line Is It Anyway?*

Aristotle: The Comeback Kid

The Christian conquest of Muslim Spain (ending in 1492) and the Muslim conquest of Christian Constantinople (1453) brought to Europe a flood of ancient texts on science, mathematics, architecture, astronomy, and theatre that had been preserved by Islamic scholars and Christian archivists. Of all the ancient books that were rediscovered, those of Aristotle had an enormous effect on the Church. His philosophies meshed so well with much of the Christianity of the time that some Church fathers even suggested he was sent by God to prepare the way for Jesus Christ. The synthesis of Aristotle's philosophy with the doctrines of the Roman Catholic Church was called **Aristotelian Scholasticism.** So powerful were Aristotle's ideas that some suggest Aristotelian Scholasticism was not the Christianization of Aristotle but the "Aristotlization of Christianity."

These rediscovered classics also launched a new breed of scholars called **humanists.** The word *humanist* first appeared in 15th-century Italy, where it was used to describe university students who rejected the traditional curriculum of theology and instead studied the classical subjects of rhetoric, literary criticism, history, poetry, painting, architecture, music, and classical literature—a curriculum much like the "liberal arts" in a modern university. Humanists revered ancient Roman and Greek philosophers, statesmen, architects, artists, and playwrights. Their studies included the surviving plays of Aeschylus, Sophocles, Euripides, and Seneca.

> What can be more absurd than the introduction in the first scene of a child in swaddling clothes, who in the second appears as a bearded man?
>
> ***Miguel de Cervantes,***
> *Author of Don Quixote, advocating the three unities*

In 1531, the first complete edition of Aristotle's writings was published. Included was the now famous *Poetics* (see Chapters 1, 4, and 10). Soon, humanists began to demand that Aristotelian dramatic principles be applied to drama of the day. Aristotle, they argued, was obviously an authority on philosophy, religion, and the natural sciences, so how could anyone question his wisdom when it came to writing a play? This was the beginning of what became known as the **three unities,** which were rigid rules for writing a play. Although these rules were attributed to Aristotle, they were a misinterpretation of Aristotle's writing by Renaissance scholars. The unities soon constituted the absolute form of classical correctness. The unities require that the action of a play take place within a period of twenty-four hours, that all the settings in a play can be reached within twenty-four hours, and that comedy and tragedy never commingle. Theatre critics' compliments and condemnations of plays were based solely on the three unities. It might seem strange that the relatively open-minded artists of the Renaissance would be so rigid about artistic expression in the theatre, but one of the hallmarks of the period was its adherence to the authority of the ancient scholars.

In France and Italy, theatre artists also sought to imitate ancient Greek plays and acting. A host of theatres revived the classical plays, and playwrights emulated the scripts of Aeschylus, Sophocles, and Euripides. An oratorical, elocutionary method called **declamatory acting** also became popular. In this style, actors delivered their lines directly to the audience in a rhetorical manner typified by order, harmony, and decorum. The actors were relying on the word of humanist scholars who believed this must have been how acting was done in the days of the ancient Greeks. In fact, the scholars were only guessing, for there is no record. Other humanist scholars believed that ancient Greek plays were entirely sung. This led to a new type of theatre at the end of the sixteenth century called **opera.**

The Italian Perspective

In Italy, not only did playwrights follow Aristotelian rules, but their patrons also built theatres that were imitations of ancient Greek and Roman stages, with a *theatron,* an *orchestra,* and a *skene* building. The sole difference was that the Italian theatres were indoors and lit with candles. This architectural change required the addition of intermissions so that the candles could be relit. Although theatres are no longer lighted with candles, today we keep the intermission as a relic of the Renaissance and those first indoor theatres.

The Italians also gave the theatre **perspective scenery.** Filippo Brunelleschi (1377–1446), the first important architect of the Italian Renaissance, is credited with inventing perspective painting. It uses converging lines and a vanishing

© Veroslav Skrabánek/Courtesy Cesky Krumlov Castle

Perspective scenery opened up a whole new world to theatre designers. Stages became rich with depth; vanishing points on distant horizons gave the illusion that the settings extended for miles. This example of perspective scenery can be seen in the Baroque Theatre of the Krumlov Castle complex in the Czech Republic. This well-preserved theatre is one of the few Renaissance theatres still standing. Once a year, a play is staged there, and it is lit by candlelight, just as it was during the Renaissance.

point to create the illusion of depth, of a three-dimensional reality on a flat, two-dimensional surface. The innovation of perspective made medieval art seem flat and cartoonish. In contrast, Renaissance art depicted depth, motion, and realism. In order to make perspective painting work in the theatre, designers added a picture frame known as the proscenium arch. Then they angled, or "raked," the stage floor up toward a vanishing point. The resulting three-dimensional set became all the rage. Today, even though stage floors are no longer raked, the area farthest from the audience is still called **upstage** and the area closest to the audience is called **downstage.**

Spanish Dreams

Due to the reconquest and the Inquisition, Spain was now strongly and almost entirely Catholic and did not have many struggles with conflicting Christian sects. This gave Spain a certain stability, which allowed it to have a larger empire in the New World than any other European country, but it also delayed the coming of the Renaissance. The Spanish failed to embrace humanism and the flood of ancient Greek and Roman knowledge. In the theatre, the unities never caught on and the Church remained fully in control. Religious dramas called ***autos sacramentales*** were still being performed in Spain two hundred years after liturgical plays had lost popularity in the rest of Europe. While Italians were building theatres with proscenium arches and perspective scenery, Spanish drama was still being performed on pageant wagons or on crude platform-stages called ***corrales,*** temporary structures built in the courtyards of inns. Secular plays were allowed, but they often had liturgical themes and were flavored with patriotism. The Golden Age of Spanish theatre arrived in the seventeenth century with two influential playwrights: Lope de Vega and Calderón.

The Renaissance through Romanticism

1300

- Bubonic plague strikes Europe (1348–1353)

1350

- Mystery and miracle plays popular in Europe (ca. 1350–1575)
- Noh drama begins in Japan (ca. 1374)
- *The Second Shepherd's Play* (ca. 1375)

- Kingdom of Ayutthaya (Thailand) established (1350)
- Filippo Brunelleschi, inventor of perspective painting (1377–1446)
- Papal Schism (1378–1417)

1400

- Morality plays popular in Europe (ca. 1400–1550)
- Zenchiku, Noh actor (1405–1470)
- Plautus's plays rediscovered (1429)

- Construction of Forbidden City begins in Beijing (1406)
- Inca Empire in western South America (1438–1533)

1650

- Nell Gwynn (1650–1687)
- Theatre returns to England (1660)
- First professional actress performs in London (1661)
- *Tartuffe*, Molière (1664)
- *Ye Bear and Ye Cubb*, William Darby (1665)
- Voltaire (1694–1778)

- Puritan rule is ended in England (1660)
- Isaac Newton formulates his law of gravitation (1665)
- Salem witch trials (1692)

1700

- *Love Suicides at Sonezaki*, Chikamatsu (1703)
- Denis Diderot, encyclopedist and playwright (1713–1784)

- Jean-Jacques Rousseau (1712–1778)

1725

- Gotthold Lessing (1729–1781)
- Pierre Beaumarchais (1732–1799)
- Licensing Act (1737)
- Johann Wolfgang von Goethe (1749–1832)

- *Gujin tushu jicheng*, an encyclopedia, printed with movable copper type in China (1726)
- *Encyclopédie*, Denis Diderot (begun in 1745)
- Ruins of Pompeii excavated, beginning of archaeology (1748)

1750

- Peking Opera begins (ca. 1750)
- Richard Brinsley Sheridan (1751–1816)
- *Candide*, Voltaire (1759)
- Audience members banned from the stage in France (1759)
- "The Paradox of Acting," Denis Diderot (1773, published 1830)

- Melody of *Twinkle, Twinkle, Little Star* is published in France (1761)
- James Watt makes first practical steam engine (1765; patented in 1769)

1775

- *The Barber of Seville*, Pierre Beaumarchais (1775)
- *Nathan the Wise*, Gotthold Lessing (1779)
- *The Marriage of Figaro*, Pierre Beaumarchais (1784)

- U.S. Declaration of Independence ratified (1776)
- U.S. Constitution ratified (1787)
- French revolution begins (1789)

1450	1500	1550
• Noh theatre is popular in Japan (ca. 1450) • *Everyman* (ca. 1495)	• Italian translation of Aristotle's *Poetics* (1549)	• Commedia dell'arte flourishes (ca. 1550–1750) • Golden Age of Spanish theatre (ca. 1550–1650) • Lope de Vega (1562–1635) • Christopher Marlowe (1564–1593) • William Shakespeare (1564–1616)
• Johannes Gutenberg invents printing press (ca. 1450) • Constantinople falls to the Ottoman Turks (1453) • Sistine Chapel is built in Rome (1473) • First ballet, danced entertainment for Duke of Milan (1489) • Christians "reconquer" Spain from Muslims (1492)	• *Mona Lisa*, Leonardo da Vinci (1503) • Martin Luther launches the Reformation (1517) • Erasmus publishes complete edition of Aristotle's writings in the original Greek (1531)	• Elizabeth I becomes queen of England (1558) • Francis Bacon, "father of the Enlightenment" (1561–1626) • Galileo Galilei (1564–1642)

1625	1600	1575
• Molière (1622–1673) • Women banned from performing Kabuki in Japan (1629) • Jean Racine (1639–1699) • Aphra Behn (1640–1689) • Puritans ban theatrical performances and close all theatres in England (1642)	• Pedro Calderón de la Barca (1600–1681) • Kabuki begins in Japan (ca. 1603) • Ben Jonson's *Masque of Blackness* (1605) • Pierre Corneille (1606–1684) • Globe Theatre burns and is rebuilt (1613)	• Queen Elizabeth bans religious dramas (1570) • Ben Jonson (1572–1637) • Inigo Jones, architect and stage designer (1573–1652) • Blackfriars Theatre opens (1576) • First professional public theatre in Spain (1576) • The Theatre is built outside London (1576) • *The Tragical History of Doctor Faustus*, Christopher Marlowe (1589) • First opera, *Dafne*, by Jacopo Peri (1597) • *Every Man in His Humour*, Ben Jonson (1598) • Globe Theatre opens (1599)
• Taj Mahal constructed in India (1630–1653) • First coffee house in Europe opens in Venice (1640) • Qing Dynasty, last imperial dynasty of China (1644–1912)	• Galileo improves design of telescope (1609) • *Mayflower* drops anchor near Cape Cod (1620)	• Pope Gregory XIII eliminates ten days from the calendar (1582) • Virginia Dare is first English child born in American colonies (1587)

THEATRICAL EVENTS AND PLAYS

HISTORICAL / CULTURAL EVENTS

© Donald Cooper/Photostage

One of the most popular playwrights of Spain's Golden Age of theatre was Lope de Vega. His most well-known play, Fuente Ovejuna (The Sheep Well)*, tells the story of a peasant community that revolted against the repeated atrocities of a brutal nobleman. So popular was Lope de Vega that his name came to be synonymous with anything the public thought superior, such as Lope horses, Lope melons, and Lope cigars. His critics were few because anyone who dared criticize Spain's greatest playwright was susceptible to anonymous death threats. This 1989 production featured David Beames (standing) and Patrick Drury. Adapted by Adrian Mitchell. Directed by Declan Donnellan, National Theatre, Cottesloe, London.*

Félix Lope de Vega y Carpio (1562–1635), commonly known as Lope de Vega, is considered one of the most influential Spanish playwrights and was certainly the most prolific. He claimed to have written over 2,200 plays, but the number is probably closer to the 400 or so that have survived. He once boasted that he wrote ten plays in one week and an entire play before breakfast. In any case, he wrote hundreds of *autos sacramentales* as well as historical dramas, intrigues, and "cloak-and-sword" plays, with fast-moving plots about love, honor, and vindication. His most popular work, *The Sheep Well* (1614), was about the murder of a tyrannical feudal lord by humble villagers. Under torture by authorities, the villagers stand strong and refuse to confess or name names. In the end, they are saved by the intervention of a good king. In his plays, Lope de Vega was an idealist: God inspires kings, common people should obey the king as well as the Church, and personal honor must not be betrayed.

© Donald Cooper/Photostage

Although over 30,000 plays may have been written during the Golden Age of Spanish drama, most were about a narrow code of honor that limited their historical significance. One exception is Calderón's Life Is a Dream, *which explores destiny, free will, and complex human motivation. Because of its universal appeal, this play is often produced today. This 1998 production featured George Anton (foreground) as Sigismund. Directed by Calixto Bieto, Lyceum Theatre Company, Edinburgh.*

Pedro Calderón de la Barca (1600–1681) also wrote hundreds of *autos sacramentales* and secular "cloak-and-sword" plays that reflected the Spanish values of love, honor, revenge, and religious servitude. But Calderón's plays had more symbolism and depth than Lope de Vega's. Of all Calderón's works, *Life Is a Dream* (1635) is regarded as having the most universal theme. The play explores the mysteries of human destiny and the conflicts between free will, predestination, and human motivation. The story is about a king of Poland who imprisons his son Sigismund at birth because the stars have told him that his son will lead a rebellion against him. Sigismund grows up chained in a dank dungeon. Cut off from human contact, he, of course, becomes a savage beast. But then his father, suffering the guilt pangs of old age, relents and allows his son to join him in the castle. When Sigismund is taken from his dungeon to court, he proves to be a violent, thoughtless, and ruthless being. The king drugs Sigismund and banishes him back to his cell. When Sigismund awakes, he finds himself back in chains. He isn't sure if his journey to the castle was real or a dream. Sigismund vows to change and become a just human being. In the end, he defeats his cruel father and becomes king. *Life Is a Dream* was a play ahead of its time because it attempted to explain the human character as being shaped by environmental and psychological causes rather than predetermined by fate.

Elizabethan England and Shakespeare's Heyday

When Elizabeth became Queen of England in 1558, there wasn't a single professional theatre in London. By her death in 1603 London had been transformed into one of the theatre capitals of the world. Actually, the theatres were not *in* London but in its suburbs, because after 1574 theatre was banned within the city limits due to the protests of a religious group called the **Puritans.** The

Puritans got their name from their zeal to "purify" the church. The only way to escape the fires of hell, according to the Puritans, was through hard work, abstinence from all profane amusements and sensual pleasures, and careful observance of religious rites. Obviously, the theatre kept people from their work, so the Puritans condemned theatre as a temptation of the devil. To avoid the London magistrates and the Puritans, theatre managers built their theatres outside the city limits. Soon there were two types of permanent public playhouses around London: small indoor theatres such as the Blackfriars, which catered to wealthy clientele, and huge outdoor theatres such as the Rose and the Globe, which were open to the general public.

In 1576, the first permanent outdoor theatre since Roman times was built just outside the city limits by James Burbage (d. 1597), a carpenter and part-time actor. The structure was simply called "The Theatre" and proved to be so popular that there were soon a host of imitators. These theatres all followed the same basic design, like that of the Spanish *corrale,* with a platform-stage jutting into the middle of an open courtyard encircled by tiers of gallery seats; on the floor around the stage was an area where people could stand and watch the show.

FOR MORE ON

THE ROSE THEATRE

"A rose by any other name," *Management Today,* June 1989 (on saving the Rose Theatre)

One of the most famous outdoor theatres was the Rose, built on the south side of the Thames in an area famous for such dubious attractions as brothels, gaming halls, and bear-baiting arenas. Bear-baiting involved tying a bear to a stake at the center of the arena and unleashing packs of dogs; the bear killed dozens of dogs, but eventually the dogs overwhelmed the bear. Here, among such less than desirable "entertainments," the Rose and several other theatres were built.

The Rose was known for its clogged drainage system, which sometimes smelled so bad that a performance had to be cancelled. When Shakespeare's

William Dudley for the Rose Theatre Trust

Built in 1587 by London pawnbroker Philip Henslowe, this is a cross-section of the Rose's interior and stage. Because theatres were outlawed in London proper at the time, the Rose was constructed in an area famous for such dubious attractions as brothels and bear-baiting arenas. Some of the most well-known plays of English theatre were staged at the Rose, including Marlowe's Doctor Faustus, *Kyd's* Spanish Tragedy, *and Shakespeare's* Titus Andronicus. *The Rose's success prompted the construction of other theatres in the same area, including the Swan (1595) and the Globe (1599).*

Romeo and Juliet was performed in the nearby Globe, Juliet's line "What's in a name? That which we call a rose by any other name would smell as sweet" most likely brought down the house with gales of laughter because the audience knew it was a reference to the Rose's less than pleasant odor.

FOR MORE ON

THE GLOBE THEATRE

"Measuring the Globe," Christopher Hawthorne, *Architecture,* August 2000

The World of the Globe Theatre

By 1600 every Londoner was within two miles of a theatre of some kind. The most famous theatre was Shakespeare's Globe, located "97 paces" away from the Rose. Performances at the Globe and the other outdoor theatres began at about two in the afternoon when daylight flooded the stage and lasted until about five. This schedule led to criticism from the Puritans because the theatre was obviously causing people to idle away their afternoons when they should be working. The Puritans, in their attempt to close all theatres in the London area, managed to get laws passed that forbade anyone from advertising a production. So theatre owners found ingenious ways to publicize their product. One method was with flags—a black flag over the theatre meant that the day's performance would be a tragedy, a white flag signified a comedy, and red signified a history play.

A trumpet fanfare proclaimed that the performance was about to begin, and the audience, as many as 3,000 people, entered the doughnut-shaped theatre through a narrow office where a box was located. The theatregoers dropped payment into the box—hence the modern phrase **box office.** The cheapest tickets were for the main floor, where about 800 people stood elbow-to-elbow in a mob known as the **groundlings.** For an extra charge, one could climb the stairs to the galleries on the second and third floors, from which about 2,000 patrons could look down on the production from the comfort of

William Missouri Downs

In 1949 U.S. actor Sam Wanamaker set out to find the spot where Shakespeare's Globe Theatre had stood. He was shocked to find that the only memorial was a blackened bronze plaque on the wall of a brewery. Determined to create a better monument, he began a campaign to raise millions of dollars to build a faithful replica of the Globe. It took decades and, although Wanamaker did not live to see the completion of his dream, Shakespeare's Globe stands again through his efforts, only a few blocks from its original site.

cushioned benches. In either case, theatre was not expensive. A ticket for a groundling cost only about as much as a quart of ale at a local pub.

During the performance vendors sold ale, water, gingerbread, oranges, and apples, all of which were occasionally used as ammunition if the audience didn't like the play or players. The behavior of an Elizabethan audience was poor by today's standards. Not only did people talk and eat during the performance, but reportedly prostitutes and pickpockets often worked the crowds.

© Donald Cooper/Photostage

During the outdoor productions of Shakespeare's day, audiences did not see complex stage sets. Instead, actors used verbal scene painting to describe the play's various settings. Only a few simple props were used to hint at the location and situation. A potted sapling might represent a dark forest; a royal chair might indicate a golden throne room; or, as in this production of The Tempest, *a ship's wheel could represent the entire vessel. This production featured Geraldine Alexander as Ariel, the spirit helper to the play's protagonist, Prospero. Directed by Lenka Udovicki, Shakespeare's Globe, 2000.*

Plays at The Globe moved fast and aimed to please. Because the unities never caught on in England, the locations of scenes were limited only by the playwright's imagination. Story lines moved freely from location to location just as modern motion pictures do. Because the theatres were outdoors, there were no candles to relight and no need for intermissions.

The scenery of Elizabethan theatre was minimal; the plays used what is called **verbal scene painting.** English playwrights, like their Spanish counterparts, let their words paint pictures so that the audience could "dress" the stage in their imagination. For example, in Shakespeare's *Macbeth* the king paints the scene of a large manor in a picturesque rural landscape when he says, "This castle hath a pleasant seat; the air nimbly and sweetly recommends itself unto our gentle senses." The Elizabethan audience needed nothing more.

What these productions lacked in sets, they made up for in costumes, which were often extravagant affairs of gold, lace, silk, and velvet, donated to the theatre by aristocratic patrons. There was no attempt, however, to make the costumes historically accurate. Actors performing Shakespeare's *Julius Caesar* (1598) wore Elizabethan costumes, not togas. Their aim was not to give a history lesson but to entertain. Performances had music and plenty of special effects and realistic swordplay. Actors hid bladders filled with sheep's blood under their costumes so that during fight sequences, when they were "stabbed," real blood would ooze out. The stage was filled with trapdoors so that actors playing ghosts and spirits could mysteriously appear and disappear. Above the stage were cannons filled with blanks that could be fired to create realistic battle sequences.

Rogues and Vagabonds (Also Known as Actors)

A company of actors in Shakespeare's day consisted of eight to fifteen players. Some of the actors, such as Shakespeare himself, were shareholders who shared the company's profits or losses, and others were hired to act in a single production and paid a set fee or a percentage of the box office. The company would also have two or three boy apprentices who were trained to play women's parts because women were not allowed on the stage. (See the Spotlight box "Women on the Elizabethan Stage.")

Men who acted were often labeled *masterless* (meaning "jobless") rogues and vagabonds. According to English law, any person roaming the country masterless could be branded on the chest with the letter *V* and taken into slavery for two years. If that person was found a second time roaming the country without a job, he could be branded on the cheek with the letter *S* and

Women on the Elizabethan Stage

Unlike Spain, England did not allow women to act in plays. Boys played the role of Juliet and other young women, and mature men played older female characters such as Juliet's nurse. The Puritans were appalled by the thought not only of women appearing on stage but also of men dressing as women. A man wearing women's clothing or a woman wearing men's clothing was an "abomination" to God according to Deuteronomy 22:5. However, there are records of women surreptitiously appearing on stage during Shakespeare's time—as portrayed in the 1998 movie *Shakespeare in Love.*

In 1611, Mary Frith (or Moll Cutpurse, as she was known) was charged by an ecclesiastical court with appearing in a play called *The Roaring Girl* at the Fortune theatre. Not only had she appeared onstage but she had been playing the role of a man and had done so for several months before she was discovered. According to court records, she "sat upon the stage in the public view of all the people there present in man's apparel and played upon her lute and sang a song." She is also reported to have gone to a Christmas celebration at St. Paul's Cathedral and flaunted her femaleness by lifting her cloak and showing her petticoats tucked up inside. She got off with light punishment.

© Donald Cooper/Photostage

Although women are allowed on most stages today, the notion of men playing women's roles and vice versa intrigues many directors. Mark Rylance, managing artistic director of Shakespeare's Globe Theatre, is well-known for playing around with gender roles. He's played Cleopatra in Antony and Cleopatra *and has staged an all-female production of* The Taming of the Shrew *and an all-male production of* Twelfth Night. *In* Twelfth Night *he played Olivia (left), the woman who has fallen in love with Cesario, the young man who is actually Viola, a young woman who decided to make her way in the world by dressing as a man. This production featured Michael Brown (right) as Viola/Cesario. Directed by Tim Carroll, Shakespeare's Globe, 2002.*

condemned to servitude for life. This law, combined with the Puritans' ceaseless efforts to banish their profession, made life hellish for actors.

To protect themselves, acting companies sought legal immunity from hostile actions. They found that the best protection was the patronage of a lord or other noble, preferably a member of the royal family. If it had the patronage of a lord, earl, or king, a theatre company could wear its noble master's colors and take his name. The actors at the Globe were "the Lord Chamberlain's Men." The Lord Chamberlain was Queen Elizabeth's cousin and was responsible for the conduct of theatres and the presentation of plays at court. An acting company couldn't have much safer patronage than that. After Queen Elizabeth's death, the Globe's players became "the King's Men" under King James I. With that title they became the premier acting company in London.

Shakespeare and His Contemporaries

Most would agree that William Shakespeare was the most influential writer of the Elizabethan theatre, but he was certainly not the only, or even the best-known, playwright of his time. Between the end of the sixteenth century and the beginning of the seventeenth, England turned out a number of noted playwrights. Before we look at the Bard, let's take a look at two of the playwrights whose work now lives on in the shadow of Shakespeare's.

Born two months before Shakespeare, Christopher Marlowe (1564–1593) was the son of a shoemaker (Shakespeare was the son of a glove maker). Unlike Shakespeare, Marlowe was formally educated at the University of Cambridge, where he received a bachelor's and a master's degree and was a member of the University Wits, a group of students who studied the classical playwrights Aeschylus, Sophocles, Euripides, and Seneca and performed their plays. When Shakespeare was a mere actor and had not yet written a play, Marlowe was already a leading member of the Lord Admiral's company at the Rose theatre and one of the top playwrights in London. He was also living a mysterious life as a spy for the Protestant Queen Elizabeth, who kept an eye on the Catholics. In many ways, Marlowe was a true Renaissance man. He loved scholarship, hated ignorance, and wrote plays that were filled with classical allusions and about characters who were seeking knowledge. Among his most famous are *The Jew of Malta* (1590), a tragedy about a hero who seeks limitless wealth, and *The Tragical History of Doctor Faustus* (1589), about a learned man who desires limitless knowledge at any cost.

In 1593 Marlowe made the mistake of publicly pointing out some inconsistencies in the Bible and was charged with heresy. The authorities couldn't find him, so they arrested his roommate, the playwright Thomas Kyd (1558–1594), best known for *The Spanish Tragedy* (1589), a bloody tale of ghosts, revenge, and so many homicides that hardly a character was left standing at the end (this play inspired Shakespeare to write *Hamlet*). Kyd was taken to a prison near the Tower of London and tortured until he agreed to attribute the offending remarks to his roommate. He said that Marlowe was "irreligious, intemperate, and of cruel heart" and that he would often "jest at the divine Scriptures." Worse torture and imprisonment than Kyd's would have awaited Marlowe, but on May 30, 1593, the twenty-nine-year-old playwright was murdered during a fight over a bill at a restaurant. Some were not entirely sorry about his death—the Church claimed that God had punished him for his atheism, and Queen Elizabeth was probably pleased to avoid a scandal concerning one of her spies.

Another of the talented playwrights of Shakespeare's day was his friend Ben Jonson. As a youth, Jonson (1573–1637) had worked for several years as an apprentice bricklayer, but the trade did not agree with him. We do not know exactly when he became an actor and playwright, but by 1597 he was in trouble with the censors. In 1597, Jonson co-wrote the play *The Isle of Dogs,* a satiric comedy that was labeled "lewd and slanderous." As a result, the Rose theatre, where the play had been staged, was closed for three months and Jonson and several other actors were imprisoned. Upon his release, Jonson joined Shakespeare's company as an actor. The following year he got into a quarrel with an actor named Gabriel Spencer and killed Spencer during a duel.

© Donald Cooper/Photostage

Christopher Marlowe's The Tragical History of Doctor Faustus *is based on the story of a German doctor who decided to sell his soul to Lucifer so that he could learn all there is to know about the nature of the world. Lucifer provides Faustus with a devil, Mephastophilis, who serves him for twenty-four years, helping him gain knowledge, riches, and fame. Despite occasional misgivings about his deal with Lucifer, Faustus never repents and his soul is eventually delivered to hell. The story of Faustus has inspired dozens of works over the centuries, including Queen's "Bohemian Rhapsody" (1975) and the movie* Bedazzled *(1967; remake, 2000). In this 2002 production of Marlowe's play at London's Young Vic Theatre, Jude Law (right) played Faustus and Richard McCabe (left) played Mephastophilis.*

Jonson once again found himself in prison, this time charged with murder. At his trial he managed to escape execution by pleading "benefit of clergy," a legal loophole that exempted clergy from common punishments. Jonson was not a member of the clergy, but he could do something that few outside the clergy could do in those days: He could read. This was enough to prove that he was at least a clerk (that is, a literate person), so he was granted a reprieve and released. However, all his property was confiscated and he was branded on the thumb with the letter *T* so that if he should kill again, he could be easily identified as a second-time offender. For the rest of his life, Jonson was a marked felon.

Soon thereafter Jonson wrote his first big hit, *Every Man in His Humour* (1598). The following year he wrote *Every Man out of His Humour.* For Elizabethans, *humour,* which comes from the Latin word for "fluid," referred to the concept of four bodily humours that control temperament. The four humours are blood, phlegm, black bile, and yellow bile—a nice way of saying urine. Depending on the relative proportions of these humours, a person could be sanguine (cheerful and optimistic), phlegmatic (sluggish or unemotional), melancholic (depressed and withdrawn), or choleric (easily angered). Jonson's "humour" plays mocked human shortcomings and foibles. A few years later Jonson wrote his masterpiece *Volpone (or the Fox)* (1605), about a rich merchant who pretends to be near death in order to acquire sympathy gifts from three fortune hunters who hope to be his sole heir. This satire of the English lust for money was performed at the Globe, where it was a great hit. Jonson also wrote lyrical poetry and court masques (discussed in the next section of this chapter) that so pleased King James I that he was made the first poet laureate of England.

William Shakespeare (1564–1616) seems to have arrived in London in 1592, when his name first appeared as an actor with the Lord Chamberlain's company. By 1598, he was a well-known performer; his name tops a list of actors in Ben Jonson's *Every Man in His Humour.* Between 1599 and 1608 Shakespeare wrote many of the plays that made him famous, including the comedies *Much Ado about Nothing* (1598) and *Twelfth Night* (1600), the history *Henry V* (1598), and the tragedies *Romeo and Juliet* (1595), *Hamlet* (1600), *Othello* (1604), *King Lear* (1605), and *Macbeth* (1606). Shakespeare was a popular playwright because he gave audiences what they wanted. He

© Richard Termine

*William Shakespeare is one of the most admired and most produced playwrights in the world. His work has been a source of inspiration for countless writers, actors, musicians, and artists. One particularly popular Shakespeare play is the comic, complex A Midsummer's Night's Dream, about a wedding, mismatched couples, fairies, and a play within a play. In this scene from a 2003 production **(left)** at the Shakespeare Theatre in Washington, DC, Titania, the queen of the fairies, is made to fall in love with the weaver Bottom, whose head has been turned into an ass's head by the mischievous Puck. This play has been made into almost thirty movies, including a 1999 version **(right)** starring Kevin Kline as Bottom and Michelle Pfeiffer as Titania.*

often started his plays with an event, a jolting moment to get the audience interested, just as many Hollywood screenwriters do today. He intensified his tragedies with comic relief and filled his plays with implied sex, overt violence, and conflict. He paid no attention to the restrictive unities so popular in Italy but instead jumped heedlessly from location to location. He stole from other writers, borrowed plots, and even on occasion pilfered lines, passages, and phrases from other plays. By the time he reached his late forties, Shakespeare was a wealthy man. *The Tempest* (1611) was the last play he wrote before retiring to his boyhood home of Stratford. At the age of 52, after a hard night of partying with Ben Jonson, he contracted a fever and passed away.

FOR MORE ON
SHAKESPEARE

"Was Shakespeare gay? Sonnet 20 and the politics of pedagogy," Casey Charles, *College Literature,* Fall 1998

Almost four hundred years after his death, Shakespeare is one of the most produced playwrights in the United States. The first production of one of his plays on these shores was in 1730 in the settlement that would become New York City. Today, hundreds of theatres specialize in Shakespeare's plays. In England he was voted "the Briton of the Millennium." Replicas of the Globe theatre have been constructed the world over, including in Tokyo. Over three hundred movies and television shows have been based on his plays, including the musical *West Side Story* (1961) and the science fiction movie *Forbidden Planet* (1956). *Hamlet* has been made into a movie more than twenty times. During the last few years, a great many of his plays have been turned into movies, including *Titus Andronicus* with Anthony Hopkins and Jessica Lange; *A Midsummer Night's Dream* starring Calista Flockhart, Michelle Pfeiffer, and

© Fox Searchlight Pictures/Photofest

Kevin Kline; and a musical adaptation of *Love's Labour's Lost* starring Alicia Silverstone. And there was also an MTV-style adaptation of *Romeo and Juliet* starring Leonardo DiCaprio and a version of *The Taming of the Shrew* called *10 Things I Hate About You.*

Shakespeare is immensely popular all over the world, and many words and phrases from his plays and poems have become part of our everyday speech. He coined over 1,600 of our common words and phrases by changing nouns into verbs and verbs into adjectives and by connecting words that had never before been connected. Among the words he invented are *assassination, eventful, dwindle, courtship,* and *lonely.* He is also the source of the phrases "to catch a cold," "fair play," and "foregone conclusion."

Masques: Entertaining in High Places

At court, the **masques** were the most popular form of theatre. They originated in the early 1500s as a form of entertainment written especially for the monarch and an invited audience. Usually staged in banquet halls, court masques were characterized by grand dances, extravagant costumes, lavish spectacle, poetry, and florid speeches all hung on a thin story line praising the monarch and demonstrating the need for loyalty. The fanciful and ornate costumes included masks—hence the name *masque,* from the French spelling of the word. These elaborate productions were staged for important occasions and holidays and for important guests of state. The characters often came from myths and allegories. Women played goddesses, nymphs, the "Beauties," and the "Graces," and men played mythological gods, heroes, and the "Sons of Peace." In England, women were allowed to perform in the private court masques even though they were not allowed to perform on public stages.

Ben Jonson wrote many of the masques for the English court in the seventeenth century, and they were staged by Inigo Jones (1573–1652), the first major architect of the English Renaissance. He studied under Italian masters of staging and brought back ingenious stage machinery and special effects—moving clouds with sky-borne chariots and simulated starlight, earthquakes, and shipwrecks—along with Italian perspective scenery and controllable lighting with candles. In 1605, Jones introduced the Italian proscenium stage and perspective setting to the English court in Jonson's *The Masque of Blackness.* (See the Spotlight on Diversity box "Multiculturalism Gets Off to A Rocky Start: *The Masque of Blackness.*")

The extravagant frivolity of the masques offended the growing religious movement led by the Puritans. However, Puritan attacks on the theatre sometimes backfired. In 1632, a Puritan named William Prynne (1600–1669) published a pamphlet titled *The Players Scourge* in which he attacked the theatre as sinful, lewd, and an ungodly spectacle of corruption. He labeled actors and playwrights "whore-masters, ruffians, drunkards and godless." He wrote that the theatre had been invented by Satan and was a form of devil worship. He went too far, however, when he called actresses "whores." He didn't know that the queen was to play a role in the next masque. For unintentionally implying that the queen was a whore, Prynne was fined, had both ears cut off, and was sentenced to life in prison.

Multiculturalism Gets Off to a Rocky Start: *The Masque of Blackness*

The fall of Constantinople severed overland trade routes between Europe and Asia as the Turks extended their power over much of the eastern Mediterranean. The Europeans needed another way to reach the East, so they launched the great transoceanic voyages to find a sea route. These explorations and contact with alien cultures could have opened European minds to new societies, but most explorers were motivated only by "gold, glory, and the gospel." With the discovery of new lands came the beginning of the modern slave trade and intolerance for non-European cultures. In 1596 and in 1601 Queen Elizabeth I issued edicts blaming Africans for social evils because they were not Christians and calling for their expulsion from Britain. As cross-cultural interactions became more common in Europe, discourses on race and Asian and African characters billed as "exotic others" began appearing in plays. However, these characters were not played by Asian or African actors. Instead, they were played by white actors wearing dark makeup. These characters included the title character of Shakespeare's *Othello* (1604).

One of the most bizarre products of this culture clash was *The Masque of Blackness* (1605), written by Ben Jonson at the request of Britain's Queen Anne. The queen had expressed a desire to appear on stage with her ladies disguised as "Blackmoors." The masque is the story of twelve black women and their leader who are floating on the ocean in a shell looking for a land foretold in prophecy, where their dark skins can be changed to white. Most Europeans at the time believed that too much sun exposure caused black skin. They reasoned that if black people could go where there was little sun, they would eventually turn white. The "promised land" for the twelve floating ladies, of course, is Britannia, where the king makes the blackface masquers fair skinned. Needless to say, the play did little to promote acceptance. By the late Renaissance, most non-European characters on the European stage were servants or supplicants. Our contemporary problems of cultural domination had already begun.

Inigo Jones created this costume design for Ben Jonson's The Masque of Blackness. *This character, the Daughter of Niger, would not have been played by a black actor, as drawn, but rather by a white actor in blackface. Jones's lush costumes and perspective scenery contributed to the popularity of masques in the seventeenth-century English court.*

© The Devonshire Collection, Chatsworth. Reproduced by permission of the Chatsworth Settlement Trustees.

A Picture Is Worth a Thousand Words: Film Versions of *Hamlet*

Have you ever been disappointed in the movie version of a favorite book? A movie made from a book sometimes seems to lack the book's depth and richness. It leaves out the best details, focusing only on the basic story line. But consider the difference between the two mediums: Books rely on words, and movies rely on images.

© Robbie Jack/Corbis

In this scene from a stage version of Hamlet, *Prince Hamlet decides to kill Claudius but finds him praying in his chamber. Believing that if he kills him now he will send Claudius's soul to heaven, Hamlet decides to wait. This 1994 production at Regent's Park, London, featured Damian Lewis as Hamlet and Paul Freeman as Claudius.*

Similarly, turning a play into a movie can be difficult. Plays, like books, are "talkier" than movies. They rely on dialogue to move the action along. William Shakespeare's most filmed play, *Hamlet,* is so wordy that onstage it's over three hours long. However, both Russian director Grigori Kosintsev and Italian director Franco Zeffirelli have made dynamic film versions of *Hamlet* that are only about two hours long. How did they do it? They left a lot out! Shakespeare himself probably cut some of the play for various performances, and in fact we rarely see the full text performed onstage today.

Hamlet is the story of a Danish prince, Hamlet, whose father, the king, was murdered recently. Hamlet's mother, Gertrude, has already remarried the king's brother, Claudius, which greatly upsets the prince. One night, the ghost of Hamlet's father tells him that Claudius murdered him and demands that the prince seek revenge and kill Claudius. Hamlet agrees, but hesitates because he is wracked with confusion. Was the ghost just a devil sent to tempt him? Is he too cowardly to kill Claudius? As the play unfolds, we see Hamlet struggle to complete his task.

Much of a play's dialogue has to be sacrificed when it is filmed, but Kosintsev and Zeffirelli managed to cut half of *Hamlet*'s words by showing us with images what Shakespeare tells us in language. Kosintsev's film (1964) includes many descriptive images such as these:

- Interior shots of courtiers eavesdropping on staircases and numerous statues of the new king Claudius imply that "something is rotten in the state of Denmark."
- Camera angles elevate Hamlet above other characters or show him downtrodden by the forces of

From Stage to Screen

© Carolco Pictures/The Ronald Grant Archive

This expansive scene from Franco Zeffirelli's movie version of Hamlet *illustrates a film director's ability to replace words with images. Compare this image with the sparse set of the staged* Hamlet. *In film, there is not such a need for soliloquies and verbal scene paintings to provide information—images do the talking.*

court. These shots reinforce Shakespeare's lines, which frequently use *up* and *down, above* and *below.*

- Hamlet's being off to one side in crowd scenes shows his isolation in a society gone wrong.
- A locked fortress looming over the sea evokes a prison like Hamlet's metaphor of a "nutshell" in the middle of "infinite space."

Zeffirelli, taking another tack in his version (1990), cuts most of the play's references to the outside world. Our attention is focused on Mel Gibson's intimate psychological portrayal of Hamlet and his relationship with the queen, played by Glenn Close. To keep Hamlet and Gertrude on screen as much as possible, Zeffirelli cuts many of the other characters' soliloquies. Because Hamlet does not appear in the first scene of the play, Zeffirelli cuts it, and he cuts most of Claudius's long soliloquy at the beginning of the second scene. Instead, the film opens by silently showing the funeral of Hamlet's father, with close-ups of Gertrude weeping, Hamlet struggling to understand what's happened, and Claudius looking on jealously. The opening is beautifully shot, effectively using images to establish the central relationships of the film. In the hands of a good director, a picture can indeed sometimes be worth a thousand words.

Aoise Stratford
Playwright

The Restoration and the Acceptance of Women in Theatre

In 1643, civil war broke out in England. The Puritans, led by soldier and statesman Oliver Cromwell, took over the government. In 1649, they convicted the reigning king, Charles I, of treason and beheaded him. When the Puritans took power, ordinances were passed in an attempt to legislate a new morality. Of course, court masques and public theatre were two of the first things the Puritans banned. (The Puritans brought their anti-theatre sentiments with them when they crossed the Atlantic. See the Spotlight "Puritans, Pilgrims, and the Beginning of Theatre in America.") Seeking to get rid of theatre permanently, Cromwell's government ordered all the theatres around London, including the Globe, demolished. Acting companies, fearing persecution, soon followed the remnants of the royal household into exile in France. Cromwell was the absolute dictator of England until his death in 1658, when once again, civil war threatened. On May 8, 1660, a new Parliament announced that Charles II, son of the beheaded king, had the inherent legal right to the throne of England, and the rule of the inflexible Puritans ended. On his thirtieth birthday, May 29, 1660, Charles II returned from France to London. With the reestablishment of the monarchy, the period of English history known as the **Restoration** began. It was a period of scientific discovery, new philosophical concepts, improved economic conditions, and a return of the theatre—in the French style.

During the Restoration, theatre did not return to the open-air, public theatres of Shakespeare's day. Because Charles II had spent his exile in France, proscenium arches, neoclassical rules, plush costumes, and upper-class patrons shaped the new drama of London. The most popular type of theatre during this period was the **comedy of manners.** These plays often featured great wit and wordplay and told stories about sexual gratification, bedroom escapades, and humankind's primitive nature when it comes to sex. One of the great playwrights of this age was William Congreve (1670–1729), whose

Once the strict rule of the Puritans ended in England, Restoration theatre rebounded with ribald comedies that exposed the social follies of the upper class. Known as the comedy of manners, the most popular plays of this period were rife with marriages of convenience, sexual confrontations, marital infidelities, and coy lovers. A classic example of the comedy of manners is William Congreve's The Way of the World, *the story of shallow, deceitful aristocrats who plot to prevent two lovers from marrying. Complex and funny, this play is notable for its witty and well-written conversations. This 1992 production featured Tom Hollander, Emma Piper, and Barbara Flynn. Directed by Peter Gill, Lyric Hammersmith, London.*

© Donald Cooper/Photostage

comedy *The Way of the World* (1700) laughed at the hypocrites, fools, and aging coquettes of the day. This line from the play shows the flavor of its humor: "You should have just so much disgust for your husband as may be sufficient to make you relish your lover."

The Restoration also brought another innovation: In 1661, thanks to Charles II, women could legally appear on stages in England for the first time. One of the most famous was the pretty and irreverent Nell Gwynn (1650–1687). Born into poverty, Gwynn had started out singing in taverns and selling oranges in theatres. Then she began taking small parts on the stage and quickly became the darling of the London theatre scene. Her specialty was "breeches roles," in which she wore men's clothing and delivered witty prologues and epilogues. Women on stage were a novelty and most audience members found them "delightful," but some still considered them indecent. One pamphleteer noted that women are forbidden by "apostolic prohibition" to speak in church, but in the theatre they "sing, discourse and are often the principal entertainment. Which is certainly inconsistent with the modesty of their sex."

All women together ought to let flowers fall upon the tomb of Aphra Behn, for it was she who earned them the right to speak their minds.

Virginia Woolf,
British novelist

The Restoration also brought the first professional female playwrights. The most famous Restoration-era woman to make her living by writing was Aphra Behn (1640–1689). Before becoming a playwright, she had been a spy for the English government in Antwerp. Her first big hit was *The Forced Marriage* (1670); before her career ended, she wrote nearly twenty more plays full of sexual intrigue, loveless marriages, and satire. Her best-known play was *The Rover, or the Banished Cavalier* (in two parts, 1677 and 1681) for which she had to endure charges of plagiarism by critics who were shocked that a woman could write a successful play. All of Behn's plays were about subjects considered inappropriate for a woman to think about, much less write about, and she was often labeled a "smutty writer."

FOR MORE ON
APHRA BEHN
"The female will in Aphra Behn," David M. Sullivan, *Women's Studies*, June 1993

© Donald Cooper/Photostage

In 1688, Restoration-era playwright Aphra Behn published what she called a memoir and travel narrative titled Oroonoko: or The Royal Slave. *It is the story of an African prince who is first betrayed by a rival king and then by English slave-owners after he is tricked into slavery. Circumstances force him to lead an army of ex-slaves in a rebellion against his masters, and he is subsequently executed. In this 1999 production by the Royal Shakespeare Company, Nigerian playwright Biyi Bandele's adaptation and director Gregory Doran's staging resulted in a play that preserves Aphra Behn's vision but brings the story up to date. Shown here are Ewart James Walters as Kabiyesi, the heartless king, and Geff Francis as Orombo, the king's deceitful vassal.*

Complaints against the theatre were not limited to allowing women on stage. The theatre in general continued to be denounced in pamphlets and from pulpits. The anti-theatre contingent chastised dramatists and performers for encouraging idleness, perverting the youth, and promoting impiety. During the Restoration dozens of books played on the public opposition to the theatre. One such book was called *A Serious Remonstrance in Behalf of the Christian Religion, Against the Horrid Blasphemies and Impieties which are still used in the English Play-House, to the Great Dishonour of Almighty God, and in Contempt of the Statutes of this Realm Shewing their plain Tendency to overthrow all Piety, and advance the Interest and Honour of the Devil in the World; from almost Seven Thousand Instances, taken out of the Plays of the present Century, and especially of the five last years, in defiance of all Methods hitherto used for their Reformation* (1718). There is little need to describe what this book was about—the title says it all.

French Theatre: Tennis, Anyone?

In French neoclassical theatre, as in French society, symmetry, balance, decorum, and harmony were the ideal. There was now a "correct" method to set a table and to stage a play. Like Italian drama, French drama followed the classical unities and was performed in proscenium arch theatres. Because there were few existing theatres, plays were often performed in indoor tennis courts; Paris had over 250 of those in 1500. Tennis was so popular that King Charles IX had the painter include two tennis rackets in his portrait.

The three unities (time, place, and action) were the litmus test for all French plays. Playwrights who did not follow them were denounced by the French Academy (Académie Française), an exclusive club of writers founded in 1634 to maintain standards of literature and language. Jean Racine (1639–1699) was a playwright who unerringly followed the neoclassical rules and adhered to the unities. His most famous work, *Phaedra* (1677), is based on *Hippolytus* (428 BCE) by Euripides. *Phaedra* is a story of desperate love, murder, accusations of rape, and suicide, yet it all takes place within a twenty-four hour period, in only one location, and never mixes comedy and tragedy.

Although Racine was one of France's greatest tragic writers, Molière (1622–1673) was its greatest comic writer. Molière (who was born Jean-Baptiste Poquelin) wrote highly political farces, comedies, and comic-ballets that satirized French life. When incompetent doctors killed Molière's son by prescribing a powder made of antimony—a metallic element used today as a flame retardant, a paint pigment, and a component of car batteries—Molière wrote a number of satires about the medical profession. The most famous were *The Doctor in Spite of Himself* (1666) and *The Imaginary Invalid* (1673). But Molière saved his boldest attacks for the church. Often considered his greatest play, *Tartuffe, or the Imposter* (1664) is about a religious hypocrite. A wealthy gentleman named Orgon brings Tartuffe, who claims to be extremely pious, into his home to attend to his family's spiritual needs. Tartuffe professes to be interested in saving souls but is really a swindler and seducer. The vicar of St. Barthèlemy said that Molière should be burned at the stake as "a foretaste of the fires of hell," but Molière wasn't finished with religion. In 1665, he wrote

FOR MORE ON
TARTUFFE
"Molière's *Tartuffe*," Pamela S. Saur, *The Explicator*, Fall 2001

© Donald Cooper/Photostage

Molière's plays are filled with stock commedia dell'arte characters: the henpecked husband, the miser, self-absorbed lords and ladies. These characters were immediately recognizable to his audiences, which freed their attention so that they could more fully absorb his stinging attacks on the hypocrisy and pretentiousness of French society. Inspired by the death of his son at the hands of incompetent doctors, Molière wrote Le malade imaginaire (The Imaginary Invalid, or The Hypochondriac), *a sparkling satire about the medical profession. Ironically, Molière collapsed while playing the hypochondriac Argan and died a few hours later. This 1981 production at the National Theatre, Olivier, in London, featured Daniel Massey as Argan (kneeling).*

Don Juan; in his version of the story about the legendary ladies' man, the hero is a freethinker who doesn't believe in heaven, hell, or devils. When one of the characters asks Don Juan what he does believe in, he answers, "I believe that two and two are four, that four and four are eight!" This was just too much. The play was banned, never to be produced again during his lifetime, and Molière was accused of being an anarchist and an atheist.

> When I have been really amused, I don't go asking whether I was wrong and whether Aristotle's rules forbade me to laugh.
>
> ***Molière,***
> *French playwright, commenting on the three unities*

A New Light: Theatre in the Age of Reason

The **Enlightenment** (ca. 1650–1800) was a time that glorified the power to reason and analyze. One of the Founding Fathers of the United States, Thomas Paine, called it "the Age of Reason." This was a period of great philosophical, scientific, technological, political, and religious revolutions. The seeds of the Enlightenment were planted when the explorers of the New World brought back stories of distant lands. Some Europeans began to wonder how, for example, could the Egyptians claim that their culture went back 13,000 years? How could the Brahmins in India claim the earth had existed 326,669 "ages," each many centuries long? Didn't they know that the world was only 6,000 years old? According to the Bible, the Great Flood had covered the entire earth, so why was there was no historical record of it in China? Even more confusing, many of these peoples had never heard of the Pope or Christianity or Jesus and yet they had laws, morals, and concepts of right and wrong.

> The Bible teaches how to go to heaven, not how the heavens go.
> ***Galileo Galilei,***
> *Italian astronomer, mathematician, and physicist*

One Renaissance thinker who helped to usher in the Enlightenment was the Italian astronomer Galileo Galilei (1564–1642), born the same year as Shakespeare. Galileo questioned the conventional geocentric (earth-centered) theory of the universe, and he published a defense of Nicolaus Copernicus's new heliocentric (sun-centered) theory in *Dialogue Concerning the Two Chief Systems of the World* (1632). Written in the form of a play with dialogue, this book has two characters, named Salviati and Sagredo, who advocate the Copernican theory and a third character, named Simplicio, a foolish man, who argues on the side of the Church.

All this new thinking and skepticism had a profound effect on religion in Europe. During the Renaissance, bloody wars had raged over which type of Christianity was God's "revealed path," but during the Enlightenment the authority and validity of Christianity itself was questioned. Books critical of Christianity began to appear. Some found fault with the Bible's "repetitions, contradictions, obscurities and multiple interpretations," and others suggested that the miracles recounted in the Bible had natural causes that could be logically explained. Thomas Jefferson went so far as to publish his own version of the Bible which omitted all references to miracles because he regarded them as contrary to enlightened thought.

© Donald Cooper/Photostage

The Marriage of Figaro by French playwright Pierre Beaumarchais is a classic example of an Enlightenment-era play. Although it is a comedy, it includes well-reasoned attacks on the clergy, the state, and censorship. Figaro, a wit with a strong sense of justice, says, "Provided in my writing I mention neither the authorities nor the state religion, nor politics, nor morals, nor the officials, nor finances . . . nor any person of consequence, I may print whatever I like, subject to inspection by two or three censors." This, of course, highlighted the playwright's dilemma—the play, banned during the reign of Louis XVI (1774– 1792) for its skewering of the elite, couldn't get past the censors. This 1991 production featured Kate Buffery (left), Sarah Payne (right), and Simon Schatzberger as Figaro. Translated and adapted by Ranjit Bolt. Directed by Lou Stein, Palace Theatre, England.

Some of the Enlightenment's great minds were Thomas Hobbes (1588–1679), a friend of Ben Jonson's, who questioned the idea of good and evil in the world; René Descartes (1596–1650), who famously said, "I think, therefore I am"; and John Locke (1632–1704), who attacked the common notion that certain ideas and dogmas are programmed into our brains. He said that the mind is a *tabula rasa* (blank slate) at birth and that all human knowledge comes from the senses. He felt that we are a product of our environment and that nothing can be known independent of experience. But perhaps the father of the Enlightenment was Francis Bacon (1561–1626), who said that if one "begins with certainties, he shall end in doubts, but if he will be content to begin with doubts, he shall end in certainties." Doubt was the key to the Enlightenment: doubt of the church, doubt of Ptolemy's geocentric universe, doubt of Aristotle. This doubt led to the Scientific Revolution, as innovative thinkers such as the mathematician Sir Isaac Newton commenced a quest for empirical knowledge that culminated in a scientific, mathematical, and mechanistic worldview.

The Enlightenment led to a new way of looking at our purpose on this earth. For hundreds of years Christians had taught that people were born to toil, suffer, and lament—that the world was a "vale of tears," but now Enlightenment philosophers said that people could achieve great happiness here on earth. The Founding Fathers of the United States borrowed this idea from John Locke. He not only proposed the separation of governmental bodies through checks and balances and the separation of church and state, but also wrote that "life, liberty and the pursuit of property" were universal human rights. *Property* had a slightly different meaning than it does today; it meant not only real estate and buildings but also one's interests, including one's well-being. Thomas Jefferson changed Locke's line by replacing the word *property* with *happiness.* One of the basic ideas of Enlightenment thought was that people naturally pursued pleasure and fled pain and that to pursue pleasure was our main purpose on this earth—as long as it didn't hurt other people. Happiness on this earth, then, was the supreme good.

Revolutionary Theatre

The revolutions in philosophy, astronomy, science, and religion had a profound effect on the theatre. The revolution in philosophy changed how playwrights viewed character. A rationalistic empiricism slowly took over as actors and playwrights began to look at the characters' environment in order to understand why they make particular decisions. In the past a character was evil simply because he was evil or was controlled by the devil, but now playwrights began to look at a character's motivation, circumstances, and upbringing, using an early form of what today we call psychology. The revolution in astronomy caused people to question religion and led to political plays that disputed the church's power and the divine rights of kings. But the most profound revolution was in the sciences, which caused a dramatic leap in technology and industry. People could control and manipulate nature in ways that had never been possible. This resulted in the Industrial Revolution, greater productivity, greater wealth, and a strong "bourgeoisie," a middle class composed of small businesspeople and manufacturers who wanted a theatre of their own.

As the middle class gained power, theatres began to turn to them for patronage and playwrights began writing plays with middle-class heroes who spoke in prose—everyday language without metrical structure. The new types of middle-class plays came to be known as **domestic tragedies** and **sentimental comedies.** Unlike the tragic plays of ancient Greece or the French Renaissance whose heroes were of noble birth, domestic tragedies told stories about common people who felt grand emotions and suffered devastating consequences. Unlike the Roman comedies that caricatured common people or the Restoration comedies that poked fun at the well-to-do, sentimental comedies

Nature and Nature's laws lay hid in night: God said, Let Newton be! and all was light.

Alexander Pope,
epitaph intended for Sir Isaac Newton

© Robbie Jack

Some sentimental comedies were known as "tearful comedies" because they featured good and virtuous characters who overcame terrible misfortunes to live a happy life, bringing a sentimental tear to the eye. In contrast, English playwright Oliver Goldsmith (ca. 1730–1774) wrote what he called "laughing comedies," meant to make audiences laugh at their own idiosyncrasies. She Stoops to Conquer *(1773), the story of a silly middle-class woman determined to marry her son to her wealthy niece even though they have other plans, is an example of a laughing comedy. Pictured here is a production of Goldsmith's play directed by Max Stafford-Clark at the National Theatre, London, 2002.*

showed middle-class characters finding happiness and true love. These new comedies and tragedies showed that all people experience the same emotions, despite income level or social standing. These plays marked a major change in the theatre, for no less than Aristotle had said that tragedy could be only about "extraordinary" people and comedy only about "lesser" people. Domestic tragedies and sentimental comedies are still with us. The movie *American Beauty* (1999), with Kevin Spacey and Annette Bening, is a perfect example of a domestic tragedy. In this story, a man suffering a midlife crisis feels depressed by his joyless marriage to an unloving, materialistic wife. He becomes infatuated with his teenage daughter's cheerleader friend and decides to change his life so he can find happiness. His behavior does indeed change his life and the lives of everyone around him.

During the Enlightenment, theatre began to fracture. Some playwrights held on to the old neoclassical rules, but others questioned and broke those rules. In *The Critic* (1779), Richard Brinsley Sheridan (1751–1816) attacks neoclassical rules and the unities, and in George Lillo's (1693–1739) *The London Merchant* (1731), it is a common man, not a tragic hero, who succumbs to a depraved woman and murders his uncle. While some Enlightenment playwrights wrote about the common man, others began voicing revolutionary sentiments against the clergy, corruption, and despotism and calling for religious tolerance and democracy. The French Enlightenment philosopher and playwright Voltaire (1694–1778) turned the stage into a philosophical pulpit. His play *Mahomet* (1742) denounced religious fanaticism. And his *Oedipus* (1718) attacked the clergy: "Priests are not what the foolish masses think. All their ideas depend on our gullibility." In *Mérope* (1742), Voltaire criticized hereditary aristocracy: "He who serves his country worthily needs no ancestry." Other famous Enlightenment playwrights were the German Gotthold Lessing and the French Pierre Augustin Caron de Beaumarchais.

FOR MORE ON

NATHAN THE WISE

"Nathan der Weise: Suffering Lessing's *'Erziehung,'"* Astrid Oesmann, *The Germanic Review,* Spring 1999

Gotthold Lessing (1729–1781) was a playwright, critic, and Enlightenment philosopher who wrote domestic tragedies and sentimental comedies. His greatest play is *Nathan the Wise* (1779). Set in Jerusalem during the Fourth Crusade, the story is about a Jewish merchant whose wife and seven sons are massacred by the Christian Crusaders. A few days later a friar brings to Nathan a Christian infant whose mother has died and orders him to raise it as Christian. Instead, Nathan takes the child and teaches her only those religious doctrines on which Jews, Christians, and Muslims agree. Years later, the child, now a young woman, is saved by a knight who discovers that she was born Christian but not raised as one. The knight betrays Nathan to the authorities. Nathan is taken before a sultan who asks him which of the three religions is best. Nathan uses an analogy of three rings, each representing one religion, to show that each faith is true only insofar as it makes its believer virtuous. The play was a grand plea for religious tolerance, yet the Catholic Church condemned it, and Lessing was attacked as an atheist.

The most famous plays of Pierre Beaumarchais (1732–1799) are *The Barber of Seville* (1775) and its sequel, *The Marriage of Figaro* (1784). Both star the character of Figaro, a witty barber, surgeon, and philosopher who is willing to tackle any problem or injustice. Wolfgang Amadeus Mozart promptly wrote an opera based on *The Marriage of Figaro* (1786), and Gioacchino Rossini later wrote one based on *The Barber of Seville* (1816). Beaumarchais's original plays encompassed many of the philosophies of the Enlightenment. Figaro's lines are full of audacious criticism of aristocrats, nobles, and politicians. He attacks the sale of public offices and the poor treatment of women in the male-dominated society. Beaumarchais was also a great supporter of the American Revolution. He not only loaned the colonists money to help pay for the war but also recruited French officers to fight in it. His plays were rarely performed in United States, however, for theatre in the States had the Puritans to contend with. (See the Spotlight box "Puritans, Pilgrims, and the Beginning of Theatre in America.")

Puritans, Pilgrims, and the Beginning of Theatre in America

For all their complaints of religious persecution, the Puritans were, more often than not, the persecutors. They sought to purify the Anglican Church, and they protested the government of England as well as the theatre. They seemed to condemn anyone who was not like them. England, before the Puritan Revolution of 1642–1648, had been one of the most religiously tolerant countries in Europe, but the Puritans would have none of it. In the early 1600s, many left to find a place more to their liking. For thousands of them, that place was the New World, where they were called Pilgrims. The Pilgrims who landed on Plymouth Rock in 1620 were Separatists, conservative Puritans who had given up trying to reform the Church of England. With them they brought the idea that theatre is sinful.

On August 17, 1665, one of the first plays was produced in what would become the United States. Three amateur actors at Cowle's Tavern in Virginia performed a play called *Ye Bear and Ye Cubb.* The Puritans made sure that the three were thrown in jail for daring to perform a play. In the end the trio was acquitted but ordered to pay all trial costs. The Puritan element would make life difficult for theatre people for the next hundred years. The Pennsylvania Assembly prohibited plays in 1700, but the British government later repealed the law. The same thing happened in New York in 1709. In 1750, the Central Court of Massachusetts quickly banned the first attempt to present a play in Boston and threatened to levy a heavy fine on anyone who attended subsequent productions. In fact, not until the British occupied Boston during the Revolutionary War was another play produced there.

In October 1774, on the eve of the American Revolution, the First Continental Congress passed a resolution to discourage "every species of extravagance and dissipation, especially all horse-racing, and all of gaming, cock-fighting, plays and other expensive diversion and entertainment." Four years later, during the Revolutionary War, the Continental Congress passed a resolution to suppress theatrical entertainments because they caused "idleness, dissipation, and general depravity of principles and manners." The resolution also recommended that any officeholder who encouraged such plays be dismissed. These laws against the theatre were later repealed, but the anti-theatre sentiment persisted. When a yellow-fever epidemic hit Philadelphia in 1792, the Quakers tried to blame the outbreak on the presence of a theatre in the community.

W. R. Pyne after John Wright, 1788

Before the American Revolution, theatre had been often denounced or banned in the colonies. In Rhode Island, one art-loving gentleman built a theatre but, to keep his critics in the dark, called it a "schoolhouse." In New York, another theatre was called "the lecture room" so that audience members might attend plays with a clear conscience. In this image from about 1790, "A Performance at a Country Barn," a converted barn serves as a theatre.

Romanticism and the Birth of Melodrama

The Enlightenment had done much to advance human reason, but some poets, novelists, and playwrights began to question the Scientific Revolution's obsession with logic. These writers, known as Romantics, felt that science was not adequate to describe the full range of human experience, and their writings stressed instinct, intuition, and feeling. They wanted to go beyond reason to a transcendent realm of emotion where experience cannot be rationally explained.

The French philosopher Jean-Jacques Rousseau (1712–1778) is sometimes called the father of the Romantic movement because he rebelled against the rationalists of the Age of Reason. Rousseau argued that people could find hap-

© Andrew Linden

English playwright Joanna Baillie (1762–1851) typified the Romantic sensibility in that her tragic heroes inevitably allowed their emotions to overwhelm their reason, leading them either to destruction or to a strengthening of their identity. In her Count Basil *(1798), a military leader is detained from joining his troops because he is infatuated with the beautiful Victoria. Basil's enemy, Victoria's father, takes advantage of Basil's emotions and manipulates the innocent Victoria and her ladies-in-waiting into using their "powers of seduction" to keep Basil preoccupied. In the meantime, Basil's troops win a critical battle and, shamed because he did not accompany his troops to victory, Basil commits suicide. This 2003 production was directed by Leslie Jacobson, Horizons Theatre Company, Arlington, Virginia.*

piness in a "state of nature" and that they should learn from nature rather than from the artificial arts and sciences. Yet, in its stress on emotions such as happiness, the Romantic movement was a continuation of Enlightenment thinking. In his book *Confessions,* Rousseau writes with great relish about the history of his feelings and sentiments. This book stands in stark contrast to St. Augustine's book titled *Confessions,* which was about life's struggles and the search for God.

Inspired by *Émile, ou de l'Education* (1762), Rousseau's multivolume work on education, German educator Friedrich Froebel would create a new method of teaching children in 1837 called *Kleinkinderbeschäftigungsanstalt.* He later shortened the name to *Kindergarten*—a place where children would not be pushed to memorize society's artificial rules, scientific constructs, or religious dogma but would be free to explore and learn about nature through their senses. Romantic writers shared Rousseau's appreciation of nature and could lose themselves in contemplation of the landscape. For the Romantics, being close to nature was unquestionably good, so any character on stage that was "of nature" was inherently better than a character hindered by civilization. Blaise Pascal (1623–1662), the French physicist, mathematician, and philosopher, expressed the essence of Romanticism when he said, "The heart has its reasons that reason does not know."

The neoclassic writers demanded reality, but the Romantics dreamed of the ideal. The English Romantic poet John Keats (1795–1821) wrote, "O for a life of sensations rather than of thought"; William Wordsworth (1770–1850) said that "all good poetry is the spontaneous overflow of powerful feelings"; and William Blake (1757–1827) admonished us to "bathe in the waters of life." Examples of romantic plays are French playwright Edmond Rostand's (1868–1918) *Cyrano de Bergerac* (1897), the story of a sensitive but unattractive man who uses poetry to express his love for a woman, and German playwright Johann Wolfgang Goethe's (1749–1832) *Faust* (1808 and 1832) about a man searching for fulfillment, meaning, ideal loveliness, and truth.

Once Romantic theatre had taken hold, cheap imitations of Romantic plays were stealing the stage, imitations that lacked the soul of the Romantic writers but exploited their excesses. These knockoffs came to be known as melodrama. The word **melodrama** is a blend of *melody* and *drama* and refers to the background music often played during these performances. Just as modern movies have a soundtrack, these plays are accompanied by a small orchestra. Like Romantic plays, melodramas are often about a working-class protagonist who sets out on a great adventure, but melodrama's writers mix in sensational subjects, stock characters, virtuous heroes, dastardly villains, and striking spectacles such as earthquakes, battles, and floods. The plots are formulaic, filled with unbelievable coincidences, disguises, mistaken identities, and oversimplified moral dilemmas. Unlike Romantic plays, melodramas seldom question authority and they usually lack depth. Melodrama never makes audience members question themselves about anything. Its carefully calculated plots are devoid of philosophical skepticism and always leave the audience feeling good because they support the values of marriage, God, and country. Today, melodrama is still with us in television soap operas, made-for-television movies, and popular films such as *Terms of Endearment, Star Wars,* and *Indiana Jones.*

Curtain Call

Theatre seems to go through cycles: A change begins when someone creates a new way of looking at the art. Some artists wish to keep an old style alive, but new artists are always inspired to provide innovations and creative ways of doing theatre. Later, imitation and complacency will creep in, followed by outright stagnation. Then someone upsets the cart once again and the cycle begins anew. The Enlightenment upset the Renaissance world, and Romanticism upset the Enlightenment, but then it stagnated as melodrama. As the nineteenth century drew to a close, the world of theatre was about to be reinvented once again, this time in a radical new form called "realism."

Summary

The word *renaissance* means "rebirth." During the Renaissance, secular theatre once again became popular in the West. Liturgical theatre declined because of the Protestant Reformation, a time when different denominations warred over interpretations of the Bible. As liturgical drama became less popular, the commedia dell'arte brought back the slapstick farces of the Roman mimes, and humanists sought to imitate the classical theatre of ancient Romans and Greeks, using Aristotle's *Poetics* as a touchstone.

Theatre in France and Italy became governed by the dramatic rules laid down by ancient scholars. During this time the Italians invented proscenium arch theatres with perspective scenery, and the French called for greater reality on stage. In Spain and England theatre was being performed in courtyards and then in open-air theatres, such as the Rose and the Globe outside of London. The Puritans' objections to the theatre kept theatre buildings outside London's city limits and gave actors the reputation of rogues and vagabonds. William Shakespeare came to prominence during this era, but he was not the only famous playwright of the age; two famous contemporaries were Christopher Marlowe and Ben Jonson. Elizabethan theatre came to a screeching halt when the Puritans took over the government of England. When the monarchy was restored so was the theatre, but it was theatre in the style of the Italians and French. During the Restoration, women first became accepted as actors and playwrights.

During the Enlightenment, philosophers and playwrights changed human thought: Bacon called for a new inductive science, Newton reduced the natural world to a mathematical equation, and Beaumarchais supported revolutionary politics. They all demanded tolerance and an end to superstition. Before the Enlightenment, the secrets of the cosmos were explainable only by miracles and theology; now the universe was mathematical and logical. Enlightenment plays included domestic tragedies and sentimental comedies, in which common people felt deep emotions and their stories were just as tragic as those of any emperor or king.

The Enlightenment had done much to advance human reason, but some poets, novelists, and playwrights began to question the Scientific Revolution's obsession with logic. These writers, known as Romantics, felt that science was inadequate to describe human experience, and their writings stressed instinct, intuition, and feeling rather than logic. Romanticism devolved into action-filled melodramas whose purpose was not to put forth revolutionary ideas but rather to make middle-class audiences feel good about their lives.

THE ART OF THEATRE ONLINE

Use the *Art of Theatre* website at **http://communication.wadsworth.com/downs1** for quick access to the electronic study resources that accompany this chapter, including a digital glossary, a link to InfoTrac College Edition that you can use to find the For More On... InfoTrac College Edition readings listed below, a list of further reading, and a chapter quiz. When you get to the *Art of Theatre* homepage, click on the cover of the book you are using and you will be redirected to the website for your book. Then click on "Student Book Companion Site" in the Resource box, pick a chapter from the pull-down menu at the top of the page, and select an option from the Chapter Resources menu. The *Art of Theatre* website also includes links to interesting and informative theatre websites. Just click on the Theatre on the Web link in the Book Resources menu. The links to these websites are maintained and updated as needed.

Key Terms

Aristotelian Scholasticism / 275
autos sacramentales / 277
box office / 283
comedy of manners / 294
commedia dell'arte / 274
corrales / 277
declamatory acting / 276
domestic tragedy / 299
downstage / 277
Enlightenment / 297
groundlings / 283
humanists / 276
interludes / 272
masques / 290
melodrama / 303
opera / 276
perspective scenery / 276
Puritans / 281
Restoration / 294
sentimental comedy / 299
three unities / 276
upstage / 277
verbal scene painting / 284

For More On . . .

Infotrac College Edition Readings

http://www.infoTrac-college.com

Commedia dell'arte / 274
"Actor-authors of the commedia dell'arte: The dramatic writings of Flaminio Scala and Giambattista Andreini"

The Rose theatre / 282
"A rose by any other name"

The Globe theatre / 283
"Measuring the Globe"

Shakespeare / 289
"Was Shakespeare gay? Sonnet 20 and the politics of pedagogy"

Aphra Behn / 295
"The female will in Aphra Behn"

Tartuffe / 296
"Molière's *Tartuffe*"

Nathan the Wise / 300
"*Nathan der Weise:* Suffering Lessing's '*Erziehung*'"

12 Modern Theatre

The 1800s was a century of invention and expansion. The telegraph (1844), the phonograph, and the telephone (both in 1876) astounded the masses. In 1885, German inventor Gottlieb Daimler constructed the first high-speed internal combustion engine. In the same year, German engineer Karl Benz built the first primitive automobile. Only sixteen years later, English poet Wilfrid Scawen Blunt described the "exhilarating experience" of riding in an automobile at the amazing speed of fifteen miles per hour. The public delighted in the new creations of chewing gum, ice cream, and Coca-Cola. At the same time, the Industrial Revolution brought immense political and social changes. Europe and the United States were moving from an agrarian economy into an era of industrialism and laissez-faire policies toward big business. Western styles, culture, and theatre were being exported around the world. Sometimes by force, sometimes through diplomacy, Western ideas about religion, economics, politics, and art were influencing the world as never before.

© Sara Krulwich/The New York Times

◀ ***On preceding page:*** Gem of the Ocean, *by August Wilson. Directed by Kenny Leon, Walter Kerr Theatre, New York, 2004, featuring (l to r) John Earl Jelks (inset), Phylicia Rashad, and Lisa Gay Hamilton. This play, the ninth in a ten-play cycle, focuses on a young black man, Citizen Barlow, to tell a story of African American history and mythology, spiritual conflict, and the search for redemption.*

I Western Influence on World Theatre

As Western influence spread around the world, so did Western theatre. European-style theatre was introduced to India during the British occupation, which began in the 1700s. At first the plays were intended only to entertain the occupying troops, but soon Western-style plays were being used to educate Indians about British ideas, tastes, and morals. By the nineteenth century, hundreds of Indian plays imitated Western models, including the use of proscenium arches and realistic acting. In the nineteenth century, Western theatre was also appearing in China. To distinguish the European theatre from the Chinese Peking opera, it was often called "talking" or "spoken" drama because it lacked the dancing, singing, and spectacle of Chinese theatre. However, by the 1950s, the Peking opera's simple platform stage had been replaced with a Western-style proscenium arch, curtains, and orchestra pit. In the 1950s in Japan, the influence of Western theatre gave rise to a modified style of Kabuki play called *Shimpa,* or "New School of Movement"; the Kabuki spectacle was toned down and a bit of Western realism made its way into performances. In the Arab world, European-style theatre was introduced by Napoleon, who visited in 1798. Colonization by Britain, France, and Italy also introduced Western-style theatre to Beirut, Cairo, Damascus, and other Arab capital cities. (For information on traditional forms of Indian, Chinese, and Japanese theatre, see Chapter 10.)

In the nineteenth century, Great Britain, France, Portugal, Belgium, Germany, Spain, and Italy divided Africa into their colonies. The Europeans imposed their languages, customs, religion, and theatre on Africa during the colonial period. During this time, Islam and Christianity also affected all aspects of African society and stifled traditional African theatre. Early European travelers and missionaries dismissed precolonial African theatre because it was so unlike anything in the West. Precolonial African theatre had grown out of centuries-old rituals and incorporated storytelling and poetry, music and dance, acrobatics, improvisation, and the liberal use of masks. Audiences often worked with the actors to write and act out performances, a form of mass participation that was an intense mental and emotional experience for audience members. In traditional African theatre there was rarely an invisible wall between the performers and the audience as in Western theatre.

In 1801, in the Cape of Good Hope region of what would become South Africa, the British opened the first European-style theatre on the African continent. European theatre companies began traveling to Africa to entertain the colonists, and soon there was a host of local imitators. The first report of a European-style play performed by Africans appeared in 1866. But these plays did not assimilate traditional African theatre. "The theatre of Europe came to Africa and established itself in complete ignorance of and indifference to [our] traditions," Ugandan playwright Robert Serumaga said. "It did not even try to superimpose itself onto the traditions, but rather led an isolated existence related only to the needs of a few who fell within its ambit." During the colonial period, traditional African theatre was devalued and even discouraged in favor of theatres with Western-style stages, curtains, and proscenium arches. Today, African theatre is some of the most diverse in the world. Plays performed in plush, acoustically perfect European-style theatres coexist with those done in open-air venues. Western plays are popular, but so are anti-colonial plays that protest Western influences as well as plays rooted in ancient rituals and community celebrations.

Let's Get Real: The Advent of Realism

Around 1840, English physicist William Fox Talbot (1800–1877) invented the photographic negative. This improvement on the daguerreotype (an early type of photograph invented by French scene painter Louis Daguerre) allowed multiple copies of an image to be produced. Now, a boy in London could see an actual image of the battlefield of Bull Run in Virginia, not an artist's depiction. A mother in Michigan who wanted to see the U.S. president's face could study a photograph of him. Soon "real" was all the rage, especially in the theatre. There was a call for sets to be more "genuine," acting to be more "honest," and dialogue to be modeled after everyday speech. But this call for reality quickly became more than a desire to mirror the world; it became a hunger to uncover the basic forces of human nature and to show people as they really are. This was the birth of **Realism.**

Contributing to the rage for theatrical realism was Thomas Edison's invention of the incandescent light bulb in 1879. By 1881, the world's first electric power plant was up and running in New York City, and four years later the New Lyceum on Fourth Avenue was the first theatre in the world to be lit with electric lights. For the first time in the history of the theatre, every kind of lighting effect—from an eerie, stormy night to a warm summer day—could be realistically presented and controlled. Because of electric lights, the audience could sit in total darkness for the first time, like peeping toms spying on the action of a play. The ideas of Charles Darwin, Sigmund Freud, and Karl Marx also influenced Realism.

© Michal Daniel

Playwrights who wrote in the Realistic style sought to portray not only events and settings realistically but also characters who reflected the circumstances they were born into. George Bernard Shaw's comment on English class warfare, Pygmalion, tells the story of Eliza Doolittle, an uneducated flower seller who continually clashes with the smug professor Henry Higgins. Eliza's Cockney accent, disheveled clothing, and defiant attitude reveal her lower-class upbringing, and Henry's haughty arrogance pegs him as an upper-class English gentleman. This 2004 production featured (l to r) Barbara Bryne as Mrs. Pearce, Henry's housekeeper; Bianca Amato as Eliza Doolittle; and Daniel Gerroll as Higgins. Directed by Casey Stangl, Guthrie Theater, Minneapolis.

The 1800s

Decade	Theatrical Events and Plays	Historical / Cultural Events
1800	• Victor Hugo (1802–1885) • Ira Aldridge (1807–1867) • *Faust*, part one, Johann Wolfgang von Goethe (1808)	• Estimated world population reaches one billion (1802) • Explorers Lewis and Clark reach Pacific Ocean (1806)
1810	• Gas lighting first used in theatres (1816)	• Stethoscope invented (1819)
1820	• First black theatre company in the United States (1821) • The Duke of Saxe-Meiningen (1826–1914) • Henrik Ibsen (1828–1906) • Minstrel shows debut in U.S. (1828)	• Mexico, including the provinces of California and Texas, declares independence from Spain (1821) • Symphony No. 9 (Ninth Symphony), Ludwig von Beethoven (1824)
1830	• *Faust*, part two, Johann Wolfgang von Goethe (1832) • First box set (1832)	
1840	• Astor Place riot (1849) • August Strindberg (1849–1912)	• Photography invented (ca. 1840) • *The Communist Manifesto*, Karl Marx (1848) • California Gold Rush (1849)
1850	• Advent of Realism (ca. 1850) • George Bernard Shaw (1856–1950)	• *On the Origin of the Species*, Charles Darwin (1859)
1860	• Anton Chekhov (1860–1904) • The *Black Crook*, Charles M. Barras (1866)	• Abraham Lincoln assassinated at Ford's Theatre (1865)
1870	• Duke of Saxe-Meiningen's theatre tours (1874–1890) • *A Doll's House*, Henrik Ibsen (1879) • *The Pirates of Penzance*, Gilbert and Sullivan (1879)	• Telephone invented (1876) • Thomas Edison invents light bulb (1879)
1880	• Electricity first used in a theatre (1885) • Eugene O'Neill (1888–1953)	• Coca-Cola invented (1882)
1890	• Vaudeville dominates U.S. musical entertainment (ca. 1880–1920) • *The Importance of Being Earnest*, Oscar Wilde (1895) • *A Trip to Coontown*, Bob Cole and Billy Johnson (1898) • The Moscow Art Theatre opens (1898) • Bertolt Brecht (1898–1956)	• First moving pictures (ca 1890) • First skyscraper (1891) • Ellis Island begins accepting immigrants to U.S. (1892) • First professional football game (1895)

THEATRICAL EVENTS AND PLAYS

HISTORICAL / CULTURAL EVENTS

English naturalist Charles Darwin (1809–1882) is, of course, famous for his book *On the Origin of Species by Means of Natural Selection* (1859), which states that all the animals on earth evolved from a common ancestry over millions of years and that the primary mechanisms for evolution are environment and natural selection. Darwin's observations implied that from an evolutionary standpoint, humans *are* animals, not simply divine creations placed on earth to rule *over* animals, and if humans had adapted and evolved over millions of years, the human character must be more mutable than it would be if it had been created, fully formed, by a divine being. This theory had an enormous impact on the theatre. Now, in order to write or portray a realistic character, the playwright or actor had to understand the character's environment and heredity.

After Darwin equated humans with all other animals, the Viennese psychologist Sigmund Freud (1856–1939) revolutionized ideas about how our animal minds worked. Freud wrote numerous books on psychology, suppressed urges, and the unconscious. His detailed analysis of the mind and human motivation became popular in the theatre as actors began researching their characters' psychological motivations in order to present fully developed characters.

German philosopher and social scientist Karl Marx (1818–1883) founded two of the most influential mass movements in modern history: democratic socialism and revolutionary communism. Marx wrote about the negative aspects of capitalism and the Industrial Revolution and expressed moral indignation over the economic plight of the working class. As Marx's ideas spread, realistic stories about human oppression began appearing in the theatre. Soon the Romantic plays popular earlier in the century were being replaced by drama that questioned society's values and discussed the social and domestic problems of the middle class. Along with economic injustice, such subjects as divorce, euthanasia, women's rights, sexual double standards, venereal disease, and religious hypocrisy were now placed center stage.

As plays became more political, playwrights often attached a lengthy preface, appendix, or manifesto to explain the political theme of a play. Some of these realistic plays simply pointed out the social problem without offering a solution. These **problem plays** were based on the idea that before a problem can be solved, society must first understand that the problem exists. This new breed of playwrights felt that if audience members were distressed by what they saw in a play, they should try to remedy that social ill rather than complain about the play—attack the message, they said, not the messenger. Swedish playwright August Strindberg (1849–1912) said that the commercial dramatist had been "peddling the ideas of his time in popular form, popular enough for the middle classes, the mainstay of theatre audiences, to grasp the gist of the matter without troubling their brains too much." Now the playwrights of Realism were purposely troubling the audience's brains. These plays of social indictment seem to have a common theme: "We have met the enemy and he is us."

Box Sets and Fourth Walls

With the advent of Realism, set design also changed. It now seemed necessary to show how people were directly affected by their environment. Theatres began building sets that authentically replicated a character's surroundings. The forestage, or "apron," was used less because electric lights allowed the action to take place behind the proscenium arch, where a realistic setting could be built. Often these realistic settings were box sets. A **box set** is a true-to-life interior containing a room or rooms with the **fourth wall** removed so that the audience has the feeling of looking in on the characters' private lives.

One of the first theaters to have box sets was the Olympic Theatre in London, which was managed by actor and singer Lucy Elizabeth Bartolozzi Vestris (1797–1856), the first female theatre manager in London. Not only did plays at her theatre have historically accurate costumes and authentic properties, but her box sets also had working doors, real windows, and ceilings. To playgoers of the nineteenth century, seeing a scene taking place in an ordinary living room was remarkable. The British actor Charles Kean's (1811–1868) production of Shakespeare's *King John* in 1852 had realistic costumes, set, and props that he had researched to make sure they were historically correct.

Local Flavor and Real People

Along with realistic sets, darkened theatres, and themes that questioned society, dramas also had realistic characters, whose speech and manners were much like those of everyday people. Characters did onstage the sorts of things that people do in everyday life. Not only did these characters have specific psychological motivations, but they also came from a particular place, which affected what they believed and how they acted. Some Realistic playwrights attempted to capture "local color" and regional dialects. For example, John Millington Synge (1871–1909) wrote plays about the rugged lives of Irish peasants, using their dialect. In addition, during this period, Oscar Wilde's comedies forced Victorian society to reexamine its hypocrisies (see the Spotlight on Diversity box "Oscar Wilde"), and George Bernard Shaw (1856–1950) wrote what might be called "high comedies," cerebral, socially relevant plays filled with witty political propaganda and criticism.

Often called the father of Realism, Norwegian playwright Henrik Ibsen wrote many plays about the moral failings of modern society. In Hedda Gabler, *the title character, a bored and destructive young woman, amuses herself by gossiping, engaging in almost-adulterous relationships with her husband's acquaintances, and manipulating the actions and emotions of those around her. Her aristocratic contempt for her husband's bourgeois family and friends leads to tragedy. This 2000 production featured (l to r) Seth Jones, Christina Rouner, Laila Robins as Hedda, and Stephen Yoakam. Directed by David Esbjornson, Guthrie Theater, Minneapolis.*

© Michal Daniel

Even Shaw's most famous play, *Pygmalion* (1912), which was turned into the hit musical *My Fair Lady* (1956), makes a political point. It is the story of gentleman and phonetics expert Henry Higgins, who, on a bet, sets out to transform an uneducated Cockney flower girl into a lady who can pass for a duchess. This comedy attacked Victorian sensibilities by pointing out that class differences are superficial. Shaw argued that the prime function of playwrights was to expose the social and moral evils of their time and to make people think. He said, "Few people think more than two or three times a year; I have made an international reputation for myself by thinking once or twice a week."

Oscar Wilde

Irish playwright Oscar Wilde (1854–1900) is famous for such comic plays as *Lady Windermere's Fan* (1892), *A Woman of No Importance* (1893), and *An Ideal Husband* (1894). Wilde was quite the character, advocating "art for art's sake" and known for aesthetic idiosyncrasies such as wearing his hair long and always having a huge flower in his lapel. His plays were filled with witty repartee that forced Victorian society to reexamine its hypocrisies and the arbitrariness of its moral and social taboos.

In 1895, Wilde wrote his most famous play, *The Importance of Being Earnest.* But just a few months later, Wilde's plays were considered unproduceable, because he had been publicly humiliated and was facing a two-year prison term: His crime was his sexuality. Wilde was in love with Lord Alfred Bruce "Bosie" Douglas, a writer and editor who translated Wilde's *Salomé* from French to English. Douglas's father, Sir John Sholto Douglas, the Marquess of Queensbury, was livid about his son's relationship with Wilde and accused him of being a "Somdomite" [*sic*]. In turn, Wilde charged the marquess with libel, but lost the case. Only a few days later, Wilde was charged with violating Section 11 of the Criminal Law Amendment Act which, when broadly interpreted, made homosexuality a crime. After three trials, Wilde was found guilty and sentenced to two years in prison at hard labor. He was released on May 18, 1897, but he was a broken man. Wilde died three years later at the age of 46. On his deathbed, he still retained his wit: "My wallpaper and I are fighting a duel to the death. One or the other of us has to go." Today, Wilde is one of the most produced playwrights of the Victorian age, and several of his plays have been made into movies. In 1999, *An Ideal Husband,* the story of a successful politician threatened with blackmail, starred Minnie Driver, Cate Blanchett, Rupert Everett, and Julianne Moore; and in 2002, *The Importance of Being Earnest,* a comedy of manners and mistaken identity, featured Rupert Everett, Colin Firth, Reese Witherspoon, and Dame Judi Dench.

© Corbis

Playwright, novelist, poet, and wit Oscar Wilde

The most famous Realistic playwright is Henrik Ibsen (1828–1906), often called the father of Realism. Ibsen wrote his first play in 1850, the year many historians choose as the beginning of Realism, but his first plays were hardly realistic. Initially, he was a Romantic writer and his early plays were verse dramas based on Norwegian history and folk literature. Not until 1879 did Ibsen change his style and write the series of plays that have brought him an international reputation as a Realistic writer.

FOR MORE ON

A DOLL'S HOUSE

"The female jouissance: An analysis of Ibsen's *Et Dukkehjem*," Anne Marie Rekdal, *Scandinavian Studies*, Summer 2002

One of his first Realistic plays was *A Doll's House* (1879), the story of Nora, a pretty housewife who is expected by her banker husband and the patriarchal society to be cheerful, obedient, and mindless. Ibsen's intent is not to condemn Nora but to makes a statement about a society that limits women by sheltering them. In the course of the play, the petted and spoiled Nora begins to examine her life. She realizes that she has always been dominated by men, first by her father and now by her husband. In the end, she leaves her husband and children and strikes out on her own to redefine her identity. When *A Doll's House* was first performed, the audience was outraged because the play did not reinforce their family values. A riot took place outside the theatre. Playhouses in Hamburg and Vienna threatened to withhold royalties unless Ibsen rewrote the ending so that Nora stayed with her husband. Ibsen went on to write many other socially relevant plays, such as *Ghosts* (1881), which examines lies and the devastating effects of venereal disease; *Hedda Gabler* (1890), a psychological study of a sexually repressed and destructive woman; and *Enemy of the People* (1882), about an idealistic doctor who tries to save a resort city from its polluted waters only to discover that the community is more interested in capitalism than in the safety and health of its citizens.

Anton Chekhov (1860–1904) is another famous Realistic playwright. Chekhov was a physician, yet he made his name as a journalist and author of comic sketches. He later joined one of the greatest theatres in the world, the Moscow

Anton Chekhov tried not to judge his characters but to be an objective observer who eavesdrops on life and reports the facts to the audience. Chekhov's plays are full of comic characters, all of whom are paralyzed by the tragedy of inaction. In this University of Wyoming production of The Cherry Orchard, *the characters take a moment to watch the sunset even though their lives are in turmoil.*

University of Wyoming photo archives

Art Theatre, run by the father of modern acting, Konstantin Stanislavsky. (See the Spotlight box "Chekhov, Stanislavsky, and the Birth of Modern Acting.") Chekhov's body of work includes four plays that changed Western theatre: *The Seagull* (1896), *Uncle Vanya* (1899), *The Three Sisters* (1901), and *The Cherry Orchard* (1904). Chekhov wrote about what he considered the stagnant, helpless, and useless people in Russian society, especially the rural landowners. Whereas Ibsen used a "hammer" to make his point, Chekhov was deceptively subtle. Shaw shouted his political opinions from the stage, but Chekhov was a master of understatement, at least in his full-length plays. Most of

Chekhov, Stanislavsky, and the Birth of Modern Acting

SPOTLIGHT

The birth of modern, realistic acting can be traced to the opening night of Anton Chekhov's *The Seagull* on December 17, 1898. The play had been a total disaster when it was first staged two years earlier in St. Petersburg. But Konstantin Stanislavsky (1863–1938) and Vladimir Nemirovich-Danchenko (1859–1943), the co-founders of the Moscow Art Theatre, decided to stage the play with a realistic set, natural staging, and acting characterized by psychological realism. These elements had been tried before, with varying degrees of success, but Stanislavsky and Danchenko wanted to bring them together into a completely realistic production. Stanislavsky had the actors draw on their own experiences and emotions to shape how their character spoke and moved, thereby creating a complex human being with well-motivated feelings and desires.

Chekhov was so nervous about the opening night that he did not attend. At the end of the first act, the audience sat silently. Backstage, most of the actors were convinced that the new realistic acting and the play were a failure. Actress Olga Knipper, who later became Chekhov's wife, fought back tears. Then "like the bursting of a dam, like an exploding bomb," as one audience member later wrote, "a sudden deafening eruption of applause broke out." Stanislavsky was said to be so happy that he danced a jig. The Moscow Art Theatre became one of the most influential theatres in the world, and Stanislavsky became the father of a new, realistic approach to acting and a new kind of actor training. (For more on Stanislavsky's ideas on acting, see Chapter 7; for more on Stanislavsky and directing, see Chapter 8.)

Before the advent of photocopiers and the Internet, playwrights often read their plays out loud to the cast during the first rehearsal. Here, in 1898, Anton Chekhov (center) reads The Seagull *to the actors of the Moscow Art Theatre.*

© Tass/Sovfoto

Chekhov's characters are decent and sensitive people who dream of improving their lives but, like most of us, haven't the vaguest idea of how to do it. Chekhov placed life as it is on stage, not life as it should be. He felt that playwrights do a disservice by showing protagonists who win against impossible odds. Such things, Chekhov argued, rarely happen in real life. In Chekhov's plays, the protagonists pass the time by, in effect, talking about nothing. In this respect, the TV sitcom *Seinfeld* is very Chekhovian.

[I]n real life people don't spend every minute shooting each other, hanging themselves, and making confessions of love. They don't spend all their time saying clever things. They're more occupied with flirting, eating, drinking, and talking stupidities. . . . Let everything on the stage be just as complicated, and at the same time just as simple as it is in life. People eat their dinner, just eat their dinner, and all the time their happiness is being established or their lives are being broken up.

Anton Chekhov,
Russian playwright

Chekhov's last play, *The Cherry Orchard,* is often considered his best. This play has no clear protagonist. Instead, it deals with a family of characters who tell many stories at once—just as in real life. At the center of this comic drama are Lyubov Ranevskaya and her daughter Anya; they were once wealthy but now have no money left. As the play begins, they return from France to their heavily mortgaged estate near Moscow. They are told that their estate and its cherry orchard are to be sold to pay back-taxes. Lopakhin, a self-made millionaire, suggests that they cut down the cherry orchard and rent the land for summer cottages. This would provide the funds they so desperately need, but Ranevskaya does nothing. In the end the estate is sold at auction. The new owner of the estate turns out to be Lopakhin, who sets out to cut down the cherry orchard, and the family is forced to leave. In one last gesture of absurdity, they accidentally lock their ancient butler in the abandoned mansion, where he dies, forgotten. The audience's reaction to such frustrating inaction is often laughter, just as Chekhov wanted. But also, after having seen characters take no action on stage, audience members may be encouraged to do the opposite in real life.

Naturalism: A Slice of Life

For some, however, realism was not real enough. A few directors, actors, and playwrights began calling for an even more extreme form of realism, an accurate "documentary" of everyday life, including its seamy side. French novelist Émile Zola (1840–1902) named this new "photographic" realism **Naturalism,** and his phrase "slice of life" is an often-quoted description of it. Naturalistic plays exposed the squalid living conditions of the urban poor and explored such scandalous topics as poverty, venereal disease, and prostitution. This earned Naturalism the designation "sordid realism." Naturalism placed the underbelly of life on stage in order to expose social ills and repressive social codes without preaching about them. The hope was that showing an appalling situation on stage would shock the audience into calling for social reform. Two proponents of Naturalism were the Russian playwright Maxim Gorky (1868–1936), whose play *The Lower Depths* (1902) took a stark look at people living in the cellar of a Moscow flophouse, and the French director André Antoine, who staged the play *The Butchers* (1888) with real sides of beef infested with maggots.

The period of Realism and Naturalism was also a time of important social change. Women's rights became an important issue in Europe and the United States. In England, the 1882 Married Women's Property Act abolished a husband's grip on his wife's inheritance, Oxford and Cambridge Universities both started colleges for women, divorce laws were changed to allow women more freedom, and there were attempts to make public schooling for boys and girls equitable. Even so, as the turn of the century approached, women still did not have the right to vote in the United States and most of Europe. The old morals

© Sovfoto

Naturalism often represented the seedy side of life in order to show the audience life as it is rather than as we would like it to be. Perhaps the best example of Naturalism is Maxim Gorky's The Lower Depths, *a study of wretched derelicts in a horrible tenement run by greedy landlords. Konstantin Stanislavsky directed this original 1902 production at the Moscow Art Theatre. It later toured Western Europe and the United States.*

and sexual prejudices, however, were crumbling. Many argued that one reason was the criticism from Realism and Naturalism. Although the great drama critic William Archer could proclaim that Realism was the ultimate dramatic style, Realism and Naturalism were facing challenges.

The Rise of the Avant-Garde

In the early 1900s, movies began to take a toll on the theatre. By 1910, there were over 10,000 nickelodeons in the United States. By 1911, 1,400 legitimate stages in the United States had been converted to movie houses. By 1915, the number of touring theatre companies had dropped from 300 to 100, and soon the number fell to less than ten. One of the reasons movies grew so popular so quickly was that their admission price was very low. Attending a movie in 1910 cost only about 5 cents, whereas a ticket to a play cost five to ten times more. Theatre practitioners took notice of the trend and began considering how the theatre could save itself. Many playwrights and directors believed that the biggest problem was Realism and Naturalism, because stories in these styles could be depicted much more easily with film. For example, depicting a sunset on stage takes a battery of lights, detailed sets, plus a crew of stage-hands, and even then it doesn't look completely real. For a movie to show a real sunset, all that's needed is a camera at the right location at sundown.

The only theatre worth saving, the only theatre worth having, is a theatre motion pictures cannot touch. When we succeed in eliminating from it every trace of the photographic attitude of mind, when we succeed in making a production that is the exact antithesis of a motion picture, a production that is every thing a motion picture is not and nothing a motion picture is, the old lost magic will return once more.

Robert Edmond Jones,
American theatre set designer

Soon there were calls for theatre to "re-theatricalize" by doing what the camera could not do. As many theatre artists began to reject Naturalism and Realism, a variety of new styles began to emerge. Unlike previous historical trends wherein one style dominates for a while and then is replaced by another style, now, several styles flourished simultaneously. These new perspectives on the human experience led to avant-garde theatrical styles, each with its own systems and theories. The word **avant-garde** can describe any work of art that is experimental, innovative, or unconventional. Symbolism, expressionism, futurism, Dadaism, surrealism, and absurdism are some of the avant-garde styles, the "isms," that playwrights, directors, and designers created in order to rebel against Realism and Naturalism and draw audiences back to the live stage.

Symbolic Acts, Hairy Apes, and the Theatre of Cruelty

In the theatre, an "ism" is a label often used to describe a set of ideas about the style, purpose, and scale of a production. Some critics and artists feel such labels help the audience understand a particular performance. Others feel that such labels only limit art by creating arbitrary rules that artists must follow—such as the Aristotelian unities during the Renaissance (see Chapter 11). Having said this, let's look at a few of the "isms" that became popular early in the twentieth century, some of which are still popular.

One of the first "isms" of the rebellion against Realism and Naturalism was **symbolism.** Symbolists argued that the Realists' objective observation of the world using the five senses was not the best way to show inner truth. They believed that such truths could be hinted at only through symbols. Whereas conventional theatre mirrored images of common life, the symbolists searched for truth beyond the physical world. Symbolist drama sought to replace the specific and concrete with the suggestive and metaphorical. Symbolist plays had rapturous moments of silence representing communion between two souls, doors and windows that mysteriously opened and closed, and lamps that dimmed on their own—all of which gave the plays mystery or spirituality or whatever truth lurks below the surface of things. Symbolist theatre did not last long because the plays had little plot or action and tended to baffle the audience. But traces of symbolism have been assimilated into almost every type of theatre in the form of symbolic acts, gestures, designs, and dialogue that hint at deeper truths.

Another short-lived "ism" was **futurism,** which flourished for less than a decade in the early twentieth century. Futurism glorified the power, speed, and

© Sovfoto

One of the most significant directors of the twentieth century was Vsevolod Emilevich Meyerhold (1874–1940). Originally a member of the Moscow Art Theatre, Meyerhold lost interest in Realism and struck out on his own as a director. Declaring that theatre should present something different from everyday reality, he began exploring avant-garde, alternative, and abstract methods of staging. In this production of Russian playwright Vladimir Mayakovsky's political satire The Bedbug *(1929), Meyerhold used symbolist staging to tell the story of a man who comes back to life after being frozen for fifty years, only to discover that the world has become a sterile place filled with dehumanized beings.*

excitement of the Industrial Age. Its opposite was **expressionism,** which held that the Industrial Age distorted the human spirit, destroyed society with false values, and turned people into little more than automatons. Expressionism started in Germany around 1910 as a reaction to a new kind of painting called Impressionism. Monet, Renoir, Cezanne, and other Impressionist painters were interested in how reality appears to the eye at a particular moment. In other words, Impressionism gives a subjective account of an objective perception. With expressionism the artist imposed a concept of the world onto the outside world itself; therefore, expressionism is a subjective account of a subjective perception. For example, if a person who is drunk says that he sees pink elephants on the walls, he isn't describing objective reality, for there are no pink elephants on the walls. Rather, he is revealing his own internal state. Unlike a realistic play, an expressionist play would show the audience those pink elephants, so they could see what the character feels. Expressionist plays often used deliberate distortion—walls slanted inward to make the room feel claustrophobic, wallpaper striped like prison bars, or trees having the form of huge strangling hands.

On June 28, 1914, a Serbian terrorist's assassination of the heir to the Austro-Hungarian throne, Archduke Franz Ferdinand, sparked World War I. At the beginning of the war, generals talked of gallant cavalry charges and grandly announced that it would all be over within "three months." No one predicted that it would last over four years and be one of the bloodiest wars in history.

The 1900s and Beyond

1900

Theatrical events and plays

- Expressionism thrives (ca. 1900–1920)
- *The Cherry Orchard*, Anton Chekhov (1904)
- Lillian Hellman (1905–1984)
- Samuel Beckett (1906–1989)

Historical / cultural events

- Ragtime is popular (1900–1918)
- *Interpretation of Dreams*, Sigmund Freud (1900)
- Wright brothers' first flight (1903)
- Albert Einstein formulates special theory of relativity (1905)
- Earthquake and fire destroy much of San Francisco (1906)

1910

Theatrical events and plays

- First western-style theatre opens in Japan (1911)
- Tennessee Williams (1911–1983)
- Women allowed on stage in China (1911)
- Actors' Equity founded (1912)
- *Pygmalion*, George Bernard Shaw (1912)
- Arthur Miller (1915–2005)

Historical / cultural events

- The *Titanic* sinks (1912)
- World War I (1914–1918)

1920

Theatrical events and plays

- *The Hairy Ape*, Eugene O'Neill (1922)
- Moscow Art Theatre troupe tours U.S. (1923–1924)
- *Show Boat*, Hammerstein and Kern (1927)
- Edward Albee (b. 1928)
- *Threepenny Opera*, Bertolt Brecht (1928)

Historical / cultural events

- First scheduled radio broadcast (1920)
- U.S. women gain right to vote (1920)
- *The Jazz Singer*, first talking movie (1927)
- Charles Lindbergh makes solo flight across Atlantic (1927)
- Stock market crashes, sparking Great Depression (1929)

1990

Theatrical events and plays

- *Angels in America*, Tony Kushner (1993)
- *Rent*, Jonathan Larson (1996)
- *The Vagina Monologues*, Eve Ensler (1996)
- *The Blue Room*, David Hare (1998)

Historical / cultural events

- Gulf War (1991)
- World Wide Web introduced (1993)
- *Pulp Fiction*, Quentin Tarantino (1994)

2000

Theatrical events and plays

- *Topdog/Underdog*, Suzan-Lori Parks (2001)
- *Hairspray*, Mark O'Donnell, Thomas Meehan, Marc Shaiman, and Scott Wittman (2002)
- *Anna in the Tropics*, Nilo Cruz (2003)
- *Avenue Q*, Jeff Whitty, Robert Lopez, and Jeff Marx (2003)
- *Caroline, or Change*, Tony Kushner and Jeanine Tesori (2004)
- *The 25th Annual Putnam County Spelling Bee*, Rachel Shenkin and William Finn (2005)
- *Spamalot*, Eric Idle and John Du Prez (2005)

Historical / cultural events

- Millennium celebrations; none of the predicted Y2K computer failures (2000)
- September 11 attacks on New York City and Washington, DC (2001)
- Iraq War begins (2003)
- Final movie in *Matrix* trilogy (2003)
- Final episode of *Friends* draws about 52 million viewers in North America (2004)
- Live 8 concerts around the world draw attention to extreme poverty (2005)

THEATRICAL EVENTS AND PLAYS

HISTORICAL / CULTURAL EVENTS

1930

- Lorraine Hansberry (1930–1965)
- Harold Pinter (b. 1930)
- Augusto Boal (b. 1931)
- Jerzy Grotowski (1933–1999)
- Wole Soyinka (b. 1934)
- Caryl Churchill (b. 1938)

- Orson Welles's radio broadcast *The War of the Worlds* causes mass panic (1938)
- World War II (1939–1945)

1940

- Luis Valdez (b. 1940)
- *Oklahoma!* Rodgers and Hammerstein (1941)
- *Mother Courage and Her Children*, Bertolt Brecht (1941)
- Sam Shepard (b. 1943)
- *No Exit*, Jean-Paul Sartre (1944)
- Absurdism flourishes (ca. 1945–1965)
- August Wilson (1945–2005)
- *A Streetcar Named Desire*, Tennessee Williams (1947)
- David Mamet (b. 1947)
- *Death of a Salesman*, Arthur Miller (1949)
- *The Bald Soprano*, Eugène Ionesco (1949)

- First TV station put on the air in Chicago by Paramount (1940)
- Atomic bombs dropped on Hiroshima and Nagasaki (1945)
- Harry Truman integrates U.S. armed forces, sparking the civil rights movement of the 1950s (1948)

1950

- Off-Broadway theatre begins (1950)
- *Waiting for Godot*, Samuel Beckett (1953)
- Tony Kushner (b. 1956)
- David Henry Hwang (b. 1957)
- *Endgame*, Samuel Beckett (1957)
- *West Side Story*, Arthur Laurents, Leonard Bernstein, and Stephen Sondheim (1957)
- *A Raisin in the Sun*, Lorraine Hansberry (1959)

- Senator Joseph McCarthy begins his anti-Communist crusade (1950)
- First color television sets sell for about $1,175 (1953)
- First space satellite launched, Soviet Union's Sputnik (1957)
- Ghana is first country in colonial Africa to declare independence (1957)

1960

- *Fiddler on the Roof*, Jerry Bock, Sheldon Harnick, and Joseph Stein (1964)
- Suzan-Lori Parks (b. 1964)
- El Teatro Campesino (The Farmworkers Theatre) founded (1965)
- Off-Off-Broadway theatre begins (ca 1966)
- *Dance of the Forest*, Wole Soyinka (1966)
- *Hair*, Gerome Ragni, James Rado, and Galt MacDermot (1968)

- Berlin Wall constructed (1960)
- First Beatles record released (1962)
- Martin Luther King's "I Have a Dream" speech at the Lincoln Memorial (1963)
- Tonkin Gulf Resolution begins major U.S. involvement in Vietnam War (1964)
- China begins Cultural Revolution (1966)
- Woodstock Art and Music Festival in upstate New York (1969)

1970

- *Jesus Christ Superstar*, Tim Rice and Andrew Lloyd Webber (1971)
- *A Chorus Line*, Marvin Hamlisch and Edward Kleban (1975)
- *Zoot Suit*, Luis Valdez (1978)

- Richard Nixon resigns to avoid impeachment for role in Watergate scandal (1974)
- First albums by Blondie and the Ramones bring punk rock to U.S. mainstream (1976)

1980

- *Buried Child*, Sam Shepard (1979)
- *Cats*, Andrew Lloyd Webber (1982)
- *'night Mother*, Marsha Norman (1983)
- *Glengarry Glen Ross*, David Mamet (1984)
- *You Have Come Back*, Fatima Gallaire-Bourega (1986)
- *Fences*, August Wilson (1987)
- *M. Butterfly*, David Henry Hwang (1988)

- Mount St. Helens erupts in Washington State (1980)
- Former Hollywood actor Ronald Reagan elected U.S. President (1980)
- Macintosh debuts Apple personal computer (1984)
- *The Simpsons* debuts (1989)
- Berlin Wall is destroyed (1989)

No one had ever seen a war with poison mustard gas, air raids, submarines, trench warfare, starvation, mutiny, and huge guns that could shell a city seventy-five miles away. When the war finally ended on November 11, 1918, all of Europe was shell-shocked, and the dying continued as outbreaks of typhus and the flu killed millions more.

Expressionist plays were often political but after World War I and the Russian Revolution, they were more likely than ever to support socialist and pacifist causes. An example is Elmer Rice's (1892–1967) *The Adding Machine* (1923), about a man named Mr. Zero who is fired from his job and replaced by an adding machine. But the most famous expressionist play is Eugene O'Neill's (1888–1953) *The Hairy Ape* (1922), the story of Yank, a stoker in the engine room of an ocean liner. At the beginning of the play, Yank thinks that his life is important and useful because he is one of the men who make the great ship move. But when the shipowner's daughter visits the engine room, she is shocked by what she sees. To her, the room seems like a steel cage, and the stokers look like Neanderthals. Overwhelmed by the sight, she faints. Because of her reaction, Yank begins to question his point of view. When he visits New York City, his perception is that it is a slave to grotesque commercialism and inhabited by identical puppets with simpering, toneless voices. When these "puppets" ignore him, Yank lashes out and lands in jail. He decides to seek revenge by destroying the complex social machine that is controlling his life, but he can find no support. He goes to a zoo, where he finds a gorilla that seems to

In 1922 New York's Provincetown Players staged the original production of Eugene O'Neill's expressionist play The Hairy Ape, *featuring Louis Wolheim as Yank (standing). The Provincetown Players was formed by avant-garde theatre artists who rebelled against the big Broadway productions of light musicals and other flimsy entertainment. The Players' no-star policy reflected their support of socialist causes, and their willingness to experiment supported many different forms of drama outside theatre's mainstream.*

Vandamm Theatre Collection, The New York Public Library, Astor, Lenox, and Tilden Foundations

understand him. When Yank frees the beast, it crushes him and throws him into the cage. In the end, Yank dies bewildered and humiliated, realizing that he had no power over the massive machine that dominated his life.

The patriotism of World War I turned into cynicism and apathy as the Roaring Twenties gave way to the Great Depression. Many began to believe that the German philosopher Friedrich Nietzsche (1844–1900) had been right when he proclaimed, "God is dead." Perhaps life was not governed by rational principles but was unjust and meaningless.

Like expressionism, **Dadaism** and **surrealism** were founded in opposition to Realism. For Dadaists, life has no purpose, and they confused and antagonized their audiences by refusing to adhere to a coherent set of principles, thereby mirroring the madness of the world. The performances of the late stand-up comedian Andy Kaufman are as close to Dada as one can find in contemporary popular culture. Like Dadaism, surrealism attacked the evils and restrictions of society. But, unlike the Dadaists, the surrealists tried to reveal the higher reality of the unconscious mind with fantastic imagery and contradictory images. They felt that if the subconscious could avoid the conscious mind's control, it would rise to the surface, where it could be used to find truth. Surrealist performances were often violent and cruel as they tried to shock the audience into the realization that "normal" realities are arbitrary.

One of the most famous surrealists was Antonin Artaud (1896–1948), who studied Asian religions, mysticism, and ancient cultures and lived with the Tarahumara Indians, an indigenous people of northwest Mexico. Artaud wrote several manifestos and the book *The Theatre and Its Double* (1938), in which he declared that theatre, above all, should wake the nerves and heart. Artaud called for a **Theatre of Cruelty,** which would agitate the masses, attack the spectators' sensibilities, and purge people of their destructive tendencies. Artaud and the surrealists disliked Stanislavsky's methods of teaching acting. They wanted stylized, ritualized performances, not realism, which they felt restricted the theatre to the study of psychological problems and society's dilemmas. Artaud argued that proscenium arch theatres create a barrier between the audience and actors and that performances should instead be staged in found spaces, such as warehouses and airplane hangers.

Life Is Absurdism

The devastation and genocide of World War II led many playwrights to believe that humans face a cold, hostile universe and that our existence is futile. Relationships seemed ineffective, language was imprecise, and the traditional structure of plays failed to reflect the ridiculousness, anxiety, and chaos of the world. Thus **absurdism** was born. There are three broad categories of absurdism which might be labeled *fatalist, existentialist,* and *hilarious.* The fatalists believe we are trapped in an irrational universe where even basic communication is impossible. The existentialists hold that God being dead is a good thing, because then it's up to us to do everything for ourselves—no excuses. Hilarious absurdism highlights the insanity of life in a comical way.

Samuel Beckett (1906–1989) is a fatalist absurdist playwright. His plays include *Endgame* (1957), *Krapp's Last Tape* (1958), and *Happy Days* (1961). His most famous work is *Waiting for Godot* (1953): Vladimir and Estragon, two clown-like tramps, meet each day on a barren plain, a dreamlike vacuum

Samuel Beckett's Happy Days *is an absurdist play about a husband and wife. The wife, played here by Felicity Kendal, spends the duration of the play half-buried in a pile of dirt. As time goes slowly by, she finds occasional happiness in chatting with her husband and engaging in petty rituals such as brushing her hair. In true absurdist fashion, her predicament is never explained. Absurdist playwrights would agree with Scottish psychiatrist Ronald D. Laing (1927–1989), who said, "Madness is a sane response to an insane world." This 2003 production was directed by Peter Hall, Arts Theatre, London.*

© Robbie Jack/Corbis

that some critics say is the aftermath of a nuclear holocaust, and wait for Godot. They try to break the monotony of waiting by bickering, doing comic routines, and contemplating suicide, but Godot never shows up. The play is about our inability to take control of our existence and the absurdity of wasting our lives hoping to know the unknowable.

FOR MORE ON

SARTRE

"Jean-Paul Sartre: Philosopher for the twentieth century," Jeannette Lowen, *Free Inquiry,* Winter 1999

A notable existentialist is French philosopher and playwright Jean-Paul Sartre. His plays included *The Flies* (1943) and *No Exit* (1944). *No Exit* was first performed in France in May 1944, just before the liberation of Paris and a year before the end of World War II. It is the story of a man and two women who find themselves in Hell, which just happens to be a living room decorated with Victorian furniture. For Sartre, existence is the will to create our future, and the opposite of existence is not having the power to create our future or giving that power away—whether through law, religion, or government. Existentialism teaches that humans have free will, but that there are no alibis, no gods to thank, no devils to blame, no original sin to account for our situation and that existence precedes essence. For example consider a pair of scissors. Scissors were created to cut paper. Sartre would say that to cut paper is the essence of a pair of scissors. He argued that human beings, however, are unlike scissors and do not have a preconceived essence, or purpose. Instead, humans must use their minds and their existence to create their essence. This idea contradicts what many religions teach, that essence precedes existence, or that we are all created with a preconceived purpose, like a pair of scissors. Sartre said, "Man is nothing else but what he proposes, he exists only in so far as he realizes himself, he is therefore nothing else but the sum of his actions, nothing else but what his life is." In *No Exit,* the character of Garcin is more succinct: "You are nothing else but your life."

Realism, whether it be socialist or not, falls short of reality. It shrinks it, attenuates it, falsifies it; it does not take into account our basic truths and our fundamental obsessions: love, death, astonishment. It presents man in a reduced and estranged perspective. Truth is in our dreams, in the imagination.

Eugène Ionesco,
Romanian-born French playwright

One of the best-known hilarious absurdist playwrights is Romanian-born French playwright Eugène Ionesco (1912–1994). In *Rhinoceros* (1959) the lead character slowly transforms into a rhinoceros. *The Bald Soprano* (1949) is a parody of the middle class. Mr. and Mrs. Smith and Mr. and Mrs. Martin, polite but empty people, spend a social evening together and engage in silly small talk, full of clichés. His comedies convey the meaninglessness of modern existence in a universe ruled by chance and irrational values.

Bertolt Brecht: Appealing to the Intellect, Not the Emotions

Bertolt Brecht (1898–1956) was a German poet, director, and playwright who also challenged traditional ideas about theatre. His great innovation was **epic theatre.** An *epic* is usually a story, play, or poem that has a large cast, covers a long period, and includes a large number of sometimes unrelated incidents. Although epic theatre has been around for centuries, the term is now most often associated with Brecht's theories. The cycle plays of the Middle Ages could be considered epics (see Chapter 10). And today Tony Kushner's sweeping two-part *Angels in America* (1993; I: *Millennium Approaches* and II: *Perestroika*) could also be called an epic (see Chapter 3).

Brecht saw the grand scope of epic theatre as a perfect way to confront the social and political evils of his day, and he took epic theatre to a new level by eliminating vicarious experience and catharsis that had been standard in the theatre for thousands of years. He rebelled against the theatrical illusion of Aristotelian drama—specifically, against the use of suspense, reversals, rising action, climax, and other plot devices to lull the audience into a trancelike state and emotional catharsis. If you've ever become so involved in the story of a play or a movie that you forget time is passing, then you know what Brecht was up against. He wanted his audiences to be aware that the play is only an illusion and to be conscious enough to consider and judge the political, social, and economic implications of the story. He wanted a theatre that aimed for the intellect, not the emotions.

Brecht wanted the audience to be both conscious and critical during a performance. He called his means the **alienation effect,** and he alienated the spectators through various techniques: by having the actors address the audience while out of character, by exposing the lights, by removing the proscenium arch and curtains, and by having the actors perform on bare platforms and simple sets sometimes adorned with political slogans. In this way, Brecht argued, the public could gather evidence, objectively perceive the moral issues of the play, and reach an intelligent understanding of them.

A few of Brecht's better-known plays are *The Threepenny Opera* (1928), *Galileo* (1945), *The Good Person of Setzuan* (1947), and *The Caucasian Chalk Circle* (1948). Perhaps his most famous is *Mother Courage and Her Children* (1941), set during the Thirty Years' War (1618–1648), a series of religious and political wars between the Protestants and Catholics that eventually involved

© Ken Howard/Courtesy South Coast Repertory, Costa Mesa, CA.

Bertolt Brecht's The Caucasian Chalk Circle, *two stories within a play, explores the themes of justice and the life-altering effects of war. In one of the stories, Grusha, a maid, has raised Michael, the child of her mistress, Natella, who fled during a war and left Michael behind. After the war ends, Natella wants the child back so that she can claim her dead husband's estate, but Grusha doesn't want to give him up. To settle the dispute, Judge Azdak draws a chalk circle on the ground. Solomon-like, he puts Michael in the middle of the circle and tells the women that whoever can pull him out can keep him. In this scene, the narrator Singer tells of the soldiers who pursued Grusha and Michael as they fled the war. This 2005 production featured Daniel Breaker as Singer. Directed by Kate Whoriskey, South Coast Repertory, Costa Mesa, California.*

FOR MORE ON
BRECHT
"The figure of the 'spectator' in the theoretical writings of Brecht, Diderot, and Rousseau," Andy Byford, *Symposium*, Spring 2002

most of Europe. The action of the play is epic: Mother Courage travels with her canteen wagon through Sweden, Poland, and Germany, profiting from the war by selling goods to the soldiers. *Mother Courage* makes a powerful statement about capitalism and war. Brecht's themes were often anti-capitalist, expressing the views that capitalism makes people work against one another and that it encourages selfishness and greed as well as injustice. After World War II, Brecht, who was in exile in the United States, was called before the House Un-American Activities Committee (HUAC) and forced to leave the country because of his Marxist ideas. (See the Spotlight box "McCarthyism, Lillian Hellman, and the Theatre.")

American Post-War Theatre

At the end of each world war, the United States, although paranoid about Communism and suffering from the deaths of tens of thousands of its sons and daughters, had seemed filled with optimism. Unlike most European plays, most American plays were still realistic. However, mixing various "isms" in

McCarthyism, Lillian Hellman, and the Theatre

The history of the United States is filled with attempts to censor plays for their content. After World War II, the United States endured one of its worst periods of censorship. McCarthyism, named for Joseph R. McCarthy, a Republican senator from Wisconsin, had actually begun in 1938 with a House committee's investigations of suspected "subversives" in Franklin Roosevelt's administration. After WW II ended, the Cold War began, and the House Un-American Activities Committee (HUAC) stepped up its work. In 1947, it gained notoriety by investigating alleged Communist influence in Hollywood. The Hollywood Ten, a group of producers, directors, and screenwriters who refused to testify about their friends' political beliefs, was found guilty of contempt of Congress and sentenced to prison. The studios blacklisted, or refused to hire, anyone said to have an affiliation with or compassion for socialism or communism. In 1950, McCarthy formed a Senate subcommittee to conduct his own investigations of other sectors of U.S. society. Conformity was coerced and political messages were restricted through intimidation. In 1954, when McCarthy claimed without any solid evidence that the U.S. Army was riddled with Communists, the Senate decided to eject him. However, the effects of McCarthyism and blacklisting lasted. For years, plays and films in the United States had to champion capitalism and Christian ethics to be produced—meanwhile in the Soviet Union, plays had to be in the style of Social Realism.

One of America's best-known playwrights in the middle of the twentieth century was Lillian Hellman (1905–1984). She is perhaps most famous for *The Children's Hour* (1934), a play about a spoiled, disturbed girl who ruins the lives of two female teachers by spreading rumors of an intimate relationship between them. On the play's opening night, there had been threats of injunctions and police actions to stop the production because it dared to suggest lesbianism. Before the Hays Office, the censor for Hollywood's studios, would let the script be used for a movie, they ordered it changed. The result was *These Three* (1936), a bowdlerized version of the play that had no hint of lesbianism. In the play, a young doctor loves one of the women, but the other woman loves her too. In the screen version, both women love the doctor. By 1961, a film version with Audrey Hepburn and Shirley MacLaine would be brave enough to vaguely allude to the central dramatic question, but it was still a pale imitation of Hellman's script.

When the play was re-staged in 1952, Hellman was called before HUAC. Her longtime companion, novelist Dashiell Hammett, had already been sent to prison for not cooperating with the committee. Hellman was willing

one play soon became popular. For example, Arthur Miller's (1915–2005) *Death of a Salesman* (1949) mixes Realism and expressionism. Most of this play—about the attempts of Willy Loman, an unsuccessful traveling salesman, to achieve the American dream—is in a realistic style. But expressionism is used in several sequences that show Willy's memories—visions of the past that are colored by his psychological biases. The realistic sections of the play show Willy's blind desire to attain the elusive, perhaps nonexistent, American dream, whereas the expressionistic sections illustrate Willy's limited view of what life should be.

Another form of realism is found in the works of Tennessee Williams (1911–1983), known for *The Glass Menagerie* (1945) and many other plays. This play tells the story of Tom; his disabled sister, Laura; and their controlling mother, Amanda, who tries to make a match between Laura and a gentleman caller. The style of *The Glass Menagerie* has been called **poetic realism** because the realism of the play is expressed through lyrical language.

Yet plenty of traditional realistic plays in post–World War II America also attacked the system and attempted to put real life on stage. Because realistic

Photofest

In this original production of Lillian Hellman's The Children's Hour, *student Mary Tilford is questioned about her allegation that two of her teachers are lovers. Because of its subject matter,* The Children's Hour *was banned initially in Boston, Chicago, and London. Even the Pulitzer Prize–selection committee refused to attend the play. This 1934 production featured (l to r) Robert Keith as Dr. Cardin, Anne Revere as teacher Martha Dobie, Florence McGee as Mary, Katherine Emery as teacher Karen Wright, and Katherine Emmett as Mary's aunt. Directed by Herman Shumlin, Maxine Elliott's Theatre, New York.*

to answer questions about herself but refused to answer any questions about her friends and acquaintances; she was, of course, blacklisted. She told the committee, "To hurt innocent people whom I knew many years ago in order to save myself is, to me, inhuman and indecent and dishonorable. I cannot and will not cut my conscience to fit this year's fashions." Hellman was blacklisted by the studios but not held in contempt of Congress.

While these witch hunts were silencing many voices in the United States, a few wrote plays that attacked the censorship and intimidation. Arthur Miller's *The Crucible* (1953) was a thinly veiled allegory about the Salem witch trials, and *Inherit the Wind* (1955) by Jerome Lawrence and Robert E. Lee defended freedom of thought in its portrayal of the Scopes trial about teaching evolution in the schools.

plays usually convey a social message, many activist writers used this style during the civil rights movement. One of the most famous plays of this period was Lorraine Hansberry's (1930–1965) *A Raisin in the Sun* (1959), a living-room drama about three generations of an African American family who struggle against economic, social, and political prejudices as well as self-doubt. Set in a small apartment in Chicago's South Side, the play tells the story of Walter Lee, a chauffeur, who dreams of a better life. He wants to use the life insurance money his family received after his father's death to open his own business, a liquor store. But his mother rejects his dream and wants to spend the money on his sister's aspiration of attending medical school and her own desire to move the family to a better neighborhood. Mama Younger even puts down a deposit on a new house in what happens to be an all-white neighborhood. When a con artist steals the majority of the life-insurance money, Walter Lee falls into despair. Then a representative of the all-white neighborhood tries to take advantage of the situation by offering to buy back their new house. Walter is ready to sell, but then he regains his integrity and decides that the family will take the house after all. With *A Raisin in the Sun* Lorraine Hansberry became the first black woman playwright to be produced on Broadway.

FOR MORE ON

LORRAINE HANSBERRY

"African/American: Lorraine Hansberry's *Les Blancs* and the American Civil Rights Movement," Joy L. Abell, *African American Review*, Fall 2001

After a disappointing audience response during the Broadway preview of A Raisin in the Sun, *Lorraine Hansberry thought the play would fail. However, at the premiere, the audience and the critics responded enthusiastically, and* A Raisin in the Sun *has become a pioneering example of African American theatre. Wanting to avoid stereotyped characters that audiences would dismiss, Hansberry created complex characters who struggled with a painfully realistic situation. Like the Naturalist plays of the early twentieth century,* Raisin *was a glimpse of life that most Broadway patrons had not seen before. This original production featured Sidney Poitier (center) and Ruby Dee as Walter Lee and Ruth Younger. Directed by Lloyd Richards, Ethel Barrymore Theatre, New York, 1959.*

© Gordon Parks/Time & Life Pictures/Getty Images

Off the Beaten Broadway Path: 1960s U.S. Theatre

The 1960s was a time of great social turmoil all over the world. During the 1950s, the United States had seen the Korean War, McCarthyism, the threat of mass annihilation with the Cold War, and the beginning of the civil rights movement. The new decade brought political assassinations, urban riots, the Vietnam War, peace protests, and start of the modern women's rights movement—filling the streets with marches, demonstrations, and civil disobedience.

Starting in the late 1950s, small theatres sprang up in several Manhattan neighborhoods to put on plays about the issues of the day. These theatres became collectively known as **Off Broadway.** Though the term was not coined until the 1950s, the movement had begun fifty years earlier as the **little theatre movement,** which staged inexpensive, noncommercial productions of artistically significant plays in small, out-of-the-way theatres. From the mid-1950s through the mid-1960s, there was a proliferation of little theatres in Manhattan, including Circle in the Square, The Phoenix Theatre, The Jewish Repertory, Circle Rep, The Manhattan Theatre Club, and The Negro Ensemble. Off-Broadway theatres produced new versions of commercial plays that had failed, neglected plays, plays of social protest, and experimental works. By 1959, there were seventy-four Off-Broadway productions, more than were playing on Broadway. During the next twenty years, these small theatres introduced many playwrights including Edward Albee, Britain's Caryl Churchill, John Guare, Sam Shepard, Megan Terry, Jean-Claude van Itallie, and Lanford Wilson, as well as the actors Jason Robards, Colleen Dewhurst, Al Pacino, and Dustin Hoffman.

By the late 1960s, Off Broadway was becoming a victim of its own success, as actors, designers, and technical unions were demanding better working conditions and higher pay. Soon, production costs grew and therefore plays had to become more commercial and less experimental in order to attract a larger audience. The result was a new wave of even smaller, less expensive, alternative, experimental theatres: the **Off-Off-Broadway** movement. These tiny theatres—less than a hundred seats—flourished in lofts, basements, coffeehouses, storefronts, cafes, and in any found space that could be adapted for use as a theatre. At Off-Off-Broadway theatres, diverse and often formerly taboo topics such as homosexuality could be frankly discussed, and political plays that denounced the Vietnam War were the norm.

Experimental theatre groups tested not only the premises of society but also of theatre. They questioned the idea that theatre had to take place in a theatre, with the audience sitting on one side and actors performing on the other. A few theatre companies even eliminated the need for a theatre by staging **happenings,** or unstructured theatrical events, on street corners, at bus stops, in lobbies, and virtually anywhere else people gathered. Some experimental theatre groups tried to bring ritual back into the theatre; others mixed movies and theatre into multimedia performances. Many of these companies were inspired by the writings of Brecht, Beckett, Artaud, and the Polish Laboratory Theatre headed by Jerzy Grotowski (1933–1999). The Polish Laboratory was famous for taking theatre back to its basics. It limited the technical side of the theatre and promoted the actor-audience relationship. Grotowski also changed the traditional seating arrangement and instead integrated the audience into

FOR MORE ON
EXPERIMENTAL THEATRE
"Experimental theatre in the 1960s," Arthur Marwick, *History Today,* October 1994

When we talk about the future of the American theater, we have to talk about the future of our economic structure. There is none supporting the theater. And that is becoming an increasing concern. Not only is it exorbitant to produce in New York, it's exorbitant everywhere. And the funding is tied up with the attitude of government officials, who can do a kind of benign censorship. So I think the whole economic infrastructure is at risk.

Paula Vogel,
American playwright

© Piotr Barącz/Photo courtesy of the Archive of the Grotowski Centre, Wroclaw, Poland.

This 1969 production of Jerzy Grotowski's Apocalypsis cum figuris *illustrates his penchant for dissolving barriers between actors and their audience. Drawing on Christian themes and the work of intellectuals such as Fyodor Dostoyevsky and Simone Weil, this play was staged at the Teatr Laboratorium 13 Rzedow, Wroclaw, Poland.*

the action of the play. For example, in *Kordian* (1962), a play that takes place in a mental institution, the audience sits on stage with the actor-patients.

The experimental theatre movement spread across the United States, as hole-in-the-wall theatres tested new ground. In Chicago, the Off-Loop theatre movement mirrored the Off-Off-Broadway movement by staging experimental plays in theatres outside the downtown area (the Loop). In California, the San Francisco Mime Troupe promoted civil rights and women's rights, and El Teatro Campesino staged plays on the backs of flatbed trucks beside the picket lines of striking Chicano and Filipino migrant workers. In New York at the same time, Joseph Papp's Public Theater gave birth to the offbeat musical *Hair* (1967), the story of hippies fighting the draft during the Vietnam War. The play raised eyebrows primarily for its use of nudity and rock and roll. (For more on musicals, see Chapter 13.)

Contemporary Theatre: It's Alive!

The five categories of theatre discussed in Chapter 1 are with us today: commercial, historical, political, experimental, and cultural. Commercial theatre—what we call "show business"—still dominates, as it always has, but the number of theatres that produce it has shrunk. In the 1960s there were 36 Broadway theatres, and the number of touring companies in the United States had fallen from 327 in 1900 to fewer than 10. Today, Broadway is dominated by small-cast comedies, blockbuster musicals, and—some feel—a lack of innovation. Theatre critics say that Broadway has turned into nothing more than one big theme park where only safe, profitable plays or Disney-imitation musicals can be staged. The major problem is cost. As with Hollywood movies, if a lot of money is at stake, producers are reluctant to take chances. Even Off-Broadway theatre, which was once the source of new ideas, has been forced to play it safe because of prohibitive costs. In spite of the problems, the commercial theatre continues to attract millions of people each year. Like most Hollywood blockbusters, the commercial theatre attracts an audience because it presents safe themes and reaffirms mainstream values.

Regional theatre is one ray of light in the contemporary theatre world. A regional theatre is a permanent, professional theatre located outside of New York City. The regional theatre movement started in 1947, when Margo Jones founded the first fully professional, nonprofit, resident theatre in Dallas. A short time later, the Arena Stage was founded in Washington, DC, and the Alley Theatre in Houston. A host of other regional professional theatres followed: the Guthrie Theatre in Minneapolis (1963), the Actors Theatre of Louisville (1964), the Mark Taper Forum in Los Angles (1967), and many others. These theatres now do what Broadway did fifty years ago. By staging new plays alongside commercial hits and historical plays, they appeal to the intellectual audiences that Hollywood seldom serves. Playwright John Guare says, "Broadway is the place where tourists come. When I was a kid at Yale Drama School back in the 60s, you dreamed about having a play on Broadway. I don't think anybody dreams that today. You dream of having a play at the Seattle Rep, or Louisville, or the Goodman, or Trinity Rep. That's where the theatre is, and that's healthy."

Thanks in part to regional theatres, historical theatre is alive and well. Productions of dramas by such playwrights as Ibsen, Shaw, Goethe, Aeschylus, Sophocles, and Euripides still dot the landscape. In 2003, Aristophanes' 2,400-year-old comedy *Lysistrata* was simultaneously produced in fifty-nine countries as a protest against the war in Iraq. In any given week, more than two hundred professional productions of Shakespeare's plays are taking place in theatres across the United States—and hundreds more in high school, community, and college theatres. College and regional theatres are the main source of historical theatre because they feel it is part of their mission to educate the public, as well as their aspiring artists, about the various styles and ideas in theatre over the centuries.

Experimental theatre is also flourishing, because playwrights, directors, designers, and actors always want to test their premises and reinvent their art. One new type of experimental theatre is **performance art,** a term used to describe performances that mix theatre, visual arts, music, dance, gesture, and rituals. Performance artists often use multimedia effects, sounds, and lighting effects to make a point and allow the audience to understand its deeper implications. They often reject the traditional elements of drama: plot, dialogue, characters, and setting. They are not interested in telling a story but in conveying a state of being. Like Dada and Theatre of Cruelty performers of the

© Lynn Goldsmith/Corbis

Performance artist Laurie Anderson (b. 1947) began her career in New York in the 1970s, a time that fostered experimentation, a blending of art forms, and a willingness to perform in informal art spaces. In addition to working as a musician and a visual artist, Anderson collaborates with other artists to create large-scale theatrical works that incorporate storytelling, music, video, and projected imagery and that often transform the ordinary into the strange. Like many other performance artists, she uses her work to explore conceptual and social issues, such as our perception of time, the challenges we face maneuvering through a digital age, and our fascination with crime and justice. Of her audiences, Anderson says, "I like it when we fall into that communal dream."

past, performance artists seek to challenge the audience. They often break social rules in order to force the observers to think about current issues. Instead of a traditional theatre or performance space, performance artists are interested in public arenas, such as galleries, parks, garages—anywhere that fits their needs. (For more on performance art, see Chapter 3.)

Political and cultural theatre, what George Bernard Shaw called "drama of thought," is practiced today by David Henry Hwang, Caryl Churchill, August Wilson, Sam Shepard, and David Mamet, among others. David Henry Hwang (b. 1957), the son of Chinese immigrant parents, often writes about the conflicts of Chinese immigrants who are expected to abandon much of their Chinese identity in order to fit into mainstream U.S. culture. His greatest success was *M. Butterfly* (1988), which won the Tony for best Broadway play. Caryl Churchill (b. 1938) is a member of the Monstrous Regiment, a feminist theatre group famous for its ensemble method of creating plays. One of her most famous plays, which used this improvisational workshop method, is *Cloud Nine* (1979), a provocative study of colonialism and sexual politics. Another of her plays, *Top Girls* (1982), is the story of a woman who has sacrificed a home and family life to achieve success in a man's world. Another prominent contemporary playwright was August Wilson (1945–2005). He was inspired to write his first big hit *Ma Rainey's Black Bottom* (1984), a play about 1920s blues musicians and their struggle against the white recording companies, while listening to Ma Rainey, Bessie Smith, and other classic blues artists. Wilson then set out to write a ten-play cycle that chronicles the black experience in each decade of the twentieth century. His award-winning plays include *Fences* (1987), *Joe Turner's Come and Gone* (1988), and *The Piano Lesson* (1987). (For more on David Henry Hwang, Caryl Churchill, and August Wilson, see Chapter 3.)

Sam Shepard (b. 1943) worked in Off-Off-Broadway before he won the Pulitzer Prize for Drama in 1979 for *Buried Child* and became famous as the playwright of *Curse of the Starving Class* (1978), *Fool for Love* (1982), and *True West* (1980). As a screenwriter, he has written *Paris Texas,* which won the Golden Palm Award at the 1984 Cannes Film Festival. As an actor, Shepard earned an Oscar nomination for his performance as Chuck Yeager in the movie *The Right Stuff.* David Mamet (b. 1947) came to prominence with the Off-Off-Broadway plays *Sexual Perversity in Chicago* (1976) and *American Buffalo* (1976). He won the Pulitzer Prize in Drama for *Glengarry Glen Ross* (1984), which exposed the greed and cynicism of real estate salesmen. Perhaps his most controversial play is *Oleanna* (1992), which looks at charges of sexual harassment of a male professor by one of his female students. Also a

© Robbie Jack

Modern plays, such as David Mamet's Oleanna, often explore current social issues. Oleanna is about a power struggle between a university professor and a female student who accuses him of sexual harassment. Inspired in part by the 1991 Senate hearings in which law professor Anita Hill brought charges of sexual harassment against Supreme Court nominee Clarence Thomas, the play addresses such timely issues as political correctness and power dynamics in relationships. This 2004 production starred Aaron Eckhart and Julia Stiles. Directed by Lindsay Posner, Garrick Theatre, London.

Nigerian playwright, novelist, poet, activist, and Nobel Prize–winner Wole Soyinka bases much of his work on the mythology and customs of his tribe, the Yoruba. Death and the King's Horseman *(1976) portrays two cultures struggling with questions of death and self-sacrifice in British-occupied Nigeria in 1946. Accompanied by West African music and dance, the story revolves around Elesin Oba, the chief horseman of a king who has just died. According to ancient custom, Oba is expected to "commit death" so that he can accompany his king to heaven. But the British colonial administrator, appalled by this ritual, puts Oba in prison to prevent his death and inadvertently brings disgrace to the entire tribe. This 2004 production featured Forrest McClendon as the Praise Singer and was directed by William Roudebush, Lantern Theater Company, Philadelphia.*

© Nick Embree/Courtesy Lantern Theater Company

FOR MORE ON
WOLE SOYINKA
"Wole Soyinka's outrage," Alan Jacobs, *Books & Culture*, November–December 2001

Theatre is the most revolutionary art form . . . because it's so prone to self-transformation. . . . That dynamic quality expresses itself in relation to, first of all, the environment in which it's being staged, then the audience, the nature of the audience, the quality of the audience. The space, the mutual space of interaction between audience and stage. And no two performances are ever the same. Theatre can respond immediately.

Wole Soyinka,
Nigerian playwright

screenwriter, Mamet's screenplays include *The Verdict* (1982), *The Untouchables* (1987), and *Wag the Dog* (1998).

Because the stage is often financially controlled on the local level, playwrights of the "drama of thought" who cannot find a voice in the mainstream can still hope to find an audience. One of these playwrights is Nigerian-born Wole Soyinka (b. 1934), whose plays are deeply rooted in African myths, dance, and rituals. But he is also influenced by Western drama—ancient Greek theatre, Shakespeare, and European nonrealistic plays. Soyinka's plays combine symbolism, mysticism, and beautiful dialogue, and they contain strong political points. His play *Dance of the Forest* (1966) celebrates Nigerian independence but also warns against returning to Nigeria's violent past and the "recurrent cycle of stupidities," dishonesty, and abuse of power he feels was caused by European colonialism. His many other plays parody tyranny and corruption in post-independence Africa and attack African dictators including Uganda's Idi Amin and Zaire's Joseph Mobutu.

Algerian-born French playwright Fatima Gallaire-Bourega also uses her plays not only to express herself but also to prompt discussions about such topics as violence against women, religious fanaticism, and female sexual desire. Her play *You Have Come Back* (1986) is about a woman named Lella who returns to her native Arab village after living in France for twenty years. At first, Lella is welcomed home, but, within a day, her family finds her ideas about men, life, and love are just too different. The women of the village are so outraged by Lella's Western point of view that they put her on trial. Found guilty of being a blasphemer who has deserted Islam, Lella is clubbed to death by the women of the village. Throughout the clubbing, Lella protests, accusing the women of being "dead for ages." The play ends with the women of the village being called to evening prayer. They leave behind Lella's lifeless body. Because of its subject matter, this play cannot be performed in Gallaire-Bourega's native Algeria, but it has been produced internationally.

FOR MORE ON

FATIMA GALLAIRE-BOUREGA

"Multiculturalism as text and context: Teaching Fatima Gallaire-Bourega's *You Have Come Back*," Lalita Pandit, *College Literature*, October–February 1992

Theatre: Will It Survive?

For the last hundred years, theatre has struggled to find its voice in a world dominated by film and television. Many have predicted its demise. Its saving grace has been its uniqueness—theatre is where the people go to hear the voices of the people—not the voices representing corporations or the government, but all those voices talking about everyday people's desires and problems as well as their diverse political and social points of view. (For more on the theatre of the people, see Chapter 3.) But even this uniqueness may not be enough for theatre to survive.

The economic crises that followed the 9/11 attacks on the United States hit the theatre hard. Declining attendance and the loss of government support forced theatres to trim their budgets to the bone. Many theatres became dependent on corporate sponsors, many of whom want to control content. For example, the Trinity Repertory Company in Providence, Rhode Island, got in trouble with a production of *Nickel and Dimed* (2002), a play based on social critic Barbara Ehrenreich's book about what it's like to be a minimum-wage worker in this country. Oskar Eustis, artistic director of the company, reported that the major corporate supporters called, "suggesting that we were doing something counterproductive to our own interests by producing this play. Now, none of those corporate supporters took their money back, but those phone calls made us sweat."

The current financial straits of the theatre have forced many artistic directors to put entertainment and big box office above social, educational, or intellectual agendas. Crowd-pleasing musicals like *Always Patsy Cline* and farcical comedies like *Greater Tuna* dominate our theatrical landscape, leaving little room for the more controversial works of Ibsen and Williams or newer experimental plays that challenge and provoke. The result, some feel, may be catastrophic. Donald Margulies of Yale University points out, "Our government, our society, has created a generation of people who simply don't think in abstraction. . . . I think that one needs to put on one's thinking cap when going to the theater or seeing a film. . . . I think that we have fostered a mentality that somehow is ill-equipped to handle abstract thought."

When the economy was really strong, we felt comfortable doing Suzan-Lori Parks's *The American Play*. Right now we're running *Always Patsy Cline* for months and months and months, as long as it will run.

Ann Ciccolella,

Managing Director, Zachary Scott Theatre, Austin, Texas

In spite of economic problems, theatres are still managing to survive and even find the resources to produce new, innovative, and thought-provoking plays. In 2003, the latest year for which statistics are available, there were over 1,200 nonprofit professional theatres in the United States that managed to

© Michal Daniel

When corporations partner with local theatres, they often want the theatre's productions to reflect their corporate values. Such was not the case with Joan Holden's Nickel and Dimed, *a play about Americans who work full-time for poverty-level wages. The story follows the undercover research of social critic Barbara Ehrenreich, who worked minimum-wage jobs in three states to see whether she could make ends meet. This 2003 production at the Guthrie Theater in Minneapolis marks the first time the play was staged in one of the cities where Ehrenreich did her research. So that Minneapolis's working poor could attend the play, the Guthrie made tickets available for $2. Featuring Robynn Rodriguez as Ehrenreich, this production was directed by Bill Rauch.*

mount over 170,000 performances of 13,000 productions and employ 104,000 artists, administrators, and personnel. They added over $1.4 billion to the U.S. economy. And this amount does not include theatre-related spending by patrons for parking, babysitters, and dinner at nearby restaurants. Add this to the money generated by professional for-profit theatres on Broadway and elsewhere and the tens of thousands of amateur and college productions staged each year, and theatre in the United States certainly appears poised for continued survival.

Curtain Call

Today's theatre is eclectic. A single production can combine elements of realism, absurdism, and expressionism and more. One play may be a cutting-edge experiment, and the next a simple, life-affirming melodrama. One play can reaffirm our values, making us feel good about who we are and what we believe, while the next challenges us as well as our country, our culture, and our values.

Today's theatre also expresses diverse points of view. Unlike film or television, most theatre is controlled at the local level, so subjects seldom addressed in the mainstream media are more likely to be given a full hearing. Divisive topics such as AIDS, feminism, race relations, and gender biases can be seriously examined. The contemporary theatre is also the place you go to find uncensored stories from seldom-heard Asian, African, Hispanic, Native American, Middle Eastern, and gay and lesbian voices. (For more on diversity in contemporary theatre, see Chapter 3.) Today, theatre audiences seldom know what to expect, nor should they. Its variety makes the contemporary theatre irreplaceable.

Though it's impossible to predict what forms and styles of theatre will arise in the coming years, the social pressures that have always inspired theatre's many directions continue to push and pull theatre today. Tomorrow may literally bring a new era in response to today's funding needs, political climate, competition from other art forms and entertainments, and a society's ever-changing view of theatre's relevance to their lives. And in the words of playwright Wole Soyinka: "Theatre can respond immediately."

Summary

Twentieth-century inventions such as the camera and electric lights changed the centuries-old art of theatre forever. There was a call for sets to be more "genuine," acting to be more "honest," and dialogue to sound like everyday speech. This trend led to Realism and naturalism, styles that were also influenced by the ideas of the modern thinkers Charles Darwin, Sigmund Freud, and Karl Marx. Plays began to feature true-to-life, well-motivated characters and themes that examined problems of society. In an attempt to be more real, Realistic plays used box sets that allowed audiences to feel as if they were spying on the action of the play. For some, Realism wasn't real enough, and so they developed Naturalism.

In the early part of the twentieth century the film industry began to take its toll on the theatre. Thousands of theatres were closed or converted into movie theatres. Movies could produce realism and naturalism better than the theatre, so theatre artists decided to "re-theatricalize" the theatre. Their efforts led to many avant-garde "isms." Symbolism was an attempt to show inner truth through symbolic acts and images. Futurism glorified the Industrial Age. Expressionism attempted to show life from the point of view of a particular character. Dadaists attempted to mirror the madness of the world, and surrealists attempted to reveal the higher reality of the unconscious mind. Absurdism was a result of the atrocities of the world wars, World War II in particular, and especially in Europe. There are three broad categories of absurdism: fatalist, existentialist, and hilarious absurdism. Fatalists show people trapped in an irrational universe where even basic communication is impossible. The existentialists believe that God is dead and that we must now do everything for ourselves. The hilarious absurdist playwrights highlight the insanity of life in a comic way.

The plays of epic theatre have a grand scope: a large cast, a long period of time, and a wide range of sometimes unrelated incidents. One of its greatest proponents is Bertolt Brecht, who also advocated an "alienation effect" so that the audience would always be aware they are watching a play and must confront the same political, social, or economic injustices.

In the United States after World War II, mixing various "isms" in one play became popular. Some plays were part realism and part expressionism, whereas others told realistic stories with lyrical language. The social unrest of the 1960s led to the Off-Broadway and Off-Off-Broadway movements in which less-commercial, more-experimental plays tested the boundaries of theatre. Today, regional theatres are growing in number and importance, as they are often more willing than big Broadway houses to stage new and experimental plays.

The Art of Theatre Online

Use the *Art of Theatre* website at **http://communication.wadsworth.com/downs1** for quick access to the electronic study resources that accompany this chapter, including a digital glossary, a link to InfoTrac College Edition that you can use to find the For More On... InfoTrac College Edition readings listed below, a list of further reading, and a chapter quiz. When you get to the *Art of Theatre* homepage, click on the cover of the book you are using and you will be redirected to the website for your book. Then click on "Student Book Companion Site" in the Resource box, pick a chapter from the pull-down menu at the top of the page, and select an option from the Chapter Resources menu. The *Art of Theatre* website also includes links to interesting and informative theatre websites. Just click on the Theatre on the Web link in the Book Resources menu. The links to these websites are maintained and updated as needed.

Key Terms

absurdism / 323
alienation effect / 325
avant-garde / 318
box set / 312
Dadaism / 323
epic theatre / 325
expressionism / 319
fourth wall / 312
futurism / 318
happenings / 329
little theatre movement / 329
Naturalism / 316
Off Broadway / 329
Off-Off-Broadway / 329
performance art / 331
poetic realism / 327

For More On . . .

Infotrac College Edition Readings

http://www.infoTrac-college.com

***A Doll's House* / 314**
"The female jouissance: An analysis of Ibsen's *Et Dukkehjem*"

Sartre / 324
"Jean-Paul Sartre: Philosopher for the twentieth century"

Brecht / 326
"The figure of the 'spectator' in the theoretical writings of Brecht, Diderot, and Rousseau"

Lorraine Hansberry / 328
"African/American: Lorraine Hansberry's *Les Blancs* and the American Civil Rights Movement"

Experimental theatre / 330
"Experimental theatre in the 1960s"

Wole Soyinka / 334
"Wole Soyinka's outrage"

Fatima Gallaire-Bourega / 335
"Multiculturalism as text and context: Teaching Fatima Gallaire-Bourega's *You Have Come Back*"

17 The Musical

No doubt about it, Americans love musicals. From Broadway theatres to high schools, from cruise ships to casinos—musicals are everywhere. Not only are they often big box office, but some of the longest running shows in the history of the theatre have been musicals. For example, the musical Cats *ran on Broadway for nearly eight years; hundreds of thousands of people saw the 7,485 performances—and then touring companies took the play to theatres around the country. Broadway shows sell over $1.5 billion worth of tickets annually, and the majority of those seats are for musicals.*

Why are musicals so popular? Perhaps it's because music—from deafening car stereos, to telephone-hold "Muzak," to our favorite CDs that get us through the day—is a daily

© Sara Krulwich/The New York Times
© Evan Agostini/Getty Images (inset)

◀ ***On preceding page:*** *Spamalot, book and lyrics by Eric Idle, music by John Du Prez and Eric Idle. Directed by Mike Nichols, Shubert Theatre, New York, since 2005, featuring Tim Curry, Hank Azaria, David Hyde Pierce, and Sara Ramirez. Based on the cult movie* Monty Python and the Holy Grail, *this musical provides a wacky spin on the legend of King Arthur and his knights.*

constant for most of us. Perhaps the rhythmic repetition of our heart beating inside of us gives music its power. Researchers have shown that music can intensify our emotions, increase our blood pressure, cause our pupils to dilate, and raise our heart rate. It also can calm our breathing and help us relax. The right music can even cause hens to lay extra eggs and help cows to produce more milk. Music can make us dance with joy or trigger depression; it can inspire us to make love or to make war. French emperor Napoleon Bonaparte summed up the power of music when he said, "Give me control over he who shapes the music of a nation; I care not who makes the laws." In this chapter we will examine one of the oldest forms of theatre, the play that combines music and drama, and its popular modern variation, the American musical.

American musical theatre is our indigenous art form. We can't claim drama, ballet, or opera, but musical theatre is our very own. . . . Musicals are in our blood and in our bones, are part of our collective personality.

Molly Smith,
Artistic Director of the Arena Stage

I Something for Everyone: What Makes a Musical?

There are two categories of theatre: plays with music and plays without. Plays without music are sometimes called **straight plays.** Plays with music come in all shapes. Let's make a quick survey of the various forms before we look at the elements and the history of musical theatre. **Opera,** such as Giacomo Puccini's (1858–1924) *Madame Butterfly* (1904), is a drama that is set entirely to music; all the lines are sung, usually to grand, classical music. **Operetta,** or "light opera," such as *The Mikado* (1885) by Gilbert and Sullivan differs from "grand opera" because it has a frivolous, comic theme, some spoken dialogue, a melodramatic story, and usually a little dancing.

The play called the *musical* is a form you probably saw performed by your high school's drama department. There are a few varieties of musicals. A **musical comedy,** such as *Guys and Dolls* (1950), is characterized by a lighthearted, fast-moving comic story, whose dialogue is interspersed with popular music. A straight **musical,** such as *West Side Story* (1957), has a more serious plot and theme. A **rock musical** uses rock music—the rock and roll of the 1950s (*Grease,* 1972), the psychedelic rock of the 1960s (*Hair,* 1967), or contemporary pop and rock (*Rent,* 1996).

A program of satirical sketches, singing, and dancing on a particular theme is called a **revue,** or musical review; a program of unrelated singing, dancing, and comedy numbers is called a **variety show.** Variety shows and revues descend from **vaudeville,** a popular form of stage entertainment from the 1880s to the 1930s and the Great Depression. An evening of vaudeville included a dozen or so slapstick comedy routines, song-and-dance numbers, magic acts, and juggling or acrobatic performances. Vaudeville descends from **burlesque,** a form of musical entertainment featuring bawdy songs, dancing women, and sometimes striptease. Burlesque began in the 1840s as a parody of the pretentiousness of opera—and of the upper class who could afford to attend it.

Whether opera, rock musical, or burlesque, no matter what your taste, you are sure to find a type of musical theatre to your liking. Now let's take a closer look at the structure and music of most forms of musicals.

© Ethan Miller/Getty Images

Avenue Q represents a new twist on the traditional musical comedy, where irreverence and racy humor take center stage. Featuring puppets manipulated by bunraku-like handlers, this innovative musical tells the story of Princeton, an eager college graduate who comes to New York with big dreams and little money. He settles into a slightly shady neighborhood populated by a motley host of characters in search of work, love, and a reason to be. A sort of Sesame Street *for adults,* Avenue Q *showcases songs such as "I'm Not Wearing Underwear Today," "Everyone's a Little Bit Racist," and "What Do You Do with a B.A. in English?" Book by Jeff Whitty, lyrics and music by Robert Lopez and Jeff Marx. Directed by Jason Moore, John Golden Theatre, New York, since 2003.*

Good Things Come in Threes: The Scripts of Musicals

Musical scripts have three components: book, music, and lyrics. The **music** is the orchestrated melodies, the **lyrics** are the sung words, and the **book** is the spoken lines of dialogue as well as the plot. Unlike most straight plays, musicals often need several writers. The **librettist** writes the book, the **composer** writes the music, and the **lyricist** writes the lyrics. For example, Joseph Stein wrote the book for *Fiddler on the Roof* (1964), Jerry Bock wrote the music, and Sheldon Harnick wrote the lyrics. Occasionally, a versatile writer, such as George M. Cohan (*Fifty Miles from Boston,* 1908) and Meredith Willson (*The Music Man,* 1957), can write all three, but the duties for most musicals are shared. And these creative teams don't appreciate it when only one member of the team is credited for the entire work, as often happens. The wife of lyricist Oscar Hammerstein, a famous name in musical theatre, once overheard someone at a party say, "I just love Jerome Kern's 'Ol' Man River'" (from the musical *Show Boat*). She indignantly corrected the guest by pointing out that her husband had written the lyrics and that all Kern wrote was "'Dum, dum, dum dum; dum, dum, dum dum.'"

Musicals with a particularly well-developed story and characters, such as *Fiddler on the Roof,* are sometimes called **book musicals.** *Fosse* (1998) and other **dance musicals** feature the work of a director-choreographer such as Tommy Tune, Michael Bennett, or Bob Fosse. Musicals that are mostly singing and have less spoken dialogue, such as *Les Misérables* and *Evita,* are known as **operatic musicals.** Operatic musicals are similar to operettas, but their tone is often much darker and more dramatic. For example, Steven Sondheim's

Based on the Romantic novel by French author Victor Hugo, the operatic musical Les Misérables *is the complex, epic tale of Jean Valjean, a former thief who spends his life trying to rectify his past by being a force for good in the world. Set in prerevolutionary France, this story of the search for individual liberty and peace inspired audiences so much that the musical ran for sixteen years on Broadway and is still performed all over the world. Like many operatic musicals,* Les Misérables *is loved mostly for its stirring, dramatic music. Music by Claude-Michel Schönberg, book by Claude-Michel Schönberg and Alain Boublil, English lyrics by Herbert Kretzmer. This production was directed by Trevor Nunn and John Caird, London, 1988.*

© ArenaPAL/Topham/The Image Works

One difference between poetry and lyrics is that lyrics sort of fade into the background. They fade on the page and live on the stage when set to music.

Stephen Sondheim,
American musical theatre lyricist and composer

A song without music is a lot like H_2 without the O.

Ira Gershwin,
American musical theatre lyricist

operatic musical *Sweeney Todd: The Demon Barber of Fleet Street* features a story of betrayal, seduction, and revenge, subjects that are far too serious for light operettas. (For more on Sondheim and *Sweeney Todd,* see the Spotlight box "Steven Sondheim.")

From Ballads to Showstoppers: The Music of Musicals

A traditional musical begins with an **overture** in which the orchestra plays a medley of the songs as a preview. The overture also lets the audience know that it's time to stop talking because the performance is about to begin; it can also provide time for latecomers to take their seats. Many contemporary musicals, such as *A Chorus Line* (1975), forgo the overture, but it is still the norm for revivals of traditional musicals.

During the show, different types of songs are used for different dramatic and theatrical purposes. Leonard Bernstein and Stephen Sondheim use a large variety in *West Side Story,* a retelling of *Romeo and Juliet* set on the streets of New York. "Tonight" is a **ballad,** a love song for Tony and Maria. "Gee, Officer Krupke" is a **comedy number** that provides comic relief. "A Boy Like That," a sung conversation between Maria and her best friend, advances the storyline. And "America" is a big production number called a **showstopper** because of the torrent of applause that such numbers often receive, literally stopping the show.

Songs are placed strategically within the story, usually at points where dialogue is not sufficient, so the characters must break into song to fully express what they are feeling. Some songs are followed later by a **reprise,** a repetition of the song, sometimes with new lyrics, sometimes with the same lyrics but with new meaning or subtext in order to make a dramatic point.

Stephen Sondheim

One of the most accomplished lyricists and composers of contemporary American musicals is Stephen Sondheim (b. 1930). Sondheim wrote his first musical at the age of fifteen, but his remarkable career officially began when be became a protégé of legendary lyricist and producer Oscar Hammerstein II (1895–1960). Sondheim's Broadway credits begin with the lyrics for *West Side Story,* including the famous "I feel pretty / Oh, so pretty / I feel pretty and witty and bright!" He went on to write the lyrics for the golden-era musical *Gypsy* (1959) and was lyricist and composer for the ever-popular *A Funny Thing Happened on the Way to the Forum* (1962).

Sondheim has also written less traditional musicals like *Company* (1970), *Follies* (1973), *A Little Night Music* (1974), and *Pacific Overtures* (1976). These musicals are known as "concept" musicals because they focus on a particular event rather than a more traditional cause-and-effect story plot. For example, *Company* follows the main character, a single guy named Bobby, through a series of dinners with his somewhat neurotic friends. *Follies* tells the story of a condemned theatre building in which a series of vaudeville-like *Follies* had run many years ago. Because the theatre is due to be demolished to make room for a parking lot, all of the old "follies girls" return to the theatre for a reunion. The story runs in both the present and the past, showing the audience the younger versions of these characters. *Pacific Overtures* (1976), which was staged Kabuki style, portrays the ways in which Japan's culture was affected when the United States forced the isolated islands to open up to international trade in 1853.

One of Sondheim's most famous musicals is *Sweeney Todd: The Demon Barber of Fleet Street* (1979), which combines a conventional plot structure with an operatic score. *Sweeney Todd* explores a subject that is highly unusual for musicals: revenge-based serial murder and cannibalism. The musical is the story of Benjamin Barker, a barber who has led a beautiful life until a corrupt and depraved judge convicts him on trumped-up charges. After serving his time on a prison island, Benjamin returns, assumes the name Sweeney Todd, and sets out on a mission of revenge, slitting the throats of men who come to his shop for a shave, and then giving them to his neighbor, Mrs. Lovett, who turns the bodies into meat pies.

Other popular Sondheim musicals include *Sunday in the Park With George* (1984), loosely based on the life and loves of French neo-Impressionist painter Georges Seurat while he was creating his famous painting *A Sunday on La Grande Jatte; Into The Woods* (1987), which combines classic fairy tales into a story that shows that life seldom ends happily ever after; and *Assassins* (1990), which explores the history of presidential assassins in America, from John Wilkes Booth to John Hinckley, Jr.

Sondheim's work proves that a musical can be about any subject. As Sondheim's mentor, Oscar Hammerstein, once said, "It is nonsense to say what a musical should or should not be. It should be anything it wants to be, and if you don't like it you don't have to go to it. There is only one absolutely indispensable element that a musical must have. It must have music."

© Robbie Jack/Corbis

One of Stephen Sondheim's most famous musicals, Sweeney Todd *is the tale of a murderous barber who wreaks havoc in eighteenth-century London to avenge his unjust imprisonment. Supposedly based on a real case, the story of Sweeney Todd fascinates audiences as much as the mystery of Jack the Ripper. Music and lyrics by Stephen Sondheim, book by Hugh Wheeler. Royal Opera House, Covent Garden, London, 2003.*

Filming All That Jazz: *Chicago* on Screen

The Broadway musical is such a self-consciously theatrical genre that it's hard to imagine it being transferred to today's silver screen. All those people dancing and bursting into song—it just doesn't feel real, and real is the way we like films to feel. Sure, it was done with *The Sound of Music* (1959, Broadway; 1965, Hollywood), but now it seems old-fashioned. Yet the 2002 film version of Fred Ebb, Bob Fosse, and John Kander's hit musical *Chicago* (1975) is very successful as a movie. Why?

The beauty of this adaptation is that form *is* content. *Chicago,* originally based on a 1926 stage play by Maurine Dallas Watkins, is a tale about fame, celebrity, and murder. But it's also about performance and theatre, which gives it license to embrace its theatrical roots and be heavily theatrical in its presentation. The film uses cuts, juxtapositions, and close-ups to establish Roxie Hart as the main character and gives us the world of Chicago's cabaret scene as it revolves around her and as she

© Sara Krulwich/The New York Times

Compared with the film version, the stage version of Chicago *tells Roxie Hart's story in a relatively straightforward fashion. In this 1996 production, Ann Reinking starred as Roxie Hart. Directed by Walter Bobbie, Richard Rodgers Theatre.*

sees it. The film ingeniously recasts the story as a blend of Roxie's fantasy and 1920s Chicago's reality.

The first image in the movie is a close-up of Roxie's eye—this tells us that we're about to see the world as she sees it. We then see the first dance number, "All That Jazz." In the musical's script, this number is performed by Velma (Catherine Zeta-Jones), Roxie's role model and rival. However, to establish Roxie as the central character, don't we need to see her in a prominent role right away? The film version solves the problem by juxtaposing Velma's dance number with shots of Roxie (Renée Zellweger) as she watches hungrily from the audience. We even see a quick fantasy shot of Roxie wearing Velma's costume and singing "All That Jazz" as she imagines herself a star.

As the opening number concludes, the choreography is juxtaposed against shots of Roxie as she goes home with Fred (Dominic West) to have an affair she hopes will help her career. In this scene, the movements of the dance are mirrored by Roxie and Fred as they tumble into bed, a comparison that makes it clear what's on Roxie's mind: fame, shiny costumes, and flashing lights. By aligning us with her point of view, the film is able to get away with delivering all the grand, over-the-top glamour of a big musical in a way that it fits easily into the reality of the story and the characters: Roxie is a dreamer, the world is a circus, and we are along for the ride.

Of course, it helps that the film's cast offers great performances to go with the fabulous costumes, solid cinematography, and seductive choreography. What's not to like? *Chicago* is a slick, stylish movie, but it is also fun with a capital F, which, after all, is what a Broadway musical should be.

Aoise Stratford
Playwright

© Miramax Films/Photofest

"Mama" Morton, played by rap artist and actor Queen Latifah in the movie version of Chicago, is imagined as a lusty cabaret singer by Roxie Hart. In fact, Mama is the prison warden who keeps Roxie under lock and key. One of the keys to Chicago's success as a movie was its reliance on elaborate fantasy to tell the tale of Roxie's rise from obscurity to notoriety.

I Musicals: Then and Now

Although it's often said that the musical is an American invention (and that may be true), music, dance, and song have been a part of the theatre since its beginnings. Traditional African dramas and ritual plays have always incorporated music and dance. Twenty-five hundred years ago, Greek tragedies depended on a chorus of singing and dancing men. Aristophanes may have been creating musical comedy when he combined parody, satire, wit, and music in his plays. Then, for hundreds of years the Roman stage was filled with bawdy song and dance, and during the Middle Ages traveling bands of performers offered popular songs mixed with stories full of slapstick comedy. Elizabethan plays often included folk songs—Shakespeare's *The Tempest* alone includes nine songs. Japanese Kabuki plays depend on dance, music, and song. Musical masques, operas, burlesques, minstrel shows, variety shows, and music hall revues are all ancestors of the modern American musical. Though Americans were not the first to add song and dance to the theatre, they did make a unique form of musical theatre by borrowing from and combining earlier forms. Let's take a closer look at musicals throughout history.

Opera: High Art and Comic Relief

In opera, there is no spoken dialogue. Instead, the actors sing and sometimes chant their speeches and conversations. Opera developed five hundred years ago during the Italian Renaissance. Its creators were attempting to imitate ancient Greek tragedies; many scholars of the time thought the plays of Aeschylus, Sophocles, and Euripides were intended to be sung rather than spoken. In the end, they created a hybrid of music and drama, an art form in which the actors sang all their lines. The word *opera* comes from the Latin for "work"; the Italians may have originally called these singing plays "works in music" or "musical works for the stage." The first operas were staged in Italy in the late 1500s, and the first public opera house was built in Venice in 1637. Opera proved to be so popular that by the end of the century Venice alone had eleven opera houses. Opera hit its peak in the nineteenth century. Notable opera composers include Richard Wagner (1813–1883), Giacomo Puccini (1858–1924), Wolfgang Mozart (1756–1791), Gioacchino Rossini (1792–1868), and George Frideric Handel (1685–1759).

Today, traditional opera is not as common as it once was. It's also often considered an elitist form of entertainment enjoyed primarily by the wealthy and well educated. But other forms of opera are still quite popular. **Comic opera,** including operetta, developed out of *intermezzi,* or comic interludes performed during the intermissions of operas. This style of opera became widely popular with the work of Sir William Schwenck Gilbert (1836–1911) and Sir Arthur Seymour Sullivan (1842–1900), including *The Pirates of Penzance* (1879), *The Mikado* (1885), and *HMS Pinafore* (1878). When Gilbert and Sullivan's *HMS Pinafore* was staged in the United States in 1879, it was a triumph. Soon, American theatres added song and dance wherever possible in their shows.

© Michal Daniel

Gilbert and Sullivan's The Pirates of Penzance *is the story of Frederic, a child mistakenly apprenticed to a band of kindhearted pirates. In his twenty-first year, Frederic has fulfilled his apprenticeship and is eager to return to respectable society. However, the pirates inform him that he was bound until his twenty-first* birthday, *and since he was born in a leap year on February 29, technically he has celebrated only five birthdays. When Sir Sullivan was working on* Pirates, *he wrote to his mother, "I think [the opera] will be a great success, for it is exquisitely funny, and the music is strikingly tuneful and catching." He was right—*The Pirates of Penzance *was an instant hit and is still performed regularly. This 2004 production featured Dan Callaway as Frederic and was directed by Joe Dowling, Guthrie Theater, Minneapolis.*

Early American Musicals: The Good, the Bad, and the Ugly

The earliest American musicals were **ballad operas,** brought from England and popular during the colonial period. These comic operas mixed popular songs of the day with spoken dialogue. About a hundred years later, around 1840, burlesque was all the rage. It featured songs, skits, and plenty of racy dancing girls in a "leg-show"; later burlesque shows often also included striptease acts. The original purpose of burlesque was to lampoon high society's operatic tradition by turning it into a kind of sexy caricature. Today, burlesque lives on in The Pussycat Dolls, an all-female group of dancers, whose lineup has included Carmen Electra and guest stars Britney Spears and Gwen Stefani. These modern acts no longer satirize high art, but they continue the tradition of striptease's sly humor and sexual innuendo.

By 1890, vaudeville had replaced burlesque as the dominant form of American musical entertainment. It was designed to be more respectable, wholesome, and family oriented. It added acts by ventriloquists, acrobats, jugglers, magicians, male and female impersonators, and monologists (early stand-up comedians) to the toned-down song and dance numbers. Vaudeville shows could also include animal acts; ballroom dancing; demonstrations of scientific discoveries; famous criminals recounting their lurid past; comic skits featuring actors playing Irish, Jewish, Italian, or "blackface" stereotypes; and sing-alongs of "Camptown Races," "Swanee River," "Oh! Susanna," and other popular songs written before the Civil War.

Most vaudeville companies were small and traveled the rails from town to town putting on one-night shows in local theatres. Big-time vaudeville was the *Ziegfeld Follies* (1907–1931), a series of lavish musical reviews on Broadway, featuring Will Rogers, Fanny Brice, and other popular stars. (In many ways, the *Follies* live on in today's Las Vegas stage shows.) Many early movie stars got their start in vaudeville, including W. C. Fields, Al Jolson, Buster Keaton, Fred Astaire, and the comedy team George Burns and Gracie Allen. The vaudeville circuit was also a popular subject of early American movies. On television, the *Ed Sullivan Show,* the *Sonny and Cher Comedy Hour,* and the many other variety shows between the 1950s and the 1970s were descendants of vaudeville.

Another popular form of musical theatre in the nineteenth century was the **minstrel show.** Unique to the United States, these shows came to prominence in the 1830s and lasted well into the twentieth century. The shows included comic scenes, dance interludes, and sentimental ballads all based on white stereotypes of black life in the South. These shows flourished for a couple of reasons. First, black music was very popular, but it was considered improper for whites to go to a theatre to hear black musicians play, so white performers put on black makeup—called *blackface*—and performed what was supposedly black music, such as Thomas Rice's song "Jump Jim Crow" (ca. 1828). (For more on blackface, see the Spotlight on Diversity box "Blackface, Redface, Yel-

© Bettmann/Corbis

In the late nineteenth century, vaudeville was the dominant form of musical entertainment in the United States. Intended as a family-friendly alternative to burlesque, vaudeville often featured family acts such as The Three Keatons (who, incidentally, shared the stage with escape artist Harry Houdini and his wife, Beatrice). The Keatons' shtick included skits that showed their audiences how to "properly" raise a child, but included throwing the youngster though fake walls and scenery. The youngest member of this act grew up to become one of America's greatest silent film stars: Buster Keaton, the great stone face.

lowface" in Chapter 2.) Second, minstrel shows provided Northern white audiences with an idea of what the lives of the slaves were like, albeit in a highly distorted and romanticized way. After all, before the abolition of slavery, it was in almost everyone's interest to depict slaves as content with their lot in life.

As the shows became more popular, their structure became standardized. The first part had musical numbers with bits of comic dialogue; the second was full of songs, dance, and standup routines; and the third segment typically featured a one-act play. The skits in the minstrel shows often contained illiterate and foolish exchanges that made fun of blacks. Yet, because the blackface makeup provided a kind of mask, some performers felt free to incorporate social commentary about abolition and women's rights into the skits. This was particularly true of shows in the 1860s, the Civil War years, when some black performers also painted their faces black and formed their own minstrel troupes. In fact, the most famous minstrel performers in the late 1800s and early 1900s were black.

FOR MORE ON

MINSTREL SHOWS

"Demons of disorder: Early blackface minstrels and their world," Thomas DeFrantz, *TDR (The Drama Review)*, Fall 2000

When Hollywood got into the act, the faces under the black makeup were once again white. The first "talkie" movie, *The Jazz Singer* (1927), featured white actor Al Jolson in blackface performing in a minstrel show, and later the famous stars Fred Astaire and Judy Garland portrayed minstrel show performers in blackface. Not until the 1950s and 1960s brought the civil rights movement did minstrel shows fall into total disrepute. Today, at best, they are seen as an imitation of the commedia dell'arte, but more often they are viewed as a low point in American theatre history.

The Black Crook, a melodrama about black magic staged in New York City in 1866, is often called the United States' first modern musical. The story was a Faust-like melodrama about a crook-backed practitioner of black magic (hence the title) who makes a pact with Lucifer that allows him to live one extra year for each soul he delivers to hell. His first victim is the virtuous Rudolphe, who has been imprisoned by an evil count. However, Rudolphe escapes, frees a trapped fairy queen, discovers buried treasure, and saves the day. In the end, the sorcerer fails to deliver any souls and is himself carted off to hell. By most accounts the play was poorly written and doomed, but just before it opened, the producers had an odd stroke of luck when the nearby New York Academy of Music caught fire, stranding a troupe of Parisian ballet dancers. The enterprising producers of *The Black Crook* hired the dancers and quickly restaged the play, combining the melodrama with music and dance into a production described as an "extravaganza" that included demons and sprites and "bare-armed" women. *The Black Crook* opened September 12, 1866, and was a massive success, running for 475 performances and making over $1 million on an investment of only $25,000—a considerable profit even today. It would be revived on Broadway an unprecedented eight times and have over 200 performances in London.

The success of *The Black Crook* spawned a host of similar extravaganzas that were, by today's standards, just musical reviews containing unrelated but toe-tapping songs by a number of composers, chorus girls dancing in elaborate production numbers, and plenty of spectacular costumes and magnificent sets without regard for the story or characters. The joke-filled dialogue was only an excuse to get from one song to the next. These early musical plays lacked strong plot and believable characters, but both were deemed unnecessary because entertainment was the primary purpose, not drama.

African American Musicals: Opening New Doors

The success of *The Black Crook* also opened the door for the first full-length musical comedy conceived, written, produced, and performed by African Americans in New York. Composer and producer Bob Cole along with lyricist Billy Johnson formed a production company and opened *A Trip to Coontown* at the Third Avenue Theater in 1898. The story of a con man, the musical used minstrel stereotypes and spoofed *A Trip to Chinatown,* a popular musical comedy. But one of its songs challenged the racist policies of the day: A young black man sings about how he and his date were denied entry to a nightclub because of the color of their skin. *A Trip to Coontown* played to both whites and blacks and had two long runs in New York and a successful tour.

That same year, the ragtime musical *The Origin of the Cakewalk* (1898) became the first all-black show to play at a top Broadway theatre. But getting onstage required some ingenuity. The play's black composer, Will Marion Cook, went to the theatre and confidently informed its manager that the white

Shuffle Along *(1921) was a wildly popular all-black musical review and a first in many respects: It introduced jazz dancing to Broadway, premiered such notable black entertainers as Paul Robeson and Josephine Baker, and featured the first realistic African American love story at a time when onstage love scenes between blacks were taboo. The show's catchy music included "I'm Just Wild about Harry," which years later became Harry Truman's presidential campaign song. Here, Noble Sissle poses with some of the* Shuffle Along *showgirls. Sissle and Eubie Blake, a team made famous on the vaudeville circuit, wrote the music and lyrics. Another famous vaudeville team, Flournoy Miller and Aubrey L. Lyles, wrote the book.*

Courtesy The Maryland Historical Society, Baltimore, Maryland

owner had sent the troupe to perform that night. They were such a success that the manager immediately signed them for a long run. Only later did he find out that the theatre owner had known nothing about Cook's players.

By the 1920s there were a host of black musicals and revues including *Runnin' Wild* (1923), *Dixie to Broadway* (1924), and *Blackbirds* (1926). They had black casts and many had black writers, but blacks and whites acting together on stage was still considered improper, at least by whites. Broadway had opened its door a crack for black librettists, lyricists, composers, and actors, but not until 1959 did a straight play by a black playwright make it to Broadway—Lorraine Hansberry's *A Raisin in the Sun.* Of course, blacks were not the only ones discriminated against. Women also ran up against discrimination. (See the Spotlight box "Unsung Heroines of the American Musical.")

FOR MORE ON

EARLY BLACK MUSICAL THEATRE IN AMERICA

"Parody and double consciousness in the language of early black musical theatre," David Krasner, *African American Review,* Summer 1995

Unsung Heroines of the American Musical

Women have always sung, danced, and acted in musicals on the U.S. stage, but for a hundred years, almost all the composers, librettists, and lyricists have been men. In 1999, the New York State Council on the Arts (NYSCA) reported that only 8 percent of Broadway plays and only 1 percent of the musicals had been written by women. Women were better represented in Off-Off-Broadway: About 30 percent of the playwrights and more than 40 percent of the directors were women. But Off-Off-Broadway is far less lucrative than big Broadway theatres.

The gender disparity goes the other way for audiences; most of the audience members are women:

- The audience for the 2001–2002 Broadway season was 63 percent female, according to the League of American Theatres and Producers.
- Of the respondents to the 1997 NEA Survey of Public Participation in the Arts, 26.7 percent of the women and 22.3 percent of the men had attended a musical in the previous twelve months.
- Of the plays produced in professional theatres at the national level in 2001–2002, 17–18 percent had been written by women, and 16 percent had been directed by women, according to *American Theatre Magazine.*

In spite of their lack of recognition and opportunity, some women have been successful writers for musicals. Dorothy Fields (1905–1974) wrote the lyrics for *Sweet Charity* (1966) and the book for *Annie Get Your Gun* (1946) and gave us such great songs as "I Can't Give You Anything But Love" and "The Way You Look Tonight." Betty Comden (b. 1919), with her partner Adolph Green (1915–2002), wrote for the smash Broadway shows *Wonderful Town* (1953), *Bells Are Ringing* (1956), and *Applause* (1970), and the musical films *Singin' in the Rain* (1952) and *The Bandwagon* (1953). Some of their best-known songs are "The Party's Over," "Make Someone Happy," and "New York, New York."

Ronald Grant Archive

Although it's true that men have always dominated the creative and business sides of the entertainment scene, women have long played a part in bringing quality shows to the stage and screen. Betty Comden and her partner Adolph Green, the longest-running creative partnership in theatre history, collaborated on many award-winning Broadway shows and Hollywood musicals. One of their most famous films is Singin' in the Rain *(1952), starring Gene Kelly and Debbie Reynolds—this movie routinely makes critics' lists as one of the best films of all time.*

The Railroad, the War, and All That Jazz

In 1869 the Union Pacific met the Central Pacific Railway at Promontory Point, Utah, completing the first transcontinental railroad across the United States. By 1900 nearly three hundred touring theatre companies were taking advantage of this new, relatively fast form of travel. All the larger towns along the tracks built a theatre where these companies could play one-night or one-week stands. Most of the plays were melodramas, but there were also plenty of musicals, which were fast becoming America's favorite form of entertainment. Even today successful musicals usually spawn one or more road companies that travel around the country.

By World War I, the music of George M. Cohan (1878–1942) and Irving Berlin (1888–1989) was dominating Broadway. Their big-ticket musical comedies, such as Cohan's *Hello, Broadway* (1914), were patriotic and sentimental. They had cardboard characters and flimsy stories in which the guy always got the girl, good always triumphed over evil, and life was all ice cream, apple pie, and the American way. The plots never stood in the way of giving audiences an evening of pure entertainment and plenty of catchy tunes such as Cohan's "You're a Grand Old Flag" (1906) and "Yankee Doodle Dandy" (1904) and Berlin's "God Bless America" (1918).

After the war, jazz began influencing the American musical. Brothers George and Ira Gershwin (1898–1937 and 1896–1983) wrote a string of successful musical comedies whose songs are still popular today: *Lady, Be Good!* (1924) with the song "Fascinating Rhythm," *Strike Up the Band* (1930) with "I've Got A Crush On You," and *Girl Crazy* (1930) with "But Not for Me," "Embraceable You," and "I Got Rhythm." Playing in the orchestra for these shows were soon-to-be-famous big band leaders Glenn Miller and Benny Goodman.

These early musicals had simple stories about charming princes, gallant young men, romantic swashbucklers, and wealthy gentlemen all of whom were looking for love. Happy endings and no mention of the dark side of life were a must; the few plays that ended unhappily always did so for the good of humanity. For example, at the end of Sigmund Romberg's *The Student Prince* (1924), the kind young heir to the throne sacrifices his personal happiness for the good of the kingdom when he sorrowfully pulls himself away from his true love, a beer-hall girl, in order to marry a princess whom he does not love. The characters and stories of these sweetheart musicals may have been simple, but most of the musical comedies we enjoy today follow the same formula.

The *Show Boat* Revolution

In 1927 lyricist-librettist Oscar Hammerstein (1895–1960) and composer Jerome Kern (1885–1945) revolutionized musical theatre with *Show Boat*. It combined musical comedy and serious drama to create what we recognize today as the quintessential American musical. The story begins aboard the show boat *Cotton Blossom* in 1880s Mississippi. Gaylord Ravenal, a riverboat gambler, comes aboard and falls for Magnolia, the daughter of the ship's captain, Cap'n Andy. When the star of *Cotton Blossom*'s show, Julie, is forced out by the local sheriff because she is a mulatto woman married to a white man, Magnolia and Gaylord fill in. Years later, Gaylord and Magnolia are married and have a daughter, Kim. After Gaylord racks up sizable gambling debts and leaves Magnolia, she looks for a singing job to support herself and Kim. She

FOR MORE ON
SHOW BOAT AND RACE RELATIONS
"Show Boat: The revival, the racism," Robin Breon, *TDR (The Drama Review)*, Summer 1995

Ronald Grant Archive

Today we are used to seeing realistic relationships between black and white characters portrayed on stage and screen, but when Hammerstein and Kern's Show Boat *premiered in 1927, such portrayals were a revelation.* Show Boat *was based on a book by novelist and playwright Edna Ferber, who was well known for strong female protagonists and strong secondary characters who managed to rise above racial or other discrimination. Adapting* Show Boat *for the stage is a testament to the courage of Hammerstein, Kern, and producer Florenz Ziegfeld; they took a huge chance staging a story of such depth for audiences accustomed to much lighter fare. This still photo from the 1936 film version of* Show Boat *features Paul Robeson (center), who sang one of the musical's signature songs, "Ol' Man River."*

runs into Julie at a club, and the kindhearted Julie lets Magnolia take her own singing job. At a New Year's Eve show, Cap'n Andy comes to the club and is surprised to see Magnolia on stage. When she is almost booed off stage, he brings the crowd around in a magnificent sing-along. He then convinces her to return to the *Cotton Blossom,* where a contrite Gaylord is waiting to be reunited with his family.

Unlike the musicals that came before, *Show Boat* had a consequential story, powerful dialogue, three-dimensional characters, and songs and dances that tied directly into the plot. Instead of a line of pretty dancing girls, the chorus was black dockworkers, and they portrayed real people rather than the black stereotypes common at the time. The theme was more serious and dealt with, among other subjects, racial issues. Moreover, black and white actors performed on stage at the same time, which was still a rare occurrence. Yet old attitudes and customs don't reverse themselves overnight; in the original production the role of Queenie was played in blackface by a white actress named Tess Gardella (1897–1950), who was famous for playing "Aunt Jemima," or "mammy," characters in vaudeville.

In spite of its shortcomings, *Show Boat* was the first to combine dancing, choruses, toe-tapping melodies, and huge spectacle with a strong plot and plausible characters. In 1932, following on the heels of *Show Boat*'s tremendous success, Ira Gershwin and George S. Kaufman's musical *Of Thee I Sing,* a

> I know the world is filled with troubles and many injustices. But reality is as beautiful as it is ugly. I think it is just as important to sing about beautiful mornings as it is to talk about slums. I just couldn't write anything without hope in it.
>
> **Oscar Hammerstein,**
> *American lyricist and producer*

biting satire of Washington politics, became the first musical to win the Pulitzer Prize—the highest award given for American drama. Although frothy love stories didn't disappear from Broadway, more musicals featured complex characters: the professional gambler who can't turn down a bet, Sky Masterson, in *Guys and Dolls* (1950); the bombastic but vulnerable king of Siam in *The King and I* (1951); the self-important but charming Professor Higgins in *My Fair Lady* (1956); and the kindhearted con man, Harold Hill, in *The Music Man* (1957). The American musical was becoming a serious art form, and more musicals won the Pulitzer, including *South Pacific* (1950), *Fiorello!* (1960), *How to Succeed in Business without Really Trying* (1963), *A Chorus Line* (1976), *Sunday in the Park with George* (1985), and *Rent* (1996).

Thoroughly Modern Musicals

During the 1927–1928 season, Broadway had over seventy theatres with a total of 264 productions, including 46 musicals—a record that has never been broken. The great stock market crash of 1929 drastically reduced their numbers. George and Ira Gershwin's operatic musical *Porgy and Bess* (1935), Marc Blitzstein's (1905–1964) labor parable *The Cradle Will Rock* (1938), and other musicals of the Great Depression took on the tone of the times. After the United States entered World War II at the end of 1941, musicals returned for a while to flimsy plots with a patriotic flair. But in 1943, Richard Rodgers (1902–1979) and Oscar Hammerstein's *Oklahoma!* came to Broadway. Like

The 1950s and 1960s produced some of the most beloved Broadway musicals of all time. These "golden age" musicals not only told entertaining and exciting stories, but also featured perennial favorites, such as "There's No Business Like Show Business" (Annie Get Your Gun) *and "Luck Be a Lady"* (Guys and Dolls). *One of the most popular golden age musicals was* The Sound of Music, *which recounted the adventures of the singing von Trapp family, featuring the timeless songs "Do-Re-Mi" and "My Favorite Things," and was made into an Academy Award–winning movie starring Julie Andrews. In the original Broadway production (1959–1963), Mary Martin played the plucky governess, Maria Rainer. Music by Richard Rodgers, lyrics by Oscar Hammerstein II, book by Howard Lindsay, Russel Crouse, and Maria Augusta Trapp. Directed by Vincent J. Donehue. Lunt-Fontanne Theatre, New York.*

Photofest

Show Boat, it had well-developed characters, song-and-dance numbers integrated into the story, and some serious plot elements, including a murder. It even incorporated classical ballet. The story of *Oklahoma!* is simple—it is the tale of a cowboy and a farmhand competing for the affections of a farmgirl in Oklahoma Territory in 1906. However, it was influential because it incorporated storytelling techniques new to musicals, the use of dance to develop the plot and the characters.

At the end of the war, Americans seemed filled with optimism, believing that they had saved the world for democracy and that the American dream of prosperity, order, and happiness was within everyone's grasp. This optimism led to the two decades that many consider the golden age of American musicals. Broadway was filled with great musicals: *Carousel* (1945), *Annie Get Your Gun* (1946), *South Pacific* (1949), *Guys and Dolls* (1950), *The King and I* (1951), *My Fair Lady* (1956), *West Side Story* (1957), *The Sound of Music* (1959), *Fiddler on the Roof* (1964), and *Man of La Mancha* (1965). All provided more than just light entertainment; they combined powerful, often serious stories with musical numbers that advanced the plot. Stephen Sondheim recalls a man walking out on *West Side Story* when it was first produced: "He wanted a musical—meaning a place to relax before he has to go home and face his terrible dysfunctional family. Instead of which he got a lot of ballet dancers in color-coordinated sneakers snapping their fingers and pretending to be tough. His expectation had been defeated." Today, a golden age of musicals exists not in the United States but in India. Although "Bollywood" musicals don't have the robust stories of America's golden age musicals, they are just as rich in spectacle and song—and they are as immensely popular as U.S. musicals once were. (See the Spotlight on Diversity box "Hooray for Bollywood.")

FOR MORE ON

THE HISTORY OF THE AMERICAN MUSICAL

"The road to *Oklahoma!*" Robert Kimball, *Opera News*, July 1993

Musical theatre in the 1960s and 1970s broke even more expectations and took more risks. *Cabaret* (1966) showed Germany's period of political freedom and cultural experimentation just before the Nazis came to power. *Hair* (1967) introduced rock music, hippies, and nudity to the musical. *The Wiz* (1975)

© Martha Swope

The Wiz is a good example of the chances musical theatre artists took in the 1970s. A funky take on the well-loved story of the Wizard of Oz, this musical not only draws heavily on African American musical forms such as gospel, jazz, R&B, and disco, it also touches on topics of concern to the black community at the time, such as drug addiction and a focus on following hip trends rather than addressing social ills. This 1975 production featured Stephanie Mills as Dorothy. Music and lyrics by Charlie Smalls. Book by William F. Brown. Directed by Geoffrey Holder at the Majestic Theatre, New York.

retold the story of the Wizard of Oz from the perspective of an African American schoolteacher and her streetwise companions, who travel through an Oz with an urban flavor in search of happiness. And *A Chorus Line* (1975) dealt with homosexuality in a matter-of-fact way. These plays once again challenged the traditions of the American musical and brought a new strain of intellectual complexity to this fun-loving form of theatre.

Hooray for Bollywood!

The term *Bollywood* blends "Hollywood" and "Bombay" and is often used in the West to refer to the cinema of India. Some consider the term pejorative slang, but others take it as a compliment—an average of 800 films are made every year in India, and many of them are musicals. That's over twice the number of films Hollywood produces per year, making India not only the top producer of movies around the world but also the top producer of musicals. Movies are India's sixth largest industry and employ more than 300,000 people.

Indian movie stars such as Madhuri Dixit, Aishwarya Rai, and Karishma Kapoor are mobbed everywhere they go and, just like Hollywood stars, must hire bodyguards to protect them from admiring fans and overzealous paparazzi. Bollywood directors such as Raj Kapoor, Gugu Dutt, Mehboob Khan, and Bimal Roy are as famous in India as Alfred Hitchcock and Steven Spielberg are in the United States.

Since the first Indian talkie in 1931, song and dance have been an integral part of Indian films; even many nonmusicals include a few songs. Bollywood musicals typically have stock love stories, heroes, heroines, love affairs, song-and-dance sequences, and happy endings. Here's how the Bollywood musical goes: A young man and woman fall in love. After their first meeting, the man sings a love song rhapsodizing about his beloved's beauty. However, some obstacle keeps the lovers apart, and they sing in a split-screen duet about their painful separation. In the end, they are reunited and celebrate their love with a huge song-and-dance number as flamboyant as any 1940s Broadway musical. Although most Bollywood musicals follow this formula, audiences are satisfied as long as the songs are fresh and exciting.

It is not surprising that musicals are so popular in Indian cinema. For thousands of years, song and dance have been an integral part of ritual, religious, and social life in India. Modern Indian theatrical music traces its roots to the Urdu Parsee theatre of the 1930s, which drew its inspiration from classic Indian literature and its staging techniques from nineteenth-century British melodrama.

Bollywood movies and musicals have helped to define the national character of this huge country with seventeen major languages, five thousand gods, and six primary religions. Now Bollywood films are becoming popular around the world. In fact 65 percent of the revenue from Indian movies comes from outside India. Bollywood musicals have even begun to inspire Hollywood movies (*Moulin Rouge!* 2001) and Broadway musicals (*Bombay Dreams*, 2005).

© Donald Cooper/Photostage

A tongue-in-cheek homage to the musicals of Indian cinema, Bombay Dreams *tells the typically Bollywood story of a poor Bombay tour guide, Akaash, who become a superstar with the help of Priya, an independent filmmaker, and Rani, a glamorous movie star. As Akaash gains money, fame, and the attentions of Rani, he wonders if these things can take the place of his family, friends, and relationship with the girl-next-door Priya. This 2002 production at the Apollo Victoria Theatre in London featured Ayesha Dharker as Rani. Book by Meera Syal, music by A. R. Rahman, and lyrics by Don Black.*

The End or a New Beginning?

During the 1920s an average of 40 musicals per year were produced on Broadway. During the depression years of the 1930s the annual average fell to about 18. During the war years of the 1940s the average was 16. By the 1990s the number had fallen even farther, to only about 5 musicals per year. In the 1994–1995 Broadway season only two new musicals were produced. Over those decades, musicals also fell out of favor in Hollywood. (See the Spotlight box "The American Musical and the Movies.") Even though the brilliant composer-lyricist Stephen Sondheim had been writing such notable musicals as *Company* (1970), *Sweeney Todd* (1979), and *Into the Woods* (1987), many felt that the golden age of the American musical had passed.

The main problem for musical theatre today is the cost. Unlike straight plays, Broadway musicals almost always cost big money. For example, *Phantom of the Opera* had 36 actors, over 50 crew members, and 30 musicians. It needed 120 wigs, 260 costumes, and a massive set—not to mention the 20,000 AAA batteries it used a year. When it opened on Broadway in 1988, the cost was $375,000 a week. In comparison, the entire Broadway run of *The King and I* (1951–1954) cost $360,000. Even taking inflation into account, production costs have skyrocketed from decade to decade. In 1956, *My Fair Lady* cost $401,000 to produce; in 1975, *A Chorus Line* cost $1,145,000; in 1986, *Phantom of the Opera* cost over $7 million. Today, a Broadway musical can cost as much as $12 million to produce.

Soaring production costs make it difficult for producers to recoup their money, so investing in a new musical is risky. When *My Fair Lady* opened in 1956, it paid off its investors after twenty-five weeks of sold-out performances. Thirty years later, it took sixty-five weeks of sold-out performances for *Phantom of the Opera* to break even. A few years after that, the revue *Jerome Robbins' Broadway* would have needed over a year of sold-out performances to break even, which it never did.

FOR MORE ON

THE COST TO RUN A BROADWAY MUSICAL

"A really, really 'Big' show: Broadway bets on a $10 million musical with hip-hop moves, tons of toys, and no Tom Hanks," Greg Evans, *Entertainment Weekly,* February 23, 1996

As production costs have increased, so have ticket prices. When *A Chorus Line* opened on Broadway in 1975, the best seats sold for $15. Fifteen years later, when it closed, the price of a ticket was $50. Today, a ticket to a Broadway musical typically costs $100. (For more on production costs, see the Spotlight box "Theatre Is Expensive" in Chapter 2.)

Today, only Walt Disney and other huge corporations can afford to foot the bill for huge new musicals. Consequently, some Broadway producers have turned to staging revivals of popular older musicals that have a greater chance of making back their investment. Others are trying to ensure success by basing "new" musicals on well-known Hollywood movies: *Sunset Boulevard* (1994), *Big* (1996), *Footloose* (1998), *Thoroughly Modern Millie* (2002), and *The Producers* (2001). Expensive musicals such as *Phantom of the Opera* and *Miss Saigon* are still popular, yet there still seems to be room for smaller musicals such as revivals of *The Fantasticks* (1960) and *I Love You, You're Perfect, Now Change* (1996) that have small casts and can be produced on a shoestring. Whenever people say the American musical is on its way out, the art form always seems to stage another comeback. Today, new musicals such as *Rent* (1996), *Urinetown* (2001), *Hairspray* (2002), *Avenue Q* (2003), *The 25th Annual Putnam County Spelling Bee* (2005), and *Monty Python's Spamalot* (2005) are keeping the art form alive and pushing it to new levels.

It is clear that the musical theatre is changing. No one knows where it is going. Perhaps it is going not to one place but to many. That would be healthy, I think, just as the search in itself can be healthy. . . . Thus it was for Shakespeare in Elizabethan times; thus it was for writers of musicals after Rodgers and Hammerstein; and thus it will be again.

Tom Jones,
American lyricist

The American Musical and the Movies

The musical became popular in Hollywood the moment talkies were invented. The very first talking movie *The Jazz Singer* (1927) had several musical numbers. Hollywood's golden age of musicals lasted from the 1930s to the early 1960s. From the dance extravaganzas of Busby Berkeley to the water ballets of Esther Williams, musicals were Hollywood's biggest moneymakers. But a decade after what has often been called Hollywood's best musical, Gene Kelly's *Singin' in the Rain* (1952), the musical was no longer a Hollywood mainstay.

By the 1980s, musicals had disappeared from the screen almost completely. Today, a few musicals are still made in Hollywood, but they are seldom *originated* by Hollywood. Rather, they are based on successful stage musicals such as *Chicago, The Phantom of the Opera,* and *Rent.* Or they are quirky independent films, such as *Hedwig and the Angry Inch* (also based on a stage show) or "straight" movies, such as Woody Allen's *Everyone Says I Love You,* that parody or pay homage to old movie musicals. An exception is Baz Luhrman's *Moulin Rouge!* (2001), starring Nicole Kidman and Ewan McGregor, though even this innovative movie musical uses songs recycled from Elton John, Madonna, Patti LaBelle, and other pop stars. In fact, the movie is considered innovative because it uses contemporary popular music in an attempt to generate in contemporary audiences an excitement similar to what the original Moulin Rouge audience felt in 1899 as they watched well-executed burlesque.

Some have speculated that the demise of the Hollywood musical is due to the demise of American optimism during the Vietnam War, others think the rise of music videos killed off the form, and still others say that movies today are far too realistic for the actors to suddenly break into song. All of those reasons may apply to Hollywood, but musicals are still as popular as ever in the live theatre.

© 20th Century Fox/Ronald Grant Archive

Baz Luhrmann's Moulin Rouge! *is the tragic tale of Christian, a young British poet who falls in love with Satine, the star of a lush cabaret show in turn-of-the-century Paris. In true modern style,* Moulin Rouge! *reflects numerous cultures and genres, including European opera, Greek myth, Bollywood movies, and American pop, rock, and disco. This scene, featuring Nicole Kidman as Satine and Ewan McGregor as Christian, alludes to the fanciful imagery of the 1902 science fiction film* Le Voyage dans la lune *(*A Trip to the Moon*).*

| Curtain Call

Depending on whom you talk to, the American musical is alive and well or on its deathbed. Musical theatre historian Denny Martin Flinn is one who has sounded the death knell for the musical: "When *A Chorus Line* gave its final Broadway performance fifteen years after it opened, the last great American musical went dark, and the epoch was over." Stephen Sondheim, who gave us such great musicals as *Sunday in the Park with George* and *Sweeney Todd,* recently told critic Frank Rich that only two types of Broadway musicals exist

© Sara Krulwich/The New York Times

Because big Broadway musicals can be so expensive to produce, smaller musicals such as The 25th Annual Putnam County Spelling Bee *are becoming increasingly popular. This musical takes an affectionate look at the mortifications of middle school via six misfits who compete for a spelling bee trophy. Because* Spelling Bee *has a small cast, a simple set, and cost a mere $3.5 million to produce, it broke even after only eighteen weeks on Broadway. As long as the public clamors for musicals—and they always do—producers will find innovative ways to keep this fun-loving art form alive. This production of* Spelling Bee *premiered in 2005 and was directed by James Lapine at the Circle in the Square Theatre, New York. Book by Rachel Sheinkin, music and lyrics by William Finn.*

today: "revivals" and "the same kind of musicals over and over again." In his opinion, most musicals today are nothing more than "spectacles" and "stage versions of a movie." "We live in a recycled culture," said Sondheim. "I don't think the theatre will die per se, but it's never going to be what it was. You can't bring it back. It's gone. It's a tourist attraction."

However, this kind of pessimism is common each time there is a new turn or major development in musical theatre. There may be good years and bad, but the American musical is far from dead. It is simply in another transition as it evolves to become what culture and business require of it, just as it evolved to allow blacks and whites together on stage with *Show Boat* in 1927. Music and theatre have been traveling hand in hand for thousands of years, and even though the shape of the musical can't be predicted, there will be musicals as long as people like a story told with song.

| Summary

Musical scripts are made up of three parts: book, music, and lyrics. The librettist writes the book, the composer writes the music, and the lyricist writes the lyrics. Musicals that feature a well-developed story and characters are called book musicals. Musicals that emphasize dance are called dance musicals, and musicals in which singing dominates are known as operatic musicals.

Music, dance, and song have been a component of theatrical traditions around the world for thousands of years. The modern American musical has evolved from a number of musical traditions, including opera, operettas, musical reviews, variety shows, vaudeville, and burlesque. The distinction of the first modern American musical is often given to *The Black Crook,* a melodrama about black magic staged in New York City in 1866. In the same year the ragtime musical *The Origin of the Cakewalk* was the first all–African American show to play at a top Broadway theatre.

By World War I, big-ticket, sentimental musical comedies dominated Broadway. They seldom told complex stories or featured well-developed characters. The first big revolution in the American musical came in 1927 when Oscar Hammerstein and Jerome Kern wrote *Show Boat,* which combined aspects of musical comedy and serious drama to create what today we consider the quintessential musical. Sixteen years later, another well-rounded musical advanced the form, Richard Rodgers and Oscar Hammerstein's *Oklahoma!* Like *Show Boat, Oklahoma!* featured serious plot points, well-developed characters, and songs and dances used to develop the plot.

The musicals of the 1960s, 1970s, and 1980s brought a new round of innovation with musicals that took on a wide variety of social and political issues. Today, there are musicals to fit every taste: rock and roll musicals, musicals based on movies, and traditional revivals of Broadway classics.

The Art of Theatre Online

Use the *Art of Theatre* website at **http://communication.wadsworth.com/downs1** for quick access to the electronic study resources that accompany this chapter, including a digital glossary, a link to InfoTrac College Edition that you can use to find the For More On . . . InfoTrac College Edition readings listed below, a list of further reading, and a chapter quiz. When you get to the *Art of Theatre* homepage, click on the cover of the book you are using and you will be redirected to the website for your book. Then click on "Student Book Companion Site" in the Resource box, pick a chapter from the pull-down menu at the top of the page, and select an option from the Chapter Resources menu. The *Art of Theatre* website also includes links to interesting and informative theatre websites. Just click on the Theatre on the Web link in the Book Resources menu. The links to these websites are maintained and updated as needed.

Key Terms

ballad / 344
ballad opera / 349
book / 343
book musical / 343
burlesque / 342
comedy number / 344
comic opera / 348
composer / 343
dance musical / 343
librettist / 343

lyric / 343
lyricist / 343
minstrel show / 350
music / 343
musical / 342
musical comedy / 342
opera / 342
operatic musical / 343
operetta / 342
overture / 344
reprise / 344
revue / 342
rock musical / 342
showstopper / 344
straight play / 342
variety show / 342
vaudeville / 342

For More On . . .

Infotrac College Edition Readings

http://www.infoTrac-college.com

Minstrel shows / 351
"Demons of disorder: Early blackface minstrels and their world"

Early black musical theatre in America / 353
"Parody and double consciousness in the language of early black musical theatre"

***Show Boat* and race relations / 354**
"Show Boat: The revival, the racism"

The history of the American musical / 357
"The road to *Oklahoma!*"

The cost to run a Broadway musical / 359
"A really, really 'Big' show: Broadway bets on a $10 million musical with hip-hop moves, tons of toys, and no Tom Hanks"

GLOSSARY

A

absurdism An avant-garde "ism" that was the result of the two world wars. It has three types: fatalist, existentialist, and hilarious.

action The characters' deeds, their responses to circumstances, which in turn affect the course of the story.

Actors' Equity Association The union that represents stage actors; often shortened to "Actors' Equity" or "Equity." See also *Equity waiver.*

aesthetic distance The audience's awareness that art and reality are not the same. Closely tied to *willing suspension of disbelief.*

aesthetics The branch of philosophy that deals with the nature and expression of beauty.

alienation effect The result of techniques to keep the audience aware that what they are witnessing is only a play; used by Bertolt Brecht. Alienation techniques include having the actors address the audience out of character, exposing the lights, removing the proscenium arch and curtains, and having the actors perform on bare platforms or simple sets that are sometimes punctuated with political slogans.

American Federation of Television and Radio Artists (AFTRA) The trade union, affiliated with the AFL-CIO, that represents talk-show hosts as well as announcers, singers, disc jockeys, newscasters, sportscasters, and even stuntpeople.

antagonist (an-TA-guh-nist) The character who stands in the way of the protagonist's goals. See *protagonist.*

apron See *lip.*

arena theatre A type of theatre with the stage in the center, like an island, surrounded on all sides by audience; also called theatre-in-the-round.

Aristotelian Scholasticism (air-is-teh-TEEL-yen skeh-LAS-teh-sizm) A synthesis of Aristotle's philosophy and the dogma of the Roman Catholic Church that was widely taught in universities during the Middle Ages.

assistant director A person who helps stage scenes and manage the production crew.

assistant stage manager A person who helps the stage manager run the show during performances and assist the director with the rehearsal process.

autos sacramentales (OW-toes sah-krah-mehn-TAH-leys) Religious dramas in Spain during the Middle Ages and Renaissance.

avant-garde (ah-vahnt-GARD) Any work of art that is experimental, innovative, or unconventional.

B

back story Dialogue about what happened to the characters before the play began and what happens between the scenes and offstage; also called *exposition.*

ballad A love song.

ballad opera Comic opera that mixed popular songs of the day with spoken dialogue; brought from England to the colonies during the colonial period.

beat A section of dialogue about a particular subject or idea; the smallest structural element of a script.

black box theatre A small theatre that generally holds fewer than a hundred people and has moveable seats so that audience groupings can be changed for every production.

blackface Black makeup used by white performers playing black characters, as in minstrel shows.

blocking The movement of the actors on stage during a production; the technique the director uses to achieve focus and "picturization."

blocking rehearsals A series of rehearsals in which the director and actors work out the *blocking,* or the movement of the actors on stage during the play.

book For a musical, the spoken lines of dialogue and the plot. Is written by the librettist. Compare *lyrics* and *music.*

book musical A musical with a particularly well-developed story and characters, such as *Fiddler on the Roof.*

bourgeois theatre (boorzh-WAH) Commercial theatre productions that, like big-budget Hollywood films, pursue maximum profits by reaffirming the audience's values.

bowdlerize (bohd-luh-RISE) To edit out any vulgar, obscene, or otherwise possibly objectionable material before publication. The origin of the word is Thomas and Harriet Bowdler's prudishly sanitized edition of Shakespeare's plays for Victorian-era family consumption.

box office Ticket office of a theatre; named for the entry room in Elizabethan theatres where theatregoers dropped payment into a box.

box set Commonly used in realistic plays, a true-to-life interior containing a room or rooms with the fourth wall removed so that the audience feels they are looking in on the characters' private lives.

burlesque (bur-LESK) A form of musical entertainment that features bawdy songs, dancing women, and sometimes striptease. Begun in the 1840s as a parody of opera and the upper class.

C

callback list During auditions, a list directors keep of actors they want to call back for subsequent auditions as they narrow the field of candidates.

casting against type Casting an actor who is very different from, or even the opposite of, the type of person who would be expected to play the part.

casting director A person who specializes in finding the right actors for parts; especially common in Hollywood.

casting to type Casting an actor who physically matches the role or who has a deep understanding of the character's emotions and motivations.

catharsis An intense, twofold feeling of pity and fear that is the goal of Greek tragedy.

cattle call An audition to which anyone may come and be given a minute or so to perform for the director; also known as an "open call."

censorship The altering, restricting, or suppressing of information, images, or words circulated within a society.

character flaw An inner flaw that hampers a character's good judgment and leads the character to make unfortunate choices; sometimes called "fatal flaw" or "tragic flaw."

character makeup Makeup that completely transforms the way actors look, such as shadows, wrinkles, and gray hair to turn a young actor into an elderly character; compare to *straight makeup.*

choreographer The person who creates the dance numbers for a play or musical, or who teaches the dance numbers to the actors.

City Dionysia (dye-oh-NYE-see-ah) One of two ancient Greek religious festivals held each year to honor Dionysus. This festival often included plays.

climax The point of the greatest dramatic tension in the play, the moment the antagonist is defeated.

closed-shop union A union to which all employees *must* belong and which the employer formally recognizes as their sole collective bargaining agent; also called a union shop. Compare *open-shop union.*

cold reading Audition in which actors read from a script without any preparation.

color-blind casting Casting actors without regard for their race or ethnic background.

comedy number A song in a musical that provides comic relief.

comedy of manners A form of Restoration comedy that features wit and wordplay and often includes themes of sexual gratification, bedroom escapades, and humankind's primitive nature when it comes to sex. See also *Restoration.*

comic opera A style of opera, including operetta, that developed out of *intermezzi,* or comic interludes performed during the intermissions of operas. Popularized by the work of Gilbert and Sullivan.

commedia dell'arte (kuh-MAY-dee-uh del-AHR-tay) Originating in sixteenth-century Italy, traveling acting companies that presented broad, improvisational comedy and were popular throughout Europe between 1550 and 1750.

commercial theatre The type of theatre that, like the majority of Hollywood screen entertainments, has entertainment and profitability as its reasons for existence.

composer For a musical, the person who writes the music.

computer-aided design (CAD) Programs used by set designers to create blueprints of set designs.

concept production A production of a play dominated by the director's artistic vision, or concept.

conflict The key to the movement of a story; the element that qualifies a theatrical work as a "play."

convergent thinking Thinking that is measured by IQ and involves well-defined rational problems that have only one correct answer.

copyright A legal guarantee granted by the government to authors, composers, choreographers, inventors, publishers, and corporations that allows them to control and profit from their creative work and intellectual property.

corporate funding Money contributed to the arts, including the theatre, from companies of all sizes. Compare *government funding* and *patrons.*

corrales (koh-RAHL-layz) Crude platform stages built in courtyards of inns in Spain for performances of *autos sacramentales* and other plays.

costume plates Drawings that indicate how a costume is shaped, where seams and folds are, how the costume flows, and what fabrics are to be used.

costume shop The sewing machines, fabric-cutting tables, fitting rooms, and laundry facilities needed to create and maintain the costumes for a theatrical production.

creative director A director who adds concepts, designs, or interpretations that are independent of the playwright's intentions.

creativity A moment of insight when something new is invented or something that already exists is transformed.

cross-cultural theatre Theatre that joins contrasting ideas—whether staging techniques or myths and rituals—from diverse cultures into a single work in order to find parallels between cultures and promote cultural pluralism.

cross-gender casting Intentionally casting men to play women's roles and women to play men's roles.

cultural theatre The type of theatre that is designed to support the heritage, customs, and point of view of a particular people, religion, class, country, or community.

culture The values, standards, and patterns of behavior of a particular group of people expressed in customs, language, rituals, history, religion, social and political institutions, and art and entertainment.

curtain Usually the start of a show, but can also be the end of a show or an act, signaled by the raising or lowering of the curtain.

cyclorama (often shortened to **cyc**) A large, stretched curtain suspended from a U-shaped pipe to make a background that can completely enclose the stage setting. Lights are often projected on the cyc to indicate a location or a mood.

D

Dadaism (DAH-dah-izm) A movement that was ignited by the atrocities of World War I and gained fame through staged performances designed to demonstrate the meaninglessness of life.

dance musical A musical that features the work of a director-choreographer such as Tommy Tune, Michael Bennett, or Bob Fosse.

dark moment The end of the middle section of a formula play, when the protagonist fails (for internal or external reasons), the quest collapses, and the goal seems unattainable.

dark night The one night of the week when a play is not performed and the theatre is closed; typically Monday night.

declamatory acting A style of acting popular from the Renaissance through the early twentieth century that features grand gestures and an exaggerated elocutionary style. The actors deliver their lines directly to the audience in a rhetorical manner typified by order, harmony, and decorum.

denouement (DAY-noo-MAH) The outcome of a play, a short final scene that allows the audience to appreciate that the protagonist, because of the preceding events, has learned some great or humble lesson.

dialogue The spoken text of the play, the words the characters say.

didaskalos (dih-DAH-sko-los) In ancient Greece, a playwright who staged the plays he wrote, instructing the performers and advising the designers and technicians.

Dionysus (dye-oh-NYE-sus) The ancient Greek god of wine and fertility, Dionysus was worshipped through theatre performances and sacrifices.

director The person who turns a printed script into a stage production, coordinating the work of theatre artists, technicians, and other personnel.

director's note An article in a play's program by the director explaining what he or she intended to accomplish.

disturbance An inciting incident that upsets the balance and starts the action of a play by creating an opportunity for conflict between protagonists and antagonists.

dithyramb (DIH-thih-RAHM) A hymn sung at the altar of Dionysus, the ancient Greek god of wine and fertility; it was accompanied by dancing and perhaps improvisations by a chorus of as many as fifty men.

divergent thinking Thinking that involves fluency and the ability to generate a multitude of ideas from numerous perspectives.

domestic tragedy A type of play characterized by stories about common people, rather than ones of noble birth, who feel grand emotions and suffer devastating consequences.

downstage The area of the stage closest to the audience.

drama A form of theatre that tells a story about people, their actions, and the conflicts that result.

dramatic criticism A discriminating, often scholarly interpretation and analysis of a play, an artist's body of work, or a type or period of theatre; sometimes called *literary criticism* or criticism.

Dramatists Guild of America (DGA) The playwrights' union in the United States; an open-shop union.

dramaturg (DRAH-mah-TURG) A literary advisor and expert in theatre history who helps directors, designers, and actors better understand the specifics and sensibilities of a play and who can also help playwrights find their voice. (Sometimes spelled *dramaturge.*)

dress parade A tryout of the completed costumes by the actors for the costume designer and director so that necessary changes can be made before opening night.

dress rehearsals The final rehearsals, when costumes and makeup are added, before the play opens.

E

electric shop Theatre workshop with equipment to maintain, repair, and hang lights.

elevations The views of a set design from front and back.

emotional memory An acting technique pioneered by Konstantin Stanislavsky in which the actor recalls the visual and auditory images, or physical circumstances, of a real-life (or imagined) event in order to relive the emotions accompanying it. Also called sense memory or affective memory.

empathy The ability to understand and identify with another's situation to the extent of experiencing that person's emotions.

enculturation The process by which we learn about our culture.

enlightenment The protagonist's realization of how to defeat the antagonist; often related to the theme of the play.

Enlightenment A period in Europe (ca. 1650–1800) that glorified the human power to reason and analyze; a time of great philosophical, scientific, technological, political, and religious revolutions.

ensemble The crews of technicians, the assistants, and the artists including actors, directors, speech coaches, playwrights, and designers who use a wide variety of art forms including painting, drawing, writing, and acting as well as set, lighting, and costume design to create a theatre production.

epic theatre Features plays that have a grand scope, large casts, and cover a long period and a wide range of sometimes unrelated incidents.

episode One scene in an ancient Greek play; alternates with *stasimons.*

Equity waiver An exception to Actors' Equity Association wage standards that allows members to work for free in small productions. See *Actors' Equity Association.*

ethnocentrism The practice of using one's own culture as the standard for judging other cultures.

event An unusual incident, a special occasion, or a crisis at the beginning of a play that draws the audience's interest.

exodos (EKS-oh-dos) In ancient Greek theatre, the summation by the chorus on the theme and wisdom of the play.

experimental play A play that pushes the limits of theatre by eliminating the distance between actor and audience, trying out new staging techniques, or even questioning the nature of theatre.

exposition Dialogue about what happened to the characters before the play began and what happens between the scenes and offstage; also called *back story.*

expressionism A style that shows the audience the action of the play through the mind of one character. Instead of seeing photographic reality, the audience sees the character's own emotions and point of view.

F

fatal flaw See *character flaw.*

fight director A specialist who choreographs stage combat from fistfights to swordplay.

final dress rehearsal The last rehearsal before an audience is invited. See *dress rehearsals.*

flats Originally, the wood-and-muslin units that made up three walls of a room on stage. Now, plain wall units as well as doors, windows, and fireplaces.

floor plan The blueprint of a set design that shows the view from above.

fly system The elaborate network of pulleys, riggings, and counterweights that allows scenic pieces to be "flown" up and out of the audience's sight in a traditional proscenium arch theatre.

focus The actor, action, or spot on the stage to which the director draws the audience's attention. See also *sharing focus, stealing focus, triangulation,* and *upstaging.*

found, or **created, space** Spaces where theatre can be performed, such as parks, churches, town squares, basements, warehouses, gymnasiums, jails, subway stations, and street corners.

fourth wall An imaginary wall separating the actors from audience; an innovation of Realism in the theatre in the mid 1800s.

french scene A structural element of a play that begins with any entrance or exit and continues until the next entrance or exit.

futurism A twentieth-century "ism" that glorified the power, speed, and excitement of the Industrial Age.

G

gels (JELLS) Sheets of colored plastic attached to the front of lighting instruments.

gender-neutral casting Casting without regard for the character's gender.

general working rehearsals Rehearsals during which the director and actors work on individual scenes and concentrate on understanding the characters' motivation, emotions, and personality.

genre (ZHAHN-ruh) A category of artistic works that share a particular form, style, or subject matter.

given circumstances Character-analysis approach that begins with examining characters' life circumstances: their situation, problems, and the limits life has placed on them. Can include general background such as upbringing, religion, and social standing, as well as what happened to the character the moment before entering the scene.

gobos (GOH-bohz) Metal cutouts placed on the front of lighting instruments to project patterns (such as sunlight coming through the leaves of a tree) on the stage..

government funding The money spent each year on the arts by federal, state, and local governments. Compare *corporate funding* and *patrons.*

green room A small room for actors waiting for their cues, located just off the stage and out of the audience's earshot.

groundlings Audience members who stood on the main floor (and therefore paid the least for their tickets) in an Elizabethan theatre.

group dynamics The functioning of people when they come together into groups.

H

hand props Any objects actors handle while on stage, such as pens, fans, cigars, money, and umbrellas.

happenings Unstructured theatrical events on street corners, at bus stops, in lobbies, and virtually anywhere else people gather.

Harlem Renaissance An African American literary, artistic, and musical movement during the 1920s and 1930s centered in the Harlem neighborhood in New York City.

Hellenistic period The two centuries when classical Greek culture spread around the Mediterranean Sea, including Egypt and the Middle East; dates approximately from the death of Alexander the Great in 323 BCE until the Roman conquest of Greece in 146 BCE. The word *Hellenistic* is derived from the Greek word meaning "to imitate the Greeks."

historical theatre Dramas that use the styles, themes, and staging of plays of a particular historical period.

house A theatre's seating area.

hubris (HYOO-bruhs) The term used in classical Greek drama for overbearing pride or arrogance.

humanists In fifteenth-century Italy, university students who rejected the traditional curriculum of theology in favor of the subjects studied in classical Greece, specifically rhetoric, literary criticism, grammar, history, poetry, painting, architecture, music, classical literature, and theatre.

I

inner conflict Some sort of unfinished business that is so compelling that it handicaps the character until it is confronted.

interludes Secular plays performed between other forms of entertainment at court in the late Middle Ages.

International Phonetic Alphabet (IPA) A system for transcribing the sounds of speech that is independent of any particular language but applicable to all languages.

interpretive artist A member of the creative team, such as a director, actor, or designer, who turns the playwright's thoughts into a play.

interpretive director A director whose goal is to translate a script from page to stage as faithfully as possible.

K

Kabuki (kuh-BOO-kee) A popular, robust, and spectacular version of the Japanese Noh theatre. The name comes from the characters for "song" (*ka*), "dance" (*bu*), and "skill" (*ki*). See also *Noh*.

L

legs The curtains at the sides of a stage in a proscenium arch theatre.

Library of Alexandria One of the first universities; its holdings included original manuscripts by Aeschylus, Euripides, and Sophocles. Located in Alexandria, Egypt, a city founded by Alexander the Great. Partially destroyed by Roman troops and later by Christian mobs.

librettist For a musical, the person who writes the book, or the spoken lines of dialogue and plot.

Licensing Act of 1737 An English law that gave the Lord Chamberlain the authority to censor plays. The term *legitimate theatre* comes from the time of the Licensing Act.

lighting plot A detailed drawing that shows the location of each lighting instrument on the hanging grid, where its light will be focused, and its type, wattage and the circuitry needed, and its color.

limelight In the mid-1800s, a gas-powered spotlight in which a jet of oxygen and hydrogen was ignited with small bits of lime. Now, the word means "the center of attention."

lip Also called an *apron,* the area of a proscenium arch stage that extends into the audience's side of the picture frame.

literary arts Arts created with written language.

literary criticism See *dramatic criticism.*

little theatre movement Inexpensive, noncommercial, artistically significant plays in small, out-of-the-way theatres. In the United States, flourished from the mid-1950s through the mid-1960s.

lyricist For a musical, the person who writes the lyrics.

lyrics For a musical, the sung words; the writer is called a lyricist. See also *book* and *music.*

M

magic if A technique pioneered by Konstantin Stanislavsky for developing empathy with a character. It involves searching for the answers to the question "What would I do *if* I were this character in these circumstances?" The magic *if* allows actors to find similarities between themselves and a character and to explore the intimate emotions and thoughts that result.

major dramatic question (MDQ) The hook (or question) that keeps an audience curious or in suspense for the duration of the play; an element in the beginning of a formula play that results from the disturbance and the point of attack.

masque Originating in the early 1500s, a form of entertainment for monarchs and their invited audiences; characterized by grand dances, extravagant costumes with masks, lavish spectacle, poetry, and florid speeches all hung on a thin story line praising the monarch and demonstrating the need for loyalty.

medium The method, substance, and technique used to create a work of art.

melodrama Most popular in the late nineteenth century, a type of play that usually features working-class heroes who set out on a great adventure; story lines that praise marriage, God, and country; and florid background music. The word is a blend of *music* and *drama*

method acting Also known as "the method," this system of realistic acting was distilled by followers of Konstantin Stanislavsky and has been taught primarily since the 1930s in America. See *Stanislavsky system.*

minstrel show Stage entertainment consisting of songs, dances, and comic scenes performed by white actors in blackface makeup; originated in the nineteenth century.

miracle plays Plays in the Middle Ages in Europe that recounted stories about the lives, suffering, and miracles of particular saints.

morality plays Allegorical plays in the late Middle Ages in Europe that taught moral lessons about how to conduct one's life.

Moscow Art Theatre A theatre company founded in the late nineteenth century by a group of Russian producers, actors, directors, and dramatists. Made famous by the plays of Anton Chekhov and the acting techniques of Konstantin Stanislavsky.

motivated light Stage lighting that comes from an identifiable source, such as a candle, a lamp, or the sun.

motivation The conscious or subconscious reason a character takes a particular action.

movement coach A specialist who instructs actors in various styles of movement.

multiculturalism The attempt to achieve a pluralistic society by overcoming all forms of discrimination, including racism sexism, and homophobia.

music In a musical script, the orchestrated melodies, which are written by the composer. See also *book* and *lyrics.*

musical A type of theatre that features song and dance interspersed with spoken text. The genre includes not only modern musicals with popular songs and impressive spectacle (e.g., *Miss Saigon, Phantom of the Opera*) but also the masques, operas, burlesques, minstrel shows, variety shows, and music hall reviews of earlier periods. Compare *straight play.*

musical comedy A type of musical characterized by a lighthearted, fast-moving comic story, whose dialogue is interspersed with popular music.

musical director A specialist who works with the musicians and teaches the actors the songs for a musical.

mystery cycle A group of plays about biblical stories performed outdoors by guilds during the Middle Ages in Europe.

N

National Endowment for the Arts (NEA) The federal agency that disburses tax dollars as grants to fund cultural programs.

Naturalism A style of theatrical design and acting whose goal is to imitate real life, including its seamy side. Also called "slice of life" theatre.

New Comedy Greek comic plays with safe themes and mundane subject matter produced after Athens lost the Peloponnesian War to Sparta.

Noh (NOH) A form of traditional Japanese drama combining poetry, acting, singing, and dancing that was developed during the 1300s. Compare *Kabuki.*

nonmotivated light Stage lighting that reinforces the mood of a scene but doesn't necessarily come from an identifiable or onstage source.

Off Broadway Originally, small experimental theatres that sprang up in the late 1950s outside Time Square to put on plays about current issues. They typically have much smaller houses than Broadway theatres do.

off-book rehearsal The rehearsal when the actors must have their lines memorized because they no longer have the script ("book") with them on stage.

Off-Off-Broadway Small, nontraditional, noncommercial theatres located in storefronts, coffeehouses, churches, and other public spaces in the New York City area.

Old Comedy Greek comic plays that directly or indirectly lampooned society and politics; they were filled with sight gags and obscene humor.

onnagata (oh-nah-GAH-tah) Men who play female roles in Kabuki theatre. See also *Kabuki.*

open-shop union A union in which membership is optional, such as the Dramatists Guild of America; compare *closed-shop union.*

opera A type of drama introduced at the end of the sixteenth century that is entirely sung.

operatic musical A musical that is mostly singing, with less spoken dialogue and usually a darker, more dramatic tone than an operetta has. Examples are *Les Misérables* and *Evita.*

operetta Like an opera, a drama set to music, but with a frivolous, comic theme, some spoken dialogue, a melodramatic story, and usually a little dancing. Also called *light opera.* Popularized by Gilbert and Sullivan.

orchestra The circular playing area in ancient Greek theatres; derives from the Greek word for "dancing place." See also *skene* and *theatron.*

overture At the beginning of a musical; a medley of the songs played by the orchestra as a preview.

P

pageant wagon Wagon decorated with a set and used as a traveling stage for performances of mystery and miracle plays during the Middle Ages.

paint shop Theatre workshop where paint is stored and mixed.

paper the house To give away free tickets to the families and friends of cast members in order to make it appear as though the play is popular.

parenthetical A short description such as *(loving), (angry),* or *(terrified)* to help the actor or the reader interpret a particular line of dialogue.

parodos The entrance of the chorus into the playing area in ancient Greek theatre.

patrons Individual contributors to the arts. Compare *corporate funding* and *government funding.*

Peking opera A synthesis of music, dance, acting, and acrobatics first performed in the 1700s in China by strolling players in markets, temples, courtyards, and the streets. Known in China as the "opera of the capital," or *ching-hsi,* it was founded by Qing dynasty Emperor Ch'ien-lung (1736–1795).

Peloponnesian War War between the city-states of Athens and Sparta and their allies (431–404 BCE). Athens' defeat by Sparta brought about the end of Athenian democracy and classic Greek theatre.

performance art An art form from the mid-twentieth century in which one or more performers use some combination of visual arts (including video), theatre, dance, music, and poetry, often to dramatize political ideas. The purpose is less to tell a story than to convey a state of being.

performing arts Arts, such as theatre, music, opera, and dance, whose medium is an act performed by a living human being.

perspective scenery A technique of set design and scene painting that gives the illusion of depth; it gave birth to the proscenium arch theatre.

pictorial arts Arts, such as drawing and painting, created by applying line and color to two-dimensional surfaces.

picturization Composing pictures with the actors to reinforce an idea in the story; a technique used by directors.

playwright's note An article in a play's program by the playwright explaining what he or she intended to accomplish.

plot The causal and logical structure that connects events in a play.

plot-structure The playwright's selection of events to create a logical sequence and as a result to distill meaning from the chaos of life.

poetic realism A style of realism that is expressed through lyrical language.

Poetics Written by Aristotle (384–322 BCE), the first known treatise on how to construct a dramatic story.

point of attack The point in the beginning of a formula plot where the protagonist must make a major decision that will result in conflict.

political theatre Theatre in which playwrights, directors, and actors express their personal opinions about current issues.

pop culture Short for "popular culture"; the fads and fashions that dominate mainstream media, music, and art for a period of time.

presentational theatre Type of theatre that makes no attempt to offer a realistic illusion on stage. The actors openly acknowledge the audience, often playing to them and sometimes even inviting members to participate.

preview Performance of a play open to the public before the official opening night (and before the critics see it).

primary artist The playwright, because he or she is the person who conceives the idea, creates the characters, and builds the story.

problem play A play that expresses a social problem so that it can be remedied.

producer In the United States, the person or institution responsible for the business aspects of a production. Producers can be individuals who finance the production with their own money or who control investors' money, or they can be institutions—universities, churches, community organizations, or theatre companies—that control the business side of the production.

production concept The thematic idea, symbol, or allegory that conveys the tone, mood, and theme of a play (e.g., a post-nuclear Hamlet).

production meeting One of a series of meetings between a director and designers to discuss how to realize the production concept as well as the play's philosophy, interpretation, theme, physical demands, history, and style.

profile An actor's position at a right angle to the audience; halfway between open and closed.

prologue In ancient Greek theatre, a short introductory speech or scene.

prompt book A copy of the play on which the production's sound and light cues, blocking notes, and other information needed for rehearsal and performance are recorded.

property shop Theatre workshop where props are designed, built, and stored.

props Short for *properties;* includes *set props* such as sofas and beds and *hand props,* or small objects actors handle on stage such pens, guns, cigars, money, umbrellas, eyeglasses.

proscenium arch A formal arch that separates the audience from the actors, or a theatre with such an arch. Also called "picture frame" theatre.

protagonist (pro-TA-guh-nist) In an ancient Greek play, the main actor . Now, the central character who pushes forward the action of a play; also called the *hero.* See also *antagonist.*

public domain The legal realm of intellectual property that is not protected by a copyright or patent and belongs to the community at large.

Puritans A strict religious group in Elizabethan England who hated the theatre and lobbied to shut it down.

R

realism A style of theatre that attempts to seem like life, with authentic-looking sets, "honest" acting, and dialogue that sounds like everyday speech. See also *poetic realism, selective realism, simplified* (or *suggested*) *realism.*

Realism The cultural movement behind theatrical realism, it began around 1850 and popularized the idea that plays could be a force for social and political change.

regional theatre Permanent, professional theatres located outside New York City.

rehearsal See *dress rehearsals, final dress rehearsal, general working rehearsals, off-book rehearsal, run-through, special rehearsal, table work,* and *tech rehearsals.*

representational theatre A style of theatre in which the actors attempt to create the illusion of reality and go about their business as if there were no audience present.

reprise In a musical, the repetition of a song, sometimes with new lyrics, in a later scene. The new meaning or subtext makes a dramatic point.

Restoration Period of English history that began in 1660 with the reestablishment of the monarchy. It was characterized by scientific discovery, new philosophical concepts, improved economic conditions, and a return of the theatre.

reviews Published or broadcast opinions of critics about whether a particular play is worth seeing. Also called *notices.* Compare to *dramatic criticism.*

revue A program of satirical sketches, singing, and dancing about a particular theme; also called a musical review. Compare to *variety show.*

rising action The increasing power, drama, and seriousness of each subsequent conflict, crisis, and complication in a play.

ritual theatre The middle stage of theatre's evolution from rituals; the theatrical techniques of song, dance, and characterization were used, but the performances' purpose was that of rituals.

rock musical A musical that uses rock and roll music, psychedelic rock, or contemporary pop and rock.

rock opera A type of comic opera that features rock-and-roll music, such as Andrew Lloyd Webber's *Jesus Christ Superstar* (1970).

royalty payment Payment to playwrights or their estates in exchange for staging a copyrighted play.

run-through A rehearsal to go through an act or the entire play from beginning to end with as few interruptions as possible.

Sanskrit theatre One of the earliest forms of theatre in India, performed in Sanskrit by professional touring companies on special occasions in temples, palaces, or temporary theatres.

satyr play (SAY-tur) In ancient Greece, a comic-relief play performed between tragic plays at the City Dionysia. Often burlesque, these plays parodied the myths, gods, and heroes in the tragedies. Named for the half-beast, half-human creatures said to be companions of the god Dionysus.

scene shop Theatre workshop with a variety of metalworking and woodworking tools.

Screen Actors Guild (SAG) The union that represents film and television actors.

scrim A curtain of open-mesh gauze that can be transparent or translucent depending on whether the light comes from in front or behind it.

script analysis The director's intensive study of a script, perhaps with the playwright, and research of the history and criticism of the play in order to understand the script's strengths and weaknesses and each character's motivations, desires, and circumstances.

selective realism A design style that mixes authentic-looking elements with stylized ones.

sentimental comedy A type of comedy that features middle-class characters finding happiness and true love.

set prop Any prop that sits on the set, such as sofas, chairs, and beds. Compare *hand prop.*

shadow theatre A form of theatre created by lighting two-dimensional figures and casting their shadows on a screen. Probably originated in China around 100 BCE and later became popular in Islamic lands, where people were prohibited from playing characters.

sharing focus A position for two or more actors, each with a shoulder thrown back (also called *one quarter*) so that the audience can see them equally. See also *focus.*

showstopper In a musical, a big production number which receives so much applause that it stops the show.

sight lines Audience members' view of areas of the stage.

simplified, or **suggested, realism** A design style that suggests rather than exactly duplicates the look of a period.

skene (SKEEN) In ancient Greek theatre, the building behind the orchestra; it housed dressing rooms and storage spaces, and its façade was used as a backdrop for productions. See also *orchestra* and *theatron.*

sound booth The room where sound effects and music cues are prepared and edited.

souvenir program Programs sold at large professional performances that have more pictures and information about the production and cast than the basic program.

spatial arts Arts, such as sculpture and architecture, that are created by manipulating material in space.

special rehearsal A rehearsal for a special element, such as fight scenes, musical numbers, dance numbers, or dialects.

stage area One of the nine sections of the stage labeled according to the actors' point of view, such as downstage right, center stage, or upstage left.

stage directions Notes that indicate the physical movements of the characters.

stage door The back door that actors use to enter and leave the theatre.

stage manager The most important assistant to a director; the person who is responsible for running the show during the performance and helping the director during auditions and the rehearsal process by taking notes, recording blocking, and scheduling rehearsals.

Stanislavsky system An individualized, psychological approach to acting pioneered by Konstantin Stanislavsky; also known as *method acting.*

stasimon In ancient Greek plays, a choral interlude between episodes.

stealing focus Taking focus out of turn; also know as *upstaging.* Compare *sharing focus.* See also *focus.*

stereotypes Generalized assumptions about people who are not like us.

straight makeup Makeup that does not change actors' looks but makes their faces look more three-dimensional and therefore more visible to the audience; compare to *character makeup.*

straight play In contrast to a musical, the category of plays without music.

subject What a work of art is about, what it reflects, and what it attempts to comprehend.

substitution Replacing a character's emotions with unrelated personal emotions; a technique used when the actor has not had the experience or emotional reaction of the character.

subtext The hidden meaning behind a line of dialogue; the real reason a character chooses to speak.

superobjective The driving force that governs a character's actions throughout the play.

surrealism A genre of theatre that emphasizes the subconscious realities of the character, usually through design, and often includes random sets with dreamlike qualities.

symbolism A design style or theatre genre in which a certain piece of scenery, a costume, or a light represents the essence of the entire environment.

synthespians Digital actors created by computer animators.

T

table work The first step in the rehearsal process; the actors read through the play while seated around a table. Afterward, the director and actors discuss the characters, motivations, and meaning, and the designers may present their ideas to the cast.

talent Natural ability; it is innate but also can be developed.

teaser The curtain that frames the top of the stage. Compare *legs.*

tech (technical) rehearsals Rehearsals that include the lights, sound, costumes, more complex props, and final set pieces.

technical approach Acting from the outside in, concentrating on physical details. Compare to *method acting.*

technical director (TD) The person who coordinates schedules and engineers all the technical elements of a production.

technique Proven procedure by which a complex task can be accomplished, such as raising a child, fixing a heart valve, auditing books, or acting in a play.

theatre A performing art that is always changing and whose every performance is unique.

Theatre of Cruelty Originated by Antonin Artaud, stylized, ritualized performances intended to attack spectators' sensibilities and purge them of destructive tendencies.

Theatre of Dionysus The largest ancient Greek theatre, located in Athens; it could seat as many as 17,000 people.

theatre of identity Plays by and about a particular culture or ethnic group.

theatre of protest Plays that criticize the policies of the dominant culture and demand justice.

theatre of the absurd A theatrical style conceived in reaction to the atrocities and devastation of World War II. Absurdist playwrights sought to dramatize the anxiety and chaos of the world.

theatre of the people A type of theatre that provides a forum for everyday people to express themselves.

theatron (THAY-uh-tron) From the Greek term for "seeing place," the seating area in ancient Greek theatres. Compare *orchestra* and *skene.*

theme A play's central idea: a statement about life or a moral.

Thespis The first known Western actor. Created theatre by stepping from a dithyramb chorus in ancient Greece to play an individual role. In 534 BCE, wrote and acted in a play that won the City Dionysia. Source of the word *thespian,* or a person who has studied the craft of acting.

three unities Rules for writing a play requiring (1) the action to take place within a 24-hour period, (2) settings that can all be reached within 24 hours, and (3) no commingling of comedy and tragedy. These rules for unity of time, place, and action were a misinterpretation of Aristotle's writings by Renaissance scholars.

thrust stage A theatre with a lip that protrudes so far into the house that the audience must sit on one of the three sides of the stage.

tragic flaw An unchangeable trait in a character that brings about his own ruin (e.g., Oedipus's arrogance in ignoring the oracle). Also known as *character flaw* and *fatal flaw.*

triangulation A technique for drawing focus when three actors or groups of actors are on stage; the person or group at the upstage or downstage apex of the triangle takes the focus. See also *focus.*

U

unities See *three unities.*

upstage The area of the stage farthest from the audience.

upstaging Taking focus out of turn; also know as *stealing focus.*

V

values The principles, standards, and qualities considered worthwhile or desirable within a given society.

variety show A program of unrelated singing, dancing, and comedy numbers. Compare to *revue.*

vaudeville (VAHD-vill) A popular form of stage entertainment from the 1880s to the 1930s, descended from burlesque. Programs included slapstick comedy routines, song-and-dance numbers, magic acts, juggling, and acrobatic performances.

verbal scene painting A technique used by English and Spanish playwrights to set the mood or place of a scene. Because the words paint pictures, the audience "dresses" the stage in their imagination.

voice and dialect coach A specialist who helps actors with speech clarity and volume and with accent reduction or acquisition.

vomitories (often shortened to **voms**) Tunnels, like those in sports stadiums, that run into and under the tiers of audience seats to allow actors quick access to the stage.

willing suspension of disbelief The audience's acceptance of the quasi-reality of a work of art that enables the playwright, director, and actors to communicate perceptions about reality; the term was coined by English poet Samuel Taylor Coleridge.

wings Areas out of the audience's sight from which actors make their entrances and in which sets are stored.

writers for hire Writers, such as screen and television writers, who sell their words to production companies rather than retaining a copyright to them.

Writers Guild of America (WGA) The closed-shop union that represents screen and television writers.

Y

Yiddish Broadway The Jewish theatre district on Second Avenue in New York City in the late nineteenth and early twentieth century.

Guide to Pronunciation of Names

Aeschylus (EHS-kuh-luhs)
JoAnne Akalaitis (ah-kah-LYE-tuhs)
André Antoine (AHN-dray AHN-twahn)
Adolphe Appia (AY-dahlf AHP-pyah)
Archimedes (ahr-keh-MEE-deez)
Aristophanes (air-eh-STAHF-eh-neez)
Aristotle (air-eh-STAH-tehl)
Antonin Artaud (ahn-tuh-NAHN ahr-TOH
Amiri Baraka (ah-MEER-ree bah-RAH-kah)
Pierre Beaumarchais (pee-AIR boh-mahr-SHAY)
Aphra Behn (AF-rah BAYN)
Augusto Boal (ah-GOOS-toh BOH-ahl)
Bertolt Brecht (BEHR-tohlt BREHKT)
Calderón (kahl-deh-ROHN)
Anton Chekhov (AN-tahn CHAY-kahf)
Chikamatsu (CHEE-kah-maht-soo)
William Congreve (KAHN-greev)
Duke of Saxe-Meiningen (SACKS MINE-ehn-gehn)
Alexander Dumas (doo-MAH)
Eratosthenes (air-eh-TAHS-thuh-neez)
Euclid (YOO-klehd)
Euripides (yoo-RIP-eh-deez)
Athol Fugard (ah-TOHL FOO-gahrd)
Fatima Gallaire-Bourega (FA-teh-meh gahl-YAIR boor-AY-zhah)
Johann Wolfgang von Goethe (YOH-hahn VULF-gahng vahn GEHR-teh)
Maxim Gorky (mahk-SEEM GAHR-kee)
Jerzy Grotowski (JER-zee groh-TOW-skee)
Uta Hagen (OO-tuh HAH-gehn)
Václav Havel (VAH-klahv HAH-vehl)
Zygmunt Hubner (ZIG-moont HOOB-nuhr)
Henrik Ibsen (HEN-rik IP-sehn)
Eugène Ionesco (yoo-ZHEN ee-eh-NEHS-koh)
Inigo Jones (EE-ni-goh)
Kalidasa (kahl-ee-DAH-seh)
Moisés Kaufman (Moi-ZEZ KAHF-mehn)
Elia Kazan (EHL-ee-ah kah-ZAHN)
Gotthold Lessing (GAHT-hohlt LEHS-sing)
George Lillo (LIL-loh)
Mario Vargas Llosa (MAH-ree-oh VAHR-gahs YOH-sah)
David Mamet (MA-meht)
Maishe Maponya (MYE-sheh mah-PAHN-yah)
Menander (meh-NAN-dehr)
Molière (mohl-YAIR)
Phrynichus (FRIN-eh-kehs)
Plato (PLAY-toh)
Plautus (PLAH-tehs)
Giacomo Puccini (JAH-keh-moh poot-CHEE-nee)
Jean Racine (ZHAHN ra-SEEN)
Edmond Rostand (rah-STAHN)
Jean-Jacques Rousseau (zhahn-ZHAHK roo-SOH)
Nicola Sabbattini (NEE-koh-lah sah-bah-TEE-nee)
Ken Saro-Wiwa (SAH-roh WEE-wah)
Jean-Paul Sartre (zhahn-PAHL SAHR-treh)
Seneca (SEHN-i-kuh)
Sebastiano Serlio (say-bahs-tee-AH-noh SEHRL-yoh)
Robert Serumaga (seh-roo-MAH-gah)
Socrates (SAHK-reh-teez)
Sophocles (SAHF-eh-kleez)
Wole Soyinka (WO-lay shah-YIN-kuh)
Konstantin Stanislavsky (KAHN-stehn-teen stan-eh-SLAHV-skee)
Tadashi Suzuki (tah-DAH-shee sooz-OO-kee)
Lope de Vega (LOH-pay deh VAY-gah)
Voltaire (vohl-TAIR)
Richard Wagner (VAHG-nehr)
Émile Zola (AY-mil ZO-lah)

INDEX

A

B

C

J

K

L

N

U

Z